LONDON
& ITS PEOPLE
A SOCIAL HISTORY FROM MEDIEVAL TIMES TO THE PRESENT DAY

A Greenwich Baptist minister, the Rev. Charles Spurgeon, commissioned a series of street-life photographs of his neighbourhood between 1884-1887. Spurgeon, the son of the famous evangelical preacher of the same name, is pictured here having his shoes cleaned. The name of the photographer is unknown.

LONDON & ITS PEOPLE

A SOCIAL HISTORY FROM MEDIEVAL TIMES TO THE PRESENT DAY

JOHN RICHARDSON

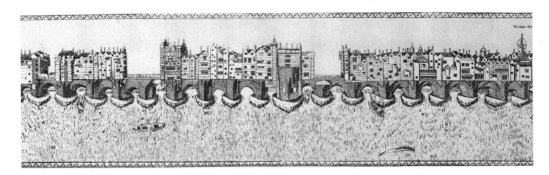

BARRIE & JENKINS

First published in 1995

1 3 5 7 9 10 8 6 4 2

Text copyright © John Richardson 1995

John Richardson has asserted his right under the Copyright,
Designs and Patents Act, 1988 to be identified as
the author of this work.

First published in the United Kingdom in 1995 by Barrie & Jenkins,
Random House, 20 Vauxhall Bridge Road, London SW1V 2SA

Random House Australia (Pty) Limited, 20 Alfred Street,
Milsons Point, Sydney, New South Wales 2061, Australia

Random House New Zealand Limited, 18 Poland Road, Glenfield
Auckland 10, New Zealand

Random House South Africa (Pty) Limited, PO Box 337, Bergvlei
South Africa

Random House UK Limited Reg. No. 954009

A CIP Catalogue record for this book is available from the
British Library

ISBN 0 09 180801 4

Designed by David Fordham

Typeset by SX Composing Ltd
Printed and bound in Great Britain by
Butler & Tanner Ltd, Frome and London

Title page: View *of the east side of London Bridge c.1600 by John Norden.*

CONTENTS

INTRODUCTION

LONDON IS NEARLY TWO THOUSAND YEARS OLD. IT BEGAN AS AN OUTPOST ON THE periphery of the Roman Empire, yet in its heyday it was the capital of the world and centre of an empire whose bounds were beyond the dreams and knowledge of its founders. Its first people were Romans and Celts, and it was subsequently occupied by Saxons and Scandinavians, and then ruled by Normans. So many nationalities have since contributed to its life and growth that the word 'Londoner' has no significance except in its residential sense. It has long been a cosmopolitan city and, by virtue of its trading history, open and amenable to other cultures. Generalizations about the character of its people are not possible or sensible, although romantics have often voiced them.

London is probably the most documented city in the world. Each neighbourhood, each activity, each institution, each notable building has its printed history. Social histories are thinner on the ground – with good reason. The lives of people are inextricably mixed with the physical history of a city so as to render their description a formidable task. In the case of London the over-abundance of material is daunting.

Buildings supply many clues to the nature of a city's people. A building, after all, is not usually a spontaneous item, erected on a whim. It is a considered consequence of an extended process of ideas and skills, and therefore accurately reflects the tastes and requirements of the day. Buildings reveal, to the observant, activities and manners, affluence or the lack of it, and often the structure of family life or the mechanics of a business. They demonstrate the ambitions of the rich and – wryly sometimes – those ambitions when curbed for want of money. In the suburbs aspirations are subtly displayed in the nuances of semi-detached houses, and in local authority estates the competing forces of thrift and official philanthropy are seen at odds. Even street patterns speak volumes. In the City narrow streets and alleyways, fronted by Victorian and modern office blocks, remind us of a medieval city crowded and busy within the shelter of a Roman wall. The planned squares and streets of Bloomsbury, Soho and Mayfair, are carefully graded in status and function and are a consequence of an exodus of people from the City and an influx of others from the provinces. To the east along the river, converted warehouses announce the river behind and the activities that once filled them.

Old town halls, opened with a municipal pomp and pride that is now rarely displayed, lie unused or else are merely reduced in status to local annexes. They tell us something about the old order – the smaller units of parishes, vestries and boroughs that were the battlegrounds of old disputes, old politics, old ways of administering the recurring problems of urban areas. Workhouses survive, dressed up as hospitals, their former role remembered and feared today by few residents. Almshouses, now gathered (sometimes with new politically correct names) into the portfolio of social services departments, may, if their foundation stones still exist, remind us that charity on such a scale came usually as a private donation. Converted mission halls and minor church buildings tell us of the evangelical zeal of the nineteenth century. The lofty naves of parish churches, which echo to the responses and hymns of small clusters of people, are stone witnesses of a London that once set Sunday aside for worship.

In local high streets old drapery-cum-department stores may still be seen, but now with their pavement floors cut up into small shop units. High above such shops and on their flank walls, proprietors engraved their names in stone, or advertisers painted their product names – but no one looks up now, and no one bothers to erase them. These inscriptions are reminiscent of the marble counters and the courtesy chairs that were once part of shopping. Occasionally a clothes shop, remarkably old-fashioned and without any kind of display sense, still survives, a tribute to a dedicated owner and a lease negotiated many years ago on advantageous terms. Nothing changes so quickly as retail trade, and the proud buildings of the old chain stores – Fifty Shilling Tailors, Dunn's the hatters, the Co-ops – are quickly devoured by smarter predators, but almost invariably something is left on the buildings, some insignia, some wording to tell us their origins and the social fashions of the day.

Old cinemas may be discerned – impressive and sometimes bizarre fronts often shielding remarkably plain buildings behind them. Their names occasionally come to light in renovation work – Essoldo, Rialto, Rio, Scala – exotic responses to people's expectations. Edwardian library buildings, resplendent in red brick and iron railings, take us back to the era when local authorities purposely delayed provision until Andrew Carnegie half paid for it. Inside these buildings, despite the new shelving and lighting and the racks of records and videos, the old atmosphere may still be imagined, one of men (on their feet, for there were no chairs) reading newspapers securely fastened within clamps. This was an age of information, but one where it had to be sought: it did not flow, in a gratuitous wash, into living rooms. And sometimes there survive other buildings that illustrate that urgent Victorian and Edwardian lust for education – the institutes for middle-class people, or those for 'mechanicks'. Most of these are now gone, merged into polytechnics which themselves have been absorbed into universities.

All these clues to how people went about their business or pleasure abound in London – it is a city reluctant to come to terms with modernity and slow to sweep aside the bric-à-brac of several centuries.

Buildings, are of course, only part of the story. London and its people have inevitably, been fashioned by national events, disasters, good fortune, geographical features and, not least, by individuals and I have tried to show how such influences have revealed themselves over the centuries.

JOHN RICHARDSON 1995

PORTRAIT of Geoffrey Chaucer from Thomas Hoccleve's poem De Regimine Principum; *early 15th century. Chaucer (c.1340-1400), was born in Vintry ward, south of Cheapside, son of a City vintner. A civil servant for much of his life, he was appointed Clerk of the Works for the Tower of London and the Palace of Westminster in 1389.*

CHAPTER I

LIFE WITHIN THE WALLS

THE MERCHANT

BEGINNINGS

THE THAMES BROUGHT LONDON INTO BEING AND FROM MEDIEVAL TIMES IT FASHIONED occupations within its walls. The river then was shallower and much wider: at times it so lacked depth and pace that in many winters it froze for weeks on end, forming a ghostly white highway that gave delight to many but brought trade to a standstill. Occasionally, a combination of tide and weather could leave the Thames so scant of water near London Bridge that its bed was hardly covered; and at Westminster, where the surge of tide from the estuary was scarcely felt, the Romans had moved armies across on a ford.

Other rivers flowed into the Thames. On the north bank the Walbrook carved a channel from swampy Moorfields through the centre of the City; the Fleet to the west of the City Wall was used by cargo ships up to Holborn; and the Tyburn came down from Hampstead to low-lying Westminster, where its arms enclosed the abbey. On the south bank the shoreline of Southwark and Bermondsey was less defined, and through this sometimes waterlogged area the river Neckinger emerged at St Saviour's Dock at Bermondsey, and the Effra disgorged into the Thames at Vauxhall. Wharves, quays and inlets coped with the congestion that each tide brought; some larger boats, obliged by lack of vacant landing space to anchor mid-stream, were off-loaded on to lighter craft that could manoeuvre to the docks, or instead hazardous arrangements of planks were constructed across other boats to the shore. Within all this activity the customs officers inspected, noted and taxed.

The Romans had come upon this place about AD 43. It was a point just above high tide, with terraces of gravel on the northern side of the river, and on the south, with ingenuity, there was sufficient standing to bear one end of a long bridge. The bridge, and therefore London, was a military requirement, a place through which soldiers and supplies might pass to assist the colonization of Britain. Yet archaeologists have found no military equipment from this period and, so far, we must conclude that London then was not a permanent encampment, but a transit place. The line of Watling Street from Richborough in Kent, where the Romans landed, to Lambeth and then northwards from the Thames at Westminster, suggests that the Romans crossed the river there, perhaps by a tied arrangement of floating rafts, before they were ready to tackle the more difficult task of bridging the Thames from Southwark. Westminster would, in any case, have been only a temporary solution for it was a marshy area, hostile to significant settlement.

Nothing is certain in all this and it is probable that too much thoughtless excavation has occurred at Westminster for some questions to be resolved. What we do know for sure is that *Londinium*, as the Romans named it, was destroyed soon after its foundation. In AD 60 the Iceni and Trinovantes, under the redoubtable Boudicca, razed it with fire – a burnt layer of earth has been found between the Walbrook and Gracechurch Street appropriate to this date. We know of a number of subsequent Roman buildings. The basilica, which served as town hall, exchange and law courts, and the forum, were on the site of Leadenhall Market, on one of the hills of the City; the governor's palace was just below Cannon Street midway between the Walbrook and London Bridge; west of the Walbrook was a bath house, its rooms heated by warm air carried beneath the floors; to

A VIEW of part of the remains of London Wall near All Hallows Church, Tower Hill, in 1818. London Wall was built towards the end of the 2nd century using stone brought up from quarries near Maidstone. It was about two miles long and about 18ft high.

the north, built *c.* AD 120, was a fort, probably used as barracks, on the higher ground at Cripplegate, projecting in such a way as to have clear vision east, north and west; in recent years a long-sought-for amphitheatre, or at least a section of it, has been found near the Guildhall; and on the east bank of the Walbrook a temple dedicated to Mithras was discovered in 1954. It has not yet been determined when the first London Bridge was built and it may have been a temporary structure, but certainly a permanent wooden bridge was built by about AD 90 on a line slightly to the east of the present bridge, ending on the northern side at today's Fish Street Hill.

The Romans' greatest achievement was the City Wall. It was built from about AD 190, presumably to guard against insurrection from within the country rather than to repel invaders from the Thames, since the wall along the Thames was the last section to be built. The landward wall was made of about one million shaped ragstone blocks obtained from quarries near Maidstone; it was about 2 miles long, 6 to 8 feet wide and about 18 feet high, surrounded by a V-shaped ditch, 6 feet deep and varying in width from 9 to 15 feet. The river wall was constructed about a century later, roughly along the line of today's Thames Street. Four gateways were originally inserted over main roads that led out of London: Aldgate, Bishopsgate, Newgate and Ludgate.

Clearly, from the extent of this wall, *Londinium* (renamed *Augusta* in the fourth century as a mark of mutual honour between the settlement and the emperor) was of considerable size and strategic importance in the Roman order of things – the basilica itself was the largest building of its kind north of the Alps. But then after about 365 years of occupation, the unimaginable happened – the Roman army was withdrawn from the province. Then began one of the two periods in London's history for which there is little available information and the two hundred years after the Romans left cannot yet be interpreted let

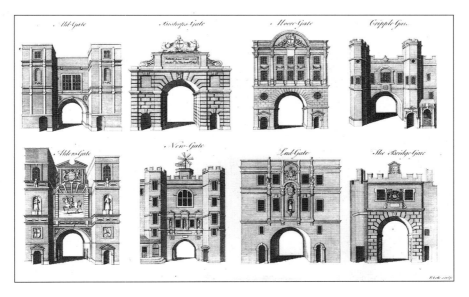

Eight gates to the London City Wall. The oldest were Aldgate, Bishopsgate, Newgate and Ludgate, from which roads led to Roman settlements. Geoffrey Chaucer lived in a room above Aldgate between 1374 and 1385.

alone accounted for. Was London abandoned altogether, or was there a rump of population? And if it were occupied in some way, were they Romans and their subjects, or were they people of Germanic tribes, such as the Saxons? It is an exquisite mystery for those who delve into such matters and one can only turn one's attention instead to the situation of London when it re-emerges once more.

In 601 London was designated by the Pope as the place where the prime archbishop should reside, but this honour went instead to Canterbury. However, the fact that London was named first signifies either that London's old importance in the Roman empire was still acknowledged, or else that it was still, by dint of its activity and influence, the natural choice in this ordered expansion of Christianity. In 604 the bishopric of London was founded and soon afterwards the first St Paul's, a wooden structure, was built with the encouragement of Ethelbert, king of Kent, then in the ascendant, whose nephew,

Saeberht, was king of the East Saxons, to which London belonged. Probably, Saeberht resided at the Cripplegate fort. The old Roman amphitheatre was also in that quarter of the city, enclosed between the curved arms of Aldermanbury and Basinghall Street: it is quite possible that, after the departure of the Romans, this arena was used for public assemblies; later it was the logical site for the centre of civic administration, which became the Guildhall. Thus we have an ecclesiastical and royal enclave in the west and north-west of the old Roman city, and possibly a civic one as well.

In effect, London within its walls had shifted westwards away from the early Roman centre between the Walbrook and the basilica. This abandonment, or so it seems, of that side of the city is further suggested by the fact that the Roman road system hardly survived there, though of course some of the old pattern was retained simply to align roads with the gates in the walls. But on the whole the road pattern of the city is medieval and even the important junction around the Bank and the Mansion House was a medieval introduction. On the other hand, the Cripplegate fort fits neatly into medieval topography, suggesting that the building remained in use when the Romans left.

Despite this seeming renaissance of London, the eighth and ninth centuries remain strangely elusive. Where archaeological evidence exists (much of it discovered in recent years), the picture is startling, for in this period a major settlement was positioned outside the city walls along and north of the Strand. This was *Lundenwic*, a trading and farming community that remained until the Viking raids in the mid ninth century sent them scuttling into the relative safety of the city walls. This area, which included Aldwych – a name meaning old port – obviously had a different function to that inside the walls where the king and bishop had their residences, but we do not know enough yet to understand the relationship between them.

THE MIDDLE AGES

WHEN THEY ARRIVED IN 1066, THE NORMANS FOUND A COMPLEX WALLED CITY which they then fortified to east and west. The construction of the Tower of London began at first as a wooden structure and then of Kentish ragstone; the White Tower, with its four corner turrets and walls about 15 feet thick, is the oldest part of the building, finished about 1087; to the west, Baynard's Castle was constructed about the same time just inside the western wall, overlooking the Thames.

It is not yet known when the parishes and wards were formed, though it was probably between the tenth and twelfth centuries. There are about four times as many parishes as there are wards and it is not known either why the boundaries of wards do not simply match those of groups of parishes. And why, uniquely in Europe, were there so many parish churches – about a hundred within the walls alone – each serving a small population? The smaller parishes and wards are grouped around St Paul's and the Cheapside-riverside area, indicating that the population was denser in these areas and could support more parish churches. There were very much larger parishes, such as St Stephen, Coleman Street, which even extended across the City Wall into Moorfields, and the relative absence of churches in that part of London implies that the land was marshy from the depradations of the Walbrook.

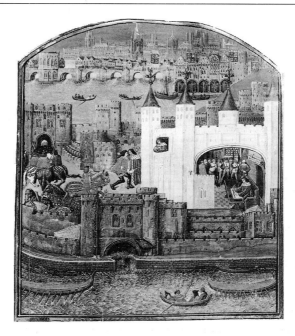

This earliest known painting of a London scene was made c.1500 as a frontispiece of a volume of poems collected or composed by the Duke of Orléans. The Duke was taken prisoner at the Battle of Agincourt and is shown looking out of the White Tower of the Tower of London. London Bridge is seen in the background and in front of that is what is assumed to be Billingsgate market building.

The two principal east-west roads within the walls ran from Newgate to Aldgate, and from Ludgate down to the area of the Tower: the line they took in Roman and medieval times differed. The main route north-south led from London Bridge up to the basilica (which it went round in Roman times) and then up to Bishopsgate; this route is now roughly that of Gracechurch Street and Bishopsgate. But in medieval times another east-west road developed by the river, on the line of the old Roman wall, called Thames Street. It was a short distance from the water: gradually over the years foreshore had been captured and revetments, dug in and reinforced, were built over. It was this long street and the alleys and lanes off north and south that dealt directly with the river.

Merchandise and commodities from the counties and the Continent were trundled up the sloping alleys, put into warehouses and there repackaged into retail bites. In and off this street was distributed hay, straw and grain brought in by boat from provincial regions, and spices, salt, wines and luxury goods from abroad. Fish was taken in at Queenhithe and Billingsgate, and just to the west of St Paul's, on the bank of the Fleet, coal from the north of England was unloaded at Seacoal Lane as early as the thirteenth century. Conversely, wool and cloth, the most valuable of English exports, went out in vast quantities. Along Thames Street, the chandlers sold a combustible mix of tar, tallow and oils, ropes and canvas, and salted food for journeys.

If Thames Street dealt with imported goods in wholesale bulk, then Westcheap (now Cheapside) and Eastcheap were its retail partners. Merchants and manufacturers settled north and south of these two roads and gradually specializations developed within defined streets. Names such as Wood, Bread and Milk Streets and Ironmonger Lane are today testimony to long-departed trades. Pudding Lane, where the Great Fire of 1666 began, was named from the offal traders there – the north country black pudding is a reminder of the old meaning of that word. Cordwainers were grouped around Bow Lane and in the fourteenth century they appear to have been replaced by hosiers. Tallow and wax chandlers were located in Candlewick (now Cannon) Street, fishmongers (in Catholic London) were in Friday Street as well as around Billingsgate and Eastcheap; poulterers were in Poultry. Butchers congregated at the far west of Cheapside and along Newgate Street: animals bought at nearby Smithfield market were, until 1371, slaughtered at the Shambles in Newgate – not a place for the delicate – and then sold as meat on the streets. Saddlers were nearby at the western end of Cheapside and so, surprisingly, were the superior goldsmiths, located, as they still are, in Foster Lane. North of Thames Street and west of the Walbrook, the vintners were gathered and wine,

South view of the Custom House in Lower Thames Street in the 16th century; this building was destroyed in the Great Fire of London. The first known customs duty in London was levied by the Saxon king, Ethelred, in 979.

unloaded at Queenhithe in tuns, was cajoled up the hill to the warehouses of the Vintry. John Chaucer, vintner, had a house here and most probably this is where his son, Geoffrey Chaucer, was born about 1340; the boy was, no doubt, baptized at one of four churches close by.

Chaucer was born into an amply governed city in which anonymity, that supposed advantage of modern times, was difficult to find: levels of control and watchfulness touched virtually everyone. Three forms of authority conspired to regulate a Londoner's life – civil, ecclesiastical and occupational. By Chaucer's time the civil administration of London was becoming sophisticated. The mayor, the Court of Aldermen and the Court of Common Council, all elected by the wards, looked after public works and the defence and governance of the City. The twenty-four wards, local units of government, pressed home the City's ordinances, and dealt with nuisances, disturbances and sanitation; some wards straddled the Wall around the City and so were obliged to maintain the gate which fell within their territory.

Then there were the parishes within and without the walls, about 120 in number. In Chaucer's Vintry ward alone four parish churches exercised influence at a time when church attendance and financial support were customary. Most were still simple structures, others rebuilt by leading citizens anxious to appease their Maker.

Trade guilds guarded entry into the most profitable occupations and encouraged the demarcation of manufacture, the maintenance of prices and standards of workmanship; unskilled workers could escape their imperatives but were, nevertheless, at their disposal. It was through a guild that an apprentice obtained his 'Freedom of the City' and hence a licence to pursue his craft. This citizen élite, which could trade retail and wholesale and buy and sell property, accounted for about a quarter of the adult male population.

The Steelyard in Upper Thames Street was the headquarters of German merchants from medieval times until the 19th century. It took its name from the large scales placed there on which traded goods were weighed.

Not only was the City of London a complex of neighbourhoods in which an outsider would be noticed, but it was also xenophobic. Time and again the London mobs turned on immigrants and overseas merchants when they felt their own prosperity at risk. Rules evolved governing the commercial activities of non-citizens. No 'foreigner', a word which embraced even a London-born person, could trade without permission; no stranger from outside the walls could easily set up business. Near to Chaucer's house, on the east side of the Walbrook, stood the so-called House of Teutons, or Steelyard, in which Germans under royal protection traded and flourished in the face of hostility and intimidation. Their building was set aside as 'a place for merchants of Almaine, that used to bring hither as well Wheat, rie and other graine, as Cables, Ropes, Masts, Pitch, Tar, Flaxe, Hempe, linnin Cloth, Wainscots, Waxe, Steele, and other profitable Merchandises.' Jews had been precluded from most things except usury and even this was denied them when, fifty years before Chaucer was born, it was expedient for the king to expel them from England and encourage Lombardy merchants to handle their business. Old Jewry indicates the whereabouts of the dispossessed and Lombard Street the domain of the incomers. In 1325 it was ordered that all 'foreigners' who had received the Freedom of the City should have that honour withdrawn, an enactment which underlined a previous generosity. Excluded from this new ruling were the merchants of Amiens, importers of onions and garlic, who had been granted their privileges a hundred years earlier for contributing to the expense of bringing water supplies to the City from the river Tyburn.

London was not unusual in its hostility to foreigners – similar rules and obstacles existed in walled cities around Europe. It was a period when those already in the ascendant were organising society so that they should remain so. At the same time the nature of citizenship was being examined and defined: if citizens had obligations, financial and martial, to the city they inhabited, then the rights they received in return ought to have some exclusivity to be of value. Thus the privilege of setting up house, shop or manufactory was hard won.

In Westminster a different kind of guild system existed – here by the fifteenth century one pre-eminent body represented numerous traders in what was essentially a small township of about 2,250 people. Only in the surrounding villages, in such places as Holborn, Islington, Hackney and Chelsea, could tradesmen do much as they pleased, though their trade with London was strictly supervised.

The City's obsession with citizenship and the rights of people within its limits was, in part, a measure of self-protection. It was also an expression of a sought-for autonomy and a jealous reaction to the royal presence at Westminster. As far as is known, Edward the Confessor was the first king to move his palace out of the City to the rather dismal terrain of Westminster where what is now Parliament Square was merely an island between two arms of the Tyburn. Here his new palace on the site of the Houses of Parliament was soon to be joined by his new abbey of St Peter, which replaced an earlier monastery. Edward's motives for moving from the City are unknown but the move was to have profound consequences for the development of London. If the Norman kings had not needed to parade a legitimate descent from the Confessor, quite possibly they would not have settled themselves in his Westminster haunts and had themselves crowned in his Westminster Abbey in sight of his tomb. But their slightly fragile claim to the throne and the violence required to enforce it resulted in an overstated attachment to the Confessor's architectural and bodily remains. More logically, the Norman kings might have based themselves, together with the instruments of law and government, in their fortified Tower of London, which was built more to intimidate the restless citizens it overlooked than to act as a bulwark against hypothetical raiders coming up the Thames. But because they chose Westminster, London – uniquely in Europe – became two cities of different functions, the one absorbed in trade, the other in court life, diplomacy and the law.

As a result the City's status became a mixture of pre-eminence and subordination, and its involvement in national affairs an unpredictable sequence of neutrality or partisanship, sometimes reluctant, occasionally full-blooded. Its relationship with the monarch was almost always one of uneasy rivalry but the dependence of the two on each other was of far-reaching importance until at least the end of the seventeenth century. The City could be and occasionally was subdued, and its leading citizens vanquished, but it could still make or break kings and despots. There were no rules in this sometimes bloody relationship. In good times, with a strong bargaining position, the City grasped a privilege or two, but in bad years it lost even its right to elect a mayor. By the Stuart period, a third force – Parliament – had stepped into this power struggle, and as its influence grew so London's city-state authority diminished.

The transfer of real power from the City to royal or parliamentary Westminster was an extended process but the prestige of being a citizen of London was still a character reference well into the eighteenth century. In court rolls in parishes around the country time and again someone is defined as not only, for example, a mercer of London, but a *citizen* and mercer. It was a long time before that distinction became superfluous.

The City was not only denied the residential patronage of the monarch but it also missed being the official centre of the Church's power. Though London contained, in St Paul's, the largest church in the country, and numerous religious houses and parish

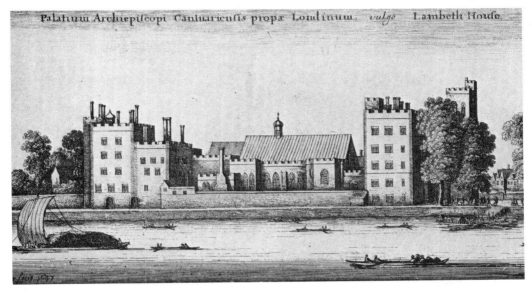

LAMBETH PALACE in 1647, by Wenceslaus Hollar. The Palace had its origins in the building of a house for canons by Hubert Walter, Archbishop of Canterbury, in about 1200. The Tudor gatehouse to the right, which may still be seen today, was built 1486–1501.

churches within its walls, it was Canterbury that was eventually designated, in the earliest days of English Christianity, as the seat of the senior archbishop. This arrangement, one that appeased Ethelbert, King of Kent, became an anomaly during the centuries when Church and politics were fatefully entwined. The Church needed the ear of the king and familiarity with the nuances of court life and national politics, and so the Archbishop of Canterbury set himself up in Lambeth, markedly near but separate from Westminster. Other archbishops and numerous bishops with similar motives established London homes, mostly outside the City walls in the neutral area between City and Westminster, along Fleet Street and the Strand. St Etheldreda's church, the former chapel of Ely Palace in Holborn, is a last remnant of this episcopal influx.

The twelfth and thirteenth centuries saw the establishment in the City of eleven major religious houses, inside and outside of the City Wall, and the founding and rebuilding of numerous churches. While the former was often the result of royal or noble patronage, the latter represented for the most part the expenditure of leading citizens of both Saxon and Norman stock. In a burst of pious construction the simple Romanesque wooden churches of the Saxons were replaced by Gothic stone edifices surmounted by the spires that were mostly to perish in the Great Fire.

THE CHURCH

IN LONDON THE CHURCH WAS EVERYWHERE. By the fourteenth century at least a quarter of the population of the City was either involved in the Church's administration or else made part of their living supplying it with goods. Jostling for trade were bakers, brewers,

THE fourth St Paul's Cathedral. This building was commenced after a fire had destroyed the third Saxon church in 1087; it was larger than today's cathedral and its spire, damaged by lightning in 1447 and again in 1561, was nearly 500 feet high.

builders, gardeners, pewterers, scriveners and candlestick-makers. Similarly, in Westminster and in Southwark the religious houses were the cornerstone of many livelihoods. As for the general population, they gave to their parish church about one eighth of what they paid in rent; in addition their charitable feelings were amply exploited by monastic appeals and mendicant friars. The Church held the last trump cards of Purgatory and Hell: an appropriate gift to the Church, it was suggested, could help lessen time spent in the former and avoid altogether an experience of the latter. It was a message the laity could hardly escape given the frequency of church attendance. Each Sunday a person *had* to attend Mass, and at least once each year *had* to make confession; fasting was ordained for about a hundred days a year, with the butchers unable to trade.

If the generally accepted estimate of London's population in the late fourteenth century is correct at around 40,000, then there was roughly one parish church relying for its sustenance on 400 people. And spread around the city, inside and outside the walls, were the conventual houses and friaries whose occupants also depended on the generosity and esteem of the citizens.

Monks and nuns usually came from the gentry and might well be from London families – in particular, the uncertain futures of unmarried daughters were resolved in this way. The convents therefore had strong links with the community outside and were not the social curiosities they are today. Preaching friars arrived in force in the thirteenth century. Backed by influential people, one after another orders – Franciscan, Carmelite, Dominican, Cistercian and Carthusian – were granted large precincts. The Dominican Blackfriars, who settled on the site of the old Baynard's Castle, were allowed even to realign London's west wall around them. Each house had its own rules of behaviour. While some, such as the Augustinians, ran hospitals like St Thomas's and St Bartholomew's, and were involved with life outside their cloisters, others, such as the Charterhouse Carthusians, remained reclusive, immersed in prayer and a vegetarian diet. Friars did not necessarily keep within their limits – they were out and about, preaching, hearing confessions, raising money, supping free meals, and, in the guise of pardoners, granting dubious pardons and peddling even more dubious relics. Even by the time of Chaucer, the friars had sunk into disrepute with many corrupted, it was claimed, by the worldliness that they daily encountered.

The largesse accrued by monks and friars was a matter of resentful concern to parish church officials. The incumbent of a parish could count on tithe income and that from baptisms, marriages and burials, but his subordinates were hard put to make a living out of the left-over crumbs. Sometimes the chantry priest, whose role in life consisted of not much more than the chanting of Masses for the souls of departed citizens who had had the money and the forethought to pay for the privilege, did better from his singular role than the vicar who had the pastoral care but not the main tithe income. The situation of the lesser clergy was unenviable, made even more penurious by the activities of hermits and anchorites who survived entirely upon charity.

Strictly speaking, a hermit was not the reclusive person we now imagine: solitary his domestic life may have been but he was familiar to the population and quite often had a civic task. For example, the hermit who lived in Highgate had the responsibility of mending the main road in the village – in return he could solicit alms. The hermit of 'St Martin, London' travelled so far abroad that he was twice fined in 1514 for digging gravel on Highgate Common without licence; his offence was related, most probably, to road mending as well. So highly regarded were hermits, so devout were they considered, that there was even competition to pay for their burial. In the case of the Highgate hermit he was able to transform his modest abode into a chapel which served for those who hadn't the energy on Sundays for the long journey to their respective parish churches in either St Pancras or Hornsey.

Anchorites excited even more admiration. Such men, and occasionally women, would seal themselves for much of their lives in a cell built within the walls of a parish church, renouncing company, worldly goods and personal hygiene. The anchorite attached to St Margaret, Westminster was better provided for, since his cell was 28 × 20 feet, and on two levels. It was believed by the laity that the anchorite's discomfort and reflective solitude equipped him or her to give advice to anyone who cared to ask and pay for it at the bars of the cell.

Chaucer's *Canterbury Tales* has made familiar the custom of pilgrimages. Canterbury was a modest destination in terms of distance, with the minor hazards of poor roads and bad weather, and hardly worth the expense of securing the protection of St Christopher or St Botolph as they left beneath a London gate. The pilgrims would have done better to have obtained the blessing of St Julien, patron saint of hospitality, to offset the deficiencies of the inn accommodation they encountered on the way. Another popular destination, Walsingham Abbey in northern Norfolk, was a different matter altogether, a place then and now inaccessible by principal roads. Pilgrimage for some was more than an act of faith or a spiritual duty: at times it was a form of self-flagellation – a number of medieval wills exist which bequeath money to those who would walk 'with naked feet' to specified shrines. This was thought to have the same beneficial effect on the soul of the benefactor as on that of the proxy. On the other hand, some observers remarked just how rowdy these groups of supposedly penitent pilgrims were, making more noise as they went through towns than 'if the King came there, with all his clarions and many other minstrels'. At the shrines the pilgrims would, like modern tourists, buy expensive nick-nacks and mementoes to take back with them, evidence of a destination reached. Likewise, pilgrims came to London, to the Westminster shrine of Edward the Confessor, and to St Paul's where St Erkenwald had lain since his body was appropriated by the canons from his own Barking Abbey. Lowlier shrines were within reach of the infirm or less resolute. Thomas Heywood mentioned those at Crooms Hill (Greenwich) and Highgate, or wayside features such as the holy well at Muswell Hill, endowed with sacred powers, which were usually on high terrain. The really determined went to shrines abroad and to the Holy Land, where danger most certainly went hand in hand with piety.

It will be seen from this that many Londoners spent a great deal of time and money propitiating God's judgement in the hereafter. Guild members had an additional method of inviting a favourable evaluation, for most guilds had an adopted church and within it a particular chapel in which Masses were said for departed members. But some charity found its way to those really in need. The hospitals attached to religious houses, such as St Bartholomew's, were for the poor; given that medical treatment was then so rudimentary, in truth they were no more than resting places in which a bed and some quiet comfort might heal an illness. Alms were dispensed at religious houses. In July 1322, so many people assembled at the gate of the Black Friars priory that in the mêlée fifty-two men and women were crushed to death.

DISEASE

THE POOR LEPERS HAD A RESTRICTED LIFE. They were refused entry to churches, inns, shops and bakehouses; they could not wash in streams, nor touch people in good health. Instead they were exiled to isolated buildings beyond the City walls, called lazar-houses (after the afflicted Lazarus) and in these they were left to manage as best they could. One such building was at St Giles's Fields, near today's junction of New Oxford Street and Tottenham Court Road, a site removed from the City and Westminster but on a busy crossroads at which alms for their support might be sought; Knightsbridge, St James's, Highgate and Hackney were other places thought suitable to seclude them. Lepers were formally excluded from the City in 1346 because the spread of the disease was helped 'by the contagion of their polluted breath, and by carnal intercourse with women in stews'. Lunatics, too, could be incarcerated. The first hospital for their containment appears to have been that attached to All Hallows Barking church, near the Tower of London, established in about 1370 for poor priests and others sick of 'the phrenzie', and it was not until the early fifteenth century that we hear of the care of lunatics at the priory of St Bethlehem (later corrupted to Bedlam) in Bishopsgate.

In some years sickness overwhelmed facilities. Plague was frequent and without remedy. It is not known how many Londoners were swept away by the Black Death in 1348-9, eight years after Chaucer's birth, but a common estimate is about a third of the population. The contagion had no impediment and the disease was ghastly and decisive – sometimes infection and death occurred within a day. It was thought that contamination, perhaps exhalations from the earth, was carried on the wind, and

The chapel of the Lock Hospital in Kent Street, Southwark, originally a hospital for lepers founded, probably, in the 12th century. Leprosy was largely extinct by the 17th century and the hospital specialized in the treatment of venereal diseases.

therefore those who could not escape the city burnt aromatic woods or powders to purify the air, or else sealed their houses with waxed cloth. It is now known that the disease was caused by infected black rats: the fleas which fed on them could spread the disease by biting a human. The churchyards could not cope with the burials and thousands were interred in pits outside the walls 'unhousel'd, unanointed, unannealed'. This was scarcely surprising since anyone handling a plague corpse did so at her peril (it was almost invariably women who dressed the dead). There is no adequate contemporary account of the desperate scenes in London, but we do know that the contagion went through whole communities – twenty-seven monks at Westminster Abbey succumbed, and all the inmates of St James's Hospital, Westminster, except one, died.

Plague raged again in London in 1394, carrying off Queen Anne and leaving King Richard II so distraught that he ordered the destruction of Shene Palace, a building which she had helped to plan. At the end of the Middle Ages, in 1485, a new epidemic called 'sweating sickness' invaded London. It took off thousands, including the mayor and his elected successor, and six aldermen. This disease, which brought high fever and in many cases sudden and unexpected death, has not yet been identified with a modern counterpart.

Disease could easily fester in a sometimes squalid London. There were no sewers; drinking water could be so contaminated that ale was safer to drink; rubbish, dung and night soil collected in piles in the streets; and in Newgate the roads might be awash with the blood and entrails of animals that had met their brutal deaths there. The activities of the butchers around Newgate are those most mentioned in records of public hygiene. A fairly mild ban was introduced in 1333 preventing them from slaughtering animals in the main streets, and those who dealt with the more obnoxious parts of the carcasses, such as the bowels, were restricted in their trade to side-streets. Ten years later the City officials, in a misguided enactment, granted the butchers a place by the river Fleet in which to clean entrails, but this merely removed the stench and nuisance away from Newgate to the already polluted area of the Fleet. The problems of street cleansing feature perennially in the City records. A Serjeant of the Channels appears in 1385, whose remit was the supervision of the streets and alleyways, but wards also employed scavengers to oversee the work of the rakyers who actually did the unpleasant job.

It is difficult to know now just how bad things were – we have only the headlines, mainly culled from City records. Complaints about people who threw their slops down to the road from upper storeys occur, references to latrines built over the Walbrook and the Fleet are frequent. But it would be unwise to infer from these selected items that life in London and its extensive rural suburbs was particularly noisome.

LAW AND ORDER

Neither should it be inferred from those same records that London was particularly violent or lawless, even though there was hardly more than the vigilance of neighbours or the rigour of community obligations to deter crime. In the City an Act of 1283 stipulated that each of the wards should supply six able-bodied householders as watchmen, and this neighbourly arrangement was hardly improved upon until the establishment of a police force in the nineteenth century. Certainly there was theft, although possessions then were few and people tended to be at home most of the time, and certainly mob rule prevailed sometimes, notably during 1326 and the Peasants' Revolt of 1381. The 1326 furore occurred when the political situation was unstable in the extreme. The Bishop of Exeter, identified with a faction detested by Londoners, was dragged from his horse before he could reach sanctuary in St Paul's, and summarily beheaded in Cheapside with a butcher's knife, and the mob then went on the rampage in the Lombard quarter. The behaviour of many Londoners during the Peasants' Revolt was unbridled. It is not possible now to determine how much of the fury was inspired by political revenge and how much by drink and mob rule, but the sacking of buildings such as the Savoy Palace, St John's Priory, Clerkenwell and the Tower of London was as barbaric as anything seen before. The unpopular Archbishop of Canterbury and others were found in the Tower and dragged to Tower Hill for execution.

Other kinds of violence resulted from disputes between guilds, when quarrels were forcefully contested by hotheads. Loriners (who made horses' bits) and painters joined forces in 1327 to fight the saddlers up and down Cheapside over a trade disagreement; several were killed in the disturbance. Twelve years later fishmongers and skinners were locked in a battle which resulted in deaths and executions. As late as 1440 law students were in trouble for attacking butchers who cleansed carcasses in the Fleet river near the students' premises. In the same year apprentice drapers and tailors fought in the streets over the election of the mayor. Apprentices were frequently in the news for riotous behaviour, especially on Shrove Tuesday, a public holiday when excessive drinking, turmoil and baiting of foreigners and prostitutes were routine.

In medieval and Tudor times prostitution was mainly confined to Southwark, and from then onwards it moved to the Strand and Covent Garden. 'Night walkers' had been

The slaying of Wat Tyler during the Peasants' Revolt of 1381. A meeting was arranged between King Richard II, and Tyler the peasants' leader, at East Smithfield near the Tower. Tyler was assassinated there by the Mayor of London, William Walworth.

outlawed in the City around 1276, but in Westminster they were not uncommon, probably because men attached to court, parliament or monastery did not care for the journey to Southwark. A clerk who had some houses at Charing let them exclusively to prostitutes in 1407, and in 1409 two women were recorded as keeping a 'bordelhouse for monks, priests, and others'. No doubt there were brothels in other places around London – one is noted as far away as Enfield in 1324.

Tolerated and regarded as inevitable prostitution might have been, but the women were still, at times, obliged to wear a distinctive badge and were buried in unconsecrated ground on the south bank; in 1352 'common lewd women' were forbidden to dress in the same manner as 'good and noble dames and damsels', and especially forbidden to use fur trimmings on their dresses. Like their modern successors who are gathered around railway stations, the Southwark women drew their customers from the numerous coaching inns in Borough High Street and from Londoners who crossed the bridge for the evening. Southwark was loosely under the City's jurisdiction but it was never closely supervised, even when the City officially took full control of it in the sixteenth century. Every city needs a 'blind eye' pocket and Southwark, until the end of the seventeenth century, was London's. It was a place of refuge, often of criminals, and the location of illicit and sometimes violent pleasures.

The array of small prisons in Southwark indicates a lawlessness disproportionate to its total population. The Clink (which itself has given a word to the language) began as an ecclesiastical prison within the Bishop of Winchester's palace in an area already notorious for the lewder attractions of life. Advice to a twelfth-century visitor included a warning against 'crowds of pimps. . ..Actors, jesters, smooth-skinned lads, Moors, flatterers, pretty-boys, effeminates, paederasts, singing and dancing girls, belly dancers, quacks,

THE Marshalsea Prison in Southwark in 1773. The building derived its name from the court held there by the king's marshal; its foundation date is unknown but it was attacked during the Peasants' Revolt of 1381. By the 18th century Marshalsea was used mainly to confine debtors.

sorceresses, extortioners, magicians, night-wanderers, mimes, beggars and buffoons', a collection of people more likely to excite the appetite than depress it. The Marshalsea Prison, off Borough High Street, was a royal prison under the control of the king's Earl Marshal, housing ordinary criminals or those who had offended the king. But it was not a fortress and, indeed, for a bribe the inhabitants could be at large in the neighbourhood. Imprisonment wasn't thought of as isolation from society and, until Victorian times, a family could live there with a prisoner – the young Charles Dickens saw his own family living in some humiliation within the walls of the Marshalsea with his debtor father.

The abundance of debtors' prisons north and south of the river emphasizes the seriousness with which this offence was viewed. It is likely that more were incarcerated for debt, and for longer, than for any other crime. Imprisonment was not the usual fate for other offenders, who were executed, exiled, mutilated, whipped, pilloried and branded instead. But a debt could usually only be redeemed if relatives of the debtor were persuaded to find the money to release the prisoner and if this didn't happen he remained in prison, kept alive by the alms of passers-by, though even then the conditions of his containment were flexible, depending on how much money he could raise. In the Fleet Prison, for example, an inmate could work and earn money in and out of the gaol – specially encouraged since he was then able to pay the keeper more for his privileges. Newgate Gaol was originally over the City gate of that name and was later enlarged and rebuilt at the expense of Richard Whittington in 1423.

The punishment of felons was a notoriously haphazard affair. Those able to read and write could plead 'benefit of clergy' and opt for trial in the more lenient ecclesiastical courts, and those with social standing could hope that this would help them with any jury. The Normans favoured mutilation as punishment for serious offences, or else

Sir John Oldcastle, a prominent follower of Wyclif, did not escape the fire that most had expected to consume his mentor. The abortive rising he led in London in 1417 led inexorably to his trial, followed by a hanging and a burning at special gallows at St Giles-in-the-Fields.

forfeiture of goods and property conjoined with exile. Execution, reserved generally for those whom the monarch wished to dispose of, became a common retribution in the later Middle Ages until it reached grotesque proportions in Tudor times as religious fervour overcame humanitarian sensibilities.

There had been an earlier blood-letting in London, also the result of religious intolerance, during the long Wyclif controversy. John Wyclif (*c.*1324-84) had endeared himself to few in authority when he claimed that the Church's involvement in temporal affairs, and its generous portfolio of temporal possessions, were contrary to the teachings of the Bible. Whatever Wyclif intended, his criticism of Church land-ownership was bound to appeal to the disaffected and was one of the contributory factors of the Peasants' Revolt of 1381. If this were not enough, Wyclif questioned the authority of the Pope, denied the doctrine of transubstantiation and for good measure translated the New

Testament into English so that more people could be familiar with its words which, he maintained, gave substance to his arguments. An English version was not welcomed by the ecclesiastical establishment because, apart from other considerations, it diminished the clergy's monopoly of the Bible's interpretation.

During his last years Wyclif was officially branded a heretic, but he survived to die a natural death under the patronage of the Lancastrian party. The same clemency, however, was not extended to his followers, the so-called Lollards. William Chatris, priest of St Benet Sherehog, was burnt at Smithfield, one of the earliest victims in a depressing chronicle at this place. In 1410 John Bradly, a tailor, suffered in the same way. Henry, Prince of Wales, was present on that occasion and did his best, we are told, to persuade the poor man to recant even as the flames engulfed him. There were not, however, enough Lollard supporters in London to gain the upper hand. When in 1414 Sir John Oldcastle,

THE cage and stocks on London Bridge, probably at the southern end. The cage was a temporary lock-up before arraignment or transfer to a larger prison. From an engraving in the New and Complete Book of Martyrs *by John Foxe.*

a leading Wyclif follower, held in the Tower until he recanted, escaped from captivity, an attempted march of his supporters on the City from St Giles's Fields was easily deterred simply by keeping the City gates secure. It was a disastrous end to a brief uprising and those who still bravely called themselves Lollards were quickly dispatched – Sir Roger Acton and thirty-six others were publicly put to death. Years afterwards men were still being executed for following Wyclif – Richard Wiche, vicar of Deptford, was burned at Tower Hill in 1440 and as late as 1475 John Goose was burnt there for the same offence. Though there might not have been an organized Lollard party in London there was a sizeable undercurrent of sympathy for them. This was exploited by the vicar of All Hallows near the Tower who took advantage of the resentment at the burning of Wiche to put spices into the ashes of the pyre and persuade the gullible that the scent given off indicated that the victim was a martyr: he then sold candles and relics at a profit.

The law's retribution was very public. Executions attracted large crowds, and by the fourteenth century the stocks and pillory provided common amusement as well. Minor offenders, such as drunks, were confined in stocks, a contraption that held the offender sat upon a bench by his ankles and sometimes by his wrists, in enforced humiliation. The pillory was a more serious matter and for more serious crimes, such as fraudulent trading and perjury; to the back of this T-shaped structure the felon was tied with his head and wrists through the crosspiece. Sometimes his ears were pinned to the board so that he could not dodge the missiles thrown at him. Ducking in a stream or river was reserved for women, particularly those thought to be gossips and shrews. The poor woman was tied in a bucket seat which was then immersed in water and brought up again only at the last moment, or else sometimes too late. One such ducking place was a pond on the site of Trafalgar Square.

Penance was less frequent. The Duchess of Gloucester was found to be guilty of witchcraft in an attempt to put her husband on the throne of England and for three days in November 1441 she was obliged to do penance in the streets of the City by walking barefoot with a lighted taper in her hand, shrouded in a white sheet. On the first day she walked from Temple Bar to St Paul's, on the second along Thames Street and on the third all the way from Queenhithe to Cornhill. A similar fate befell Jane Shore, mistress of Edward IV, in 1483.

If a criminal were fast enough and had little to lose he could flee to the sanctuary of a church which still held the right to shelter criminals without molestation. In so doing he placed himself beyond the reach of the law for forty days and caused a great deal of inconvenience – to the church officials, who were obliged to feed him, and to the local ward watch which had to guard the church every day and night to ensure that he did not leave again.

The usual procedure if the offender wanted to retain his liberty was to send for the coroner and announce his intention to abjure the realm. He was deprived of his possessions, assigned a port of embarkation from which to leave the country and given a precise route to get there. Even the most serious offenders could escape punishment by this method. But while the Church jealously guarded its right to shelter criminals it could also withdraw its protection if the offender had injured the Church itself. In 1321 a woman who had slain the clerk at All Hallows at London Wall took refuge in the building, but the Bishop of London ordered her removal and she was hanged at Newgate; five thieves who robbed the convent of St Martin-le-Grand in 1480 were similarly expelled: three were hanged and two pressed to death. Westminster Abbey's sanctuary was particularly favoured, empowered as it was to shelter debtors.

In the City, Smithfield and Tower Hill were customary places of execution, though it was not uncommon for the event to take place opposite the scene of the crime. It is not known when and why the remote crossroads at Tyburn, near today's Marble Arch, became a place at which to hang City prisoners. Roger Mortimer (d.1330), implicated in the death of Edward II, may have lost his life there, though more likely his execution was at Smithfield, but certainly from the fourteenth century the 'Tyburn tree' was in frequent use for increasingly barbaric hangings. By the eighteenth century Tyburn was the destination for rowdy and macabre processions that wound their way from Newgate through the western suburbs, an example, if one were needed, of the retribution that faced wrongdoers.

Spectacle and Entertainment

THE CHURCH, CONTROLLING AS IT DID the religious or formerly pagan celebration days, was the most prodigious provider of spectacle: Christmas, Easter, Midsummer and May Day were notable occasions. On May Day 'every man, except impediment, would walke into the sweete meadows and greene woods, there to rejoyce their spirites with the beauty and savour of sweete flowers, and with the harmony of birds.' They would return with armfuls of flowers to decorate their houses, or else put them around the traditional maypole – there was a particularly important maypole at the eastern end of the Strand.

There were also corporate occasions of mayor-making, livery company processions, coronations, funerals, weddings and receptions for celebrities. City officials in 1290 escorted Edward I on the last stage of his journey with the cortège of his queen, Eleanor,

MAYPOLES were the centrepiece of the 1 May holiday. After branches and flowers were brought from surrounding fields to decorate houses, the May queen was crowned at a ceremony which included dancing around the maypole.

who had died in Grantham: this melancholy procession came into the City and then along the Strand to a burial service at Westminster, and by the King's command elaborate stone crosses to mark resting-places were erected at Cheapside and near the hospital of St Mary Rounceval at the little settlement of Charing at the top of Whitehall. Charing Cross, rebuilt in the nineteenth century in a fancied replication of the old monument, is a reminder of this event. After victory over the French at Poitiers in 1356 the Black Prince was received triumphantly in London, where civic leaders met him at Southwark to escort him across a Thames bedecked by boats. The captured King of France was a prominent part of this occasion, dressed in purple and mounted on a magnificent white horse; tapestries, ornaments and silks decorated the streets, and bows, arrows, shields and spears were hung from balconies to emphasize London's appetite for battle. In 1396, the seven-year-old Isabella of France, betrothed to Richard II, was welcomed to London via

Blackheath and in the crush to glimpse her on London Bridge seven people were pressed to death. In 1415, victory at Agincourt was celebrated when City dignitaries met King Henry at Blackheath 'in magnificent copes, and preceded with rich crosses, and censers smoking with frankincense'. In Cheapside the water conduits ran with wine.

Tournaments took place in Cheapside, the widest street in the City. The London historian, John Stow, writing in the sixteenth century, described a typical tournament in the presence of Edward III in 1331: 'the stone pavement being covered with sand, that the horses might not slide when they strongly set their feet to the ground, the King held a tournament three days together, with the nobility, valiant men of the realm, and other strange knights'. London Bridge was used on one occasion for an unusual needle match. In 1390 an argument between English and Scottish ambassadors as to which country contained the bravest men was brought to the test in a joust on the bridge between the two ambassadors. The two countries were, in fact, in a state of hostility at the time, and the Scottish party was granted safe conduct to take part. The King, courtiers and probably half of London watched as the Englishman was thrown and injured; the Scot is reported to have sat by his rival's bedside for some days afterwards. The area outside Westminster Abbey was another venue for tournaments, such as that to mark the coronation of Queen Margaret in 1445, or for the wedding of Prince Arthur in 1501.

Though jousting was a rich man's amusement and a poor man's spectacle, the sport of archery was a common one. It was, in any case, obligatory for a man to learn the use of a bow in case of need by sovereign or City, but the number of proclamations over the years urging its practice suggests that less formal sports such as wrestling and football had gained ground at archery's expense. By John Stow's time things were so lax that he wrote in his *Survey* that young men had abandoned archery and did 'creepe into bowling-alleys and ordinarie dicing-houses where they hazard their money at unlawful games'.

William Fitzstephen, from whom in the late twelfth century we obtain our first proper taste of the recreations of the period, describes races, skating, javelin throwing, putting stone, and mimic battles with sword and buckler. Wrestling had official sanction in London where it took place with the Lord Mayor's blessing on St Bartholomew's Day. In 1222 a wrestling match occurred between men of the City and Westminster which the City won; the return match a week later ended in riots, indicating perhaps not just a disposition to violence but a deep-seated rivalry between the two parts of London.

Tilting at quintains was popular for those who could ride, though a version of this sport was common on the Thames where the trick was to strike a target while standing in a rowing boat moving in the fast current of the river.

THE FRIAR

T. Cook sculp

Sᴿ. THOMAS MORE.

Sɪʀ ᴛʜᴏᴍᴀs ᴍᴏʀᴇ (1475–1535). Born in Cheapside, More was placed by family influence in the household of the Archbishop of Canterbury. He studied at Oxford and there formed friendships with Erasmus and Colet. He published his most famous work, Utopia, *in 1515. In 1529 he became Lord Chancellor but, unable to support Henry VIII's divorce from Catherine, he resigned and, in 1534, refused to take the Oath of Supremacy.and so was beheaded.*

CHAPTER II

THE OTHER LONDON

LONDON WAS NOT A CITY IN ISOLATION. TO ITS WEST LAY WESTMINSTER, A RELATIVELY small township, but nevertheless, because of the presence of the royal household, abbey and law courts, a force to be reckoned with. Between lay Fleet Street and the Strand, a thoroughfare which became increasingly prestigious, the eastern end a legal centre and the western end one of large mansions overlooking the Thames. Around were numerous villages which supplied the City, and which were trapped within its financial orbit.

The rivalry between the City and Westminster noted earlier persisted throughout the Middle Ages as an extension of the City's relationship with the Crown. In terms of population and affluence there was no comparison between the two places, since the residents of Westminster were scarcely more than attendants and suppliers to the Court, Abbey and law courts. But even so, royal patronage of Westminster was certainly an irritant to the City, no more so than in 1245 when Henry III granted Westminster the right to hold two annual fairs in January and October. Initially, these were of three days

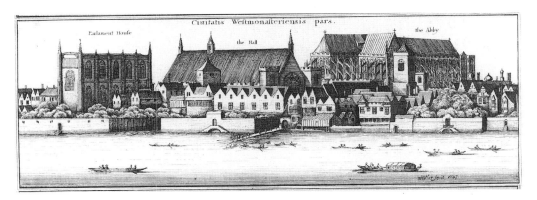

THE Palace of Westminster and Westminster Abbey in 1647, by Wenceslaus Hollar. To the left is St Stephen's Chapel, built in the early years of the 14th century; since secularization it had been the home of the House of Commons. In the centre is Westminster Hall, built by William II in c.1097, and altered between 1397 and 1399 by Henry Yevele. The Abbey is to the right.

each, but the October event, large enough it seems to be a European affair, was later extended to three weeks, during which time the shops of the City had to remain closed. The contemporary chronicler, Matthew Paris, tells us that this fair was intended to raise money for the rebuilding of the Abbey, and to tax the City. Its effect on City tradesmen, manufacturers and merchants may be imagined, and extravagant gifts were pressed on the King, to no avail, in efforts to lift the ban on City trade. These fairs eventually disappeared, hampered by poor facilities and the fact that they were held in months when the weather was inclement, and they were superseded by a small fair in the Abbey grounds, while a much older market in Tothill Street continued.

Westminster was an odd concoction. Sometimes it was full to bursting, and at others, when the Court was absent, those who made their livings supplying it had to look elsewhere for income. Many of the properties which lined what became Whitehall were

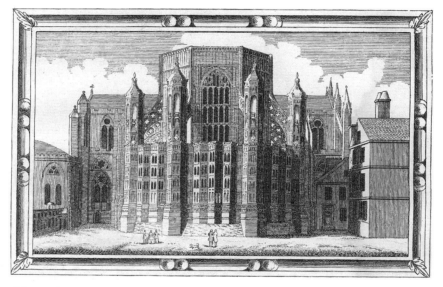

The Henry VII Chapel in Westminster Abbey. Henry VII originally intended this building, begun in 1502, as a memorial to his uncle Henry VI. Henry VII was himself buried here as was Oliver Cromwell until he and his followers were disinterred after the Restoration.

occupied by members of the royal household, which could number between 300 and 400 when the Court was resident. The law courts, based in Westminster Hall, became firmly established there in the fourteenth century; and many of the personnel involved and those who came from the provinces to plead or defend cases would have needed accommodation.

Parliament, though it met infrequently (and for much of the fifteenth century hardly at all), created another seasonal demand for bedroom space. The numerous residents of the Abbey could rely on the produce of its landholdings. Included in those lands, which stretched up to Hendon, was the Convent Garden, north of the Strand, an estate of about forty acres later developed by the Bedford family. During the Middle Ages this garden contained a mixture of orchard, meadow, pasture and arable land.

Westminster was thus a place which had a permanent feature in the Abbey (which owned most of the land), a royal household which could be absent for long periods, regular law courts and an occasional parliament. A further element was to develop after a fire destroyed much of the Palace of Westminster in 1512. Henry VIII, with palaces elsewhere, abandoned Westminster to the growing number of civil servants and only in 1529 did he return to Wolsey's York Place, which he renamed Whitehall Palace.

THE STRAND

AS EARLY AS THE 1170S WILLIAM FITZSTEPHEN, who was not short of a glowing phrase or two, remarked upon 'a populous faubourg' which connected the City to Westminster. He was here describing Fleet Street and the Strand, the first taking its name from the river that it ended at, the second denoting what it was originally, the shoreline

THE Savoy Palace from the Thames in 1736. The Palace was begun by Peter, the future Count of Savoy. It was inherited by John of Gaunt in 1361, partially destroyed in the Peasants' Revolt of 1381, and rebuilt as a hospital in the 16th century by Henry VII.

of the Thames: Maitland's *History of London* (1756) noted that during the construction of St Mary-le-Strand church in 1714, natural ground level was found to be not much higher than the Thames. The character of the Strand in its early days is elusive. We know from a petition of 1315 that the roadway was so bad that the 'feet of horses and rich and poor men received constant damage', and that the 'footway was interrupted by thickets and bushes'; in 1353 a tax was levied to repair the highway because it was 'so deep and miry, and the pavement so broken and worn as to be very dangerous both to men and carriages'. Again, in 1532 the Strand was described as 'full of pits and sloughs, very perilous and noisome' – hardly resembling the highway of rich men's mansions that is sometimes suggested. It was in the Strand that Peter of Savoy, uncle of Henry III, built a palace from c.1290, a building virtually destroyed in the Peasants' Revolt of 1381 – the site was then apparently left derelict until 1505, again implying a thoroughfare of low social standing.

Numerous bishops and abbots had London homes, some of them along the Strand. The Bishop of Durham resided here (opposite today's Bedford Street) from medieval times, but the street's heyday of aristocratic residents properly began in 1549 when the grasping Duke of Somerset appropriated the ground east of today's Waterloo Bridge, demolished premises belonging to bishops and an Inn of Chancery, together with the church of St Mary-le-Strand, and there built himself Somerset House, the first Renaissance palace in the country. By the end of the Tudor period noblemen, state officials and courtiers had followed his example. Families such as those of Burghley, Essex, Arundel and Bedford – those who needed a home near Whitehall – erected mansions with grounds fronting the unpredictable Thames. As the sites filled up on that side of the street so houses of quality were built on the northern side. This transformation was spread over about a hundred years, and yet by the end of the seventeenth century they had almost all disappeared.

SOMERSET HOUSE from the river in 1755. Somerset House was built from 1547 to 1550 for the unpopular Lord Protector Somerset, then exploiting his guardianship of the young Edward VI. The acquisition of the site entailed the demolition of numerous buildings.

FURTHER OUT

IT WAS DURING THE TUDOR PERIOD too that we find some Londoners setting up second homes in the rural hinterland of the metropolis. Sir Thomas More, who was to follow Wolsey as Chancellor and was to lose his life and not just his reputation in dealing with the King, bought land at Chelsea on which he erected a house for his large family. More himself exemplified the class of citizen whose fortune was in the ascendant. He was the son of a barrister, then living in Milk Street, Cheapside, and after education at St Anthony's, Threadneedle Street, he became part of the household of the Archbishop of Canterbury in Lambeth Palace. His wit, knowledge and ability ensured a rapid rise in his career but his opposition to the Boleyn marriage and the Act of Supremacy brought about his downfall and death. In his Chelsea house on the banks of the Thames, described as 'surrounded with green fields and wooded hills', he is reputed to have lived in simple style together with his children and eleven grandchildren, a monkey and an aviary.

Nearby in Chelsea was the house of the Earl of Shrewsbury, a rambling, gabled mansion around a courtyard, built in the early sixteenth century and which, by the nineteenth century, was a 'stained paper manufactory'.

Successful Spanish merchants called Balm built themselves a large house in Hackney complete with moat, parterre, orchards and lawns. Up in Highgate – to become a favourite retreat for City men and lawyers – Sir Roger Cholmeley, a Chief Justice who narrowly escaped with his life in the perilous years after the death of Henry VIII, had a house overlooking London across what is now Waterlow Park; it was Cholmeley who founded Highgate School. The Lord Mayor of London in 1536, wool merchant Ralph Warren, escaped to a handsome house called Passors in Fulham, and in Enfield the formidable

BEAUFORT HOUSE, Chelsea. During his retirement from state politics Sir Thomas More bought land at Chelsea and there erected a large house, described by Erasmus as 'not mean, not invidiously grand, but comfortable'. Beaufort Street is now across its site.

City businessman, Sir Thomas Wilmot, a man almost always dressed entirely in black, occupied a mansion called Elsings that Queen Elizabeth I was later to own.

THE VILLAGES AROUND

ONLY IN ITS VERY EARLY DAYS was the City self-sufficient. Then there was space for agriculture, horticulture and the keeping of animals but, even by the time the Normans were overlords, it relied for many of its day-to-day needs on the villages around. The citizens found they could make more money, and faster, from trade and manufacture, than from farming, and they exchanged their remaining rural occupations for those of a growing commercial city. And while pigs may still have roamed some of the streets of the

City, and cows were still kept in some back rooms, the residents as a whole turned to the suburbs for their necessities. In this way the outlying villages and London became interdependent, especially once the gardens of the City monasteries were built upon after the Dissolution.

At the same time the gap between the wealth and aspirations of City-dwellers and those of their suppliers in such villages as Stratford, Kentish Town and Fulham grew wider. In part this was due to the almost inevitable consequence of wealth, bravely used, multiplying itself; also, the activities of London's traders and merchants were less labour intensive, less dependent on the weather's hazard, and could be turned to profit in most circumstances.

But another factor encouraged a disparity of wealth between the residents of the City and the villages. While the framework in which Londoners sought to make a living permitted enterprise, in the villages feudalism diminished only slowly and restricted innovation. Even Westminster was a patchwork of manors and liberties involving a variety of land-tenures, customs and regulations derived from Saxon and early Norman traditions.

In the City those who governed also worked there, whereas in the villages the landowners, mostly ecclesiastical bodies, were absent and without interest in the problems or the prosperity of the community. In the villages the occupier of the manor house was rarely the landlord, and not necessarily even his representative. At assemblies of tenants it was the manorial steward or bailiff who presided, not the owner of the land.

This arrangement prevented any natural development of parochial government, especially so when there were several manors within a parish. Whereas in the City the wards, comparatively large units, were responsible for local government, in the villages the manor courts were the most active bodies of administration. The parish, bereft of responsibilities, played a minor role. It elected a few officers at meetings in the church vestry each year, had the fabric of the church and its burial ground in its care and administered local charities, but the manors had the day-to-day concerns such as the state of the roads, the silted streams, the occasional crime, the ownership of land and houses, the provision and management of common fields, and the standards of ale and bread. Thus, until the 1601 Poor Law Act, which put the care of the poor into the reluctant hands of the parishes, the manors, with their absentee and unconcerned landlords, were the prime local authorities. It is unsurprising then that no parochial mechanism evolved, or was felt to be necessary by those who owned the land, so that the villages and the small towns they became could govern themselves adequately.

Usually, there were two kinds of manor courts functioning around London. One, the Court Baron, dealt with land transactions; the other, the Court Leet, controlled the management of manorial lands, dealt with misdemeanours, encroachments, the blockage of streams, immorality and unlawful retailing of ale. It was this court which appointed manorial officers, such as the reeve, aletaster, hayward, constable and highway inspector. It is the Leet records which illustrate, even if erratically, early social life in these London suburbs. In Fulham a man in 1475 was fined for persuading others to gamble at dice all night; many court rolls have examples of women punished for being scolds and gossips. In Cantelowes manor (Kentish Town) a man was arraigned for harbouring a single woman in his house. But apart from these more entertaining items generally the records are of uncleared streams, pigs roaming the commons unringed, farmers breaking into the manor pound to reclaim their cattle without payment, people digging gravel illegally and tenants removing wood that had not already fallen to the ground.

Most tenancies were copyhold, their title recorded on a copy of the lord's court roll: no transfer of property was legal without that record. Almost invariably the lord charged a fee for that transfer, and what was called a heriot was often levied after the death of a tenant on the assumption, by the lord of the manor anyway, that the late tenant probably owed him money in lieu of weapons or services. Usually, the best beast of the deceased was impounded. Nor was a tenant necessarily free to leave his property to whom he wished. Often inheritance was governed by the custom of 'Borough English' in which the *youngest* son inherited, or, in the absence of sons, property was divided equally among daughters. In Kent and some parts of Middlesex, such as St Pancras and Hornsey, the potentially disruptive system of gavelkind prevailed in which the estate was equally divided among sons, which often led to a division of a holding into impossibly uneconomic plots, causing jealousy and ill-feeling among those in receipt of them.

Copyhold tenants were obliged to work for periods as free labourers on the manorial lord's land, probably at times also crucial to themselves. Gradually this liability, undignified and inconvenient, was commuted in most areas to a money payment. This was the case in Bexley, for example, where a hired force of labourers worked on the lord's demesne land, with gradated scales of pay from the ploughman down to the swineherd, and at appropriate times village boys were employed to scare birds or look after ewes with young lambs. Quaint gifts of produce are recorded as a condition of tenancy or, more mundanely as in Plumstead, water and wood had to be occasionally collected and taken to the local abbot. In return for these payments and services the tenant was afforded the protection of the lord of the manor, an advantage both dubious in definition and rare in performance.

These rural outposts of London had a precarious existence and famine was no stranger. There were very bad harvest years from 1315 until 1320, which led to severe hardship in the winters, and there was acute hunger in London and elsewhere in 1391 at a time when the King was said to employ 300 domestics in his kitchen alone, and to occasionally entertain 6,000 people at a sitting. Cattle plague, especially severe in 1319, was endemic. Animals, let out on common fields to graze, could easily infect others, and in large open fields where tenants worked adjacent strips of land, crop diseases could also travel at will. Many of the cattle were, in any case, slaughtered as winter began – there was scarcely any feed to keep them alive and most root crops had yet to be introduced.

The poorest houses were wood-framed, the walls a lattice-work of strong twigs contrived between main supports, and then secured by mud. Humans and animals commonly lived beneath the same thatched roof, separated by an interior wall. The floor would be rushes or straw straight on to the earth; walls and chimney (if it existed), were of mud – alternatively, the smoke from the fire in the middle of the room went straight up through a hole in the roof; windows had no glass and were therefore shuttered or covered in the colder months. To add to the smoke from the fire there was the stench of tallow grease burnt as crude candles. In all these cottages furniture was scarce and primitive, utensils crude, diet monotonous and deficient.

For the poor, it was a mean living in a lush landscape. The monk, William Fitzstephen, who in the 1170s wrote a buoyant and much quoted description of London, was enthusiastic too about its suburbs. To the north of London, he said:

are pasture lands and a pleasant space of flat meadows, intersected by running waters, which turn revolving mill-wheels with a merry din. Hard by there stretches a great forest with wooded glades and lairs of wild beasts, deer both red and fallow, wild boar and bulls. The cornfields are not of barren gravel, but rich Asian plains such as make glad the crops and fill the barns of their farmers with sheaves of Ceres' stalk.

The 'great forest' was that of Middlesex, a panoply that once spread up and over the northern ridge above London and in which enclaves such as Hampstead, Highgate and Hornsey were hard-won clearings. Hampstead Heath and Highgate Wood are truncated successors of that forest as are the wooded areas of the Kenwood estate at Highgate. Kenwood was owned, at about the time of Fitzstephen's description, by the Blemont family, one that has left its name in London, being corrupted to Bloomsbury and translated to Cornhill. However, the deer, boar and game that enthused Fitzstephen were the preserve of the king or such families as the Blemonts, and the penalties for poaching them were heavy even when famine made it imperative. On the links of Highgate Golf Club today can clearly be seen the outline of the moated lodge owned by the Bishop of London, used as a base for hunting parties.

The villages probably had little diversity in their composition: a parish church of late Saxon or early Norman foundation, a churchyard still with space for burials, a vicarage, an alehouse or two, at least one smithy, some country-seat houses, a water supply and a watermill, and farmhouses and cottages scattered as land-ownership permitted.

The alehouse was the lowest category of drinking-place, and even then might just be a small brewhouse from which to buy pitchers of the thick, poorly fermented, short-life ale for home consumption. Larger villages, such as Islington, might boast an inn, where accommodation, food and wine could be had, but taverns, a third class of public house which also sold wine – an expensive drink – were rare in villages. Chaucer's ale-wife appears repeatedly but prosaically in court rolls where she is frequently fined for 'regrating' ale, almost certainly a licence disguised as a fine. Some alehouses developed into small parlours where ale could be drunk and some served as a local shop for daily necessities. It was an intermittent business for the ale-wives, as ingredients were available and the custom was forthcoming. If the village were on a cattle route almost certainly she would sell along the way, or she might take ale to a fair or market, and there were local celebrations such as scot-ales, bride-ales and those that attended the end of harvest, which needed extra supplies. But until the fifteenth century, when hops were introduced from Holland, ale was a crude concoction, notoriously difficult to keep.

Buying and selling of most commodities was done at markets and fairs. Westminster had a market under royal protection and the Archbishop of Canterbury procured one for Lambeth so long as it did not injure the interests of the City. A charter was granted to the City in 1327 in which no market, with the exceptions of those at Southwark, Lambeth and Westminster, was permitted within seven miles of the City. This prohibition, generally enforced until the seventeenth century, is reflected in the shape of a number of town centres outside the proscribed radius. In Middlesex, Staines, Uxbridge and Brentford were particularly important as market towns, as were Hounslow, Enfield, Harrow and Pinner. In Kent, only Bromley and Eltham had markets near London although there was possibly one at Woolwich; Surrey boasted markets at Croydon and Kingston, and Essex at Barking, Havering, Romford, Rainham and Epping.

Slaughtering of cattle had been expelled, at least in theory, from the City streets to those of the suburbs of Stratford and Knightsbridge, though it probably went on everywhere on the main droving routes into Smithfield – centres like Islington depended on the transit, feeding and housing of cattle. The ancillary industry of the manufacture of leather was also barred the City. Tanning was exiled, mainly to Southwark and Bermondsey where the water supply was good. Here ox, cow and calf skins were immersed for months in vats of tannin, an unpleasant-smelling liquid derived from the crushed barks of trees, especially oaks, and from these the skins went the demarcational London round of curriers, who stretched, shaved and greased them, and then on to leathersellers, cordwainers, glovers and saddlers.

Fitzstephen's rural fields were also disturbed by tile- and brick-making. From the thirteenth century the City, learning from many fires, urged the use of tiles instead of thatch on roofs, and conical tile kilns became a common feature in the outer London landscape. Brickfields played havoc with the natural contours of the land as the taste for brick houses developed. We know from the records of Westminster Abbey that the enormous total of 400,000 bricks was made at its estate in Belsize Park, Hampstead in 1496, presumably to build an early Belsize House, since the transportation of such a bulk to Westminster would not have been feasible.

On the whole the houses of the suburban wealthy were made of timber or stone at best. One we know about stood not far north of today's King's Cross, owned by William Bruges, the first Garter King-of-Arms. It was here, in 1416, that he entertained the Emperor Sigismund during his visit to England. The assembly of people gathered was immense, and one may imagine the impressive display of colour and ornament in the low-lying fields of that area. Present were the Lord Mayor, aldermen, livery company representatives, king's trumpeters, knights and esquires, the Bishop of Ely, the Dukes of Briga and Holland, the Prince of Hungary and their retinues, all at a smallish stone house in fields on the bank of the river Fleet. Presumably, many stayed the night, probably under canvas, for the feast laid on would have impeded much movement later. While minstrels and sackbuts diverted them, the guests ate nine pigs, seven sheep, one hundred pullets, one hundred pigeons, thirty capons, twenty hens, hares, rabbits, kids, salmon, eels, crabs, oysters, wild boars and red deer.

This elaborate choice of food says something about the diet of the affluent. The lord of Tooting manor had vineyards, fishponds, dovecotes and a rabbit warren and could survive easily through a winter, but it is doubtful if much of his largesse was distributed among tenants dependent on rye bread and those vegetables that could be obtained in the colder months. There was a desperate, if unrecognized, lack of vitamin C for much of the year, resulting in scurvy, emaciation, skin blotches and bad teeth.

Thomas Linacre, M.D.
Founder of the College of Physicians in London.
Was born in Canterbury, 1460, & died in London 1524.
From a very curious old Drawing in the Collection of the Rev. M.C.M.Crache rode
London, Pub. Sept. 1.1794, by J. Thane, Spur Street, Leicester Square.

JOHN GERARD (top left) (1545–1612), herbalist. Gerard, a barber-surgeon, kept a herbal gar-
den at Holborn and also supervised a herb garden in the grounds of Lord Burghley's house.
William Caxton (top right) (c.1422–91), the first English printer. He set up his business by
Westminster Abbey in 1476. Thomas Linacre (bottom left) (c.1460–1524), founder of the
College of Physicians. Richard Whittington (bottom right) (d.1423), merchant and Lord
Mayor of London. Whittington was appointed Mayor in 1397 when the elected incumbent
died, and he was elected in 1398, 1406 and 1419. The legendary Dick Whittington and his
cat began to take shape in the 17th century.

CHAPTER III

MERCHANTS AND PROFESSIONALS

THE MERCHANT CLASS

NOTHING SO INDICATES CIVIC ASPIRATIONS THAN THE BUILDING OF A SEAT OF government. England at the beginning of the sixteenth century was about to participate in a cultural and organizational upheaval that would wrench it from its medieval ways, but the City of London had begun to come of age in 1411 when work commenced on the rebuilding of its Guildhall. A form of Guildhall existed before 1150 but the 1411 project, which took twenty years to complete, was a major building designed to embellish a city proud of its appearance and corporate status. It still lacked a roof when the legendary Richard Whittington was Lord Mayor of London for the fourth time in 1419, and it was his bequest four years later which provided its Purbeck marble floor. This 'fayre and goodly house' was designed by John Croxton, master mason, a protégé of Henry Yevele who had, about ten years earlier, completed *his* masterpiece, the rebuilt Westminster Hall. It is possible, of course, that the magnificence of Yevele's Hall had persuaded an envious City to erect a rival structure, but the rush of London's fortune would have made it necessary anyway.

The project denoted prosperity: in this era of trade expansion the fine guildhalls of Norwich, York and King's Lynn were also built. London's Guildhall was not, however, the only thing afoot. In 1411 the City also took in charge a large mansion called Leadenhall, used previously as a market for poultry and cheese, for civic use. Croxton was commissioned later to convert this into a granary to tide London over bad harvest periods – evidence again of a city administration taking itself seriously. (Leadenhall continued to function as a market and its Victorian glass-and-iron successor survives on the same site.) In 1449 the City bought land next to the Billingsgate inlet on the Thames and at an unknown date before 1500 erected a handsome arcaded market building there. By 1477 the City had appointed its first 'Clerk of the City's Works', a title which survived down to the nineteenth century, when he became the City Architect.

The guilds, who virtually ran the City, had also been active. By 1400 at least five of the companies had halls of their own and in the next one hundred years about another twenty of them were settled in their own premises.

Sir John Crosby exemplified the growing wealth of the City merchant class. His life touched three trades – his father was a successful fishmonger, he himself was a member of the Grocers' Company, and yet he made a great deal of money trading in silks. In 1466 he leased a large house in Bishopsgate, which he then enlarged to match his position in life, transforming it into a building described by Stow as the highest in London in its own time. Its grandeur may be judged by the fact that the Duke of Gloucester (the future Richard III) used it as his London residence before his accession to the throne – Shakespeare mentions the house three times in his play about the king. Much of Crosby Hall still remained in 1907, when it was taken down and re-erected on the Chelsea Embankment, where it still stands. It was a grand house denoting a class able to live and entertain almost royally. Influential in the City, Crosby also had a foot in the Westminster camp – he was employed several times by Edward IV on diplomatic missions.

Crosby died soon after his house was completed and one of his bequests emphasized a new mood of civic pride and confidence in London. He left a substantial £100 towards

CROSBY HALL, *drawn by Thomas H. Shepherd in the 1820s. This mansion was built in Bishopsgate by the London merchant, Sir John Crosby, between 1466 and 1475. It was later owned by Sir Thomas More.*

the repair of London Bridge. It was a timely gift. The old stone bridge, lined on both sides with shops and houses, crazily cantilevered, was showing signs of strain made worse by the reverberation of new-fangled iron-shod cart wheels – these were prohibited on the bridge in 1481; by 1497 the drawbridge was unused except in emergencies. Crosby here was participating in a new vogue of civic rather than ecclesiastic endowment, in which road and bridge maintenance and the provision of almshouses were common concerns. Whittington's will of 1423 contained a mixture of endowments. During his lifetime he had rebuilt his own church of St Michael Paternoster Royal, provided a library at Greyfriars, and established a ward at St Thomas's Hospital in which unmarried mothers could spend their confinements in privacy. His executors provided the money for the construction of a College of Priests, some almshouses and a rebuilding of the fetid Newgate Prison. His oddest gift to London was a public lavatory, situated by the Thames near the mouth of the Walbrook river at Dowgate. It consisted of two rows of sixty-four seats, one for men, the other for women; above it almshouses were constructed. A City Public Cleansing Department building is now on the site of this extraordinary bequest.

In 1431, John Wells, Lord Mayor of London and member of the Grocers' Company, was responsible for the rebuilding of the important Fleet Bridge, which connected Ludgate Hill to Fleet Street across the river Fleet. It was, according to Stow, made of stone and 'fair coped on either side with iron pikes; on which, towards the south, be also certain lanthorns of stone for lights to be placed in the winter evenings for commodity of travellers.' The widow of Stephen Forster, fishmonger, who had been mayor in 1454, enlarged Ludgate Prison in his memory with a chapel, tower and exercise area. In 1491 Cripplegate, traditionally kept in good order by the Brewers' Company, was rebuilt at the expense of a former mayor, goldsmith Edmund Shaw.

LONDON BRIDGE *from Visscher's* Panorama of London, *published in 1616. By then the structure was overloaded with buildings; the drawbridge, for which Crosby bequeathed a sum for repair, is to be seen to the right of the top of the church tower of St Mary Overie.*

Normally London merchants were unencumbered with the time-consuming and wasteful duties involved in playing court to a usually capricious monarch: not for them the doleful days of the courtiers at Westminster whose lives were fashioned by the king's partialities. And while the Renaissance in art, philosophy, architecture and religion came slowly to England, the merchants of London and elsewhere in the country were free to rid themselves, if they wished, of traditional ties. The merchants, at least in their business lives, were able to make choices and could, and did, make their own fortunes, while most others could not escape a status they were born into nor the occupation and earning power allotted them.

Those belonging to the élite of tradesmen and merchants had some schooling, enough to manage the paperwork of business transactions and the administration of guild affairs. But schools were in short supply. In 1447 the rectors of All Hallows the Great,

St Andrew's Holborn, St Peter's Cornhill and St Mary Colechurch had petitioned the king for permission to establish grammar schools as there was not a 'sufficeant nomber of Scholes and good Enfourmors in Gramer'. They pleaded the disappointment of those who came up to London for 'lack of schoolmasters in their own country' and shrewdly pointed out to the receptive Henry VI that lack of learning produced ignorant clerics. All this may well have been true but there had already been a history of protest by ecclesiastical authorities in London at the number of *'escoles generales de gramer'* conducted by men who had neither the blessing nor the authority of the Church to do so, and possibly what we see here is the Church, in the guise of parochial authorities, seeking to keep control of education.

Apart from these maverick enterprises that so infuriated the rectors, schools were, as a rule, formal or informal appendages of churches or conventual institutions. Boys were taught to sing church services and at the same time received a grounding in Latin and grammar. A school was attached to St Paul's by the twelfth century and Westminster Abbey had an almonry school; both these institutions have modern successors. By 1386, Westminster School had twenty-eight pupils and is thought to have had higher standards than the school run at the adjacent church of St Margaret's. From about 1434 another important school, that attached to the Hospital of St Anthony in Threadneedle Street, taught boys free of charge – Sir Thomas More and possibly Dean Colet were pupils here. The evidence points to an excessive discipline and a liberal use of the birch at these schools. At Westminster there was to be:

> *No laughing, talking, giggling or smirking if someone reads or intones poorly. No open or surreptitious scuffling, and don't answer back if asked to do something. . ..whosoever presumes to speak in English or French in reply to Latin, be it with friend or cleric, let him endure a stroke for any word. . .if dice are found in anyone's hand, let him feel a birch blow on naked flesh for each point.*

For most, education was little more than being literate and familiar with religious texts. This was made more difficult by the competing merits of the three languages in use. French, once the language of Court, was waning, the process encouraged by the 1362 statute which ordered that while all court records should be in Latin the proceedings should be in English. Latin, the *lingua franca* of the Law and the Church, had a structure and consistency that English lacked, but English, the common tongue, was gaining respectable ground. Wyclif had encouraged the reading of the Bible in English, and if conservative Londoners could see some reason for retaining Latin for religious and legal documents there seemed no point in perpetuating it in matters civil. The Brewers' Company in 1422 gave up keeping its records in Latin, which probably only its Clerk and officials could understand, and used English instead. Other livery companies followed suit, but the court rolls of the manors around London continued to be in Latin since they were, for the most part, legal documents.

Caxton, the first English printer, set up his press in the precincts of Westminster Abbey in 1476 near to the royal palace. It was in this area, whose residents were described by Fitzstephen three hundred years earlier as 'everywhere known and respected above all others for their civil demeanour, their good apparel, their table and their discourse', that Caxton saw his market. Palace, law courts and the Abbey dominated, with Parliament in sporadic attendance. His protégé, Wynken de Worde, however, favoured Fleet Street, near to the City and adjacent to the Inns of Court, and in moving here began an industrial speciality that survived in this area until modern times. It was to be many years, and in the context of the flowering of the Renaissance in England, that the printing press was to have much impact. For the time being printed books were rare and expensive.

THE PROFESSIONAL CLASS

THE MEDICAL PROFESSION

Professions stifled by the complacency of the church and the conservative obstinacy of received opinion included those of the physician and surgeon. Empirical deduction made little progress in a period when disease and plague were regarded as God's wrath,

A DISSECTION. *Illustration from* Bartholomaeus Anglicus, *printed by Wynken de Worde in London in 1495. Anatomical research was hampered by religious prohibition, although the bodies of criminals were later used and were much sought after following executions.*

with no remedy save prayer or propitiation, and no prevention but astrology and devotion: this followed inevitably because the physicians themselves were usually priests and their medical diagnoses were influenced by religious beliefs and a strong regard for supernatural factors. After the Council of Tours in 1163 pronounced that ecclesiastics should not shed blood, even in medical operations, priest-physicians became increasingly academic and remote from their patients. Instead they left operations, amputations, tooth-drawing or common blood-letting and other such intimate matters to barbers or to a new breed of lay surgeons who, for hundreds of years, were regarded as straightforward craftsmen and distinctly lower in the social scale than physicians. The devolvement of surgical work to barbers and surgeons led to connection which culminated in the formation of the Barber-Surgeons' Company in 1540 and to the appearance of one of our more enduring trade signs, the red and white barber's pole, which signifies the letting of blood. At the same time the preparation of drugs became the prosperous domain of apothecaries who themselves were often spicers belonging to the Grocers' Company.

While physicians were constrained by religious beliefs, surgeons were hampered by an inadequate knowledge of anatomy, a subject that could hardly be explored since the Church forbade dissection of a corpse except in exceptional circumstances. Indeed, artists of the Italian Renaissance probably knew more anatomy than most surgeons.

Often the practice of medicine was undertaken by nuns, and for childbirth 'wise women' were usually employed. In theory, difficult births were handled by surgeons, who alone were permitted to use surgical instruments, but midwives were charged with the same responsibilities if no surgeon could be found, even to the extent of attempting a Caesarean section on the body of a dead mother in the hope of delivering a live child. She was also obliged to baptize a child likely to die before a priest arrived.

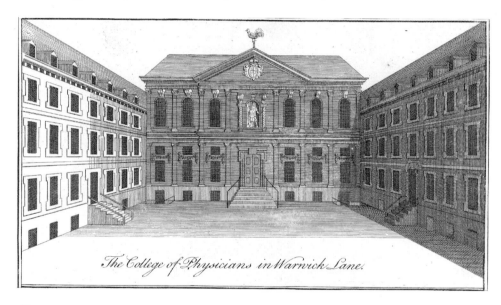

The College of Physicians in Warwick Lane, c.1756. The College was founded in 1518 by Thomas Linacre, Henry VIII's physician. At first, and after his death, meetings were held in Linacre's house in Knightrider Street, then in a new building in Paternoster Row before moving to Warwick Lane.

The doctor in Chaucer's *Canterbury Tales* made much use of astrology and of charms through which healing powers could reach the patients and cure them of their ills. Apothecaries who made up the complicated drugs also used astrology to determine just when and in what proportions components were mixed to ensure maximum effectiveness.

At a time when impurity of the blood was perceived as a frequent cause of illness, blood-letting to excess, and in conjunction with the phases of the moon, was carried out, especially with the unpleasant use of leeches. Lithotomy was attempted as were amputations, but without the benefit of anaesthetics they must often have done more harm than good. Nor did greater skills exist in the hospitals of St Bartholomew and St Thomas, where a physician was a rare visitor. In the wards illnesses and fractures took their course for good or for bad, ameliorated only by care and attention. As late as 1544,

Thomas Gale, who became Queen Elizabeth's Sergeant-Surgeon, records that he did see in the two hospitals of London:

> *300 and odd poore people that were diseased of sore arms and legs, feet and hands, with other partes of the body so greaviously infected that 120 of them could never be recovered without the loss of a limb. All these were brought to their mischief by witches, by women and by counterfeit worthless fellows that take upon themselves the use of art, not only robbing them of their money but of their limbs and perpetual health.*

In the physicians' absence the quacks prospered, particularly in the later sixteenth century when syphilis was common. Someone who frequented St Bartholomew's Hospital estimated that of each twenty patients taken in, half had 'the pockes'. There was no effective treatment for this scourge, but at least during this period the curse of leprosy diminished for reasons unknown. The dreadful practice of the priest administering last rites to someone diagnosed as having that disease, and of pronouncing over him the awesome sentence, '*Sic mortuus mundo, vivas iterum Deo*' (Henceforth be dead to the world, and live in God), was now a rare occurrence.

Plague persisted and appeared most years with severe epidemics in 1499, 1513, 1531, 1563; in this latter year it is estimated that it affected a quarter of the City's population. The traditional methods of quarantine were enforced: public assemblies were banned, the Court moved to one of the king's numerous palaces in the country and others who could go to rural retreats did so. Westminster School went no further than Chiswick, where it possessed a large house by the Thames.

It was against this background that Thomas Linacre established a College of Physicians in 1518, a year in which a particularly virulent sweating sickness epidemic ravaged London. Seven years earlier the first steps had been taken to upgrade the quality of those practising physic. The Medical Act 1511 noted that:

> *Physic and Surgery is daily within this Realm exercised by a great multitude of ignorant persons as common artificers, smiths, weavers and women who boldly and customably take upon them great cures and things of great difficulty in the which they partly use sorcery and witchcraft to the grievous hurt, damage, and destruction of many of the King's liege people.*

Linacre, as so many did in the next one hundred years, went to Italy to escape the conservative scholasticism that pervaded London, Oxford and Cambridge. He returned, enthused by an intellectual atmosphere that encouraged curiosity and investigation, though it was widely felt that the new breed of scholars was merely rediscovering the finite knowledge of the Greeks. Linacre was not only the father of medicine in this country, but an important figure in the development of learning generally. The College of Physicians, which met in his house in Knightrider Street, near St Paul's, was granted the right to license physicians in London and within seven miles around it, a measure to counteract the charlatans noted in the 1511 Act. As the physicians at that time knew little more about the nature of illnesses than those who had no licence, this was of no great significance, but the importance of the College was that it was able to study medicine unfettered by the influence and opinions of the Church. Gradually the perceived relationship between disease and sin was challenged by science and a fragile bridge was erected between medieval dogma and empirical thought.

At the same time there was greater competence in the practice of pharmacy. New elements and drugs, made familiar by the spread of Arab medicine through Spain, became widely used by physicians and apothecaries. Cloves, cinnamon, ginger, opium, sugar and special woods were imported. In the garden of the College of Physicians the herbalist, John Gerard, created a herb garden to provide a nearer supply of those plants which could brave the English climate.

THE LEGAL PROFESSION

WHILE MEDICINE WAS TAUGHT BADLY in the universities, the teaching of Common Law was even worse, and then only in Latin. Those intending to be lawyers therefore came to London and there joined one of the loose organizations called an Inn of Court or

THE present Middle Temple Hall, shown above in a 19th century engraving, was completed in 1573. Its roof consists of a magnificent oak double hammer beam. The 29ft- long Bench Table, made from one piece of oak, is believed to be the gift of Queen Elizabeth I.

Inn of Chancery, for tuition. 'Inn' in this sense derived from the hostel-like houses in which students lived. The first Lincoln's Inn, for example, was a large house on the south side of Holborn owned originally by Thomas of Lincoln, himself a lawyer, who by the 1330s rented out lodgings to apprentice lawyers; the Inn had moved down to the Bishop of Chichester's old premises in Chancery Lane by 1422. Gray's Inn was on the site of the manor house of Purtpool in Holborn, owned by Sir Reginald Grey, Chief Justice of Chester, who died in 1308. By at least the 1370s his house was also used by law students. Another concentration of lawyers existed south of Fleet Street, where, in the 1320s, the former headquarters of the Knights Templar were leased – over half of the grounds was taken by law students and divided into the 'Middle' and 'Inner' Temples, while the remainder (to the west) was taken by the Bishop of Exeter – this 'Outer' Temple area then became a separate entity and the name gradually died out.

The origins of these organizations remain obscure, partly because the Temple records were destroyed by the mob during the Peasants' Revolt of 1381, but it is thought that when law schools within the City were banned by Henry III they removed to the nearest suburb, Holborn. In effect, they constituted a law university, but their studies were not confined to legal matters. Sir John Fortescue, Henry VI's Lord Chief Justice, wrote *c.*1468, that the Inns of Court constitute:

> *a sort of an academy or gymnasium fit for persons of their station; where they learn singing and all kinds of music, dancing, and such other accomplishments and diversions, which are called revels, as are suitable to their quality, and such as are usually practised at Court. At other times, out of term, the greater part apply themselves to the study of the law. Upon festival days, and after the offices of the Church are over, they employ themselves in the study of sacred and profane history. Here everything which is good and virtuous is to be learned, all vice is discouraged and banished.*

It is hardly surprising, given these distractions, that the tuition of law students took many years, and was not helped in the Middle Temple by the lack of a library for at least two hundred years.

Writing about one hundred years after Fortescue, Sir Henry Chauncey, Master Treasurer of the Middle Temple, noted that the Inns of Court 'were excellent seminaries and nurseries for the education of youth, some for the Bar, others for the seats of judicature, others for the government, and others for affairs of State.' We see here the changing nature of the civil service and those who advised the monarch, for Chauncey is observing a professional class, versed in the Law, Latin, the Classics and probably theology, who were the real inheritors of the kingdom.

Earlier the practice of law revolved around Westminster where the Great Hall was used, but the relocation of Chancery records and much of the Chancellor's legal work to what became Chancery Lane, which took place about 1338, meant that much of the background work was done around Fleet Street, an area already, as we have seen, settled by legal practitioners.

Four Inns of Court emerged – Lincoln's Inn, Gray's Inn and the Middle and Inner Temples and in time they developed firm relationships with the nine minor inns, called Inns of Chancery, such as those of Tavy, Furnival, Barnard and Clifford, all of them around Fleet Street and Holborn; the latter seemed to have acted as nurseries to the Inns of Court, so that students progressed from one to the other.

THE DOCTOR OF PHYSIC

DESIDERIUS Erasmus (top left) *(1466–1536), Dutch scholar and theologian who came to England in 1498, where he formed a friendship with John Colet, Thomas Linacre, founder of the College of Physicians, and Thomas More. William Tyndale* (top right) *(c.1484–1536), a leader of the 'New Learning' movement. He translated the New Testament into English, published from 1525. John Colet* (bottom left) *(c.1467–1519), priest and scholar. With money left to him by his father he founded St Paul's School in 1509. Edmund Bonner* (bottom right) *(c.1500–69), Bishop of London. He opposed the use of the new Prayer Book during the reign of Edward VI, and was imprisoned in Marshalsea. Restored to his see under Mary, he rigorously persecuted Protestants.*

CHAPTER IV

A BLOODY REFORMATION

LONDON PROVIDED THE STAGE FOR THE SIXTEENTH-CENTURY REFORMATION OF THE English Church. This significant and at times wretched drama, dignified by people who died bravely, and occasionally by fine rhetoric, was played out in the streets of the City and Westminster so publicly that it touched most residents. Everyone of mature age would have been affected, whether from the abandonment of religious forms practised since childhood, the closure of well-known conventual houses, or by the dreadful procession of martyrs to their deaths. In a London whose population was still only about 150,000 it was difficult to remain anonymous and neutral, and without opinon. But danger went hand in hand with taking sides. Yet, for all the ferment of religious viewpoints, in the end it was not, perhaps, commitment to either reform or orthodoxy which counted, but political wild cards that usually swayed the issue in favour of reform. So indecisive was its victory that had Elizabeth I been a Catholic, and a wise Catholic into the bargain, the Church might well have turned again to Rome with London's approval.

RELIGIOUS INFLUENCES

THERE WERE SEVERAL STRANDS IN THE MOOD FOR REFORM. One was the remnants of the old Lollard movement which, despite suppression and executions, existed in London still, but driven underground. Their criticism of the Catholic Church was much the same as it had ever been – that it had traduced the life and meaning of Christ. In so doing they said it had conjured up an apparatus of saints, images and priestly hierarchy to sustain it; it had invented Purgatory and transubstantiation so that its power over the congregation was ever present. Even the Mass, which once had been shared by priest and congregation, was now a ceremony conducted by the priest alone, intoned in a language foreign to most, and barely heard anyway. The Lollards wanted, among other things, services in English rather than Latin, and an English Bible available for free study and interpretation by the laity. For them, understanding the Scriptures was paramount.

There were also orthodox scholars such as John Colet and Erasmus who from their studies of the humanities had come to the conclusion that reform of the Church was necessary, that it was too idolatrous and too superstitious for its own good. This New Learning, which sought the purification of the Church, was especially strong in the intellectual atmosphere of the Inns of Court at the time when Thomas Cromwell, later to play a pivotal role in the drama, was there.

Then, from about 1523, when William Tyndale arrived in London, the teachings of Luther provided a base for a radical reform movement which urged that salvation might be found only through faith in Christ, and through Christ as discovered through the Scriptures.

POLITICAL EXPEDIENCY

THESE INFLUENCES AFFECTED MOST the necessarily small ecclesiastical and intellectual élite of London, but they came to prominence just when resentment against the clergy was simmering among ordinary people. Particularly there was disgruntlement at the amount of tithes taken by clergy who hardly put in an appearance, although there appears to have been no objection to tithes in principle. A number of clergymen were notorious for being pluralists and living a sumptuous life on the backs of hard-earned money. Above them was the awful example of Wolsey, Archbishop of York, who had, it seemed, more riches than Henry VIII himself. As Lord Chancellor he was the most powerful man in the country below the King and in a typical display in May 1521, bedecked in gold, he had ridden to Paul's Cross in the City and there harangued the London crowd on the dangers of Luther. Sitting at his side, as though his junior, was the Archbishop of Canterbury. Wolsey and the City were already old enemies, with the former always ready to bring down the latter in the King's eyes. In 1516 he had issued an order to the City to curtail what he described as sedition, disobedience and disorders caused by vagabonds and 'masterless folk' who roamed its streets.

The following year occurred what became known as 'Evil May Day'. Trade had become precarious and this led inevitably to resentment of foreign merchants in London. A cleric was persuaded to preach a rousing sermon in Bishopsgate against the evils of foreigners, and as the May Day holiday approached the mob in the City became threatening. A contemporary chronicler relates that once trouble had begun people arose from every quarter, including servants, watermen and courtiers, and by eleven at night there were seven hundred assembled in Cheapside and a further three hundred in the churchyard of St Paul's. The compter prisons, small prisons for petty offenders, were broken into, the houses of foreigners ransacked, and even the diplomacy of Sir Thomas More could not quell them.

Although it was a bloodless demonstration, King Henry and Wolsey decided that the City's wings should be clipped. Those rioters captured were tried for treason rather than for riot, and ten pairs of mobile gallows saw off prisoners in various parts of the City. It was a remarkably severe and ill-judged reaction to the events and did not, in any case, cure Londoners of their long-held prejudices against foreigners. The Duke of Wurtemberg in 1592 observed that Londoners cared little for foreigners, 'but scoff and laugh at them; and moreover one dare not oppose them, else the street-boys and apprentices collect together in immense crowds and strike to the right and left unmercifully without regard to person.'

Henry was at one with Wolsey in persecuting those thought to be heretics and, with sufficient repression, radical reform might well have been crushed or delayed indefinitely. But the first wild card – the first unpredictable factor – turned up. Henry, needing a male heir, wanted to divorce Catherine of Aragon in order to marry Anne Boleyn. Annulment of the marriage was hoped for, on the grounds of it being illegal in the eyes of the Church because Catherine had been the widow of Henry's brother. However, the Pope, for political reasons if no others, declined and Cardinal Wolsey went away empty-handed from Rome. From that time Wolsey was doomed. He fell into disgrace in 1529 and the King took over the Whitehall palace on which the Archbishop had squandered so much money. In 1530, Wolsey was arrested for treason and died on his way to stand trial.

Londoners, both reformist and orthodox, were opposed to the King's plan to marry Anne Boleyn, as was Sir Thomas More, his new Lord Chancellor. More had in his younger days been an enthusiast for the New Learning, but by the time of his appointment he saw his task as stamping out heresy, which he did with great persistence, so that the grim gathering of martyrs at the stake became a familiar London sight. As it became clear that the King intended to marry Anne Boleyn regardless of the Pope, More was permitted to resign on the grounds of ill health. This left the King free to force two Acts through a compliant Parliament, one which made him supreme head of the Church in England, and the other, the Act of Succession, which recognized the annulment of his marriage to Catherine, the illegitimacy of his daughter Mary as a consequence, and the right of Anne Boleyn to be Queen and any children of the new marriage to be heirs to the throne.

It was in the context of the Act of Supremacy that the King began to look more favourably towards the people he had so far burnt as heretics. If he were to face down the Pope he needed the support of reformers in the Church and his new enemies were those who upheld the papal authority. From the evidence available and so ably assembled by Susan Brigden in her *London and the Reformation*, there was no consensus among Londoners or their clergy on the matter. By 1534 the clergy were already in effect servants of the King rather than of the Pope, but in that year they were obliged to swear an oath to accept the Act of Supremacy. Henry was in no mood for compromise: he had already married Boleyn and had by her another daughter, Elizabeth. Any further delay was out of the question.

The Act of Succession affected everyone, not just the clergy. This was for many a more difficult stumbling block, even for the religious reformers who were happy to break with papal authority under the Supremacy Act. Once again, Henry would brook no delay or opposition and the execution of the 'Holy Maid of Kent' on the day that the oath of allegiance was to be signed by the principal citizens of London was a demonstration, if one were needed, of the fate that might befall objectors.

The Holy Maid was a simple-minded woman, Elizabeth Barton, who had been exploited by clergymen for their own ends (and even believed in by others), and built up in the public's imagination as a prophetess and receiver of visions. She was also a forthright opponent of the Boleyn marriage, and prophesied that if any wrong were done to Catherine then Henry 'should no longer be king of this realm. . . .and should die a villain's death.' In 1532 a Franciscan friar had warned Henry against proceeding with the divorce, saying that should Henry marry Anne the dogs would lick his blood as they had licked Ahab's. In this the friar was nearer the truth than the Holy Maid, for when in 1547 Henry's mountainous body was housed at Syon House on its way to burial at Windsor, it is said that the coffin sprang open in the night and dogs were discovered licking at his remains.

THE SUPPRESSION OF THE MONASTERIES

THOMAS CROMWELL, HENRY'S NEW ADVISER, was a reformer as was the new Queen herself, and from the time of his appointment momentum for change increased. Images were destroyed, church walls whitewashed, crosses – including the famous rood at St Margaret Pattens – were taken down, and saints obliterated. Even London's own revered saint,

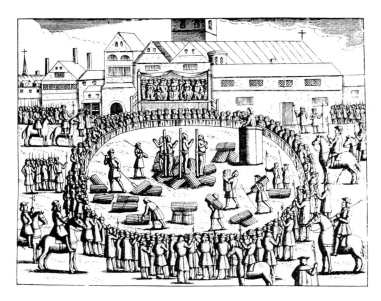

THE burning of Anne Askew, John Lacels, John Adams and Nicolas Belenian at Smithfield in 1546. Askew, a zealous Protestant, underwent interrogation by Bishop Bonner in 1545, but declined to sign a confession that would have saved her life.

Thomas Becket, had his shrine at Canterbury dismantled and his festival day abrogated; St Thomas's Hospital, a casualty of the suppression of the monasteries, was dedicated to a different St Thomas on its refoundation during the reign of Henry's son, Edward VI.

Cromwell's main opponent was Stokesley, the Bishop of London, who did his utmost to sustain non-conforming clergy. It was Stokesley who managed to persuade the devout friars at Charterhouse to accept the Act of Succession but they declined to accept the Act of Supremacy and for this they were hung and quartered at Tyburn in 1535, an execution which shocked Londoners for whom the Carthusians were model Christians. As he faced his death, the prior of Charterhouse, John Houghton, made a speech, saying to the assembled people,'Our holy mother the Church has decreed otherwise than the king and parliament have decreed, and therefore, rather than disobey the Church, we are ready to suffer.'

There seems no doubt that the Church in London was in disarray, with both sympathetic and unwilling clergy conforming to the evangelical zeal of Cromwell, but it is difficult to know if hearts were won and converts made. In the meantime the suppression of the monasteries, which combined for Henry a snub to the Pope and the acquisition of a vast amount of land and wealth, was under way. It had begun in London in a small way in 1531 when the Convent of St Clare, Aldgate was surrendered to the Crown, as was St James's Hospital for Lepers, on whose site St James's Palace was later built. But in 1536 the programme began in earnest when monasteries with an income of less than £200 per annum were taken. These included Kilburn Priory, Elsing Spital and Greenwich monastery. Westminster Abbey had already been traduced by the placing there as Abbot of a Cromwell man, and in 1536 the King acquired most of its London estates, including what became Hyde Park, Pimlico and Covent Garden. In 1537 ten more

Canonbury tower, Islington, from a print of 1816. The house, much of which survives, was built by the last prior of St Bartholomew's, Smithfield, in the early part of the 16th century. At the Dissolution in 1539 the estate was given to Thomas Cromwell.

monks from Charterhouse were imprisoned at Newgate, and there were chained and fettered upright for days. Nine died of starvation and another was sent to the Tower. The major establishments fell to the King in 1538, including the Greyfriars, Blackfriars, Whitefriars, Austin Friars and Charterhouse.

Cromwell was brought down, as he knew he would be, in 1540, his usefulness to the King over and his views overtaken by the King's political needs. By that time, Henry was convinced that Cromwell had gone too far and that heresy and not reform was in the air. A sign of the change of mood was the appointment of an anti-reform Mayor of London in 1539. But the executions continued. In 1540, when it was politic to dispose of both heretics and Catholics, three clergymen were burnt at Smithfield without trial for being heretics, within sight of six Catholic priests being hanged outside St Bartholomew's church. In 1546, Anne Askew, a young woman educated in theology, refused to recant

Protestant heresy, even after torture had left her almost too weak to stand; she was carried in a chair to the fire at Smithfield.

Despite further persecutions and a king now surrounded by orthodox ecclesiastics, reform managed to survive until Henry's death. Much of the property belonging to the dispossessed monasteries had found its way into the hands of the nobility who therefore had a motive for not reviving that part of the old establishment, but the day-to-day church ritual was a different matter and was fiercely contended for at least one hundred years. Henry VIII died a Catholic and at his death each City church celebrated a requiem mass in Latin.

Henry's son, Edward VI, who was only ten when his father died, came immediately under the control of his uncle, the Duke of Somerset, an ardent reformer. During Somerset's arrogant protectorate there was a further spate of church spoilation even to the

Souтн view of St Pancras Church, Middlesex, in 1815. This church, modernized and enlarged from 1847–1848, stands on a rise above a road and the river Fleet. The view of an uncluttered burial ground is at odds with the number of burials recorded in this space in the 18th century.

extent of demolition. Somerset, intent on building a Renaissance palace on the Strand, dismantled other buildings, among them the church of St Mary-le-Strand, which at that time stood on the south side of the road and not in the middle as it does today. He pillaged stone from here and there, disturbed the charnel house at St Paul's and threatened to take down St Margaret's Westminster in an excess of authority that alienated many Londoners from the cause of reform. Intolerance of Catholic rituals and images, rather mute during Henry's last years, emerged again with vigour.

In the villages around London the events were less dramatic. Excessive ornamentation in parish churches was taken down, the saints extinguished, the walls whitened, the royal coat of arms emblazoned, and wooden Holy Tables in the naves replaced stone altars. Possessions redolent of the past were disposed of. In Dagenham old church, for example, vestments were sold, as was a chalice studded with jewels; the stone high altar and the chantry altar were both taken down. Those clergymen unable to agree to reform were dismissed. On the other hand, there were zealots who went too far in their enthusiasm for reform and were an embarrassment. The vicar of St Pancras, Middlesex, one John Bedow, was forced out of office for his radical views: in 1549 he had taken to preaching from a high tree in the churchyard there, rather than from the pulpit. He advocated not only the renaming of churches, so that the Catholic saints should disappear, but that all the names of the days of the week, with the exception of Friday and Saturday, should be changed. After his open-air sermon he would then enter his church and sing High Mass in English facing north, and he caused such a disturbance in the neighbourhood that the Sheriff of Middlesex imposed martial law and executed ring leaders.

As with Cromwell, who was faced by the implacable Stokesley, so Somerset had a persistently uncooperative Bishop of London – Bonner. Somerset, however, was even more ruthless than Cromwell and packed Bonner off to the Marshalsea Prison. But soon Somerset himself was deposed. In 1552 he was executed and replaced by the equally zealous Duke of Northumberland. In the meantime, the Catholic Princess Mary, who had been restored as an heir to the throne in 1544, defiantly rode with a retinue through London in 1551, each carrying a rosary. The early death of Edward VI in July 1553 brought religious matters to a head once again.

For ten days Lady Jane Grey was Queen. Cousin of the late King and daughter-in-law of Northumberland, she represented the only way in which the accession to the throne could be diverted from Mary. She seems to have been a reluctant bride and an unwilling queen, and the City of London, though cowed by Northumberland, were hesitant in their acceptance of her. Ridley, the reforming Bishop of London, preached a sermon at Paul's Cross which declared the two royal princesses to be illegitimate, and he spoke in Jane's favour. But it was a doubting crowd that heard him, 'sore annoyed with his words, so uncharitably spoken by him in so open an audience'.

Poor Jane Grey was easily swept aside in the political events that followed. Mary took the throne with the approval of the London crowd and its City corporation and one can only assume that the Londoner's distaste for usurpation of the throne was stronger than any Protestant notions they might have had, for she seems to have been genuinely welcomed. They were not to know, though they might have guessed, that an horrific sequence of executions was to follow.

'BLOODY' MARY AND THE BRIEF RETURN TO CATHOLICISM

MARY BEGAN WITH SOME CIRCUMSPECTION. Only Northumberland and two supporters went to their deaths for their part in previous events. The City of London was let off lightly and even Lady Jane remained alive in the Tower. The religious edicts of the reign of Edward VI were repealed so that the clergy reverted to the forms of worship that pertained during Henry's last year.

It was then that another unpredictable event took place which was a godsend, so to speak, to the reformers. Mary, urged by her advisers to marry as soon as possible, and flattered by the suggestion of her cousin, Charles V that his son, Philip of Spain, was eager for the match, made clear her intention to marry him. Philip's reputation was that of a devout and zealous Catholic, detested in the Low Countries for his behaviour to

Protestants, and of a cold and remote demeanour unlikely to appeal to the volatile English. The fact of his being Spanish was sufficient in itself to arouse the opposition of all but Mary's most devoted supporters, and the French and Venetians were not slow to suggest that in future England would be subordinated to Spain's kingdom. It was an appalling political blunder on Mary's part – she had never met Philip and no emotion was at stake – but against all advice she insisted on the match. Inevitably her action set in train campaigns to replace her. Some canvassed for the reinstatement of Lady Jane, others for the accession of Mary's sister Elizabeth, daughter of Anne Boleyn, in each case putting those women in danger. The greatest peril to them came from an uprising in Kent led by Sir Thomas Wyatt in 1554. This force was welcomed at Southwark, but prevented from crossing London Bridge. It crossed the Thames at Kingston and then came into London, camping at the village of Knightsbridge before approaching Westminster. Denied entry to Whitehall, it pressed on to the City where the corporation opted for Mary and refused the rebels entry. As a rebellion it fizzled out, though with determination it might have succeeded given the poor defences of both Westminster and the City.

The end of the Wyatt Rebellion was marked by executions of the rebel leaders and then of Lady Jane Grey. At the same time, by royal edict, the Catholic religion was ordered back into the churches and Bishop Bonner, now out of prison and restored as Bishop of London, pursued this with fervour. Catholic images were reinstated, married clergy were ousted, street processions again entertained the crowds. Reformers who could flee and felt inclined to do so went to Europe; others died for their faith in the terror years of 1555 and 1556 – denial of the Mass alone was sufficient excuse for burning. By the end of Mary's reign nearly three hundred Protestants had been burned as heretics.

The intemperate nature of Mary's suppression of the reformers was to prepare the way for a ready acceptance of a return to the reformed religion that Elizabeth, when she came to the throne in 1558, was happy to revive.

THE ECONOMIC CONSEQUENCES

THE SUPPRESSION OF THE MONASTERIES was more than just the immediate concern of the monks, nuns and friars who were pensioned off. Their quiet precincts were emptied and freed for development, providing a sudden deluge of space in a crowded city. Mostly these properties were snapped up by the nobility, and some were converted into large houses and others used for storage, such as Austin Friars which contained coal and corn; St Anne's Blackfriars was turned into stables. The precincts of St Katharine's by the Tower were soon covered with tenements. Their poor quality was inevitable since much of the adjacent land of Wapping had been reclaimed from the marsh as late as 1544 and the neighbourhood was the domain of transient dockers, mariners and their suppliers: it was not an area for speculators to build houses of quality. Even more importantly, all around London the church estates, with few exceptions, came into lay ownerships to whom profit motive, and therefore the appetite for development, came more naturally.

While some profited from the demise of the monasteries, others were distinctly worse off, for at a stroke the long-established system of helping the poor via the almonries of the City conventual houses was dismantled. A census in 1511 of the number of beggars in the

City revealed that there were about one thousand, but by 1594 the Lord Mayor estimated that they stood at over 12,000, many of whom were impoverished provincials come to escape the misery of their home villages. In the past these people, or many of them, could have been sustained by the monasteries but now they were destitute street beggars. The problem was recognized in 1563 when new legislation provided for the appointment in each parish, of 'two able persons or more' to gather and collect charitable alms of 'all the residue of people inhabiting in the parish'. In 1572 the post of Overseer of the Poor was created, but the matter was not tackled comprehensively until the 1601 Poor Law Act – legislation which, from a combination of its own worth and the sloth of successive governments, was hardly altered until the nineteenth century. Parish officials set to work those who could not maintain themselves and were also charged with the relief of the impotent, old, lame and blind. However harsh, it was still a vast improvement.

BRIDEWELL PALACE and the entrance to the Fleet river in 1660. Bridewell was built by Henry VIII from 1515 to 1520, but was a short-lived royal home. It was given to the City of London in 1553 as a home for destitute people.

In 1561 a proposal was made for a 'House of Correction' in Westminster in which the inmates were to be put to work. This building appears not to have opened but one scheme which did materialize was the conversion of the old Bridewell Palace near Blackfriars as a City House of Correction. In this building, destitute and criminals alike were set to work or else punished in a draconian attempt to get the poor, the beggars and their children off the streets.

The closure of monasteries during the Reformation had also resulted in the sick being ousted from their hospital beds. It is doubtful if there were any lepers left at St James's Hospital, but there were plenty of patients at St Bartholomew's, which seems to have carried on with reduced funding when the priory was dissolved, until it was revived and placed in the hands of the City of London. St Thomas's was closed and lay derelict for eleven years.

SIR THOMAS GRESHAM (top left) *(1519–79), London merchant and founder of the Royal Exchange. Inigo Jones (top right) (1573–1652), architect of Covent Garden piazza and St Paul's church. Sir Hugh Myddleton (bottom left) (1560–1631), promoter of the New River scheme. Edward Alleyn (1566–1626), actor, theatre manager and founder of Dulwich College.*

CHAPTER V

A GATHERING PACE

FROM MARKET TOWN TO METROPOLIS

JOHN STOW, LONDON'S FIRST HISTORIAN, WAS BORN ABOUT 1525 AND THUS HAD THE melancholy fortune to watch the London he loved and chronicled change rapidly. His life, which ended in 1605, two years after Queen Elizabeth's, saw the City's medieval nature diminish and its Catholic life replaced by a reformation he did not in his heart embrace. The exploitation of land in the City distressed him, and the materialistic spirit in the air offended him who was never happier than when bringing back to his house a previously unregarded old manuscript or book. His concern is clear when describing the old de Vere mansion in Lime Street, near his own house, now 'letten out to Powlters for stabling of horses and stowage of poultrie, but now lately new builded into a number of small tenements, letten out to strangers and other meane people.' The former house of Lord Mayor John Philpot, in Eastcheap, was now divided into 'sundry small tenements', and the Earl of Shrewsbury's house in Dowgate ward had been taken down and replaced by 'a great number of small tenements now letten out for great rents, to people of all sorts'. East of the Tower the precinct of St Katharine's was now 'of late yeres enclosed about, or pestered with small tenements and homely cottages, having inhabitants, English and strangers more in number than in some cities in England'. In the manor of Shadwell, to which as a boy Stow had walked daily to fetch milk, 'there hath been of late, in place of elm trees, many small tenements raised towards Radcliffe.' At Aldgate, where he had first lived, there were filthy cottages and laystalls which presented a 'horrid entrance to the City'. Because of building and encroachment on the highway there was no 'fair pleasant or wholesome way for people to walk on foot, which is no small blemish to so famous a city to have so unsavoury and unseemly an entrance or passage thereunto'.

Stow's *Survey of London and Westminster* (first published in 1598) describes a London becoming unpredictable and unstable, spreading in all directions as it shed its market-town nature. It was the first period in London when perpetual change and mobility were inevitable and beyond anyone's control. Legislation might be passed to prevent it, but London was escaping the City's strait-jacket to become a metropolis.

What we also find in Stow's survey are the beginnings of the East End of London, a jerry-built, ill-regarded, catchpenny blot. Though the area remained important for

London's trade, especially as the docks stretched eastwards seeking ever deeper water, its more affluent population was already moving west and, as the 17th century gathered pace, decamped in great numbers.

While Stow was pessimistic about the City his contemporary, Dekker, was still proclaiming that 'our Worthiest Citizens are from home, they goe into Milk Street, Bread Street, Lime Street, St Mary Axe or the most priviest places where they keep their residence.' City houses still contained a number of courtiers: Thomas Cromwell had property in Throgmorton Street and Sir Francis Drake lived for a time in Thames Street. In the grounds of some of the dissolved monasteries good-class buildings were erected, or mansions were made of the existing structures. The merchants remained as there was little development permitted near the City and Westminster, and commuting by horseback to villages outside the metropolis was tiresome and difficult.

*N*ORTH-EAST *view of Cornhill, published in 1814. To the left is the Cornhill Pump at the inter-section of Gracechurch Street, Cornhill and Bishopsgate. Until the supply of water made available by the New River project, much of London's water came from pumps in the streets.*

Stow's undisguised lament at the amount and quality of development would not, of course, be heard, any more than that of anyone else in later centuries who despaired as fields, hedgerows and streams around London vanished. Official action to contain the spread of London was only partially successful. A royal proclamation in 1580 was concerned on the face of it with the poor and the likelihood of plague in crowded tenements, but the authorities were also aware that a large number of poor and disaffected people in London was a danger to public order. Queen Elizabeth noted:

> *great multitudes of people brought to inhabit in small roomes, whereof a great part are seene very poore. . .heaped up together, and in a sort smothered with many families of children and servantes in one house or small tenement*

and she commanded that

all manner of persons, of what quality soever they be, to desist and forbear from any new
buildings of any house or tenement within three miles from any of the gates of the said citie
of London, to serve for Habitation or Lodging for any person, where no former house hath
bene knowen to have bene in the memorie of such as are now living.

As with many pieces of planning legislation this had the opposite effect to that desired: with a prohibition on building in the immediate London suburbs the density of population and development within the walls, illegally or not, became higher. And once available space in the City had been exploited the same process occurred with the conversion of buildings in the suburbs, most notably in Clerkenwell and Holborn. Families took in lodgers and then, when that proved profitable, subdivided their houses. Cellars were dug, upper stories were jettied out above the street, and gardens were built over. Supervision of the legislation appears to have been lax, for in 1598 the Justices of the Peace for Middlesex, were summoned before the Privy Council and warned as to their negligence in allowing building in the suburbs. In 1602 an even stiffer announcement commanded that there should be no new buildings, and no subdivision of buildings, and that all infringements of the legislation in the last seven years were to be torn down. There is reason to suppose that these regulations, pursued assiduously by James I and Charles I, were not much more than fundraising activities, since it was the custom for an illegal dwelling to be compounded by the payment of a fine to the Exchequer. In 1637 a list was compiled of properties built in London since the accession of James I: there were 1,361 of them, of which Covent Garden accounted for a good number, but there were over four hundred north of the City in the areas of Holborn and Clerkenwell. Hardly any new buildings had been erected south of the river.

The City was also alarmed enough to send a letter to the Privy Council about 'the vast increase of new buildings and number of inhabitants within the City and suburbs of London'; it warned of the 'dangerous consequence, not only to this great metropolis, but likewise to the Nation in general if not timely remedied'. Though James I was, ostensibly, opposed to more development in his capital he was, more positively, prepared to permit new houses provided that they were built of brick. He wrote:

As it was said of the first emperor of Rome, that he had found the city of Rome of brick and
left it of marble, so Wee, whom God hath honoured to be the first of Britaine, might be able
to say in same proportion, that we had found our Citie and suburbs of London of stickes,
and left them of bricke, being a material farre more durable, safe from fire and beautiful
and magnificent.

To restrain house building within three miles of London (at times the limit was five) seems rather stringent given that by present standards London was still essentially a large country town and that places within that radius such as Islington and St Pancras were no more than villages.

At the time of the first proclamation in 1580 there was development up Bishopsgate, along the Strand, around Charterhouse, the Barbican and Aldgate, but the fields are there on the maps to see, decorated with images of cattle, archers practising and women laying out linen to dry; and for all the density of housing inside the walls a Londoner had not far to walk before finding an agricultural landscape. St Giles-in-the-Fields still warranted its name and was separated from London, Soho was open, and Holborn went no further than Gray's Inn. No doubt it was the speed with which development was happening that perturbed the authorities. For example, the manor of Holborn, which in 1516 contained twelve houses, had at least one hundred in 1580.

For reasons related to land drainage and accessibility to the City, development on the south side of the river had so far been negligible. There was a concentration of buildings along Borough High Street, whose inhabitants mostly made their livings from travellers across London Bridge, and there was also a ribbon of development along the waterfront of Tooley Street past the mariners' church of St Olave; Lambeth Palace stood in brooding isolation opposite Westminster. Otherwise in Southwark there was a stretch along the south bank, between London Bridge and today's Blackfriars Bridge, which was celebrated for its theatres and louche pleasures.

ENTERTAINMENT

THEATRES IN LONDON were first contrived in the courtyards of inns, but they achieved their notoriety in this riverside stretch of Southwark where the audiences were as happy to watch plays as to see animal baiting before, perhaps, visiting a local bar or brothel. Some inns were ready-made auditoria, with a captive audience that could view the actors either from ground level or else from the galleries that went around the sides of their courtyards. Productions are recorded at the Saracen's Head in Islington and at the Boar's Head in Aldgate in 1557, but a proclamation two years later banning plays in hostels and taverns indicates that such theatres were common – the City introduced a similar prohibition in 1574. Not only were theatrical occasions regarded as possible causes of violence, but the spread of plague was also a concern. There were complaints that watching plays led to immorality and crime and while the Court and its hangers-on generally encouraged groups of players, the early representatives of England's Puritans were already inveighing against them. Certainly a description of an evening at the Red Bull, Clerkenwell, when 'the Benches, the tiles, the laths, the stones, Oranges, Apples, Nuts, flew about most liberally and. . .there were mechanicks of all professions who fell everyone to his own trade, and dissolved a house in an instant, and made a ruine of a stately Fabrick' explains the anxieties of the local authorities.

An Act of 1572 which provided for the punishment 'of Vagrants and Vagabondes', with whom travelling players might be included, obliged actors to seek the patronage of aristocracy, including the Lord Chamberlain, whose later role was to censor any play performed. As a result, the major companies were named after these protectors, such as the Earls of Pembroke or Leicester. They performed at the first purpose-built theatre called, simply, The Theatre, erected c.1576 at the junction of Curtain Road and New Inn Yard in Shoreditch, slightly beyond the clutches of the City fathers. The building's promoter was carpenter-cum-actor, James Burbage, who borrowed the £666 needed to build it, and whose sons, Cuthbert and Richard, transported it in 1599 to Southwark for re-erection as the Globe, an operation which suggests that the building might well have been some kind of pre-fabricated structure in the first place.

By the time the Globe, by then owned by seven men including Shakespeare, opened on the south bank, two theatres already existed there, to the great benefit of ferry watermen: the Rose, whose remnants have recently been discovered between Rose Alley and

Southwark Bridge, was begun *c.*1587, and the Swan (*c.*1595), west of today's derelict Bankside Power Station. It was at the Swan that a play called the *Isle of Dogs*, partly written by Ben Jonson, so enraged the authorities for 'contanyng very seditious and slanderous matter' that the Privy Council ordered the demolition of all theatres. What actually happened was that for the remainder of Elizabeth I's reign only two London companies were permitted and performances continued, especially at the Globe where, by the time the building was burnt down in 1613, at least sixteen plays by Shakespeare had been performed. Richard Burbage played the first Hamlet at the Globe in 1602, the same year that the volatile London crowd wrecked the Swan Theatre when an advertised play was not performed.

The main disadvantage of the Southwark theatres, apart from a possible boat journey to reach them, was that they were open-air buildings and therefore unusable in the colder

A bird's-eye perspective of the Globe Theatre and a bear-baiting auditorium on the south bank, in 1647. The first theatre here, in 1587, was the Rose, the remains of which were recently discovered near Southwark Bridge Road.

months. To rival them were theatricals mounted by a company of children in a converted room in the old Blackfriars monastery, a development from those children who performed plays in cathedral schools in the thirteenth century. They enjoyed considerable success, with plays written for them by Dekker, Beaumont and Massinger – even the ribald '*Tis Pity She's a Whore*' was staged at Blackfriars – and were sufficiently competitive for Shakespeare to rile against them in several plays. Rosencrantz in *Hamlet* refers to them as 'an aery of children, little eyeases, that cry out on the top of question, and are most tyrannically clapp'd for 't'.

Actors and playwrights, on the same footing as casual workers, were not well paid. They endured the unpredictability and discomforts of any touring company and dealt with hostile audiences; theirs was a penurious existence led somewhere between art and violence. The playwright, Ben Jonson, killed an actor in a duel in 1598 near the Theatre in Shoreditch; he escaped with his life, but was imprisoned and branded. Christopher Marlowe, always a controversial figure, was killed in a tavern brawl in Deptford in 1593, in circumstances still shrouded in uncertainty. In 1617 the unruly London apprentices attacked the 'new playhouse, sometime a cockpit in Drury Lane, where the queen's players used to play. . .cutting the players' apparel into pieces, and all their furniture and burnt their playbooks'. It was not an auspicious beginning for the first theatre in Covent Garden.

Given the ambivalent view of theatre held by those in authority, ownership of a playhouse could be a hazardous investment, but it was sometimes profitable. James Burbage was a wealthy man when he died, and Edward Alleyn, an actor who went into management with his father-in-law, Philip Henslowe, retired in middle age and for £10,000 bought the manor of Dulwich, where he founded what became Dulwich College.

THE baiting of animals was undoubtedly the most popular entertainment of the early 17th century, appealing to all classes. By 1546 baiting was established at Southwark, with the enthusiastic support of Henry VIII and Elizabeth I.

Alleyn and Henslowe built the Fortune Theatre in Golden Lane, Cripplegate, and Alleyn also had an interest in a baiting house at Paris Garden, near the southern end of today's Blackfriars Bridge. From this latter enterprise he was well placed to acquire the lucrative office of Master of the Royal Game of bears, bulls and mastiff dogs, and he then had some monopoly of this popular form of entertainment. He could not have chosen a better time to buy this privilege, for James I was unhealthily obsessed with displays of animal harassment and courage. Alleyn it was who supplied mastiff dogs for a contest involving a lion at the Tower of London in 1604; though two dogs were savagely killed, a third survived and enjoyed extra rations commanded by the King. Alleyn, no doubt, was around in August that year when James entertained the Constable of Castile at Whitehall Palace with song and dance, followed by bears fighting greyhounds.

Near the Southwark theatres were at least three arenas for bull-baiting and bear-baiting

– two of the buildings, both circular, are clearly shown on a map of *c.*1559. Here were attractions for all classes. Stow enjoyed baiting except on Sundays, and Elizabeth I herself took the Spanish ambassador to see bear-baiting at Southwark in 1575 and remained so enthusiastic that she later persuaded the Lord Mayor to prohibit theatrical performances in Southwark on the same days. He announced that 'in divers places the players do use to recite their plays to the great hurt and destruction of the game of bear-baiting and such like pastimes which are maintained for her Majesty's pleasure.'

The Spanish ambassador might well have found the entertainment savage and raw compared with the formalized brutality of Spanish bullfights. Bears often had their teeth ground down – a dangerous operation in itself – and were therefore reliant on their heavy forepaws for the kill. Even so it was considered fair sport to face a bear with several dogs at a time, whereas a bull would fight each dog singly. Gambling on the result was an

*T*HE *Royal Cockpit, Westminster, published in Ackermann's* Microcosm of London *between 1808 and 1810. A royal cockpit was built at the instigation of Henry VIII in Whitehall, but the one shown above was near Queen Anne's Gate.*

attraction, as it was at cockfights. Stow remarks that 'Cocks of the game are yet cherished by diverse men for their pleasure, much money being laide on their heades, when they fight in pits, whereof some be costly made for that purpose.' Henry VIII had had his own cockpit ring near his tennis court in Whitehall, and in 1609 a public cockpit was built in Drury Lane.

The Court occasionally saw theatrical performances – Shakespeare's *Love's Labours Lost* was performed at Whitehall Palace, for example, in 1598, and the following year Queen Elizabeth saw *The Merry Wives of Windsor* there. But the main interest in aristocratic circles was the growing sophistication of masques. These elaborate productions, part play, part opera, part dance, sometimes allegorical, were staged and designed by artists of celebrated calibre and performed mostly by members of the Court. They were usually held in the Banqueting Hall in Whitehall. The second Hall was erected, like the first, for a specific occasion, and was a temporary, canvas-walled affair, but richly decorated inside. It was built in three weeks to impress the Duc d'Alençon, the last foreign suitor to press his unwelcome attentions on Queen Elizabeth.

James I saw *The Masque of Blackness* at Whitehall in 1605, written and designed by Ben Jonson and Inigo Jones, in which his queen, Ann of Denmark, and numerous courtiers took part. 'For the scene was drawn a landscape consisting of woods and hills, and here and there a void place filled with huntings; which folding, an artificial sea was seen to shoot forth as if it would flow to the land, lashed with waves that seemed to move.'

James enjoyed his spectacle and pomp but, as was the custom then, he was not so remote from his humbler subjects in the way that later sovereigns became. He dealt personally with many things brought to his notice. In 1605 he interviewed one Butler, a man renowned for his prophecies which bordered, it was thought, on the realm of witchcraft; after interrogation James passed him on to the Lord Chief Justice. At about the same time some Levant merchants came to see him to petition personally against a new taxation on the import of currants. And when plague was not rampant, he touched people who believed in his power to cure their illnesses.

CRIME AND PUNISHMENT

THE SEVENTEENTH CENTURY WAS A TIME IN WHICH ASTROLOGERS AND PROPHETS could make respectable livings. The dread of witchcraft, in particular, took hold of the public. No one was more prone to accusation than the local midwife, for there was a popular belief, derived from Christianity, that a still-born child unrelieved of original sin by baptism was possessed of an evil spirit. It was usual for the midwife who delivered such a child to secretly bury it in unconsecrated ground, but there were accusations that some had retained the 'evil' foetus for witchcraft purposes. Given, too, a midwife's reputation for intimacy with the human anatomy and things sexual, she was more likely than most women to incur suspicion. Legislation followed the popular beliefs. Witchcraft was made a felony in 1543, a capital offence in certain circumstances in 1563, and was pursued by James I with vigour. In 1615, Agnes Berry of Enfield was hanged for exercising witchcrafts, enchantments, charms and sorceries on another woman; the following year in London, Margaret Wellam was accused of being a witch and for sucking and feeding on evil spirits; the wife of an Edmonton brewer was accused in 1617 of bewitching a child. This was not the most celebrated Edmonton case: there were numerous ballads, pamphlets and even a Jacobean play entitled *The Witch of Edmonton* on the subject of Mother Sawyer, a labourer's wife, who was hanged at Newgate. At least seven women from Whitechapel and Stepney were accused of witchcraft in the 1650s.

It was often the maligned local midwives, otherwise described as 'honest and discrete matrons' when it suited the authorities, who were appointed as 'Searchers' in the City and surrounding parishes. Their job, which still survived in the nineteenth century, was to inspect corpses and to report on the causes of death. This bizarre system was introduced so that local authorities might have notification of any deaths from plague, and the fact that the women had no medical training was not an issue, since plague was thought to be recognizable by almost anyone. It was inevitable perhaps that the Searcher would accept a bribe to describe the cause of death differently, so that the deceased's family would not themselves have to go into quarantine.

A city which had seen so many grotesque public executions in the previous eighty years was one that, by the seventeenth century, was accustomed to capital punishment for quite insignificant offences. The records of the Middlesex Sessions are witness to a savage regime of sentencing in an era when religious devotion was at its most fervent. As early as the reign of Edward VI, small-time theft was a capital offence. A burglary in Charterhouse Lane in 1558, in which a linen handkerchief valued at twelve pence and a key worth eightpence were taken, resulted in a hanging. Two men who stole five shillings at Marylebone went to Tyburn, and a man living in St John Street was executed for stealing a curtain and some woollen stockings, as were two men at Notting Hill for robbery with violence.

The authorities were having to cope with an increased crime rate and this resulted in a revival of Houses of Correction, one of which had been established by the City of London in 1556. An Act of 1609 instructed counties to erect buildings, equipped with 'mills, turns, cards and suchlike necessary implements to set the rogues or other such idle persons on work'. The City had found that it was convenient to house the poor and criminals together and, indeed, to treat them in much the same way. All were obliged to labour at the most wearing and monotonous tasks such as on treadmills, or picking oakum; punishments became, at least in Bridewell, a public amusement, particularly whipping, which was carried out in a large room with a gallery especially erected for spectators. Middlesex built a House of Detention in 1615, just off Clerkenwell Green and Westminster followed in 1618, with a building at Tothill Fields. As was the custom in London prisons, management was farmed out to private individuals and an inmate's conditions depended largely upon any money he could raise from friends. In the communal rooms in which prisoners were usually kept, there was excuse to fetter and weigh them with irons, which could be increased or reduced at the whim of the gaoler or the production of the right amount of money.

These buildings, mixtures of poorhouse, workhouse and prison, were added to the motley collection of London's gaols, compters and lock-ups. The playwright, Thomas Dekker, who was imprisoned in Poultry Compter in the City, described what it was like there:

> jailers hoarsely and harshly bawling for prisoners to their bed, and prisoners reviling and cursing jailers for making such a hellish din. Then to hear some in their chambers singing and dancing, being half drunk; others breaking open doors to get more drink to be whole drunk. Some roaring for tobacco; others raging and bidding hell's plague on all tobacco.

A new Sessions House was erected for Middlesex in 1621 in St John Street, near Smithfield, at the expense of Sir Baptist Hicks. A pattern of sentencing can be found in the records of this court. People charged with a serious offence were still able to plead benefit of clergy and put themselves at the mercy of the more lenient ecclesiastical courts. To qualify for this the prisoner had to read correctly a passage from the Bible, in which case he was branded with the letter T (for Tyburn) on his thumb. As elementary education became available during the reigns of Edward VI and Elizabeth more and more prisoners found escape this way. Women delayed hanging for the time being if pregnant, but could be executed after the birth. Occasionally, the accused stood mute and if found guilty endured an excruciating death by *peine forte et dure*, in which he was stretched naked in a dark cell, pressed down with heavy weights, and fed occasionally over the days in which he took to die with sour bread and even worse water. The dubious advantage to the prisoner of this kind of death was that although his chattels would be seized by the authorities, his lands were free to go to his heirs.

A new punishment, which was to have inadvertent but lasting consequences, was transportation. Although this was to reach its peak in the eighteenth and nineteenth centuries, it began with an Act of 1597 which included provision 'for the punishment of rogues, vagabonds and sturdy beggars' by deportation, as slaves, to the new colonies. The first such occasion which appears in the Middlesex records was not until 1614, when a man convicted of burglary was transported, not to Virginia, but to an even more inhospitable Greenland, which had been discovered by Frobisher in his quest for the North-West Passage.

Whipping was a frequent punishment for prostitution or petty larceny. This could take place in the local high street, or outside the prisoner's home, or in a prison. The humiliation of being whipped while pulled along at the tail of a cart through the streets was common. The stocks and the pillory were used in cases of fraud, unruly behaviour, minor poaching, fornication outside marriage, and for being a scold – the last an offence usually applied to women.

THE GROWTH OF TRADE

SWARMS OF DESTITUTE PEOPLE AND A MOUNTING CRIME RATE went hand-in-hand with a rampant increase in prosperity, not for the only time in London's history. Business was good as London assumed the position it was to hold for the next three hundred years, that of the most important trading city in the world. The English at last exploited their earlier footholds in the New World, realizing their potential quite late in the day, and the generally peaceful reign of Elizabeth I enabled London merchants to establish serious and continuous trade links abroad. These were prosaic things compared with the drama and legend of naval battles on the Spanish Main or the heroic explorations of English navigators, but they were, despite that, of more importance in the development of London. As the Low Countries suffered the rapacity and suppression of their Spanish masters, so England, and in particular London, usurped their trade and, indeed, became home to many of their more vigorous citizens. The fall of Antwerp demolished that city's European trading dominance, one that was seized by a London rejoicing in new-found wealth and moral superiority. As City merchants increased their trade with counties such as Russia, Turkey and India they became, because of their wealth and enterprise, even more superior to the craftsmen of the City, and to complete their dominance in London the merchants controlled the most influential guilds, and the guilds controlled the City of London. And yet, depite their forwardness in business, merchants remained a conservative class, far removed from the extravagances of Westminster.

For a city that depended on trade London was decidedly unorganized for day-to-day business. Men promenaded in Lombard Street or in the aisles and nave of St Paul's, or met in company halls and inns to do transactions. It was the wealthy merchant, Sir Thomas Gresham, who created an Exchange in which traders could stand in rather more comfort and expect to meet others of like mind. This innovation, copied from Antwerp (where Gresham had lived for a while and where the original bourse and his house there still survive), was the forerunner of the trading floors in which London achieved its pre-eminent financial position –– the Stock Exchange, the commodity exchanges, Lloyd's insurance, all derived much of their character and business methods from Gresham's building.

The Exchange (originally named after Gresham, but Queen Elizabeth insisted that it should be the *Royal* Exchange) was a quadrangle of buildings enclosing an open courtyard. A cloister, which provided a covered walk, ran at ground level, and above this were shops called 'pawns'. These retail outlets were slow to prosper when the Exchange began and it was not until the Queen officially opened the building in 1571 that they began to flourish. The Bohemian artist Wenceslaus Hollar's view of the interior of the building shows traders of many nations gathered in the courtyard transacting business; by the time the second Exchange was erected after the Great Fire of 1666, categories of

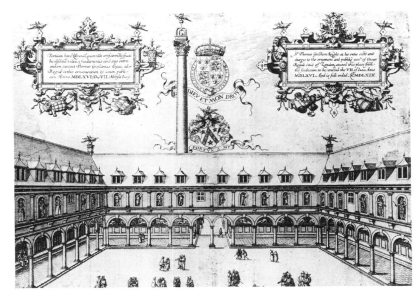

THE first Royal Exchange. Thomas Gresham's Exchange derived from his admiration of a similar building in Antwerp. He believed that a central place for merchants to do business was better than the haphazard arrangement of meetings in livery halls and churches.

merchants had marked out their pitches. Druggists and grocers, silkmen and dyers could immediately be found, as could dealers in goods from the different countries of Europe and the New World. 'At every turn,' remarked Dekker in 1607, 'a man is put in mind of Babel, there is such a confusion of languages.'

Dekker was not exaggerating. With Europe in turmoil during Elizabeth's reign, London had become a refuge for Flemings, French and Dutch in particular; there were also a great many Scots who had come down with James I. The East India Company had been formed in 1600 and other companies traded with places as disparate as Guinea, Turkey, Africa and the Canary Islands. It was a visiting artist, George Hoefnagel, who with his engraver, Frans Hogenberg, produced the earliest complete map of London we have (surveyed *c.* 1550), and it was Anthony van den Wyngaerde who produced a panoramic view of London from the Thames in the same period. Wenceslaus Hollar's drawings of London were to be the most important in the depiction of mid seventeenth-century London

Tradition has it that the Exchange Gresham built commemorated his only legitimate son, who had died young. It is just as likely that he was being perfectly businesslike and had expectations of shop rentals. In this, as we have seen, he was initially disappointed, but he had a shorter time to wait for a return on his money than another entrepreneur of the period, Hugh Myddelton, who had the initial funds, imagination and patience to construct the New River from Hertfordshire to the heights of Clerkenwell, and so bring fresh water to London. He was not being altruistic, but the difficulties he had to overcome, the bankruptcy he nearly faced, and then the poor response from the citizens of London, transformed him from an ordinary capitalist into a patron. In truth, the New River should have been a civic project, but the City declined to fund it.

THE New River Head was at Amwell Street, Clerkenwell, and from here water was pumped to London houses. This was augmented in the 18th century by the use of a reservoir near the Pentonville Road and later still, illustrated above, a proper reservoir was built.

London by the late sixteenth century was ill-supplied with fresh water. Much of it came from the Thames, pumped by the London Bridge Waterworks using a machine by the most northern arch of the bridge that took advantage of the swift flow of the river there as it squeezed through the openings. The intake of water was downstream from the outlets of the rivers Fleet and Walbrook, both of which were not much more than sewers, and it is as well that Londoners did not, as a matter of habit, drink water. Other supplies came from wells in and around London, such as St Clement's Well in the Strand but, by 1598, when Stow published his Survey, Holywell was 'much decayed and marred with filthiness', the Horsepool in Smithfield was 'much decayed, the springs being stopped up', and a pool by St Giles's Churchyard was 'for the most part stopped up'. Free water was obtained from medieval conduits running from Oxford Street and Paddington which tapped the river Tyburn and springs in those rural areas. A small banqueting house had been erected in what is now Stratford Place so that the City fathers could dine there when they paid their annual visit to inspect the head of the conduit; the lead pipes ran down what is now Conduit Street, along the Strand and Fleet Street, over the Fleet river and thence to Cheapside. Other supplies came from Canonbury, Islington and Bloomsbury – the last denoted today by Lamb's Conduit Street. Over such distances leakage was significant and as London's population grew it was evident that a substantial augmentation was needed.

Myddelton – like so many London merchants, from a country family – had made his fortune as a goldsmith. He was to need it. Not only was construction expensive but it was necessary to placate landowners through whose estates the river was cut and whose appetite for compensation was equalled only later by those courted by railway companies. Myddelton's scheme had its origins in 1607 when a Captain Edmund Colthurst applied for Letters Patent to construct such a river, but the City, ever fearful of private enterprise, applied for its own licence and so scotched Colthurst. The City did not, however, proceed with the venture and Myddelton took it under his own wing. The City's reluctance may have stemmed from a preoccupation with draining the Moorfields marshes, a task that was begun that same year, and which transformed an area used for recreation in the drier months into one which could be used for most of the year.

Myddelton's scheme was saved by the enthusiasm of James I and the King's willingness to buy half the shares and pay half the costs. The river, actually a canal, wound 39 miles from springs at Chadwell and Amwell near Ware, to a large reservoir at what is now Amwell Street, Clerkenwell. From there, in elm tree trunks, it was piped by engine and gravity to households in the northern parts of the City which could not be reached by the pumps at London Bridge where a primitive water supply system existed. On a September day in 1613, sixty neatly-dressed labourers shouldered their digging tools and marched in procession around the empty reservoir. The gates were opened and 'the streame ranne gallantly into the cisterne drummes and trumpets sounding in triumphall manner, and a brave peal of chambers [cannon] gave full issue.' City people, deterred by rumours spread by resentful water-carriers, did not take to the New River with the hoped-for enthusiasm. It was believed that piped water was unhealthier than that from the Thames or from the wells. Myddelton was fortunate that James was also concerned about his own investment, for the King insisted that the City made use of the water from the New River and blocked the proposal of the Brewers' Company to erect its own waterworks at Dowgate.

The lasting significance of Myddelton's brave venture was not that the City had an alternative and abundant source of water (especially later when the river was also supplied from the Lea), but that it opened up the clay lands of inner north London for development.

FURTHER DEVELOPMENT

WATER SUPPLY WAS OF CONCERN also to the 4th Earl of Bedford as he set about developing his Covent Garden estate in the 1630s. This was the first planned development of any size in London and in this sense was the first significant consequence of the transfer of land from monastic to lay hands. The garden of the Convent of St Peter, Westminster, consisting of 40 acres on the north side of the Strand, was taken by Henry VIII in 1536, and by 1552 was in the hands of John Russell, Earl of Bedford. Later that century there were, as we have seen, restrictions on the growth of building in the London area, and for these we must be grateful, for the Covent Garden estate might well have been built earlier as a hotch-potch similar to that in nearby Long Acre and St Martin's Lane, which was partly there in speculative disorder before Covent Garden was laid out. But new buildings to house an ever increasing population could not forever be delayed. In fact, what appears to be the first planned street in London was nearby Great Queen Street. Begun in 1605, this threatened the unspoilt nature of Lincoln's Inn Fields and stirred the lawyers into action to prevent encroachment on what they regarded as their own public open space. Their petition to the King was hardly different from the modern protests at the seemingly permanent residencies erected by the homeless on the same land: they remarked on 'such persons as daylie seeke to fill upp that small remaynder of Ayre in those partes with unnecessary and unproffittable Buildinges.'

The scheme benefited from the conjunction of three men – Charles I, who had architectural ambitions for his capital, the 4th Earl of Bedford, who had energy and business acumen, and Inigo Jones, an architect whose influence on English architecture cannot be underestimated.

The Earl eluded the building prohibitions of the day and created a development which set the tone for a new London. Neatly positioned between the overcrowded areas of the City and Westminster it pointed out the deficiencies of their unplanned environments, and its classical architecture and orderly and relatively wide streets were intimations of what a capital city could look like. The concept of the Piazza itself was entirely new to an astounded London and it remained unique. Here was a large open space, faced by Inigo Jones's handsome church of St Paul, but otherwise unadorned, and around it arcades were inserted beneath the protruding upper floors of the houses, rather like the cloisters of Gresham's Exchange. In both these areas the public was invited to feel at home.

When London later lurched westward in neighbourhoods concentrated around squares, their central gardens were not open to the public. Covent Garden, in fact, represented a development in which exclusivity and privacy were not purchased with the house; in spirit it was a continuation of the London style of living in which rich and poor still had encounters, and in which it was possible for a pedestrian to walk unchallenged through the precincts of the King's palace at Whitehall. Increasingly after Covent Garden the architecture of London buildings reflected the wish and the ability of the well-to-do to separate themselves from the poorer classes, and all the squares which followed the Piazza were planned to that end.

The Piazza houses were designed to attract 'Persons of the greatest Distinction' and, indeed, the early lists of residents include a large sprinkling of aristocracy, Members of Parliament, lawyers, eminent soldiers and fashionable painters, a mix that lasted well past the end of the seventeenth century. But the Piazza's accessibility to the general public was, in the end, the undoing of Covent Garden, and its adjacency to the *demi-monde* of two large theatres, and the growing use of the square by vendors of fruit and vegetables, brought into it people whom the well-heeled wished to avoid.

Civic projects were also in the air. One was the scheme, prepared by Inigo Jones *c.*1638, for the rebuilding of Whitehall Palace as a huge rectangle of buildings that stretched from the Thames into St James's Park, obliterating Whitehall as a thoroughfare. This was Charles I at his most optimistic, since he had no funds and his own position was in jeopardy, but he pursued this scheme to outshine the grandeur of the French and

Spanish kings even to the time of his capture by Parliamentary forces. All that was built was Inigo Jones's fine Banqueting House, a perfect double cube, which still stands in Whitehall.

Jones in his buildings, such as the Queen's House at Greenwich, broke free of English vernacular architecture, but a more hesitant approach was displayed in the mansion in Bishopsgate built in the 1620s for Sir Paul Pindar, a merchant, which was basically an Elizabethan structure with classical decorative features. The quality of the wood carving was exceptional and may be assessed now in the rather incongruous surroundings of the bookshop of the Victoria and Albert Museum, where the oak frontage of the house is now kept. Pindar, who like Jones had also spent some time in Italy, was influential in its design. His mansion, probably the last to be built in the City before the Great Fire of 1666, had a frontage of about 90 feet, and was 'equal, if not superior, in splendour and extent

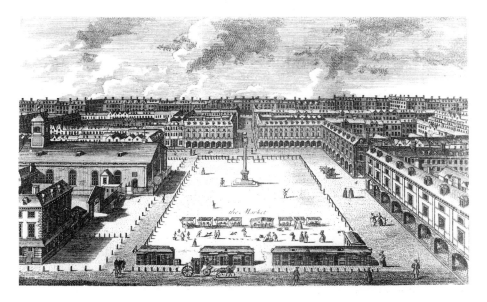

COVENT GARDEN PIAZZA in the 18th century. The Piazza was the first 'square' to be built in London – it was also the last for a very long time to allow access to the general public. Wooden posts and a rail surround the square, and a column, erected by local residents, decorates the centre.

to any structure, not only within its immediate vicinity, but probably to any in the metropolis.' Its prestige (and that of its owner) may be judged by the use of it in 1617 as a London home by the Venetian Ambassador to the Court of James I while Pindar was off representing the King at the Court of the Sultan of Turkey. The Ambassador noted in his diary that he was:

> *fortunate to secure a house in an airy and fashionable quarter. . .It was a little too much in the country; but it was near the most fashionable theatres, especially those that keep the best trained dogs for bear and bull baiting. It was spacious and handsome, and had a gallery which was easily turned into a chapel, by putting up a decent altar at the farther end.*

FISHERWOMEN at Billingsgate Market. The women, whose reputation for rowdiness was formidable, sold fish in the streets.

CHAPTER VI
MAKING A LIVING

THE MARKETS

THE NICETIES OF ARCHITECTURE WERE WELL REMOVED FROM THOSE WHO EKED OUT A living on the land. In the villages around London a reliance on agriculture and a dependence on the weather were still the stuff of life; their communities of farmers and small-time craftsmen earned modest livelihoods either in London or else at weekly markets and continued to live in unpretentious wooden houses. The proximity of London was both a blessing and a disadvantage, for the City had ensured that there were few markets in its suburbs. A saddler, for example in Highgate, had to travel as far as Barnet to sell his surplus goods at a market if he didn't wish to compete in London and whatever venue he chose he would have to pay for a pitch.

By the seventeenth century the City had acquired by tradition, purchase or charter, control over the markets within its boundaries, and the one in Southwark. The Stocks Market, on the site of the Mansion House, and Leadenhall were buildings which belonged to the City. Supervision of the stands and shops in Cheapside, Newgate Street, Eastcheap and Old Fish Street was, by long custom, in its hands although there was uncertainty, which surfaced when relations between Crown and City were strained, about authority over the stalls actually erected on the king's highway. The port and market, Queenhithe, was rented from the Crown, and Billingsgate and Smithfield had been officially granted to the City in 1400, although they were probably under its control earlier.

Armed with this monopoly the City ensured that only its own citizens could open shops, leaving country people the less hospitable streetside market stalls. Itinerant vendors seem to have been tolerated – bread was sold around the streets as, indeed, it was in the villages around London, where women particularly are noted in court rolls as 'regrators' of bread and of ale as well. The notoriously boisterous Billingsgate fishwives, were permitted to hawk it in the streets. An observer in 1632 described them thus:

> These crying, wandering and travelling creatures carry their shops on their heads and their storehouse is ordinarily Billingsgate or the Bridge-foot. They set up every morning their trade afresh. They are easily set up and furnished, get something and spend it jovially and merrily. . . If they drink out their whole stock, its but pawning a petticoat in Long Lane or themselves in Turnbull Street for to set up again.

The fishmongers were almost a law unto themselves. On the whole they were able to prevent fishermen, other than those who fished the Thames, supplying direct to the public; instead the catches went wholesale to the fishmongers, mainly at Billingsgate, and they therefore controlled the retail price structure.

A print of *c.*1600 depicts numerous itinerant vendors. The range of produce sold from their baskets (the women, generally, have the baskets balanced on their heads) includes pins, pears, rushes, strawberries and hat-cases. This suggests that these are people from the city's suburbs, who came in daily with as much produce as they could carry.

The City enforced regulations that stemmed from a hotch-potch of religion, tradition, self-interest and expediency. Butchers did not trade on Fridays or during Lent; measures and weights were based on London standards that did not necessarily correspond with those of the country vendors. For example, weight in Essex, Suffolk and London was

STOCKS MARKET, early 18th century, on the site of the Mansion House. The market, which specialized in fish and flesh, was established in the 13th century near some permanent stocks; it was demolished in 1737.

assessed by wildly different standards, and the custom of topping up a quantity, such as supplying thirteen for a baker's dozen, was widespread but inconsistent. The value of some commodities, particularly of bread and ale, was determined by the City, based on the prevailing price of raw materials. Bread was sold in farthing, halfpenny or penny loaves and, depending on the price of grain, the authorities in the City and in the manors around determined the *size* of the loaves for those prices; ale, which was sold for a penny a gallon, had its *strength* varied with the price of ingredients while the measures sold remained the same. Hours of market opening were controlled – this prevented sales in poor light, ensured that all traders sold under the eyes of market or guild inspectors, and it was contrived that the country vendors often got the worst selling periods. These incomers were, in any case, subject to the City's whim. For example, those who traded in Leadenhall Street on open stalls were obliged in the 1530s to use instead the courtyard of

Leadenhall market on Wednesdays and Saturdays, but later on, in a straightforward protectionist move, the Wednesday facility was withdrawn.

The most important general market was Cheapside, where the stalls merged into those of the Newgate Street butchers to the west, and into the Cornhill market to the east. Here, apart from grain, meat, poultry, fruit and vegetables, would be clothes, domestic goods and specialist items produced in the surrounding streets.

Food markets were not of paramount importance outside the City since most households had land on which they could keep for their own needs poultry, pigs, sheep, cattle and horses. All but the poorest classes farmed some acres and therefore had grain. Bread was made at home and if no oven was available, as was often the case, taken to a baker to finish. There was usually a shortage of grain in the months leading up to harvest, just as there were few fruits and vegetables available in the winter. As a rule meat was cheap, sea fish more expensive and fresh-water fish difficult to come by because it was almost always taken by the owner of the river.

Durable items, such as clothes, leather goods, furniture, utensils and vessels were mainly sold at fairs; at the larger events, such as Bartholomew Fair, manufacturers also bought raw materials, such as iron or cloth. Second-hand clothes markets flourished at Long Lane near St Bartholomew's Hospital and at Houndsditch, the forerunner of today's Petticoat Lane. Donald Lupton, writing in 1632, has left us a vivid account of the latter:

> A man that comes here as a stranger would think there had been some great death of men and women hereabouts, he sees so many suits and no men for them. Here are suits for all the lawyers of London to deal withal. The inhabitants are beholden to the hangman for he furnishes their shops. The jailer and broker are birds of a feather; the one imprisons the body and the other the clothes and both make men pay dear for their lodging.

The medieval Bartholomew Fair had begun in the precincts of St Bartholomew's priory, which had controlled its activities and received the tolls. Originally, it took place on three days around St Bartholomew's Day, and was primarily a cloth fair, attracting tailors and clothiers from far around – this speciality is denoted in the little street, Cloth Fair, nearby. The event was considerably enlarged and the administration complicated when the City began holding a cattle fair on adjacent Smithfield at the same time and there was until the Reformation, when the two fairs came under the single control of the City, a joint administration of the two events.

The Growth of the Retail Trade

IN THE SEVENTEENTH CENTURY, shops and retailing, in the modern sense, became common in London. Though grocers and pepperers in shops had, from the Middle Ages, progressively specialized in durable foods such as cheese, rice, currants, herbs and sugar, trade in meat, fish, fruit and vegetables and most other commodities was generally the province of the markets. There were pockets of shops: haberdashers and hosiers lined the sides of London Bridge and Gresham included shops in his Exchange in the City. Goldsmiths' Row, a prestigious line of shops, stood in Cheapside, almost entirely monopolized by goldsmiths at one time: this was one of the wonders of Tudor London, but by 1622 many of the businesses had moved out to the lower rents of Fleet Street and the Strand, so that in 1629 Charles I ordered the Lord Mayor to close any shop in Cheapside that was not a goldsmith and encourage the former tenants to return. They did not, of course, and Cheapside continued to be the mixture it had become. As we have seen, in 1609 the New Exchange in the Strand was opened on a site opposite today's Bedford Street. This was a combination of bourse and bazaar which signally failed to entice City merchants away from the City, but which had in it 'several rows of great numbers of very rich shops of drapers and mercers filled with goods of every kind, and with manufactures of the most beautiful description.'

Retailing had once been frowned upon. In medieval times, when it was usual to buy direct at market from a farmer, a market gardener, or small-time manufacturer, there was little reason for an entrepreneur to buy in bulk and resell in smaller quantities for a profit.

THE NEW EXCHANGE in the Strand, from a watercolour by T.H. Shepherd. The New Exchange was opened in 1609 by James I who named it 'Britain's Burse'. It did not succeed in drawing commercial trade from the Royal Exchange in the City.

But in the seventeenth century retailing became respectable in London and, indeed, a desirable occupation. Stow noted the trend at the end of the sixteenth century when he said that, 'In wealth, merchants and some of the chief retailers have first place.' This did not please him since, he complained, 'the people of London began to expend extravagantly.' There were on sale, he noted, 'French and Spanish gloves, and French cloth or frigarde, Flanders-dyed kersies, daggers, swords, knives, Spanish girdles, painted cruses, dials, tables, cards, balls, glasses, fine earthen pots, salt-cellars, spons, tin dishes, puppets, pennons, ink-horns, toothpicks, silk, and silver buttons.'

A number of factors made this possible. In a London then bursting at the seams there was a heavier demand for goods and for more expensive goods: this encouraged retail stockists to invest against an anticipated and consistent demand and items previously made or procured to order were held in stock instead. As well, the frequency with which ships now came into London with tonnes of merchandise from newly discovered parts of the world required a ready and reliable network of retail outlets on which to offload before the consignment became inedible or unsaleable. Sugar, for example, a rarity in the Middle Ages when it was brought only from Arabia and India, was being imported in bulk from the Caribbean in the seventeenth century, and each importer had to be sure that he could sell it quickly and efficiently. Tobacco was another case in point.

Corn chandlers, theoretically prohibited from buying up corn direct from farmers within 35 miles of London, began to buy in bulk outside that radius, arousing the ire not only of the City Corporation but the burgesses of those towns whose own markets were denuded of supplies from local farmers. Moreover, enterprises in London, such as brewers, which converted basic materials into something else, were obliged to find sources of supply larger than could be procured through the traditional City markets and, inevitably, it became common for such manufacturers to buy direct in bulk: in effect, they forestalled the markets. It was a trend that the City authorities could not in the end resist.

TRANSPORT AND TRAFFIC

A CONSEQUENCE OF LONDON'S GROWTH and its voracious appetite was traffic. Wheeled carts there were in plenty (but not until the 1620s were coaches common), and the number of animals coming into London was prodigious. Norfolk farmers brought in flocks of geese or turkeys, manoeuvring them, one imagines with great difficulty, along the East Anglian roads down to Aldgate and into Poultry. More damaging to the highways were the herds of cattle that churned up the mire which passed for road surface on their way to Smithfield; quite often they were rested for several weeks at places like Islington that had a thriving trade in fattening cattle made lean from their journey: the sunken level of the highway today at Islington and at Highgate is testimony to those milling animals. Market gardeners brought their produce on carts or on their heads from all points of the compass. Bakers, in particular from the Stratford area, came in large numbers into the City each morning to sell bread. Coal came into Billingsgate and then by heavily laden carts up the slopes to those homes which could not afford wood for fuel.

The repair of roads was rather more organized in the City than it was elsewhere. The highways outside the City were the property of the Crown and at first their upkeep fell to the reluctant manors through which they ran. An Act of 1555 then transferred responsibility to the parishes, but there was no provision for the collection of a highway rate so that men might be employed to do repair work. Instead, each able-bodied householder and each landowner was required to contribute a fixed amount of labour or equipment each year under the supervision of a Surveyor of Highways, who had the thankless and unpaid task of making sure that his grudging crew fulfilled their quotas. There was a practical difficulty around London where much of the land was clay, with only pockets of gravel available for surfacing. Any gravel deposits found were therefore worked intensively – on the evidence of court rolls it is thought that the steep slopes of the land on either side of Highgate village were formed from years of digging on outcrops of gravel there.

To a large extent, congestion in the City was caused by the narrowness of its thoroughfares: it has been remarked that many of the medieval streets of the City were built to take wheelbarrows. But height was also a problem. Time and again the authorities tried to ensure that someone mounted on horseback would not hit his head on an obstruction such as a hanging trade sign, or a storey of a house jutting out at an upper level. Even more vainly they sought to keep the alleys clear of accumulated garbage which itself got ground into the stinking mud that formed the road surface. Outside the City walls it was only in 1543 that steps were taken to enforce the paving of London's streets.

The inadequacy of the road system was disguised by the use that Londoners made of the Thames for day-to-day journeys. They took open wherries on the wide stream, in all degrees of weather, to an extent that modern Londoners would shy from; but by the middle of the seventeenth century London was growing northwards and therefore the river could not be used for many journeys. It is one of the disadvantages of an unplanned city that by the time a need is apparent there are often too many vested interests involved to accommodate it. And so it was with the provision of wider (and straighter) roads in London. Later, when London was rebuilt after the Great Fire of 1666 property interests even then prevailed and there was little change in the road pattern or the width of roads.

The City in the seventeenth century was still irritated by the use of carts which had wheels shod with iron. These had been banned in the fifteenth century, but an Ordinance of 1586, levying a hefty fine on their use, implies a widespread contravention; Westminster had a similar prohibition. The sheer number of carts, unshod or not, was remarked upon by Horatio Busoni, Chaplain to the Venetian Ambassador in 1618. Carts in London 'in passing along the streets, whether narrow or wide, do not choose to yield or give way as due to the coaches of the gentry when they meet them.' And he notes the 'multitude of them, large and small, that is to say on two wheels and on four, that it would be impossible to estimate them correctly.'

Busoni touches here on an innovation in London – coaches. Stow notes that the first one in England was made for the Earl of Rutland in 1555, although they were already common in Holland – there were about six hundred in Antwerp alone in 1560. (The word 'coach' derives from the Hungarian town, Kocs, where, it is claimed, the vehicle was invented.) Queens Mary and Elizabeth had each possessed one. 'Little by little,' writes Stow, 'they grew usual among the nobilitie and others of sort, and within twenty years became a great trade of coach-making.' The prestige and convenience of owning a coach had a considerable influence on the spread of London westwards, where a progression of generous streets and squares had stable accommodation in their hinterlands.

An early coach was little more than a box mounted on wheel axles, bereft of springs or any other device to prevent passengers from being tossed about as each pothole was encountered. Windows were at first either made of tin perforated with peepholes, or else were leather curtains. By the time Samuel Pepys took delivery of his 'little chariot' in 1668 coaches were more civilized and had become multifarious in their design. At the robust end of the scale, a system of hiring Hackney coaches was established by John Bailey in 1634, when he stationed four coaches at the Maypole in the Strand which could be had for set rates. It was a popular idea.

Other hackney men seeing this way they flocked to the same place and performed their journeys at the same rate, so that sometimes there is twenty of them together which disperse up and down, so that they and others are to be had everywhere as watermen are to be had at the waterside. Everyone is much pleased with it.

Well, nearly everyone, for the householders of the Strand were soon petitioning the Privy Council against the number of coaches waiting for fares in the Strand. So congested did London's principal roads become that in 1636 it was ordered that a hackney coach could not be hired unless it were for a three-mile journey, or else to take a Londoner to his country home, and severely limited the number of private coaches permitted in the City. No doubt, this proclamation was disregarded along with most other attempts to constrain a growing city and by 1694 when new legislation was passed, hackney licences were limited to 700.

Coaches for households rich and not so rich were bespoke items, usually made in the Long Acre area where still today buildings survive that have arched door openings that once took a coach height. Pepys bought his own second-hand model for £53 in Cow Lane, Smithfield, where he spent all afternoon of Guy Fawke's Day in 1668, 'going up and down

COACHES were hardly to be seen in London in the 16th century, except those owned by the very rich. At first they were regarded as effeminate, and the Pope advised cardinals and bishops that they should be used for the transportation of women only.

among the coachmakers', and eventually chose one at premises run by a widow, but he had it refinished in Long Acre. Like most models it had a wooden frame encased with leather, and was gilded as abundantly as the owner could run to. Pepys was inordinately proud of his purchase, having himself progressed from wherry to private carriage as his career blossomed, but he encountered, as did everyone else, the downside of ownership. Passing through the butchers' quarter at Newgate Shambles one day he dislodged two pieces of meat off a stall into the mud and had to pay a shilling compensation.

Stage coaches were numerous enough by 1637 for the poet John Taylor to include the coach routes and the inns and hostelries in London from which they began in his Carriers' Cosmography. It was at once a leisurely and tedious method of travel: a journey to Oxford from London, for example, took two days along a deeply rutted road. But the dependence of coach operators on inns for good-class accommodation and, just as importantly, for stabling, feeding and changing of horses, encouraged the upgrading of inns in London and elsewhere into comparative oases of comfort after the rigours of a journey. The accommodation of the growing trade from coaches was most probably the reason for the rebuilding of the famous Tabard Inn in Southwark, c.1629, when it became the Talbot in the process.

Those who couldn't afford even the outside passenger seats on a stage-coach used the very slow, large covered stage-wagons. These vehicles, usually hauled by at least six horses, carried up to twenty passengers, but they also took freight. The length of a stage-wagon was a hopeless obstruction in the centre of London.

It was difficult and sometimes impossible for coaches of any sort to penetrate many of the smaller streets and alleys. A solution was found in the adoption of the sedan chair, a contraption imported from Continental cities with the same problem. In 1634 Sir Sanders

The Talbot Inn, Southwark, by T. H. Shepherd c.1829. The Talbot succeeded the Tabard Inn made famous as the starting point for Chaucer's pilgrims to Canterbury. The older inn was destroyed by fire in 1676 and when rebuilt the landlord inexplicably called it the Talbot.

Duncombe was granted the sole right for fourteen years to operate sedans in London. The 'covered chair' was economic for short journeys, though the wife of the French ambassador unaccountably went from Edinburgh to London in a sedan in 1603, which must have been as tiresome for her as for the carriers. Pepys exclaimed in his diary, 'Sir John Winter, poor man! come in a sedan from the other end of the town.'

THE DOCKS

THESE DEVELOPMENTS IN TRANSPORT did not please the Thames watermen, whose trade in the later seventeenth century diminished anyway as the attractions of the south bank were duplicated on the north side of the Thames. In concert with the City

Corporation they were able to delay the construction of another bridge across the river at Westminster until 1750, and their complaints about coachmen were frequent and vociferous. It was not merely the trip from the City to Westminster that gentlemen now took by road, but also the longer journeys to prime riverside destinations such as Windsor, Maidenhead, Richmond, Greenwich and Gravesend. The plight of the watermen, exacerbated by an influx of labour as the great Tudor navy was reduced, was taken up by the self-styled 'water poet', John Taylor, whose doggerel is of more interest to the historian than to the litterateur. He complained that 'This is a rattling rowling and rumbling age. The world runs on wheels'; 'Carroaches, coaches, jades and Flanders mares Do rob us of our shares, our wares'.

Superfluous watermen turned to the docks for employment: these, at least, were growing. The East India Company had taken a lease of ten acres of Blackwall, east of the Isle of Dogs, in 1614, and here they developed a deep-water dock for the larger ships that came ever more laden. The merchandise was off-loaded on to lighters and taken to quays in the Pool of London where customs evaluation took place. This inconvenient arrangement, leaving the East End with most of the labour but none of the administrative prestige, persisted until the early nineteenth century.

By moving so far east to an uninhabited and damp wasteland the East India Company had anticipated by well over one hundred years the necessity to do so: ships did not outgrow the capacity or the depth of the Thames until the late eighteenth century. In the meantime, the neighbourhoods of this part of the Thames consolidated slowly around Wapping, Ratcliff and Limehouse, taking advantage of the partially drained marshland between Ratcliff Highway and Wapping. By 1617, Wapping, part of the very large parish of Stepney, had its own church of St John to serve a community isolated by class and poverty from the City, and separated from Whitechapel by acres of market gardens criss-crossed by drainage channels.

It was an area almost entirely settled by mariners, dockers, watermen and nautical craftsmen and suppliers. Between 1606 and 1610 as many as 90% of the Shadwell fathers noted in the Stepney baptism registers were occupied on the river or the sea, and the corresponding figures for Ratcliff were 70%, Limehouse 67%, Poplar 54% and Wapping 41%. It was the Limehouse mariner, Sir Humphrey Gilbert (half-brother of Raleigh) who took possession of Newfoundland in 1582, the first dominion overseas, and it was at Wapping that the third most famous London gallows stood, at Execution Dock, used primarily for hanging pirates. It was from Woolwich, in 1601, that the first trading fleet of the East India Company departed, containing many watermen in its crews.

Ships were repaired and maintained in yards at Ratcliff, while actual construction had shifted to Deptford and Woolwich. Shipbuilding by the seventeenth century was a profitable business and one of some status. Phineas Pett, the best-known shipwright of the period, had his portrait painted by an unknown Dutch artist in c.1612 (it is now in the National Portrait Gallery), and his son was rich enough to commission Sir Peter Lely for his own likeness.

Painted by Vandyke.

Charles 1st King of England

Engraved by Cosmo Armstrong.

London Pub. for the Proprietor. March. 1821.

CHARLES I (1600–49), from a painting by Van Dyck.

CHAPTER VII

A WAR AROUND THE CITY

THE WAR

T HE DEEPLY UNPOPULAR REIGN OF JAMES I SOURED THE RELATIONSHIP BETWEEN SUBJECTS and monarchy that had been made good by Elizabeth I. Charles I was to follow his father's example, but to excess. He married a Catholic, which was unpopular in a country increasingly Puritan in its tastes; he exacted taxes but gave the least existence to Parliament that he could; he bullied the City into loans arousing its hostility; he championed two favourites detested by their countrymen; and he propounded the doctrine of the Divine Right of Kings at a time when Parliament and the City were strong enough to withstand him. His unsuccessful attempt to arrest five prominent members of Parliament in 1642, and his further visit to the Guildhall to find them, were but the last events of a series of disagreements and blunders which led to Civil War.

Parliament was not called at all from 1629–40, obliging Charles to extract money from the City to pay for his schemes, expenses and wars. He resorted to fines and punishment of aldermen where he was unsuccessful. During this time the religious reforms urged by Laud, the Archbishop of Canterbury, were attempted; these were interpreted as a return to Catholicism and strengthened the already strong Puritan coalition facing the King – one that was to fall apart once victory was achieved. For the time being Puritans were able to command the sympathy of both religious radicals and conservatives in the face of a common enemy, but it is a measure of the malaise and misery of the age that in those same eleven years about twenty thousand men and women, mainly from the younger generations, emigrated to the hard shores of North America to escape religious and political persecution. All this is properly national history, but the role of the City and its temporary alliance with Parliament was pivotal in the conduct of the war and its ending.

For London, the Civil War, which began in 1642, was more alarums than excursions. In the earlier stages it was certainly under threat and worried about its security, but no battle took place nearer than Brentford. And although some citizens found themselves engaged in combat, or else were dispossessed for being on the wrong side, London was never in real danger. It suffered more from the restriction of trade and the expense of the war and, in the later stages, the marauding presence of unpaid soldiers.

There was at that time no standing army and each side had to find and pay its own soldiers. This was to the disadvantage of Charles for he had little income, and the resources of his supporters could only be increased by selling off land and property in a depressed market. Parliament on the other hand had the City's income, which though diminished was continuous. London also financed the Trained Bands, part-time soldiers who since 1616 had been organized in four regiments; these were increased to nine regiments, with five auxiliary units when hostilities began and they then constituted 16,000 men, co-ordinated and trained by the Guild of Artillery of Longbows, Crossbows and Handguns, later to be the Honourable Artillery Company, which still today meets in the mock fortress in City Road. This large force of men, mainly artillery and pikemen, was never called upon to defend the City, but did turn out in numbers at Turnham Green at the end of 1642, soon after the Royalists had overwhelmed the Parliamentary forces at Brentford, threatening invasion of the City. If the Royalists were going to take London it

THE *execution of Charles I outside the Banqueting House in Whitehall in 1649. The King had spent his last night in St James' Palace, and from there was escorted on foot across the park to a scaffold outside the only completed part of his scheme to rebuild Whitehall Palace.*

had to be quickly before the capital could be defended, but the far superior numbers facing them at Turnham Green persuaded them to retire.

Meanwhile, the defence of London had to be seen to. In October 1642 the City proposed a ring of fortifications – 'trenches and ramparts' – at St James's, St Giles-in-the-Fields, Islington and St Pancras. The King's advance on the capital in 1643 resulted in a much larger defensive system. The City ordered the construction of trenches and ramparts around London's perimeter. In May 1643, it was reported:

> The whole company of gentlemen Vintners went out with their wives, servants and wine porters. On Thursday, the Shoemakers of London took 4,000 and all the inhabitants of St Clement Danes. On Friday at least 9,000 men, women and children of St Giles in the Fields, Queen Street and other parts there about.

The Billingsgate fishwives marched through Cheapside to their stretch of trench near Tottenham Court Road, 'the goddess Bellona leading them in a martial way'.

It is difficult to discover just how much of this vast rampart was constructed, although it is likely that the redoubts or forts were. Probably the defences north of the Thames were given priority since Charles's army was based in that direction.

The Civil War ended in 1648 and ushered in a period of discord between Parliament, its army and the City, further complicated by religious disputes between Puritan factions. In 1649, Londoners gathered to witness the execution of Charles I in front of the Banqueting House at Whitehall, and by then the mood of the City, discouraged by the events of the last few years, had changed. In particular the City was at odds with the army whose Puritan leaders had reduced the power of the aldermen and impeached the lord mayor during its successful campaign to extract money to pay for its soldiers. It was the army that seized Charles I from Parliamentary forces so as to prevent an agreement being privately reached by the King and Commons. The King's subsequent plans to escape and his involvement with the Scots led almost inevitably to his dignified death in Whitehall in front of a hostile crowd.

Puritanism was to fully run its course in the next few years, but it was sufficiently extreme and joyless to make the Restoration a fond wish.

THE COMMONWEALTH

THE CITIZENS OF LONDON might well have had second thoughts about their support for the forces of Parliament even before the king was dead. Religious mania was already prescribing their lives before that fateful execution in Whitehall and it continued to do so until its force was spent and the political situation was such as to ensure a restoration of the monarchy. Theatres were closed, sports were prohibited, even Christmas Day was abolished as being a papal festival. By 1642 religious radicals had taken over the City government, ousting the existing aldermen, and impeaching the Royalist Mayor. The City's administrative system, however, was retained despite the upheavals of the time which saw the abolition of both the monarchy and House of Lords. To what degree the citizens of London supported the enthusiasms of the Radicals is not known, but the City, once the King had fled to Nottingham, there to take up arms, had no option but to nail its own colours to the Parliamentary mast.

Nothing much was solved by the execution of the King in 1649 and the Civil War continued. The City found itself financing the demands of the army at a period of depressed trade and there was heavy taxation. On top of these were the costs of the 1652 war with Holland. A contingent of recruits which set out in 1651 from London to march to the north of England to join the army fighting the Scots was only half its original size by the time it got there, the deserters tired of the conditions and were without the enthusiasm to continue.

A bewildering array of sects, particularly those championed by artisans, confused the situation. Typical of these was that formed by Lodowicke Muggleton, a London tailor, but there were many other self-appointed preachers on the extremes of the Baptist movement. The bizarrely-named Fifth Monarchy Men, a sect that rejected the authority of both Church and Parliament, were troublesome to the authorities and were eventually put down by force in 1661 after an abortive attack on Kenwood House in Highgate.

CHRISTOPHER WREN (top left) *(1632–1723), architect of the rebuilt City of London. Thomas Killigrew* (top right) *(1612–83), dramatist and founder of Drury Lane Theatre. Samuel Pepys* (bottom left) *(1633–1703), diarist and recorder of London life during one of its most eventful periods. John Evelyn* (bottom right) *(1620–1706), diarist and man of many parts.*

CHAPTER VIII

DEATH, DESTRUCTION
AND REVIVAL

Astrologers, astronomers, broadsheet-mongers and religious madmen were right for once. Their most commercial messages of imminent disaster came true at last when the Great Plague (1665) and the Great Fire (1666) struck London. A dubious seer, Mother Shipton, had prophesied London's destruction as early as 1641, and in 1658 Walter Gostelo had predicted that the City, as sinful as Sodom and Gomorrah, would burn unless it mended its ways. As it happened, it was Westminster and Southwark that enjoyed most of the sin, and it was the strait-laced City that got burnt. Another seer, Humphrey Smith, peddled a vision of London burning, and in April 1666 papists were hanged for an alleged plot to burn the City down on the forthcoming 3rd September which, those who indulged in such things agreed, was a propitious date for the deed according to the stars. The fire actually began on 2 September, without the aid of papists.

Before that were comets. In December 1664, Charles II and his queen, Catherine of Braganza, and many London citizens watched a moving star as it rose in the east and disappeared in the south-west. And when, in the following March, another one appeared above London, many feared the worst. An eminent doctor of the day wrote:

> That comets, or blazing stars, do portend some evil to come upon mortals is confirmed by
> long observation and sad experience, as likewise phenomena of new stars, battles fought,
> and coffins carried through the air, howlings, screechings and groans heard about
> churchyards, also raining of blood, unwonted matter etc., all of which, having something
> extra naturam, are portentous and prodigious.

He did not expand on the moving star which heralded, we are told, the birth of Christ. But in a London of which the pamphleteer, John Gaule, could remark that almanacs were consulted by the common people more often than their Bibles, a doom-laden pronouncement was heard clearer than a clarion of better tidings. And in a London used to plague, and one which could go up like a tinderbox anyway, there was good reason to be morbidly pessimistic.

The two events, the Plague and the Fire, so close together, entered London folklore as an awesome conjunction. And, as plague virtually disappeared in the years that followed

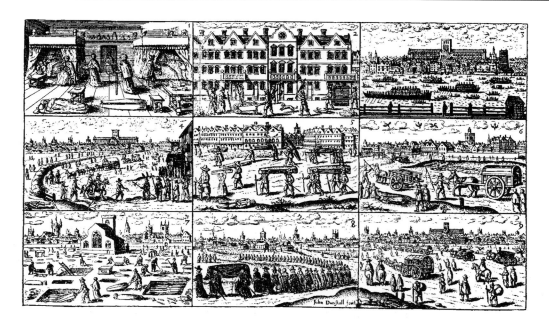

SCENES from the Great Plague of 1665, from a contemporary broadsheet. They depict the transportation of the dead by cart and by hand, the death pits hastily constructed, people living on ships in the shadow of St Paul's, and the flight from London. The scenes show the typical street architecture of London, which was to be lost in the Great Fire the following year, and the dominance of the old St Paul's, even without its spire, over the landscape of the City. Numerous pits were dug in the outer fringes of London to contain plague victims.

the fire, it is commonly supposed that the heat sterilized the pavements and the basements of the plague's infection: in popular mythology the hell-fire cleansed London for a new start. In fact, those areas destroyed in the fire were, with few exceptions, those which were the least infected. Conversely, locations that were hit the hardest by the epidemic, such as St Giles-in-the-Fields, were untouched by flame. Southwark too was infected but was not harmed by the blaze and yet plague did not return to the south bank either. Some other factor made sure that its shadow came no more.

THE PLAGUE

IN 1665 THERE ALREADY WAS IN LONDON memory a 'Great Plague' – that of 1625. But after 1665 that earlier event was relegated in status, just as in our own century the Great War was later given a number. The 1625 epidemic is thought to have claimed the lives of 35,000 people so that John Taylor could write:

All trades are dead, or almost out of breath
But such as live by sickness and by death.

How many died of plague in 1665 is uncertain, but the figure probably lies between 70,000 and 100,000 out of a population of about half a million. How many plague deaths were attributed to other causes so as to avoid panic or the curtailment of the liberty of the deceased's family can only be conjectured. How many causes of death in those early parochial records, or Bills of Mortality can be relied upon, even when honestly compiled, is unknown since it was rare for doctors to visit the dead and pronounce on such matters and the parish clerks were dependent on the diagnoses of unskilled women 'searchers'. As was remarked at the time: 'The old-women Searchers after the mist of a Cup of Ale, and the bribe of a Two-groat fee instead of one given them, cannot tell whether this emaciation or leanness were from a Phthisis or from a Hecktick Fever.'

Given the circumstances of the time it would be wrong to assume that there was a clear-cut beginning to the main epidemic: cases in Westminster, St Giles-in-the-Fields, Covent Garden and St Clement Danes in the last months of 1664 could well have been the routine ones expected each year. Their numbers did not gather momentum because London endured an unusually severe winter of black frost which rarely lifted in the first three months of the new year: even the Thames was frozen. But when the weather warmed the plague appeared in dreadful earnest.

Badly hit was St Giles-in-the-Fields, where the poor were tended by a valiant apothecary, William Boghurst. St Giles had some of the worst slums in the London area – and still had in the nineteenth century. Boghurst recalls in his account of the plague year that in 1664 smallpox had been rife in St Giles. Between the church and pound (at the junction of today's New Oxford Street and Tottenham Court Road) there were forty families afflicted and in the summer of that year flies were thick on the walls and ants covered the highways.

The Bills of Mortality were still showing no more than a handful of plague deaths each week in May 1665 when a Privy Council was appointed to deal with a plague epidemic, an indication of just how much the authorities (and, no doubt, the population) knew of the real extent of the problem, in contrast to the official local records. There was agreement, at least, on where the epidemic raged most fiercely. As the figures went up weekly in St Giles-in-the-Fields, adjacent parishes posted guards to prevent vagrants or other dubious people moving out from St Giles into new territory. It was quarantine too late. On 10 June Pepys recorded in his diary that 'to my great trouble hear that the plague is come into the City', in the house of his friend, Dr Burnet, in Fenchurch Street.

In the excess and emergency of the outbreak, customs and Christian niceties were not to be had by those who could not afford them. The dead were speedily removed from their homes, naked at worst, on to carts that called at night, and were buried with peremptory blessing in anonymous pits. And then there were so many that, as Pepys remarked in August, 'The people die so that now it seems they are fain to carry the dead to be buried by daylight, the nights not sufficing to do it in.' The nightmare begat nightmares. Tales were told of men pulling the dead carts themselves dying on the trek to the pits, leaving the horses and their awful rotting cargo to wander on aimlessly until someone was brave enough to rein them in.

There was no effective treatment. Dogs and cats, thought to carry the infection, were slaughtered in their thousands. Potions and remedies found ready buyers as quacks risked their own lives in selling them. Only one thing seemed to halt the plague and this was the burning of brimstone, saltpetre and amber in the house. It did not kill the infection, as was thought, but merely deterred the rats which carried the infectious fleas.

Those who could, including most physicians, decamped from London, taking plague with them into the countryside. In June, Pepys observed 'all the town almost going out of town, the coaches and waggons being all full of people going into the country.' Those who were left had little employment, as trade came to a standstill. The law courts closed, churches were abandoned by their clergy, businesses collapsed through lack of customers or proprietors, houses were shut up and many of their occupants lived on squalid boats on the Thames, and carcasses of animals littered the streets attracting even more rats.

By August a tangible silence in this once bustling city invoked the memorable prose of the Rev. Thomas Vincent:

> Now there is a dismal solitude in London streets: every day looks with the face of a Sabbath day, observed with a greater solemnity than it used to be in the city. Now shops are shut, people rare and very few that walk about, insomuch, that the grass begins to spring up in some places; there is a deep silence in every street, especially within the walls. No prancing horses, no rattling coaches, no calling on customers nor offering wares, no London cries sounding in the ears. If any voice be heard it is the groans of dying persons breathing forth their last, and the funeral knells of them that are ready to be carried to their graves.

For Vincent, as the title of his recollections reminds us, this was 'God's Terrible Voice'.

Somehow, the poor and the unemployed who survived the plague also outlasted its financial disaster and by the end of the year, with the epidemic abated, London was in business again.

THE FIRE

By THE TIME THE COURT RETURNED TO LONDON in February 1666 about one fifth of the population of the City, its liberties, Southwark, Westminster and outlying parishes had perished from the plague. In the seven months that the Court kept itself away and secure the Privy Council discussed the catastrophe only three times, and two of these occasions were devoted to ensuring that plague was kept away from the royal drawbridge. Of senior courtiers only Monck, Duke of Albemarle, stayed to encourage what measures could be taken in Westminster. The City officials showed greater resilience: in July it was ordered that no alderman should leave the City, and those that had already were to return.

On the other hand, the City did not distinguish itself when London caught fire. The inadequate labour force it marshalled, the ineffective measures it took and the slowness with which it faced up to the seriousness of the blaze appear to have been the decisive factors that allowed the fire to get out of hand. But that is with hindsight – fire, like plague, was part of the life of the City and of no overriding significance when it broke out.

The cause of the catastrophe was mundane, as it usually has been for spectacular London fires. This did not prevent Londoners accusing Catholics, the Dutch or the French of starting it, and some twelve years after the Monument was erected to commemorate the fire, the culpability of Catholics was newly-engraved on the base of that structure. The story of the fire's origin is well known – it began in the bakehouse of Thomas Faryner in Pudding Lane, just north of Billingsgate, in the middle of the night. This commonplace incident coincided with lethal circumstances, the first of which was the time of night, when most were asleep or reluctant to be disturbed. The blaze spread through a neighbourhood of premises full of combustible material to stock ships. Pitch, turpentine, rope and tar went up quickly and, at the same time these burning buildings, lining Thames Street, prevented easy access to Thames water. When the fire reached

London Bridge not only did it claim the church of St Magnus but it put out of action the pump of the waterworks beneath the bridge, and also prevented help coming across the bridge from Southwark.

When Pepys got up the next morning in his house at Seething Lane to the east of the City, he went over to the Tower to have a look at the fire; it was then entrenched in the area of Fish Street Hill, but a strong east wind was pushing it fast along Thames Street. By boat Pepys went to Westminster and there reported to an apparently uninformed Charles II as to the extent of the blaze. Armed with the King's exhortations to leave no house standing if it could be demolished to create a firebreak, Pepys eventually found the Lord Mayor in Cannon Street in despair. 'Lord, what can I do?', he asked. 'I am spent! People will not obey me. I have been pulling down houses. But the fire overtakes us faster than we can do it.'

THE Great Fire of London, 1666, depicted by Hollar. As a result of the blaze London lost St Paul's Cathedral, 87 churches, 6 chapels, the Guildhall, public buildings such as the Royal Exchange and the Custom House, 52 Company Halls, 4 prisons, 3 City gates and over 13,000 houses. The fire, which began in the middle of the night in the premises of a baker, was impossible to contain with fire-breaks once it had become established. Despite the fire's ferocity, very few people are known to have been killed by it.

Effectively, the fire was stopped on the 6 September and by that time about four-fifths of the area inside the walls was destroyed – as was a large district to the west as far as the Temple. It has been calculated that 13,200 houses, St Paul's Cathedral, 87 parish churches, public buildings such as the Guildhall, Royal Exchange, Custom House, 52 Company halls, four prisons and numerous shops and warehouses, were lost. In these statistics the medieval city of London had virtually disappeared.

THE REBUILDING OF LONDON

THE ASTRONOMERS, whose speciality was scarcely distinct from that of the catchpenny astrologers, could not have predicted that one of their number would rebuild London. It is a remarkable fact that a mathematician and astronomer, who by 1666 had built only a chapel in Cambridge, then designed and supervised the construction of fifty new parish churches in London, the Royal Naval Hospital at Greenwich, the Chelsea hospital for Army pensioners and the great St Paul's before he died full of years. It was Christopher Wren who within weeks of the fire produced a plan to redesign the layout of London. Others who rushed to do so included John Evelyn, who was not an architect, Robert Hooke, a mechanically-minded philosopher who was later appointed to the lucrative post of City Surveyor, and Richard Newcourt, a topographical draughtsman.

These gentlemen and their nominal occupations remind us that the status and profession of architect did not exist in their modern sense. Men of money, taste and interest in buildings went on European tours to study classical architecture and sometimes returned enthused. Some, like Wren and Inigo Jones before him, were able to translate their enthusiasm into designs, but they were not trained as architects in the way

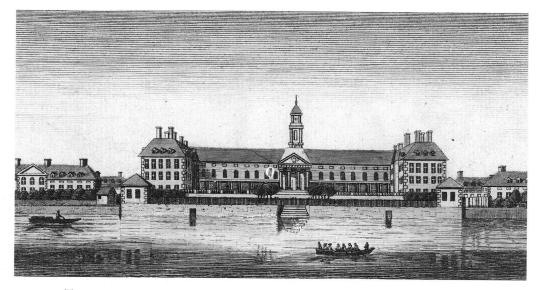

THE south front of Chelsea Hospital. The hospital, modelled on the Hôtel des Invalides in Paris, was founded by Charles II and designed by the ubiquitous Christopher Wren. It opened in 1689, when 476 army pensioners were admitted.

that lawyers took lessons at the Inns of Court. Others who had seen what opportunities existed once traditional thinking had been jettisoned, went into science, medicine and mathematics, and there developed an upper echelon of learned men who between them made up the Royal Society, which met in London from 1659.

Generally speaking, the designs for rebuilding saw London as a new-planned city. The Anglo-Saxon and later medieval street pattern was mostly abandoned, to be replaced by wider roads in orderly grids which occasionally led to setpiece features. The schemes foundered not so much on the disapproval of the authorities, nor on the innate conservatism of Londoners, but on the sheer impossibility of redistributing the thousands of plots of land which were so jealously held. It was difficult enough in the years of negotiations to trim land off plots simply to widen a medieval street, but to rearrange landholdings altogether was beyond the patience of men and the expense of lawyers.

Despite the rush to plan anew and Wren's industry, the reoccupation of the City was slow. A year after the fire only 150 buildings had been completed and by the end of six years it was estimated that about 3,500 of the new properties were empty. It is likely that the City was only full again when its commercial life made that necessary. The drift of private residents, particularly those who had a choice in the matter, away from the City has already been noted. The poorer Londoners had for the most part squeezed into Spitalfields and Tower Hamlets after the fire, there to pay rents which were lower, inevitably, than those in rebuilt City properties; the more affluent City trader found that the more orderly, spacious and hygienic new developments of the West End and Holborn suited him better.

The fashionable had briefly flirted with Covent Garden and with Lincoln's Inn Fields but found the one too public and the other too far east. But other squares had better

Bloomsbury square from the south in 1787; drawing by Edward Dayes. This square was built for Thomas Wriothesley, 4th Earl of Southampton, in the 1660s. The family mansion, later called Bedford House, may be seen in the centre of the picture.

fortune. Dressed in an English architectural compromise that toned down the fastidious Italian correctness of Inigo Jones, they were the single most important element in London's development for the next 150 years. Bloomsbury Square, laid out in the early 1660s, set the standard and was, indeed, the first designated as a square. It had both exclusivity and the convenience of smaller roads in the hinterland containing service premises. It was, as John Evelyn remarked, 'a little town'. By 1665 building had also begun in Piccadilly and on the St James's Square estate owned by the Earl of St Albans; as the Earl remarked persuasively to Charles II when seeking a permit to develop the estate to accommodate the more illustrious of his subjects, there were few fit houses in London for that class of resident. The Earl's partner in this was the enterprising Nicholas Barbon, who not only promoted the first fire-insurance scheme but was also London's first real property developer. He moved on from St James's Square to buy up the Essex House property south of the Strand, opposite St Clement Danes church, and there on his own account developed an area for middle class and gentry, again with services provided. He was later to be found at the west end of the Strand, building Villiers and Buckingham Streets. The Strand, with its large sites on the banks of the Thames and its crucial location between City and Westminster, was to be quickly shorn of its aristocratic residences in the years following the fire.

These building schemes had one thing in common – they were planned and sometimes begun before the fire and were not a response to it. Indeed, it was not until 1675 and 1680 that the next major developments, Golden Square and Soho Square, were started. They must have benefited, of course, from the City's disaster, and in the case of St James's Square the earlier concept of a closed enclave of large mansions to house a few aristocratic families was changed to a square of large town houses for a less demanding upper class, though there is good reason to think that the change in plan had already occurred before the fire made it desirable. However, though City merchants undoubtedly settled in the West End, the earliest rate books of the new developments, from Bloomsbury to Golden Square, suggest that many of the occupants made up a new class of London resident – an urban gentry supplied and cosseted by traders and manufacturers of everything from tea to wigs.

THE CITY

IT WAS IN THIS PERIOD OF BUILDING DEVELOPMENT and in the early eighteenth century that the two parts of London, City and Westminster, became physically part of one metropolis. Yet paradoxically the same period saw the City become in its nature and functions a separate entity, isolated almost from the mainstream of London life. The rebuilt City immersed itself in commercial opportunities, foreign trade and colonies, but the west end of London went its own way to develop a new style and substance – in effect to acquire the identity of a modern international city. Less fortunate were the poor ousted by the fire from the City, who could never afford to get back in; they found themselves instead tenements in an increasingly ravaged and crowded East End.

The last quarter of the seventeenth century was one of trade expansion in the City made difficult by an economic system that was disorganized and unstable and a currency that was debased. These drawbacks were a consequence of much earlier events. The pre-eminence of the big trading companies, such as the East India, had in some ways distracted London from European trade. As early as the beginning of the century, Raleigh in his *Observations on Trade and Commerce* had bemoaned the fact that the Dutch did far more trade around the North Sea, and that even the Danes and Norwegians were fishing in waters off the English coast. Complacency was engendered by the riches brought in from afar by the companies, and nearer opportunities were neglected. The East India Company also creamed off the available labour stock – by 1620, importing everything from diamonds to calicoes via Madras, it employed 2,500 mariners and 500 ship's carpenters alone.

There was outside meddling in the handling of business. Charles I had been particularly adept at selling trade monopolies in his zest to raise money, which encouraged inefficiency and prevented enterprise; he himself was no stranger to dabbling in trade – he made the sale of tobacco a royal monopoly and prevented Virginia from selling it elsewhere; he put a tax on all coal exported; he bought up all the pepper imported by the East India Company and sold it on his own account. No change in such matters could be engineered in the years of the Civil War, but even so the underlying strength of England's trading position was higher a few years after the Great Fire had destroyed London's business heart than it was in 1663. The flurry of business was increased as well by the immigration of Huguenots who brought over silk-weaving, of French with paper-making skills and of Venetians who established glass manufacture here, and in 1676 the printing of calicoes was begun in London.

For all this the basis of London's financial position was insecure. In 1672, faced with a Dutch war, Charles II closed the Exchequer so that the sum he owed to the goldsmiths of London, which amounted to over £1,300,000, was frozen, losing them both the interest and the use of the principal. The system whereby the Crown (and therefore the government) borrowed from the City was still substantially unchanged since the Middle Ages. The Crown put up security and the City via its wards and livery companies raised the loan, which meant that the Crown was often dependent on them. The establishment of the Bank of England, which opened in the premises of the Mercers' Company in 1694, provided a way for the Crown to borrow without going politically cap in hand to the City fathers.

The Bank was the project of a Scotsman, William Paterson. He was a man of many parts. Only the year before the Bank opened, he had received licence to tap the springs and streams of Hampstead and Highgate to provide water for London – the Hampstead Water Company, which dug the ponds in Hampstead and Highgate, was the consequence. And in 1695 he at last began his pet project of forming a colony, mainly Scots, in the Darien isthmus which would control trade to the east and west, to the benefit of England and Scotland.

Although the Bank of England took away the City's hold over the Crown whenever it was in need of money, as confidence grew it brought stability into the London banking system. This was to be sorely tested soon after its formation, when the goldsmiths of London caused a run on the Bank in a panic to obtain ready money. This had a knock-on effect on the value of stocks of the trading companies. Confidence returned but not quickly enough to rescue Nicholas Barbon, who died in reduced circumstances in 1698, with his building schemes, heavily financed by loans, in trouble. Worse was to come in 1720 when the so-called South Sea bubble burst.

The South Sea Company had been formed in 1711 with the object of trading with Spanish America, although it was not until the Treaty of Utrecht that limited trading opportunities were permitted there by the Spaniards. From that time the shares were pushed up by speculators until there was a classic frenzy of buying, based only on the possibility of selling them for a profit, for there were no financial securities in the scheme itself. Other bubble companies were formed at the same time as London succumbed to the fever. At the height of speculation the *London Journal* reported that 'The hurry of stock-jobbing bubbles has been so great this week as to exceed all ever known. Nothing but running about from coffee-house to coffee-house, and subscribing without knowing what the proposals were. The constant cry was, "For God's sake let us subscribe to something; we don't care what it is".'

When the crash came, ruin and bankruptcy occurred all over London. Thomas Guy had done well to sell out at a good time and with his profits he founded his hospital, but John Gay lost a stock value of £20,000 and the Duke of Chandos £300,000. The inquiry afterwards revealed that there was corruption in the government as the directors of the company used bribes to increase the standing of the stock. The Chancellor of the Exchequer, guilty of taking bribes, was sent to the Tower, and the Secretary of State had his estates confiscated.

THE THEATRE

A FEATURE OF THE NEW LONDON was its theatrical development. Theatres had flourished before the Civil War despite official restrictions, but they had been lost during the Commonwealth. Exile on the Continent had given the Court an appetite for new dramatic forms, the most important of which were opera, farce and comedies of manners; in addition, John Dryden popularized heroic drama that lent itself to declamatory and histrionic performance.

A fresh start was made on the design of theatres. The circular Bankside auditoria were not reinvented but the coarse informality of the audiences remained. Pepys, an avid theatregoer, was witness to audience behaviour that would be remarkable today. In January 1661 he notes:

> To the Theatre, where a lady spit backward upon me by mistake, not seeing me, but after seeing her to be a very pretty lady, I was not troubled at it at all.

And in November 1667:

> To the King's playhouse, and there. . .a gentleman of good habit, sitting just before us, eating of some fruit in the midst of the play did drop down as dead, being choked; but with much ado Orange Moll did thrust her finger down his throat, and brought him to life again.

The proscenium-arch stage was now the fashion and elaborate scenery was commonplace – both encouraged a separation between players and audience which has survived to this day. But the new theatres were undoubtedly more comfortable buildings than those of the Elizabethan and Jacobean eras. Pepys is again our witness:

> The stage is now. . .a thousand times better and more glorious than ever heretofore. Now, wax candles, and many of them; then, not above 3lbs of tallow: now, all things civil, no rudeness anywhere; then, as in a bear-garden: then, two or three fiddlers; now, nine or ten of the best: then nothing but rushes upon the ground, and everything else mean; and now, all otherwise.

The only theatre allowed by the Puritans had been the Cockpit in Drury Lane where Sir William Davenant produced declamatory musical entertainments that were no threat to a repressive government. At the Restoration Davenant and Thomas Killigrew were each given patents to 'erect' two companies of players which, to most intents and purposes, restricted the number of theatres in London to two. On the site of Davenant's Cockpit,

From Elkannah Settles   Empress of Morocco

*Sᴏᴜᴛʜ view of the Duke's Theatre, Dorset Gardens, in 1671. This theatre, designed by
Wren, was built for William Davenant's Duke's Company of players, in the grounds
of Dorset House, south of Fleet Street. It was at the time the most opulent theatre in
London, but its heyday was short and the building was demolished c.1720.*

Killigrew built the first Theatre Royal in 1663 and here his company, the 'King's Servants'
performed. Davenant, a Catholic, had the 'Duke of York's Servants' and for the time being
set up home in a building in Salisbury Court between Fleet Street and the river before
opening his own Duke's Theatre in Portugal Street near Lincoln's Inn Fields in 1662. He
was to return to the riverside after the Great Fire when Wren built him the magnificent,
but short-lived, Dorset Gardens theatre, which had a landing-place for those coming from
Westminster by boat.

In effect the theatrical companies were extensions of the Royal Court and, indeed, ten
of the company which opened the Theatre Royal with Beaumont and Fletcher's *Humorous
Lieutenant* were members of the royal household.

A SCENE *at Bagnigge Wells in the 18th century. The location of Bagnigge Wells was south of today's King's Cross and north of Mount Pleasant, on the bank of the river Fleet. The old house here, set among fields, is one of many houses reputed to have been used by Nell Gwyn. In the 1750s the water here was found to be impregnated with iron – fortunately for the owner, as such medicinal waters were very much in vogue. He charged threepence for a drink and one guinea for a season ticket. A banqueting house was erected and the place continued to be a popular spa until it was demolished in 1841.*

CHAPTER IX

PASSING THE TIME

L EISURE WAS DISCOVERED IN THE EIGHTEENTH CENTURY. THIS IS AN OVER-SIMPLIFICATION, of course, but certainly for the first time in London entertainment was pursued zealously by all classes, and its provision became a lucrative and full-time occupation. In part this was due to those many new and affluent Londoners who had leisure thrust upon them by their social standing and had neither the wit nor the humility to do more than manage or waste their inherited wealth. These men and women, sustained by cheap servants, uninhibited by family duties once children had been entrusted to nurse or governess, secure in incomes that burgeoned as the country became more prosperous, had time on their hands to devote to pleasure or to charity. It was these men who made the coffee-houses and the gentlemen's clubs possible, these women who made the pleasure gardens an exotic and erotic attraction, and it was these people who supported good causes, learned societies, theatres and music rooms and who, in the end, were also responsible for organized sport. In their wake trailed the less fortunate – in the cheaper seats at the theatre, at the less expensive nights at the Vauxhall pleasure gardens, and familiarly mixed with their betters at prize fights, horse races and hangings.

Just as the appetite for pleasure is revealed in this century so is its complexity: members of all classes were equally at home at executions or at decorous evenings at Vauxhall.

PLEASURE GARDENS

P LEASURE GROUNDS AND TEA GARDENS, those quintessential eighteenth-century amusements, were a development of the medicinal wells that had become the rage at the end of the seventeenth century. Wishful faith in the healing qualities of certain types of water was not new – the spa town of Bath had been in and out of fashion since the Romans, but Tunbridge Wells, where a chalybeate spring was discovered in 1606, had revived it. It was therefore with some business acumen that a Thomas Sadler, on discovering an unspectacular chalybeate spring on his Clerkenwell land in 1683, had it recommended by a medical man and built a 'musick-house' to add *divertissement* to the place and provide distraction from the awful taste of the water. Others followed in quick succession – nearby Islington and Exmouth spas, Pancras and St Chad's Wells and Lambeth Wells, and at Hampstead Wells a Long Room was built to house concerts, dancing and gambling for a more discriminating clientele. At each of these sharp water was drunk but at the Cold Bath, near today's Mount Pleasant Post Office, opened in 1698, immersion took place. It was declared that the water there was 'of the nature of St Magnus's in the north, and St Winifred's in Wales, and famed for the curing of the most nerval disorders.' The Cold Bath was open from five in the morning and the charge was half-a-crown (a very large sum indeed) for those who needed to be lowered into the water on a mechanical chair contraption. Typical of what became pleasure gardens was Bagnigge Wells, to the east of Gray's Inn Road. A contemporary described the

Sadler's wells in 1792. Thomas Sadler discovered his medicinal well in the 1680s and soon added a 'musick house' as a side attraction. Although popular at first, it was not until 1746 when Thomas Rosoman took over, that the theatrical attractions took precedence.

several beautiful walks, ornamented with a great variety of curious shrubs and flowers, all in utmost perfection. About the centre of the garden is a small round fish-pond, in the midst of which is a curious fountain, representing a Cupid bestriding a swan, which spouts the water through its beak to a great height. Round this place, and indeed almost over the whole garden, are genteel seats for company. . .At a little distance from the pond is a neat cottage, built in the rural style; and not far from that, over a bridge leading across a piece of water that pours through part of the garden, is a pretty piece of grotto-work, large enough to contain near twenty people.

Numerous pleasure gardens were opened without the benefit of medicinal waters. The curiously named Jenny's Whim, by Ebury Bridge, had surprise monsters in alcoves, a cockpit and a bowling green and was, by the middle of the eighteenth century, visited by 'the lower sort of people', a commercial fate that befell even the grander places such as Hampstead as they competed, later on in the century, with other attractions which lured away their fashionable clientele. The curious of Kensington went to Florida Gardens at Brompton which had arbours 'well adapted for gallantry and intrigue'. At Belsize House in Hampstead Charles Povey, a retired coal-merchant and inveterate inventor, opened up the mansion and grounds as a pleasure haunt and also provided a chapel for cheap weddings with catering facilities. By 1723 Belsize had a considerable reputation:

> *Bellsize House is open every day; the public days are Mondays, Thursdays and Saturdays, with a good Concert of Music in the Long Gallery during the whole season. The Proprietor is now provided with a Pack of good staunch Hounds, and a Huntsman, ready to show the Diversion of Hunting whenever the Company pleases; the Walks in the Garden and Parks are made very pleasant, where Gentlemen and Ladies have frequent Egress and Regress to Walk without any Expence. Any company that stays late, there are Servants with Fire-Arms to see them safe to London.*

At the White Conduit House in Islington the visitor commanded

> *a most agreeable view of the metropolis and the surrounding country. The garden is formed into several pleasing walks, prettily disposed; at the end of the principal one is a painting, which serves to render it much longer in appearance than it really is; and in the middle of the garden is a round fish-pond, encompassed with a great number of very genteel boxes for company, curiously cut into the hedges, and adorned with a variety of Flemish and other paintings.*

All over London such descriptions were appropriate, from Highbury Barn to Bermondsey Spa. Cuper's Gardens (where Waterloo Road now joins Waterloo Bridge) had serpentine paths and arbours decorated with statues brought from Arundel House in the Strand when it was demolished; the Red House at Battersea had pigeon-shoots; the Eel-pie House at Highbury had, as its name suggests, its own delicacy, but it also had rat-killing matches.

These were not just establishments in which Londoners savoured a fast disappearing rurality, as has often been suggested. Apart from anything else there was a new-found interest in gardening as travellers throughout the colonies brought back ever more exotic plants. Other factors were present too. First was the realisation that the refreshments, music and ambience had been contrived to *please* them. Londoners, used to rough and ready arrangements at public entertainments or the unpretentious fare and hospitality of inns, were delighted to find delicacy and taste in what was offered and an assumption that they themselves would respond in kind. Secondly, Londoners were enticed into the fantasy of inhabiting grounds of a stately home, surrounded by cultivated arbours and paths, increasingly Gothic as the century wore on, that only the rich could afford.

All of these gardens were overshadowed by the immense popularity (and size) of Vauxhall Gardens. A pleasure ground of sorts called Spring Gardens had existed here (at the southern end of today's Vauxhall Bridge) in the seventeenth century and was visited by Pepys and Evelyn; but its heyday, helped by the building of Westminster Bridge in 1750, was the eighteenth century. Patronized by the Prince of Wales and the writer Horace Walpole, and decorated by the artist Hogarth who lived nearby in Lambeth, the gardens were successful at all levels of society. Behind the myriad of lights that shone out over the river Londoners of all classes took advantage of the summer months to listen to orchestras, to dance or to promenade. The Gardens did well from spectacular events. The *Gentleman's Magazine* in 1749 tells us of a rehearsal for Handel's 'music for the fireworks, by a band of 100 musicians, to an audience of above 12,000 persons (tickets 2s 6d). So great a resort occasioned such a stoppage on London Bridge that no carriage could pass for three hours. The footmen were so numerous as to obstruct the passage, so that a scuffle happened, in which some gentlemen were wounded.' And a contemporary desciption notes its 'shady groves, and most delightful walks, illuminated by above 1000 lamps, so disposed that they all take fire together, almost as quick as lightning, and dart such a sudden blaze as is perfectly surprising.'

Vauxhall's main rival was Ranelagh Gardens, just to the east of Chelsea Hospital, opened in 1742, which had as its centrepiece a rotunda designed by William Jones. This building, whose circular interior was about the size of the present British Library Reading

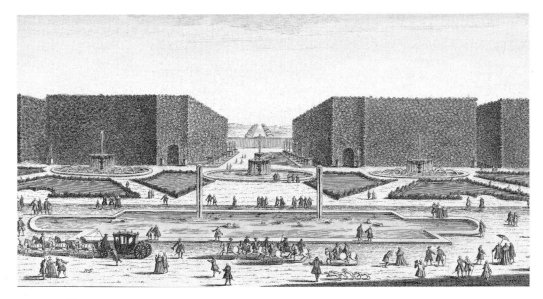

Vauxhall gardens in the 18th century. This began as the New Spring Garden in the 17th century and became the best known of the London pleasure gardens. Its heyday was after the construction of Westminster Bridge in 1750, although it was already very fashionable.

Room, had boxes around its circumference, those on the ground floor open to promenaders, others above more exclusive and reached only by stairways. In the centre of the room a vast pillar, decorated in Gothic Revival style, held up the ceiling: this at first housed the orchestra but was later converted to a chimney. Entrance to the place could be half-a-crown (but this included some refreshment), and the evening concerts usually began at about 6.30 p.m., in contrast to Vauxhall where entertainment started much later.

ASSEMBLY ROOMS

VAUXHALL AND RANELAGH WERE PLACES FOR THE WARMER MONTHS and their success is evidence, perhaps, of consistently finer summers than we now have. At other times Society retreated indoors, principally to Carlisle House in Soho Square where a Mrs

Cornelys was hostess. Her background was suitably obscure and scandalous – Casanova claimed paternity of one of her children. Was she German, perhaps?; a courtesan, possibly?; a singer, almost certainly; but undoubtedly with money, for she not only took the lease of a substantial house in Soho but transformed it in 1760 for the extravagant staging of assemblies, balls, concerts and masquerades to which only Society people were admitted. The setting entranced everyone who saw it – Walpole and fellow writer Fanny Burney included. Surprisingly, this upstart reigned supreme until the opening of Almack's and the Pantheon, but sadly she finished in prison for debt. The site of the house itself is now taken by St Patrick's church.

Almack's threatened to bring Mrs Cornelys' enterprise to a swift closure when it opened in 1765 in premises in King Street, St James's, specially designed by Robert Mylne. These new assembly rooms were, after an indifferent start, so popular that Mrs Cornelys

The Pantheon, opened in Oxford Street in 1772, was a spectacular building with a classical exterior and an interior which derived from St Sophia in Constantinople. It was considered by many to be the most spectacular building in London.

was obliged to invest large sums of money to bring Carlisle House into competition again. A correspondent that year wrote:

> *There is now opened at Almack's in three very elegant new-built rooms, a ten-guinea subscription for which you have a ball and a supper once a week for twelve weeks. You may imagine by the sum, the company is chosen; though, refined as it is, it will be scarce able to put old Soho out of countenance. The men's tickets are not transferable so, if the ladies do not like us, they have no opportunity of changing us.*

Despite teething troubles Almack's attracted a class of society avid for what it thought was exclusivity and the opportunity to spend money. Tickets for the balls were allocated by a committee of Society women who were 'a feminine oligarchy less in number but equal in power to the Venetian Council of Ten'.

William Almack's origins were as obscure as those of Mrs Cornelys. Thought by some to be a Yorkshireman and by others a Scotsman who had transposed his name from Macall to avoid the contemporary suspicion of Scots, he had long experience of managing entertainment and gambling. It was indeed the gambling which gave Almack's its special reputation and the stakes were high enough, as Walpole put it, to be 'worthy of the decline of our empire'.

The most spectacular place of such entertainment was undoubtedly the Pantheon in Oxford Street – the eastern branch of Marks and Spencer is now on the site and bears its name. Opened in 1772 and designed by James Wyatt, its interior was based on that of St Sophia in Constantinople. Walpole, at least for a time, thought it the most beautiful building in England, and Charles Burney wrote that it was 'regarded both by natives and foreigners as the most elegant structure in Europe, if not on the globe.' A Mrs Philip Lybbe Powys recorded in her diary in 1772 that:

> This week the town was in a vast bustle at the opening of the Pantheon, and Mr Cadogan was so obliging as to send me his tickets for the first night. As a fine room I think it grand beyond conception, yet I'm not certain Ranelagh struck me equally on the first sight, and as a diversion 'tis a place I think infinitely inferior, as there being so many rooms, no communication with the galleries, the stair case inconvenient, all rather contribute to lose the company than show them to advantage.

The staple form of entertainment here was masquerade, on which vast sums were spent, but the Pantheon's heyday was a short one. The building was destroyed by fire twenty years later at about the time that the fashion for its offerings was on the wane and its successor, using Wyatt's frontage but with a different interior, was a disappointing attraction.

COFFEE-HOUSES

MORE MODEST IN THEIR DEMANDS ON THE POCKET were coffee-houses. The selling and drinking of coffee had emerged unscathed from its half-hearted persecution in the seventeenth century to become respectable, and coffee-houses were now indispensable venues to show off one's erudition, exchange news and opinions, and do business. Coffee-houses began in the City as convenient places for commercial transactions, and as a consequence some became specialized in their clientele. The most famous (at least in retrospect) was Lloyd's, whose customers eventually founded the insurance market; Jonathan's in Change Alley contained stock-jobbers, the Jerusalem and Jamaica houses in Cornhill specialized in Indies merchants; at Garraway's in Exchange Alley auctions of imported goods were held; and at Hain's in Birchin Lane marine traders sold their wares. These were, in essence, business premises and, indeed, were often the official address of merchants who met in them.

Coffee-houses elsewhere, even though for the more leisured, also tended to be patronized by like-minded men. Around St Paul's churchyard and Paternoster Row were those for booksellers and publishers: the impecunious Chatterton wrote to his mother in 1770 that he was 'quite familiar at the Chapter Coffee House, and know all the geniuses there.' Others in that area were frequented by clergy. In Covent Garden actors and writers

GRIGSBY'S COFFEE HOUSE *near the Royal Exchange in the City, from the early 18th century until c.1830. It is thought that coffee was introduced into London in the 1650s, when a house in St Michael's Alley was opened by Pasqua Rosee, the Greek servant of a London merchant. By 1698, despite clumsy attempts by the authorities to limit them, there were over two thousand coffee houses in London. The most famous of the period were those devoted to business, such as Jonathan's and Garraways in Change Alley, Cornhill, and Lloyd's, devoted to shipping intelligence.*

gathered and most coffee-house anecdotes revolve around Tom's, Will's and Button's coffee-houses in Covent Garden where Dryden, Addison and Steele held court. In Greek Street, Soho, the Turk's Head was used by artists and writers and it was here that Dr Johnson and Sir Joshua Reynolds founded the Literary Club. Dean Swift and Matthew Prior were familiar customers at the Smyrna Coffee House, established by a Turkey merchant who also imported tobacco. Macky in his *Journey Through England*, published in 1722, tells us about the West End houses:

THE interior of White's Chocolate House before 1733, from The Rake's Progress *by Hogarth. White's in St James's Street is the oldest of the gentlemen's clubs. It began in the same street (on the site of Boodle's Club) as a chocolate house in 1693. It was renowned for its gambling.*

I am lodged in a street called Pall Mall, the ordinary residence of all strangers, because of its vicinity to the King's Palace, the Park, the Parliament House, the Theatres and the Chocolate and Coffee Houses, where the best company frequent. If you would know our manner of living, 'tis thus: We rise by nine, and those that frequent great men's Levées find entertainment at them till eleven. About twelve the Beau Monde assembles at several Coffee or Chocolate Houses: the best of which are the Cocoa-Tree and White's Chocolate Houses, St James's, the Smyrna, Mrs Rochford's and the British Coffee-houses, and all these so near one another that in less than an hour you see the company of them all. We are carried to these places in chairs (or Sedans) which are here very cheap, a guinea a week or a shilling per hour, and your chairmen serve you for porters to run errands.

In Cheyne Row, Chelsea, Don Saltero's was the main coffee-house. It was run by a former servant of Sir Hans Sloane, John Salter; on these premises he also practised as a barber and, as was the custom in those days, drew teeth. He gathered a 'museum' of curios there, allegedly from Sloane's own collection; however, the nature of many of the exhibits, which included a dead cat found between walls in Westminster Abbey, a shoe that was put under the Speaker's chair in the reign of James II, Robinson Crusoe's and his Man Friday's shirts and the Queen of Sheba's fan, suggest a spurious assembly that Sloane would not have given house room to. As Steele in the *Tatler* remarked: 'There is really nothing, but, under the specious Pretence of Learning and Antiquity, to impose upon the World.'

Macky mentions chocolate-houses which, for a time, rivalled coffee-houses. The drink was not to everyone's taste. Parkinson in his *Herbal* referred to it as 'a drink that might do well enough for natives, but for Christian tastes it must be reckoned as nothing more or less than a wash for hogs.' White's Chocolate House became White's Club, the most aristocratic (and now the oldest) of the London men's clubs to be formed – George IV, William IV and Edward VII were all members, as were most senior politicians. It was renowned for its gambling, the number of men ruined at its tables, and for bets between members, all studiously recorded in a betting book. Lord Arlington bet £3,000 on one raindrop falling faster than another to the bottom of a window and in 1763 Lord Masham lost the same amount in an evening playing hazard; others would bet on whether one person would live longer than another and, as Walpole described in 1750, members wagered on whether a man who had dropped down at the entrance of the club was dead or not. A description of White's in the *London Journal* (1727) remarks that 'At White's we see nothing but what wears the Mask of Gaiety and Pleasure. Powder and Embroidery are the Ornaments of the Place, not to forget that intolerable Stink of Perfumes which almost poysons the miserable Chair-men that beseige the Door.'

CLUBS

IN THE REIGN OF QUEEN ANNE there were two political clubs which met either in taverns or else in private houses. The October Club was noted by Swift:

> We are plagued here with an October Club; that is, a set of above a hundred Parliament men of the Country, who drink October beer at home, and meet every evening at a tavern near the Parliament, to consult affairs, and drive things on to extremes against the Whigs.

Around 1700 the Kit-Cat Club was formed. Meeting in taverns and houses in Barnes and Hampstead, it was at first a club for literary men such as the bookseller and publisher, Jacob Tonson, who founded it, and the likes of Addison, Steele, Vanbrugh and Congreve, but it was soon to become identified with the cause of the Whigs and the Hanoverian succession to the throne. In 1734 the Society of Dilettanti was formed at the Thatched House Tavern in St James's Street, ostensibly for those who had been to Italy to admire the arts but mainly, as Horace Walpole put it, for those of them who had been drunk during the tour.

Boodle's and Brooks' are of the mid-eighteenth-century period, both emanating from gatherings at Almack's rooms before going off to new premises under eponymous management. Though Boodle's was essentially country-gentlemen with a sprinkling of London notables, Brooks' was initially an aristocratic club which became the meeting place of Whig politicians: Sheridan was blackballed three times before he was accepted as a member with the connivance of the Prince of Wales. Both clubs witnessed the absurd high-stake gambling which obsessed many wealthy men of the period when cards were 'the opium of the polite'.

MUSIC-ROOMS

SOCIETY WAS ALSO TO BE FOUND AT MUSIC-ROOMS, the best-known of which was in Hanover Square, opened in 1775. This establishment, run by Sir John Gallini, formerly a manager of Italian opera, contained both a concert hall and ballroom. An early performer here was Johann Christian Bach, as we know from a letter to the Earl of Malmesbury during the first year:

> *Your father and Gertrude attended Bach's concert, Wednesday. It was the opening of his new room, which by all accounts is by much the most elegant room in town; it is larger than that at Almack's. . .'Tis a great stroke of Bach's to entertain the town so very elegantly. Nevertheless Lord Hillsborough, Sir James Porter, and some others (who live nearby), have entered into a subscription to prosecute Bach for a nuisance, and I was told the Jury had found a bill against him.*

The *General Advertiser* in 1750 announced a concert of vocal and instrumental music at 'the Great House in Thrift [Frith] Street, Soho (late the Venetian Ambassador's)' and a similar notice in 1751 says, 'Coaches are desired to come to the Door in Frith Street, and Chairs to the Door in Frith Street, or Dean Street, as happens to be convenient.' This handsome building, later numbered 67 and in which Alfred Novello began his music-publishing business, was an occasional venue for music, but the Hanover Square rooms were possibly the first proper concert-hall in London. However, the upstairs room of the house of a Clerkenwell coalman, Thomas Britton, used from 1678, appears to be the first London address where the performance of music for the public was taken seriously. In this bizarre and humble location Britton's guests and visitors met each Thursday for over thirty years, attracting at times a distinguished gathering. Thoresby's *Diary* in 1712 records that:

> *In our way home called at Mr. Britton's, the noted small-coal man, where we heard a noble concert of music, vocal and instrumental, the best in town, which for many years past he has had weekly for his own entertainment, and of the gentry, &c., gratis, to which most foreigners of distinction, for the fancy of it, occasionally resort.*

Performers included Handel on a five-stop organ, and Pepusch on harpsichord. The versatile Mr Britton, who had begun his working life as an apprentice coalman, was also an acknowledged bibliophile and chemist.

Handel settled in England in 1712 and became so much a part of Society that he is now included in any list of English composers. He was immediately taken up by the Earl of Burlington, who gave him accommodation in Burlington House for about five years and there he wrote part of the *Water Music*. He then moved on to Canons Park, Edgware, where another patron, the Baron Chandos, was rewarded by the first productions of *Esther* and *Acis and Galathea*. *The Messiah*, *Alcina* and *The Royal Fireworks Music* were written from Handel's residence in Brook Street – the latter was performed first in Green Park in 1749. Handel was, without doubt, the principal musical figure in London of the first half of the century, with Dr Thomas Arne as his only rival. Poor Arne, who spent much of his life learning music in secret away from the attentions of his father, a Covent Garden upholsterer, is now remembered chiefly for *Rule Britannia*, a piece he wrote (the music only) in 1740 to celebrate the accession of George I.

By the time the music-rooms in Hanover Square were opened the public performance of music was beginning to have fashionable importance. This was partly due to the introduction of the pianoforte – first heard in London, it seems, at a performance of *The Beggar's Opera* at Covent Garden in 1767 when it was played by Charles Dibdin. But the

The boy Mozart came to England together with his formidable father, mother and talented sister in 1764. The family lodged first with a barber in Cecil Court, off St Martin's Lane, from April to early August, and then moved to 180 Ebury Street. In September they moved again to 20 Frith Street (shown right but since demolished) and it was here that advertisements went out proclaiming his gifts and talents.

emergence of London as a musical city (and its corresponding absence of suitable concert rooms) was highlighted by the visit of Mozart, together with his father, mother and sister in 1764. They stayed first at the White Bear in Piccadilly, moved to Cecil Court off St Martin's Lane and then from September until the following July lived at 20 Frith Street, Soho. The prodigy's first concert in London had been in June 1764 (at the age of eight) at the Spring Gardens, but we find him in March the following year performing at his lodgings. An announcement in the *Public Advertiser* proclaims:

> *For the Benefit of Master Mozart, of eight Years, and Miss Mozart, of Twelve Years of Age, prodigies of Nature, before their Departure from England, which will be in six Weeks Time, there will be performed at the End of this Month, or the Beginning of April next, a Concert of Vocal and Instrumental music. Tickets at Half a Guinea Each. To be had of Mr Mozart, at Mr Williamson's in Thrift Street, Soho; where those Ladies and Gentlemen, who will honour him with their Company from Twelve to Three in the Afternoon, any Day in the Week, except Tuesday and Friday, may, by taking each a Ticket, gratify their Curiosity and not only hear this young Music Master and his Sister perform in private; but likewise try his surprising musical capacity, by giving him any Thing to play at sight, or any Music without Bass, which he will write upon the Spot, without recurring to his Harpsichord.*

OPERA

OPERA HAD INCONSISTENT FORTUNE in the eighteenth century. A principal venue was the Queen's Theatre (later to be Her Majesty's), opened in the Haymarket in 1705 under the management of William Congreve. This enterprise was the work of Vanbrugh, tired of what he thought was the mismanagement of the Drury Lane Theatre; but his building was unpopular and there were complaints that the architecture took precedence over productions to such an extent that not a word could be heard. Vanbrugh retired bruised and out-of-pocket from this venture as did his successor, despite the successful staging of Handel's *Rinaldo*.

Opera was also heard at the new Covent Garden theatre, opened in 1732, whose proprietor, John Rich, held the second of the two patents enabling him to produce plays in London – the other was held by the owners of the Drury Lane Theatre. Christopher Rich and his son John had earlier produced plays at their theatre at Lincoln's Inn Fields and it was in that building, in 1728, that John Rich had one of the most spectacular successes in theatre history – *The Beggar's Opera*. It ran for nearly seventy performances – not high by today's standards, but then an unheard of number.

This ballad opera came at the right time. Theatre had been in the doldrums without

A SCENE from The Beggar's Opera, *as depicted by Hogarth in 1728. This unexpected success was produced at the theatre in Lincoln's Inn Fields. It had an unprecedented initial run and then returned for another.*

royal patronage – Queen Anne did not like it and George I could not understand it – and the London audience was weary of the tedious and dramatically sterile works on offer: the sentimental and moralistic offerings of Cibber and Steele and bombastic dramas of the sort popularized by Dryden in the latter part of the seventeenth century had come to an artistic impasse. The appeal of *The Beggar's Opera* lay in its reality and humour. John Gay, its compiler and librettist, thrust actual and contemporary characters on to the stage, ranging from corrupt legal officials and gaolers to heroines whose virtue, thank goodness, had long since been abandoned.

In Peachum we are introduced to the scarcely veiled character of Jonathan Wild, who had made his living organizing robberies and then selling the stolen items back to the owners as though performing a public service: this rogue, in league with thieves, was also in tacit association with the authorities to whom he occasionally shopped a felon in exchange for his own liberty, and his own execution in 1725 was a day of rejoicing in London. The escapes and bravado of MacHeath, the hero of the plot, were reminiscent of those of folk-hero Jack Sheppard, a small-time thief made notorious by his ability to escape London gaols, and who, to the dismay of the general public, had been hanged only four years earlier. The opportunity given to the audience at the end of *The Beggar's Opera* to have MacHeath freed was a dangerous tilt at authority, and the question asked by one of the highwaymen as to why the law was levelled at them and not at those who made the laws was an alarming and revolutionary intrusion. It was no wonder that Gay's next piece for the stage was banned.

PANTOMIME

PANTOMIME APPEARED IN THE EARLY EIGHTEENTH CENTURY. It is thought that *The Tavern Bilkers*, the work of a dancing master called Weaver, produced at the Theatre Royal, Drury Lane in 1702 was the first. It may have been a ballet of sorts but, in any case, it lingered only five days and was probably not significant in the development of this dramatic form which owed more to the repertoire of visiting French and Italian companies in this period. They mixed classical stories and dance with a harlequin as a central character, and in 1717 a troupe of French pantomime artists arrived in London with a set of performing dogs as well.

The pantomime in London changed its form distinctly as familiar folk tales were adopted by the London impresarios – *Dick Whittington* was one, and Whittington's legendary liberality to the people of London was interwoven with a quite fanciful and romantic background. The rags-to-riches theme, as in *Cinderella*, fascinated audiences who also delighted to find in pantomime that those in power, such as kings and queens, were actually under the thumb of their servants.

DRAMA

PANTOMIME WAS NOT, HOWEVER, CONDUCIVE TO GOOD DRAMA, which mostly languished in the first half of the eighteenth century and then entered a golden age when the London public found new folk heroes on the stage and dramatists such as Sheridan and Goldsmith made their marks. David Garrick made his debut as Shakespeare's Richard III in a theatre in Goodman's Fields, Whitechapel in 1741 and soon the carriage trade went in numbers to this unprepossessing place, just as over two hundred years later West End theatregoers went in their cars to the unfamiliar territory of Stratford East to Joan Littlewood's domain.

A contemporary reports, no doubt with some exaggeration: 'Mr Garrick drew after him the inhabitants of the most polite parts of the town. Goodman's Fields were full of the splendour of St James's and Grosvenor Square. The coaches of the nobility filled up the space from Temple Bar to Whitechapel.' Even Pope went over from his Twickenham retreat to see the new sensation who, needless to say, was persuaded to Drury Lane for the next season for the majestic fee of £600 a year. The Goodman's Fields theatre was the victim of its own success; having transgressed the law which enabled only Drury Lane and

Covent Garden to present drama, it was forced out of business once the Garrick star was shining elsewhere.

Garrick lorded it at Drury Lane for the next twenty years, to be followed in the public's esteem by the Kemble family, John and Philip in particular and their sister, Sarah Siddons. Sarah made her London debut in 1775, a year before Garrick made his last appearance, but she found herself unwanted after a few performances in the West End and went back again to the obscurity and hardships of the provinces. It was not until 1782 that she was persuaded to return to Drury Lane where she was an immediate success. There was a rich harvest of productions in the mid-1770s: Goldsmith's *She Stoops to Conquer* (1773), Sheridan's comic opera, *The Duenna*, which broke box-office records by running for seventy-four nights in 1775, and, in the same year, *The Rivals*. By the end of 1776 Sheridan had become manager of the Drury Lane Theatre and in 1777 *School for Scandal* had its first performance.

As we have seen in the case of John Gay, censorship was imposed. Each play had to be licensed before performance because the authorities saw theatre as a possible threat to them. This was not an atmosphere in which drama could flourish and, for the most part, it did not. Enterprise was also inhibited as we have seen above by the patent law whereby only two managements could stage drama – in effect, giving a monopoly to the Theatre Royal and Covent Garden. As a consequence these two large auditoria needed catch-all dramas to fill them. The Little Theatre in the Haymarket (forerunner of today's Theatre Royal) flouted the patent regulations consistently by such devices as allowing people in to consume cake and tea for which they paid and, by-the-by, to watch satirical comedies. In the same street Her Majesty's Theatre lived precariously on opera, which was outside the patent prohibition, reluctant to be too blatant in breaking the law.

Apart from the theatre at Lincoln's Inn Fields and those just to the east of the City, the only other theatre in the London area in this period appears to have been at Richmond. In this royal stronghold William Pinkethman, an inadequate actor turned producer, hired the 'Royal Ass House' (a building used to house donkeys for both pleasure and transportation), and turned it into a theatre. It was to last six years until his death, whereupon an actor called Thomas Chapman built another small theatre in Richmond Hill for summer performances. Since Pinkethman was described as 'the flower of Bartholomew Fair and the idol of the rabble' it is unlikely that the Richmond enterprise was of any great quality.

CIRCUS

ANOTHER DIVERSION WAS CIRCUS. A temporary structure was erected by a former cavalryman, Philip Astley, in the Westminster Bridge Road in the 1770s, for the exhibition of equestrian skill on the one horse he possessed. In this venture he flouted the law because he had no licence, but he was allowed to continue by the Lord Chancellor whose daughters he had taught to ride. By 1780 his rough amphitheatre had been covered over and divided into pit, boxes and gallery, and the entertainment was expanded to include jugglers and acrobats. Horace Walpole is once again our witness, in 1783:

ASTLEY'S AMPHITHEATRE, Westminster Bridge Road c.1808, by Pugin and Rowlandson. This is the third theatre erected by Philip Astley to display his equestrian skills. Astley, who died in 1808, is described as having the 'proportions of Hercules and the voice of a Senator'.

London at this time of year [September] is as nauseous a drug as any in an apothecary's shop. I could find nothing at all to do, and so went to Astley's, which indeed was much beyond my expectation. I do not wonder any longer that Darius was chosen king by the instructions he gave to his horse; nor that Caligula made his Consul. Astley can make his dance minuets and hornpipes. But I shall not have even Astley now; Her Majesty the Queen of France, who has as much taste as Caligula, has sent for the whole of the dramatis personae to Paris.

BAITING AND FIGHTING

THE COARSER PLEASURES OF BAITING AND PUGILISM had no need of licence. A place called Hockley in the Hole, just off today's Farringdon Road, provided most of the baiting once the establishments on the south bank of the Thames had lost their prominence. The proprietor of one pit at Hockley in about 1710 was eaten by his own bear, which certainly increased the takings of the place thereafter. In 1716 an advertisement which begins, 'At the request of several persons of quality', promises:

one of the largest and most mischievous bears that ever was seen in England to be baited to death, with other variety of bull and bear baiting, as also a wild bull to be turned loose in the game place with fireworks all over him. To begin exactly at three o'clock in the afternoon, because the sport continues long.

An African tiger was 'worried' by six bull and bear dogs at Hockley, according to one advertisement, and at a bear garden behind Soho Square a leopard was baited to death in 1716.

Hockley was also home to contests between men using swords, daggers and bucklers. In effect, these were exhibition contests with well-known inhibitions on the moves that might be attempted.

These gladiatorial entertainments were also to be seen at Figg's amphitheatre, to the north of Oxford Street, where Mr Figg was himself an expert and teacher in 'self-defence', though a number of black patches on his head denoted sword-cut scars. And it was here, too, that prize-fighting, in which fists were used instead and to more awful effect, took place.

Boxing was not new as an entertainment though it had yet to achieve much status. Figg's enterprise, however, made it popular with all classes and the procedures he evolved for the weapon contests already described were adopted for boxing as well. Challenges were issued in the public prints and seconds, as in duelling, were allowed. In boxing the system of rounds was introduced as was the rule that no contender should be hit when he was down.

Jack Broughton, a former Thames waterman, became the best-known exponent, frequently appearing at the amphitheatre; he was sustained by the financial patronage of the Duke of Cumberland until he lost a fight on which the duke had wagered £10,000. Broughton went on to found his own establishment in Hanway Street off Oxford Street and a boxing academy in Haymarket, and when he died he was worth the enormous sum of £7,000.

The East End had its own hero in 'Mendoza the Jew', born in Whitechapel in 1764. His prowess developed from necessity, as he relates in his memoirs:

> I was here frequently drawn into contests with the butchers and others in the neighbourhood, who, on account of my mistress being of the Jewish religion, were frequently disposed to insult her. In a short time, however, I became the terror of these gentry, and when they found that, young as I was, I was always ready to come forward in her defence, they forbore to molest her.

Mendoza became the acknowledged champion prize-fighter in the country, until he lost to John Jackson, four inches taller and 40 pounds heavier, in 1795. However, he was still fit enough, in 1806 at the age of forty-one to go over 50 rounds at a match in Essex.

Straightforward sexual titillation was the attraction of women's boxing. This was in vogue in the 1720s at Figg's. A notice issued in 1723 advertised:

> I, Martha Jones of Billingsgate, fish-woman, who have fought the best fighting women that ever came to that place, and hearing the fame that is spread about the Town of this noble City Championess, of her beating the Newgate basket-woman, think myself as brave and stout as any, therefore invite her to fight me on the stage for ten pounds.

The rule in women's contests was that they were to clench coins in their fists so that the temptation to pull hair could be resisted.

Just as Figg and Broughton introduced rules that became standard in their own sport, so others were beginning to regulate their obsessions. The Jockey Club was formed in London in 1751 at the Star and Garter in Pall Mall; this was also the venue for a committee in 1784 which again revised the laws of cricket, and it was in the 1780s that organized cricket, as we know it today, began.

CRICKET

CRICKET MATCHES WERE HELD IN THE GROUNDS of the White Conduit Tea Gardens in Islington at least by 1754 when the landlord advertised the purity of the milk from his cows and the availability of bats and balls. By about 1785 his ground was being used by a cricket club prominent in the formulation of the Star and Garter rules. It boasted dukes among its players and indeed, took only gentlemen as players. By this time there were three stumps instead of two, surmounted by a single bail; bowling was still underarm and the bat was curved at the end, rather like a wide hockey stick; the ball was slightly lighter than today's and the players wore no gloves or pads. Inevitably this influential group of players moved on to a venue nearer their own West End residences to some ground taken by their general attendant, Thomas Lord. Seizing his opportunity,

TATTERSALL'S Repository, c.1808, by Pugin and Rowlandson. The bloodstock auctioneer, Richard Tattersall, groom to the Duke of Kingston, established his business in 1766 near Hyde Park Corner.

Lord had leased some land on the Portman estate and erected a high wooden fence around it: it was open for business in May 1787 for a game between gentlemen mainly of Middlesex against others of Essex, with a bet of 100 guineas on the result. Thus, on this modest plot, the site of today's Dorset Square, the Marylebone Cricket Club was born and the role and status of its members in the formation of cricket's rules have ensured that the MCC is still the law-making body of the sport. They ensured, too, that a game which had been mostly enjoyed by the poorer classes was taken up and administered by patricians.

AUCTIONS AND FAIRS

TATTERSALL'S HORSE AUCTION HOUSE, beside St George's Hospital at Hyde Park Corner, developed strong connections with the Jockey Club once two rooms there had been reserved for betting under the Club's supervision. Tattersall was the former groom of a

Duke of Kingston and his impeccable connections and the honesty with which he managed his business acquired this arrangement for him.

By the eighteenth century fairs, originally held for the trading of goods, were to all intents and purposes festive and sometimes rowdy occasions. Bartholomew Fair at West Smithfield was now three weeks long and full of sideshows, freaks and performers. Southwark or Lady Fair, which was originally licensed for three days in September in the middle of Borough High Street, was now extended to a fortnight, to the ire of some residents who complained of traffic obstruction and the ill-behaviour connected with it. The London historian, Strype, writing in 1720, said that it was noted for its 'shows, as drolls, puppet-shows, rope-dancing, music booths and tipping houses'. The fair was abolished in 1762. May Fair, held between today's Curzon Street and Piccadilly, was alleged to be disreputable conveniently at the time that developers wanted to capitalize

Bartholomew fair, Smithfield c.1808, by Pugin and Rowlandson. This fair, held in August, was London's principal fair. It began in the 12th century, when it's tolls were part of the revenue of St Bartholomew's priory and hospital. After the Dissolution the City assumed control.

on the empty fields there. An advertisement of 1700 notes that the fair was to last for sixteen days, beginning on 1 May, of which three days were for cattle and leather with 'the entertainments as Bartholomew Fair'. Among the many performers was a famous ginger-bread seller called Tiddy Doll, whose name is today commemorated by a local restaurant in Shepherd's Market; dressed in a white and gold suit, a laced ruffled shirt and white silk stockings, he was a familiar figure at the Lord Mayor's procession and at Tyburn execution days. The authorities claimed that the fair was 'one of the most pestilent nurseries of impurity and vice. . .the stalls and booths were not for trade but for musick, shows, drinking, gaming, raffling, lotteries, stage plays and drolls.' By 1708 the parish had managed to suppress the event, but it functioned again after an interval of some years until its final abolition mid-century.

Another fair which troubled the authorities was held at Tottenham Court, at the junction of Tottenham Court Road and today's Euston Road. Other fairs were to be found in London's outer ring – including those at Edmonton, Mortlake and Brook Green. Fairlop Fair, near Epping, began about 1725 at the instigation of a ship's blockmaker, Daniel Day, who merely wanted to provide a day out for his own workpeople and friends on land that he owned in Essex; from this the great fair on Fairlop Heath developed, held around the famous Fairlop Oak, a tree whose girth measured 36 feet and whose foliage was renowned for 'overspreading an area of 300ft in circumference'. The *Literary Chronicle* of 1823 notes that the workpeople of Day's firm still went to the fair each year 'in a boat, shaped like an Indian canoe from one piece of timber; this amphibious vehicle was covered with an awning, mounted on a carriage and drawn by six horses, and adorned with flags and musicians.' This fair, nurtured by East Enders, lasted into the twentieth century and was recalled as a childhood enjoyment by George Lansbury, leader of the Labour Party from 1931 to 1935.

The last Frost Fair on the Thames was in 1814 – it is unlikely that the river will freeze sufficiently again as it is now too deep, too fast, and the recipient of too much warm matter. Furthermore, the temperature in London is rarely cold enough for long enough. Undoubtedly the most spectacular Frost Fair had been that of 1683/4, when the bitter weather began in December and lasted until the beginning of February, so that the Thames froze to a depth of 11 feet. A street of stalls, taverns and cookhouses, known as Blanket Street or Freezeland Street, was erected from the Temple to Southwark, and diversions included the roasting of an ox and the erection of a printing press which did a ready sale in souvenir cards with the customers' names on them to mark the occasion. Other Frost Fairs took place in 1715/16, 1739/40 and in 1789; in 1768 the river froze over enclosing a fishing boat in which, eventually, a petrified young man was found sitting bolt upright as though alive. *The Times* was on hand to report the freeze of 1815:

> The ice, however, from its roughness and inequalities, is totally unfit for amusements. The whole of the river opposite Queenhithe was completely frozen over; and in some parts the ice was several feet thick, while in others it was dangerous to venture upon; notwithstanding which crowds of foot passengers crossed backward and forward. Through the whole of the day we did not hear of many lives being lost; but many who ventured too far towards Blackfriars Bridge were partially immersed in the water by the ice giving way. Two coopers were with difficulty saved. Midway between the two bridges and nearly opposite Queenhithe above 30 booths were erected for the sale of porter, spirits, ginger bread etc. Skittles were played by several parties, and the drinking tents filled by females and their companions dancing reels, while others sat round large fires, drinking rum, grog and other spirits. . .Several printers brought their presses, pulled off various impressions which they sold for a trifle. . .On February 3, a sheep was roasted, or rather burnt, over a charcoal fire, in a large iron pan. . .On Thursday a plumber named Daws, attempting to cross near Blackfriars Bridge, with some lead in his hand, sunk between two masses of ice, and rose no more.

Waxworks were sometimes to be found at fairs. A Mrs Salmon appears to have been the first to show a waxworks, and by 1711 was in a building on the north side of Fleet Street near Chancery Lane. Her exhibits, some of which were operated by clockwork, included tableaux such as the execution of Charles I, and the Countess of Heningbergh 'Lying on a Bed of State, with her Three hundred and Sixty-five children, all born at one Birth'. Tussaud's waxworks did not arrive in London from Paris until 1802.

A CARICATURE of Thomas Guy (1644–1724) who, despite his founding of a hospital, was renowned as a miser. Guy was born in Southwark and apprenticed to a bookseller in Cheapside. He set up his own business in 1668 in Cornhill and participated in the unlicensed selling of bibles printed in Holland, but he then became respectable as one of the offially designated printers of the Bible for Oxford University. This was the basis for his later wealth, but he put it to shrewd effect during the South Sea investment frenzy, selling out at the right time. With the proceeds he bought land opposite St Thomas's Hospital (of which he was a governor) and founded his own hospital which was completed just about the time he died.

CHAPTER X

INSTITUTIONS IN THE MAKING

MUSEUMS AND LIBRARIES

I N JANUARY 1759, ON WHAT WAS THEN A FRINGE OF LONDON, THE BRITISH MUSEUM WAS opened. That is, opened to those of whom the Trustees and its employees approved, and only then for a few hours a day with a maximum of ten visitors at a time. It was not an auspicious start for what was to become one of the great institutions of the world, but at least the parsimony of its foundation reflected accurately the attitude towards it of successive governments. Its contents, on the other hand, were the glory of its benefactors.

It is safe to say that were it not for the generosity of Sir Hans Sloane and the heirs and successors of Sir Robert Cotton and Robert Harley, this great enterprise would not have begun when it did, and by the time some similar institution was invented – as it most certainly would have been by the civic-minded Victorians – the collections of those three men would have long since been dispersed. But it had been hard work to sell their vast numbers of antiquities, manuscripts, artefacts and volumes, even at knock-down prices, to governments which had no imagination in such matters. London, for all its sophistication and its wordly power was, before the British Museum came into being, almost entirely bereft of public libraries. Thomas Carte, Jacobite historian, declared that, 'There is not a great City in Europe so ill provided with Public Libraries as London'. Apart from theological libraries and one small public library in St Martin-in-the-Fields, there was nothing other than two circulating libraries reported as being in the Strand.

This was an odd state of affairs for a nation which had included so many discerning collectors. Sir Robert Cotton (1571-1631) had amassed not only thousands of manuscripts, cartularies, coins and state papers, but also the Lindisfarne Gospels and two copies of the Magna Carta. As with London historian John Stow before him, his collection of documents was viewed with suspicion by the authorities and in the reign of Charles I Cotton was thought to have aided the disgraced Earl of Somerset; to his immense distress his collection was sealed up and he was forbidden its access, almost to the time of his death. Nevertheless, his grandson, Sir John, was instrumental in the passing of an Act in 1700 which transferred the ownership of the Cottonian collection to the State. Unfortunately it was allowed to remain in a damp apartment of the Cotton house in Westminster and there it deteriorated within a stone's throw of an ungrateful government.

Charles I himself amassed an array of Dutch and High Renaissance paintings, which was then wantonly sold off by the Commonwealth administration. Thomas Howard, 2nd Earl of Arundel (1586–1646), was renowned for the art collection housed in his mansion in the Strand, part of which is depicted in a painting today at Arundel Castle showing him with his antique marbles against the background of the Thames. After his death, some of his statues found their way to the dubious environment of Cuper's Gardens, and the diarist John Evelyn persuaded the heir to present others to the University of Oxford; Howard's grandson gave what was left of the library to the Royal Society in 1667, and genealogical material went to the College of Heralds, but otherwise this magnificent assembly, brought together by a man who was among the first to appreciate the importance of art in Asia Minor and Greece, was dismantled. A collection of rarities and botanical literature was brought together by John Tradescant the elder (d.1637), gardener

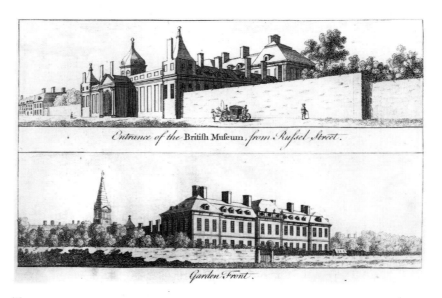

Entrance of the British Museum, from Russel Street.

Garden Front.

Two views of Montagu House, Great Russell Street, after its acquisition in 1755 by the British Museum. The Museum became the natural (and virtually the only) repository for the collections of scholars, although the trustees were particular about letting the public view them.

and traveller, of South Lambeth. This found a new home, via Elias Ashmole, at Oxford University together with Ashmole's own collection of books and manuscripts. We learn from Evelyn that the naturalist Sir Hans Sloane (1660-1753) had at his Chelsea house 'plants, fruits, corails, minerals, stones, Earth, shells, animals, Insects &c collected by him with great Judgement' and there were, at the time of his death, drawings by Dürer and Holbein, 50,000 volumes and 32,000 coins. Robert Harley, 1st Earl of Oxford (1661–1724), began acquiring his famous library in 1705 and by 1721 had 6,000 volumes of manuscripts, which included the archives of John Stow, and 14,000 charters.

It was only when Sloane died in 1753 that anything positive was done to bring together a national museum and library. His will directed that his collection be offered to the State for the low sum of £20,000 and if no sale was made within six months then it was to go elsewhere. An unusually sympathetic House of Commons accepted his terms. It was

THE Hall and Grand Staircase of the British Museum in 1808, by Pugin and Rowlandson. Extensive rebuilding began in 1823 when Robert Smirke planned buildings around a courtyard at the rear of Montagu House, which itself was replaced by the present Greek facade in the 1840s.

agreed, also, that Sloane's collection should be joined by the Cotton library, still languishing virtually unused in Westminster, and that the Harleian collection should be purchased at the same time. Later, the old Royal Library, which dated from Tudor times, was added; this had the priceless advantage of the gift of any book registered at Stationers' Hall and was the origin of the right of the British Library to every book published. All this was to be housed in a suitable building and mostly to be paid for by public lottery.

The lottery itself became a corrupt scandal but eventually the money was raised. Once Buckingham House (later transformed into Palace) had been declined the Trustees settled for Montagu House in Great Russell Street, which had over seven acres to the north of it with open views all the way to Hampstead and Highgate. It is one of the fascinations of London that the future characters of both the Bloomsbury and the St James's Park areas were determined by this decision.

Even so, the general public was denied access to the galleries of the British Museum until 1879 and the availability of libraries in London remained severely restricted until the nineteenth century. Dr Tenison, vicar of St Martin-in-the-Fields and later to be Archbishop of Canterbury, had founded a library in his parish in about 1684 and this was all that was available to the public. Evelyn was involved, as he was with most things:

Dr Tenison communicated to me his intention of erecting a Library in St Martin's parish, for the public use, and desired my assistance, with Sir Christopher Wren, about the placing and structure thereof. A worthy and laudable design. He told me there were 30 or 40 young men in Orders in his parish, either governors to young gentlemen, or chaplains to noblemen, who being reproved by him on occasion for frequenting taverns or coffee-houses, told him they would study or employ their time better if they had books.

This library was demolished in 1861 to make way for an extension to the National Gallery.

Ten years after the British Museum opened its doors the Royal Academy of Arts was founded. As its name suggests the principal intention was to teach art – Constable, Turner and Blake were all pupils – but from the earliest years the Academy held exhibitions of its members' and pupils' works; furthermore, an academician had to present to the Academy

THE Royal Academy c.1808, by Pugin and Rowlandson. The Academy was founded in 1768, holding exhibitions in a house in Pall Mall, and teaching students at Somerset House. Eventually the Academy held exhibitions there.

a work of his or her choice (there were two women members in the original thirty-six founders), a rule that has enabled the Academy to gather a notable collection. It was a flourishing period for painting and architecture in London – the early members of the Academy included Reynolds, Gainsborough, Cipriani, the Sandbys, West and Zoffany and the architects, Chambers and George Dance.

In 1789 a remarkable venture was launched by Alderman John Boydell, a wealthy City print-seller. In Pall Mall he opened an art gallery in which to exhibit scenes from Shakespeare's plays by the foremost artists of the day – from these prints were made for sale. Painters of the calibre of Romney, Kauffmann, West and Fuseli were commissioned and well over £100,000 was spent, but Boydell's hopes were dashed eventually by a recession caused by the French Revolution and the consequent loss of many European sales. Boydell was no ordinary businessman – he was highly regarded by the artistic community and was lauded for his enterprise. J.T. Smith, antiquary and Keeper of Prints and Drawings at the British Museum said that he had done more for the advancement of the arts in England than the whole mass of nobility put together. At the Royal Academy dinner in 1789, the year Boydell opened the Gallery, political theorist Edmund Burke proposed his health as 'the Commercial Mœcenas of England'. Smith's description of him throws light on Boydell's daily life and the conditions of the day:

> It was the regular custom of Mr Alderman Boydell, who was a very early riser, at five o'clock, to go immediately to the pump in Ironmonger Lane. There, after placing his wig upon the ball at the top of it, he used to sluice his head with its water.

By 1802 the Gallery contained over 160 works, but Boydell faced bankruptcy. He took the unusual course of applying to Parliament for an Act enabling him to sell his stock by lottery. All the tickets were sold but he died in 1804 before the tickets were drawn.

THE SOCIETIES

THE ENGLISH TALENT FOR ORGANIZING BOTH SCIENTIFIC AND ARTISTIC INTERESTS, and almost anything else, within societies was to flower in the nineteenth century but a few such bodies were to become prominent in the eighteenth century. The Royal Society, formed for the study of natural philosophy and science, had grown in strength since its charter at the Restoration and was affluent enough to help organize Cook's expedition to the Pacific in 1768 to observe the transit of Venus, and to send one of its members, Joseph Banks, on its voyage to collect botanical samples. The Society of Antiquaries, banned by James I, was reconstituted in 1707 and met at various taverns in the Strand and Fleet Street for the study of 'Antiquities, and more particularly such things as illustrate or relate to the History of Great Britain prior to the reign of James I'; by the end of the century they were esconced in Somerset House in apartments granted by the King.

The Royal Society of Arts was founded in 1754 by a drawing master, William Shipley. It is claimed that in 1760 the Society held the first organized art exhibition in England, which included works by Reynolds, Morland, Roubiliac and Wilson. The founding title of the RSA was 'The Society for the Encouragement of Arts, Manufactures and Commerce', which more closely identified its full aspirations: its persistent encouragement to mix good art and design with the manufacture of mass goods was to find its most influential champion when Prince Albert took a close interest in its work.

Another society concerned with practical matters was formed in 1717 in the industrious Huguenot area of Spitalfields. The Mathematical Society, which consisted of weavers, optical instrument-makers and the like, met in a local tavern and there:

> lent their instruments (air pumps, reflecting telescopes, reflecting microscopes, electrical machines, surveying instruments, etc) with books for the use of them, on the borrower's giving a note of hand for the value thereof. The number of members was not to exceed the square of seven, except such as were abroad or in the country, but this was increased to the squares of eight and nine. The members met on Saturday evenings; each present was to employ himself in some mathematical exercise, or forfeit one penny; and if he refused to answer a question asked by another in mathematics, he was to forfeit twopence.

This admirable organization, which inspired the young John Dollond in his optical measurement studies, survived until 1845, and by then had accumulated a library of some three thousand volumes which it donated to the Royal Astronomical Society.

THE PRESS AND PUBLISHING

THESE FIRST STEPS, HOWEVER MODEST, in the dissemination of arts and science to a slightly wider public were accompanied by a relaxation of restrictions on printing and publishing, although censorship was still a threat. Illiteracy was common and the market for newspapers and for books which were not academic or theological was still small. Even so, it was possible for a publisher to make a good living: Thomas Guy, who began in trade selling books in Cornhill, became wealthy enough, on the basis of selling Bibles and his profits from South Sea Company speculation, to found Guy's Hospital; and Jacob Tonson's later affluence was based on his publishing and bookselling business in Chancery Lane, bolstered by a half-share in the right to publish Milton's *Paradise Lost*. James Lackington, who established *the* bookshop in London in Chiswell Street in the City, is the most reliable observer as to the increase in book sales during the century. He notes in his *Memoirs*, published in 1792:

> I suppose that more than four times the number of books are sold now than were sold twenty years since. The poorer sort of farmers, and even the poor country people in general, who before that period spent their winter evenings in relating stories of hob-goblins etc. now shorten their winter nights by hearing their sons and daughters read tales, romances, etc; and on entering their houses, you may see Tom Jones, Roderick Random, and other entertaining books stuck up on the bacon racks.

The publication of newspapers was a more hazardous occupation. The diet of the general public in the seventeenth century had been one of pamphlets, news sheets and almanacs, fed by printers and publishers concentrated around St Paul's churchyard and Fleet Street. These gentlemen walked a fine line between publication and imprisonment. The Restoration hardly changed this, since both Charles II and James II continued to operate a censorious regime. News, open to interpretation, was thought to be dangerous and divisive and the Crown appointed Roger L'Estrange, an ardent royalist, as Surveyor of Printing Presses in 1663. He was no friend to the spread of literature and news and comments:

> I find it in general with the printers as with their neighbours, there are too many of the trade to live by one another. But, more particularly, I find them clogged with three sorts of people – foreigners, persons not free of the trade, and separatists.

His attitude to news was summed up in a prospectus he issued:

> Supposing the press in order, the people in their right wits, and news or no news to be the question, a public mercury should never have my vote, because I think it makes the multitude too familiar with the actions and counsels of their superiors, too pragmatical and censorious, and gives them not only a wish but a kind of colourable right and license to the meddling with the government.

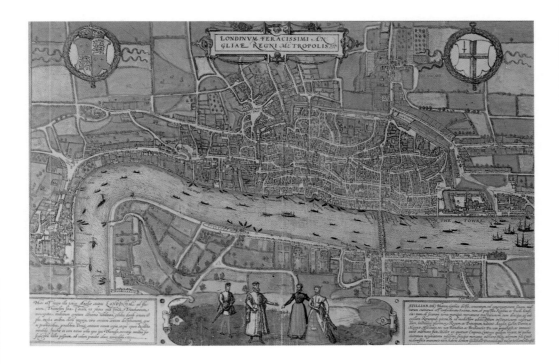

Plate I

This map of London, probably surveyed c.1550 and engraved by Frans Hogenberg from a drawing by George Hoefnagel, gives a clear indication of the size of London in Tudor times. The buildings around Westminster are shown to the left of the picture, and the Tower of London and the precinct of St Katharine's Hospital are on the right. In Southwark there are two animal-baiting auditoria but, apart from the cluster of houses at the southern end of London Bridge, it is still a rural place.

PLATE II

Flamsteed House, Greenwich, aquatint published in 1824. In the 17th century astronomers, of whom Christopher Wren was one, were examining the heavens with new energy. An Astronomer Royal, John Flamsteed, was appointed in 1675, and with bricks left over from the building of Tilbury Fort, Wren built the small observatory on the top of Greenwich Hill. The Observatory here became the most important astronomical research building in the world until modern times. Its status was such that the meridian, by international agreement, was fixed at Greenwich, dividing the world here between eastern and western hemispheres, and until the development of atomic clocks, the Greenwich time signal was relied upon everywhere.

John Flamsteed, Astronomer Royal, (1645-1720); oil painting by Thomas Gibson.

PLATE III

The Adelphi, oil painting by William Marlow, 1771. In the 18th century the large houses of the nobility along the Strand were demolished to make way for modern developments. One of the most striking was that planned and built c.1770 by the Adam brothers on the grounds of Durham House. It comprised 24 terraced houses built above a series of arches erected to counteract the slope of the bank of the Thames. The dark, often flooded, interior of this basement was used by many traders, particularly those offloading coal for the West End. Most of the development was taken down in the 1930s. The octagonal water tower is that of the York Buildings Waterworks Company.

The York Buildings Waterworks on the bank of the Thames, at the end of Villiers Street, were begun in 1675 when a licence was granted to erect an engine which extracted water from the river. The works were destroyed by fire in 1690, and when rebuilt included a water tower, seen above, 70ft high. Though at one time it served over 2,000 properties, the company was always in financial difficulties and it did not replace its steam engine when it ceased working in 1731.

Plate IV

View of London from Caen Wood, by John Wootton, 1760. Landscape gardening was an obsession of the wealthy in the 18th century. At Kenwood House, Highgate, natural ponds were transformed into scenic attractions, overlooking the panorama of London. That view is now obscured by trees, but in recent years the ponds have been dredged and their shapes redefined in an attempt to bring back the 18th century landscaping.

The Adam Library at Kenwood House in Highgate. The original house on this site on the northern heights above London was largely replaced at the end of the 17th century. Then, from 1764, Robert Adam refaced and enlarged the property for William Murray, 1st Earl Mansfield.

PLATE V

London from Hampstead Heath, 1803, by an unknown artist. At this time fields extended virtually all the way down to the City and West End. St Paul's Cathedral dominates a city of church spires.

PLATE VI

THE combined efforts of the City of London and the Thames watermen prevented the building of bridges across the Thames to add to the convenience afforded by the old London Bridge. The first to be built upstream from the City was that replacing the ferry between Fulham and Putney. Made of wood, it was constructed in 1727-9, but its numerous spans were a serious impediment to river traffic. The 18th century view above is from the Putney side, showing Fulham parish church in the background.

THE last toll being paid at Putney Bridge in 1880.

*P*LATE *VII*

*A*LBANY, *Piccadilly in the 1820s. The area to the west of today's Regent Street as far as Park Lane, was fashionable for the whole of the 18th century. The house shown above was origi- nally built in 1770-74 for the 1st Viscount Melbourne to the designs of William Chambers, but soon after it came into the possession of the Duke of York and Albany. From 1802 the house was converted into bachelors' apartments and two additional wings were added in the garden to the rear. This residential enclave is probably the last to survive in the inner West End.*

A DISCREET *entrance to the Albany apartments built in the grounds of the house which fronts Piccadilly, with shops on either side of the gate. From a drawing in the Sir John Soane Collection.*

PLATE VIII

*K*ING'S *B*ENCH *P*RISON, *St George's Fields, c.1809 by Pugin and Rowlandson. This building of 224 rooms, was renowned for the freedom of its inhabitants. It was quite easy to buy 'liberty' of the walls, and was a much desired place of incarceration. Women were allowed to live there, and traders such as bakers and tailors could move freely in the building – at the height of the gin epidemic there were at least 30 gin shops in the precincts.*

*T*HE *1869 Debtors Act abolished imprisonment for debt other than for money owed to the Crown. It also provided that those who were already in prison for debt could be freed with their debts cancelled. This produced a rush of people anxious to be incarcerated for a few days so that their debts could be erased, and a good many people crowded into the last City debtors' prison at Whitecross Street. In this picture from the* Illustrated London News *the last prisoners are being discharged from the gaol.*

He then went on to solicit information of unlicensed publications. H.R. Fox Bourne, in his two volumes, *English Newspapers* (1887), recites the 1663 case of a printer in Cloth Fair who, having been raided by the authorities at midnight, was then tried for printing material which urged that 'the execution of judgment and justice is as well the people's as the magistrate's duty, and if the magistrates prevent judgment, the people are bound by the law of God to execute judgment without them and upon them.' For this seditious prose the poor man was sentenced to the most barbarous death at Tyburn.

L' Estrange's power diminished only gradually and was finally ended when James II was obliged to flee to France in 1688. The *London Gazette*, published twice weekly, bore L' Estrange's imprint: it was the official newspaper and confined itself to news that the Crown permitted. The lack of real news and independent comment was made good by evenings spent in the increasing number of coffee-houses, to the extent that a Royal Proclamation in 1675 attempted their extinction. They were, it said, 'places where the disaffected meet and spread scandalous reports concerning the conduct of His Majesty and his Ministers'.

Charles II prorogued Parliament in 1679 before the existing law regulating the press could be renewed, and briefly newspapers were free of licensing. It was a turbulent period during which James, then Duke of York, was accused of plotting to assassinate his brother the King in order to usurp the throne and re-establish the Catholic faith. Charles II, rapidly losing favour with the populace, teetered on the brink of another civil war. But by 1682 he had re-established his position and was powerful enough to reimpose restrictions on the press.

The Act licensing newspapers was abandoned in 1695, opening the way for new ventures. In 1702 the first daily newspaper, *The Daily Courant*, appeared in Elizabeth Mallet's bookshop in what is now Ludgate Hill; it had a circulation of about 800, was printed on one side of each sheet and consisted mainly of news, rather than comment, since the editor supposed 'other people to have sense enough to make reflections for themselves'. According to the writer Daniel Defoe, the *Courant* was run by a group of twenty booksellers, as indeed were most of the newspapers which appeared in the earlier part of the eighteenth century.

Yet though the Act might no longer be in force, publishers and printers were still at the mercy of the law and a number were punished for their opposition to the government. Defoe was pilloried in 1703 for a pamphlet entitled *Shortest Way with the Dissenters*. A notorious case was that of Nathaniel Mist, publisher of *Mist's Weekly Journal*, which from its inception in 1717 had supported the Jacobite cause (Defoe, planted in the newspaper office on behalf of a suspicious Whig government, was an occasional contributor). In 1723 Mist found himself in serious trouble for alleged libel against the government and had not only his bail recognisance of £1,000 appropriated by the court, but was fined an additional £100 and sent to prison for a year. Undeterred, Mist was again in court in 1727, when he was once again fined. Richard Steele, writer, publisher and Member of Parliament, was expelled from the House for two articles he had written, but undoubtedly the most famous case was that of John Wilkes, profligate Whig MP for Aylesbury. In the complex political situation of 1763, with the Whigs in disarray, Wilkes complicated matters further by publishing in his own newssheet, the *North Briton*, what was adjudged to be a libel against George III. He was imprisoned in the Tower, but released by Chief Justice Pratt on the grounds that his position as MP protected him from arrest in the

THE *first edition of* The Gentleman's Magazine *in 1731, depicting St John's Gate, Clerkenwell, where it was published and printed. It was the first journal to use the term 'magazine' in its title.*

matter. In November that year the Whig government, urged on by the King, declared that the attack in the *North Briton* was a libel and two months later expelled Wilkes from the House. He fled to France to escape prosecution and was later to be the hero of the populace as they turned against the King.

A brief period of innovative journalism occurred with the publication of *The Tatler* in 1709 and its successor *The Spectator* in 1711. These journals, closely identified with coffee-house life, were enterprises of Richard Steele in collaboration with Joseph Addison, both of them Whigs. The Tories were sustained by *The Examiner*, a newspaper edited by Jonathan Swift in 1710. But their appearance and their quality was short-lived for all newspapers were badly affected by the passing of the Stamp Act in 1712, which imposed a tax of a halfpenny on papers of half a sheet and a penny on papers of a whole sheet.

Another influential London journal, the first to be called a 'magazine', was the *Gentleman's Magazine*, founded in 1731 in premises above St John's Gate in Clerkenwell. Its proprietor was Edward Cave who had been a regular contributor to Nathaniel Mist's much-harassed journal, and had then specialized in the conveyance of country news to London journals and London news to provincial publications. His intention when founding the *Gentleman's Magazine* was to publish a digest of articles and news which appeared in other publications. He circumvented the ban on reporting parliamentary debates by paying spies in the House with good memories and using initials for speakers. When Samuel Johnson was employed to write up these debates he composed speeches far more interesting than the originals. Johnson declared:

I never was in the House of Commons but once. Cave had interest with the doorkeeper. He and the persons under him got admittance. They brought away the subject of discussion, the names of the speakers, the side they took, and the order in which they rose, together with notes of the various arguments. . .The whole was afterwards communicated to me, and I composed the speeches in the form they have now in 'Parliamentary Debates'.

Yet while some Members secretly sent Cave written versions of their speeches to enhance their own reputations, the House itself expressed outrage at the intrusion. Cave and his rival, Astle of the *London Magazine*, were both obliged to pay fines and beg pardons on their knees for reporting the sensational trial of Lord Lovat, the Jacobite rebel who was hanged at Tower Hill for treason in 1747.

London newspapers came and went rapidly in the 1760s and 1770s. The most successful was the *Morning Chronicle*, a Whig publication, which included Lamb, Hazlitt and Coleridge among its writers, and the *Morning Post*, founded principally to obtain advertising revenue by a syndicate that included the auctioneers Christie and Tattersall. These two papers had much larger circulations than what began as the *Daily Universal Register* in 1785 and which in 1788 changed its name to *The Times*. By the time John Walter brought out the *Register* there were eight other morning newspapers in London

THE Times *newspaper, which had begun as the* Daily Universal Register *in 1785, pursued a policy of technical innovation – even, much later, commissioning its own typeface. Pictured here is a printing press constructed by its own engineers in 1827.*

and it was not until his son, John Walter II, became proprietor and editor that *The Times* rose to prominence. The first Sunday paper, the *British Gazette & Sunday Monitor*, was launched in 1780, but its history was undistinguished and in 1803 it was bought to be used as a propaganda sheet for the deluded religious fanatic, Joanna Southcott. Ten years later *The Observer* was founded.

Noon *by Hogarth, 1738. It depicts Huguenots of Soho, by then a prosperous and respected community manufacturing and selling luxury goods. They are emerging from their church in Hog Lane (now part of Charing Cross Road). Hogarth shows them as being decorous, in contrast to the ill-disciplined indigenous population. Three other Huguenot churches existed in Soho by the end of the 17th century and there were so many Huguenot residents in the area that one contemporary historian noted that 'it is an easy Matter for a Stranger to imagine himself in France'. Huguenot craftsmen were particularly known for their silverware and musical and optical instruments.*

CHAPTER XI

BUYING AND SELLING

ADVERTISING

PROCLAMATIONS IN 1762 AND 1763 BANNED THE PROFUSION OF TRADE SIGNS OVERHANGING the pavements of the City and Westminster. It is doubtful if Londoners conformed *en masse*, since other means had to be developed to advertise a business or a private address to the illiterate. The signs had their disadvantages – occasionally they crashed to the ground, or else they dripped water long after the rain had finished and they creaked ominously in the night wind. But they *were* colourful and with their disappearance went a miscellaneous array of heraldry, symbolism, and trade history.

Craftsmen in Harp Alley off Shoe Lane specialized in painting these signs but superior specimens were made by the coach and sedan painters of Long Acre. Some trade signs were enormous, sometimes sufficiently large and heavy to pull the front of a house out; others, before the alleyways of the City were widened after the Great Fire, might be extensive enough to touch across the divide. Most began as signs indicating the business of the premises, but a change of proprietor and trade didn't always result in a fresh and appropriate sign; sometimes a new owner might, just as in heraldry, quarter the old emblem so as to keep a sign that was familiar to customers yet put something of his own identity into it.

The signs were more than advertising boards. They were, in effect, addresses or else were used as signposts to other locations. There were no street numbers and, quite often, no street name plaques – it was only in 1765 that the Common Council in the City required the wards to fix name tablets to each street, alley, square and court, and it was another two years before an Act of Parliament legislated for the numbering of houses in the City, Westminster and the liberties. Yet despite the obvious advantages of clear signposting and numbering the problem still persisted in the environs of London as they were developed. The *Illustrated London News* in 1853 reported that 'Islington Vestry have caused the name of every street and court throughout the parish to be painted – a course which would be a great accommodation to strangers if generally adopted throughout the metropolis.'

As a result of the hanging-sign ban shopkeepers fixed new signs to the fascias of their buildings and engraved their names in stone high up on the parapet wall. Other changes were taking place in dressing up retail trade. As larger panes of glass became available so the shop window was used for display and bow windows were introduced to take even more advantage. It is thought that a draper called Gedge was the first, in 1782, to have a shopfront in the modern sense – his bay windows were on two sides of a building at the corner of Leicester Square and Cranbourn Street. Daniel Defoe in his book *The Complete English Tradesman* (1727) had already noted a new ostentation in the decoration of shops:

> It is a modern custom and wholly unknown to our ancestors to have tradesmen lay out two-thirds of their fortune in fitting up their shops. By fitting up, I do not mean furnishing their shops with wares and goods to sell; but in painting and gilding, fine shelves, shutters, boxes, glass doors, sashes and the like, in which, they tell us now, 'tis a small matter to lay out two or three hundred pounds.

By the time Sophie von La Roche visited London in 1786 she was able to report that:

> every article is made more attractive to the eye than in Paris or in any other town. . .Whether they are silks, chintzes or muslins, they hang down in folds behind the fine high windows so that the effect of this or that material, as it would be in the ordinary folds of a woman's dress, can be studied.

Retailing was coming of age and just as the proprietors of the pleasure gardens appealed to people who were increasingly fastidious, so the shops of London, or at least those in the West End and some parts of the City, were taking part in the same process.

THE WEST END AND THE HUGUENOTS

THE MOST PRONOUNCED CHANGE IN SHOPS AND SHOPPING HABITS came as London developed westwards. Wealthy people filled St James's, Cavendish, Hanover, Grosvenor and Berkeley Squares and their more visible hinterlands, and ambitious tradesmen followed. Pepys had presaged the departure of lucrative trade from the City. After the Great Fire he had gone with his wife to the New Exchange in the Strand to buy linen at a shop whose owner

> is come out of London since the Fire, says his and other retail tradesmen's trade is so great here, and better than it was in London, that they believe that they shall not return nor the City be ever so great for retail as it was heretofore.

In particular the Huguenots, who by and large handled luxury goods, followed their market, especially to Soho where they made their livings from jewellery, watch-making, carving, gilding, picture framing, wig-making and glove-making. (It was the Huguenots who developed the use of papier mâché for ornament.)

By 1711 there were 612 'ffrench inhabitants' in Soho together with 192 of their children under ten and 158 of their servants, and 3,318 'Lodgers who are chiefly French'. Elegant trade cards depict their shop interiors of beautiful wood and glass display cases and panelled counters – that of Peter De la Fontaine, goldsmith of Litchfield Street, shows not only the comfortable showroom but an open fire-cum-forge with assistants heating and beating metal. This card was designed by Hogarth as was that of Ellis Gamble, a goldsmith in Cranbourn Street who had taken the trouble to engrave his advertisement in French as well. (Hogarth had been apprenticed to Gamble in 1712. The Huguenots joined indigenous craftsmen in Soho where for much of the eighteenth and nineteenth centuries the City of London custom of both manufacturing and selling on the premises was preserved.

French silversmiths did very well in Soho. From the 1680s, there was a great demand for silver plate to decorate the tables of the rich; as a consequence, silver coins were melted down and turned into tableware, leaving the public to cope with a shortage of small currency.

Violin- and other instrument-makers, some of them French, were also numerous in the Soho area. Samuel Pepys noted the growing taste for violin playing after the Restoration, and French music in particular was the fashion. Manufacturers were at first congregated at the eastern end of Piccadilly and in Coventry Street, but later spread to Soho. One man

LIVERY stables in Swallow Street, off Regent Street, in 1801, formerly belonging to Foubert's Riding Academy. The original academy was founded by Solomon de Foubert at the end of the 17th century, near what is now Foubert's Place.

gained notoriety at the assemblies at Mrs Cornelys' masquerades in Soho Square by playing the violin while on roller skates, but on one occasion 'impelled himself against a mirror of more than five hundred pounds' value, dashed it to atoms, broke his instrument to pieces, and wounded himself most severely'.

Other Frenchmen went into teaching. Solomon de Foubert founded a riding academy, carried on by his son, Major Henry Foubert, just to the east of today's Regent Street on a site now commemorated by Foubert's Place. This was thought to be of considerable advantage to London since it made unnecessary the 'vast expence the nation is at yearly in sending children into France to be taught military exercises'. Mathematics and its application to geography and navigation was also taught there; John Evelyn went to see the Academy in 1684 and recorded various members of the aristocracy going through exercises that consisted of riding and firing weapons at the same time. A later pupil was the Duke of Cumberland, responsible for the savage dispatch of the Jacobite soldiers who survived the Battle of Culloden in 1746.

Hubert Gravelot began a drawing school in the Strand after his arrival in London in 1732, and was active in the affairs of the St Martin's Lane Academy, an art school which was managed in 1718 by another Huguenot, Louis Chéron. Another French academy in Long Acre, begun c.1686, taught fencing, dancing and painting.

There are still today shops in Soho which recall this earlier concentration of craftsmen, but not many, and certainly the Huguenot connection (which had almost entirely disappeared among lists of tradesmen in the 1820s) hardly survives excepting the French Protestant Church in Soho Square, which was built in the 1890s.

FURNITURE

THE FURNITURE TRADE WAS GATHERED MAINLY IN OLD COMPTON, Berwick and Wardour Streets; in St Martin's Lane, Chippendale's famous workshops stood opposite Old Slaughter's Coffee-house, used by many cabinet-makers including French craftsmen. It was a trade fragmented between subcontracted carvers, gilders, veneer and inlay artists, upholsterers, ironmongers and so on, with very few entrepreneurs taking the whole responsibility of a commission. Yet, to make much money and a reputation, it demanded the gamble that Chippendale took. As Robert Campbell emphasized in his *The London Tradesmen* (1747):

> *A Master Cabinet-Maker is a very profitable Trade; especially if he serves the Quality himself; but if he must serve them through the Channel of the Upholder, his Profits are not very considerable.*

Thomas Chippendale's career in London coincided with one of the most remarkable periods of English furniture design, when the availability of many talents was matched by a custom derived from an extraordinary boom in the building of country and town houses. There was, too, an abundance of superb wood – mahogany in particular and other hard woods, imported from colonial territories.

Chippendale began in 1749 with small premises in Conduit Court, off Long Acre, and at the end of 1753 took the lease of three adjoining houses in St Martin's Lane (there is now a plaque on No. 61), together with their rear buildings. Apart from the pieces that Chippendale designed and produced himself, his main influence was in his publication of the *Directory,* a compendium of designs which set standards and style benchmarks for much of the rest of the century. It was much more than just a catalogue intended to advertise his wares, as the prospectus printed in the *Public Advertiser* in 1753 makes clear. It is, he claimed:

> *a New Book of Designs of Household Furniture in the GOTHIC, CHINESE and MODERN TASTE, as improved by the politest and most able Artists. Comprehending an elegant Variety of curious and original Drawings in the most useful, ingenious, and ornamental Branches of Chair, Cabinet and Upholstery Work. With the Five Orders and Principles of Perspective, explained in a more easy and concise Method than ever hitherto has been made publick.*

China

THE MOST ILLUSTRIOUS BUSINESS IN SOHO was Wedgwood's china showrooms at Nos. 12–13 Greek Street. These premises were earlier known as Portland House (and still are in their modern form), the largest house in the street. By the late 1680s they were used for a Huguenot school and in 1774 were taken as a London showroom and warehouse by Josiah Wedgwood. He had been originally in Chandos Place off Grosvenor Square and then in Great Newport Street, having decided that Pall Mall was 'too accessible to the common Folk' and that his customers 'will not mix with the Rest of the World'. The subsequent move to two addresses in Soho is therefore perplexing because although the area had a high reputation in the latter part of the eighteenth century, it was never as exclusive as Pall Mall. In 1774 Wedgwood exhibited the famous dinner service made for

Wedgwood's Rooms in York Street, St James's, 1809. Josiah Wedgwood was not only a good potter, he was also a good salesman. His showroom, before he moved into Soho was opulent and tasteful and allowed customers to browse and make up their minds.

the gluttonous Catherine of Russia (it is now in the Hermitage in St Petersburg); consisting of 952 pieces, displayed in five rooms. Wedgwood devised too a series of plates featuring country houses and one depicting famous people. Sophie von la Roche saw these in 1786:

> At Wedgwood's to-day I saw a thousand lovely forms and images; vases, tea-things, statuettes, medallions, seals, tableware and a service on which pictures of the finest villas and gardens of the last three reigns were painted.

Wedgwood realized the importance of display. While eighteenth-century trade cards typically depict shop interiors where the stock is mostly behind the vendor, usually on shelves or in glass cases inaccessible to the browsing customers, Wedgwood put the merchandise right in front of them, within touching distance.

The increase in tea drinking helped Wedgwood. Mostly it was China tea at this stage since the Indian variety was not imported in quantity until the 1830s. It was outrageously expensive at about 10 shillings a pound, which is hardly surprising given that the East India Company had the sole right to import it – the price, even with a heavy duty, sank to 3 shillings a pound in the nineteenth century when the Company lost its monopoly. Furthermore, the Company was reluctant to sell tea to retailers in small lots, so that it was common for small concerns to join together in buying one large consignment. Despite its price the drink became popular with all classes and for the better off its consumption became a ritual and a meal of its own, needing its own blending procedures, crockery, silverware, utensils and furniture, and sometimes a special room as well. Rachel, Lady Russell, who lived in some splendour in Bedford House in what is now Bloomsbury Square, discovered in 1698 the delight of adding milk to tea, but that was a habit slow to develop and when it did it needed, of course, special small milk jugs as well.

Tea was denounced in much the same way as coffee had been in the seventeenth century. Some thought it addictive and others suspected that it was adulterated with almost anything that could pass for tea leaves – it was sold loose and lent itself to unscrupulous trading. The Methodists, however, approved of it as conducive to discipline (especially during the gin-drinking years which so demoralized the working classes – see Chapter 12) and it was drunk at weekly Methodist meetings. Happily, it was necessary to boil the water in which it was infused, which was an advantage given the quality of London's water supply.

FROM HATTERS TO MAD ELEPHANTS

ST JAMES'S STREET WAS VIRTUALLY A MALE PRESERVE of hatters, tailors, shoemakers, gunsmiths and wine suppliers, some of whom have survived since the eighteenth century, and Jermyn Street was noted for its shirtmakers, wigmakers, tobacconists and barbers. Piccadilly, even as late as the 1820s, was a street of general shops: what became the prestigious Fortnum & Mason was virtually next door to a bricklayer and mason, Hatchard's bookshop was two doors from a wax and tallow chandler, and the oilman to the royal family was next door to a breeches-maker. Charles Fortnum had been a footman in the household of George III until ill-health obliged him to resign about 1788, but he appears to have opened his shop in 1770, selling, it is said, the remains of wax candles from the royal household that were a perk of the job. He also supplied St James's Palace with an increasingly exotic range of foods brought to this country by the East India Company.

John Hatchard began his business in 1797 at No. 173, before taking larger premises four years later on the present shop site. As with other quality booksellers, it was possible to treat the shop as a club, read newspapers there in front of a fire, leaving servants on the benches outside. It was here, in 1804, that the inaugural meeting of what became the Royal Horticultural Society was held. Hatchard is described in the *Dictionary of National Biography* as a publisher: his output included the publications of the Society for Bettering the Condition of the Poor and a newspaper entitled the *Christian Observer*.

Women, until the development of Bond Street, still went into the City for clothes, otherwise to Covent Garden or the Strand where the New Exchange, defeated in its bid to entice away City merchants from the Royal Exchange, traded instead in gloves, fabrics, ribbons and stockings. Also in the Strand was Exeter Change, on the north side where Exeter Street now marks its position. This had, remarkably, a number of toy shops. Southey described it as:

> precisely a Bazaar, a sort of street under cover, or large long room, with a row of shops on either hand, and a thoroughfare between them; the shops being furnished with such articles as might tempt an idler, or remind a passenger of his wants – walking-sticks, implements for shaving, knives, scissors, watch-chains, purses etc.

In effect, an arcade, but instead of being at right angles to the pavement a section of it actually ran parallel and was part of the street. Exeter Change had another unusual feature – a menagerie. In 1793 the stock of a dealer in wild animals and birds was taken over and

Exeter change in the Strand, by Thomas Shepherd, 1829. Exeter Change, built about 1676 on the site of Exeter House, extended over the Strand footpath as well. Mostly consisting of drapers and hosiers, its most famous occupant was the menagerie owned by Edward Cross.

displayed together with human freaks. In the 1820s Cross's Menagerie here was one of the sights of London, for it contained an elephant which went mad in 1826 from its confinement, and had to be shot by soldiers who needed over one hundred rounds to do so.

By the mid-century Bond Street had turned fashionable shopping into an occupation. A German visitor remarked:

> Here elegant ladies appear in different costumes for every hour of the day, changing them as simple folk do for the different seasons, displaying the latest creation of the restless world of fashion, buying and paying for everything twice and three times as much as would be charged in other parts of London. Everything must be bought in the shops of this renowned street if it is to find favour with refined taste.

Another remarked, describing a shoemaker's premises in Bond Street and the high cost of such an address of consequence:

> One is taken into a boudoir, elegantly equipped with a divan, fine lamps and silk curtains. The 'artist' here would not dream of touching a foot unless it had just stepped from an elegant carriage. The result is that each 'piece of art' costs two guineas. Such is the way of the world.

At Schomberg House, a mansion in Pall Mall, Harding, Howell and Company opened what might be described as a department store in 1796. There were five sections in different rooms containing, according to Ackermann's *Repository of the Arts* (1809), 'articles of haberdashery of every description, silks, muslings, lace, gloves etc', and there was also a restaurant.

The front of Schomberg House, Pall Mall, c.1850; watercolour by Thomas Shepherd. This house was reconstructed for the Duke of Schomberg in 1698, but was divided into three in 1769. A dubious Temple of Hymen operated here in 1779.

Oxford Street did not become a shopping street until much later in the eighteenth century and even then its retail history is more properly that of later times. In part this was due to it being an outer border to London until the Cavendish-Harley estate was developed; but it had also been the road to Tyburn gallows at what is now Marble Arch, and its route was associated in the public mind with those melancholy and noisy occasions. Oxford Street was not, therefore, a place where polite society would shop. Thomas Pennant, who was born in 1726, reminisces in his *London* (1790):

> I remember Oxford Street a deep hollow road, and full of sloughs; with here and there a ragged house, the lurking place of cut-throats; insomuch that I never was taken that way by night, in my hackney coach, to a worthy uncle's, who gave me lodgings in his house in George Street, but I went in dread the whole way.

Samuel Johnson's biographer, James Boswell, had a meal here in 1763 at Chapman's Eating House when the road still had a bad reputation and, in 1776, seven years before the last execution took place at Tyburn, the Earl of Malmesbury noted that a large house, opposite Stratford Place, was the last, or nearly the last, of any decent size in the street. Work on the Cavendish-Harley estate had begun in about 1717 but languished once the financial effects of the South Sea Bubble catastrophe had taken their toll. Building began again in earnest about 1770 and by the end of the century the grid pattern of St Marylebone extended to the New Road, and on its southern boundary Oxford Street was built up from one end to the other.

No 'good' or 'bad' end of Oxford Street may be discerned from a list of retail outlets taken from a 1793 directory – a jumble of businesses is characteristic of the whole street. Shoemakers and haberdashers, china shops, cheesemongers and upholsterers, stove

*I*NTERIOR *of Harding, Howell's drapery store at Schomberg House, 1809. The company established five shops or departments which sold haberdashery, cloth, jewellery, millinery and dresses. Another section was devoted to small furniture and another to foreign manufactures.*

manufacturers and carpet-sellers mix haphazardly. There are shops which have pretensions: one claims to be baker to the Duke of York, two say they are sadlers to His Majesty, and there is even a bootmaker to the Infanta of Spain, but despite these claims to fame the list does not indicate a carriage trade. Yet the street directory belies the actuality, it seems, for the cosmopolitan Sophie von la Roche, writing in 1786, is enthusiastic about the street and impressed by the crowds:

> *Just imagine, dear children, a street taking half an hour to cover from end to end, with double rows of brightly shining lamps, in the middle of which stands an equally long row of beautifully lacquered coaches and on either side of them there is room for two coaches to pass one another; and the pavement, inlaid with flag-stones, can stand six people deep and allows one to gaze at splendidly lit shop fronts in comfort.*

By the 1820s there was a marked gathering of linen drapers and haberdashers, particularly on the northern side of the street and it was eventually these trades that gave Oxford Street its unique status.

The fashions of the period, the ability of women of all classes to make clothes and the sumptuous draperies demanded by fashion, all contributed to the rise of the multi-shop draper and his successor, the department store. Most important of all were the industrial developments in the north of England and the Midlands which facilitated cloth production by machines in factories – variety and cheapness were a consequence and so too was the transformation of the East End of London where traditional weavers, undercut and much slower, were superseded by ill-paid workers in the converting and finishing trades. Of the famous Oxford Street names the shop that can claim the earliest origins is Debenham's, which for much of its existence was actually in Wigmore Street. It

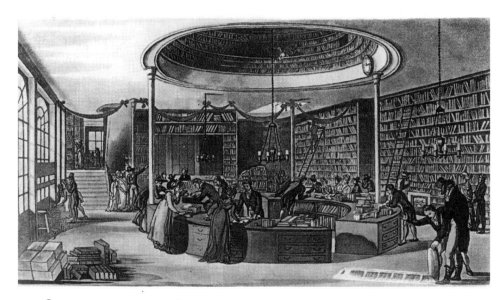

JAMES LACKINGTON'S Temple of the Muses, a spacious bookshop in Finsbury Square, 1809. Lackington was unusual among booksellers in that he established a fixed price for books and would not haggle.

was begun about 1778 by William Franks just as the building of the Cavendish and Portland estates was proceeding apace. By the 1790s the business had passed into the hands of Thomas Clark and in 1813 William Debenham became a partner.

While the mistress of the house might patronize the haberdashers and drapers, the servants were sent off to buy basic foods. A market existed between Haymarket and Lower Regent Street, which served St James's Square; another was just south-west of Bloomsbury Square; Oxford Market, east of Great Portland Street, served the Cavendish Estate and Hanover Square; Shepherd's Market looked after Mayfair and Newport Market the Leicester Square area. It must have been a perilous existence for some of these market suppliers and, indeed, for many a tradesman, for the eighteenth century was notorious for the credit extracted by the very people who, if they limited their own lifestyle to a small degree, could have afforded prompt payment. We are familiar from numerous novels with the way suppliers were treated and of how they were dismissed as contemptible for pressing their invoices. Defoe declared:

> *I have known a family whose revenue has been some thousands a year pay their butcher and baker and grocer and cheese monger by a hundred pounds at a time and be generally a hundred more in each of their debts. And yet the tradesman have thought it well worth while to trust them, and their pay has, in the end, been very good. . .Yet they do not lose by it neither, for the tradesmen find it in the price, and they take care to make such families pay warmly for their credit in the rate of their goods.*

James Lackington, who opened a luxurious bookshop in the 1790s called The Temple of the Muses in Finsbury Square (the shop was large enough, it was said, for a horse and carriage to be driven around the central sales counter), resolved not to give credit at all, for he had observed that if he did then customers did not pay their bills for at least six months, and he was therefore the poorer for the interest and the cash with which to buy new stock:

> *When I communicated my ideas on this subject to some of my acquaintances I was much laughed at and ridiculed. It was thought I might as well attempt to re-build the Tower of Babel as to establish a large business without giving credit.*

Lackington was in a minority. He was also unusual in that he marked all his books at the lowest price he would accept for them, whereas haggling was still the accepted way of buying and selling anything. He was not the pioneer in this. We learn from the autobiography of the co-operative pioneer, Robert Owen, that the shop where he was apprentice, Flint and Palmer's haberdasher's and draper's on London Bridge, was the first:

> *It was a house established, and I believe the first, to sell at small profit and for ready money only. . .Not much time was allowed for bargaining, a price being fixed for everything and, compared with other houses, cheap. If any demur was made or much hesitation, the article asked for was withdrawn, and as the shop was generally full from morning till late in the evening, another customer was attended to.*

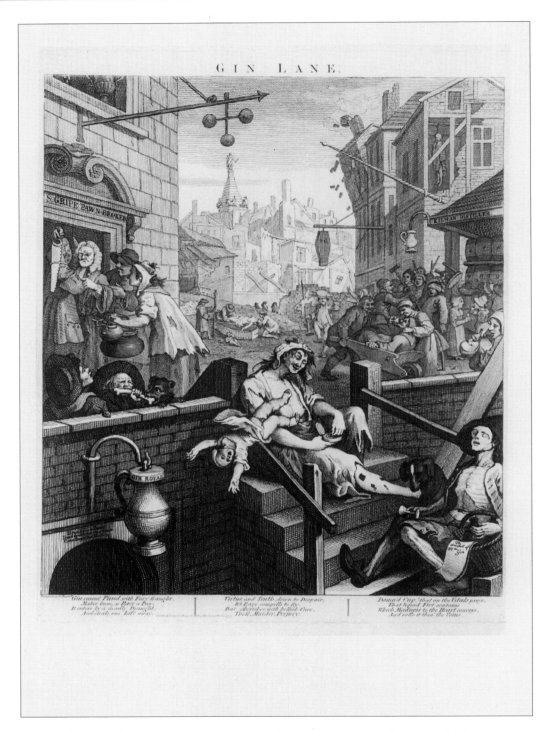

GIN Lane *by William Hogarth, 1751. Hogarth was of modest origins but he married Jane,*
the daughter of the eminent painter, Sir James Thornhill. His satirical depictions of London
life in the 1740s and 1750s are unforgettable images. Here, Hogarth vents his anger against
those who allowed the gin distillers to trade without restraint.

CHAPTER XII

A TROUBLED MULTITUDE

The Gin Epidemic

IT WAS AN OPTIMISTIC DANIEL DEFOE WHO IN 1713 EXTOLLED THE ADVANTAGES OF distilling the country's corn surplus into gin:

Nothing is more certain than that the ordinary produce of corn in England is much greater than the numbers of our people or cattle can consume. The distilling trade is one remedy for this disaster as it helps to carry off the great quantity of corn in such a time of plenty.

Furthermore, he went on with conviction:

It has this particular advantage, that if at any time a scarcity happens, this trade can halt for a year and not be lost entirely as in other trades it often happens.

Defoe was writing before the gin epidemic so absorbed London; by 1728 he was lamenting that:

Our common people get so drunk on a Sunday they cannot work of a Day or two following. Nay, since the use of Geneva has become so common many get so often drunk they cannot work at all, but run from one irregularity to another, till at last they become arrant rogues.

In 1751 the House of Commons was informed that the loss of children to the capital, either by ill-health due to the drinking of spirits by their mothers or themselves, or from the lower birth-rate that had occurred as a result of the dissolute habits of the lower classes, was over 9,000. By that time there was said to be one spirit-selling house in every fifteen houses in the City, one in every eight in Westminster, one in every five in Holborn and more than one in four in St Giles-in-the-Fields, and more than half of the grain sold in London was converted into alcohol. The retailing figures did not take into account the numerous vendors who sold gin in the streets off wheelbarrows. Two years later, physician and novelist Tobias Smollett revealed that conditions were hardly different in the London suburbs:

The suburbs of the metropolis abounded with an incredible number of publick houses, which continually resounded with the noise of riot and intemperance; they were the haunts of idleness, fraud, and rapine, and the seminaries of drunkenness, debauchery, and extravagance, and every vice incident to human nature.

The drink's name is derived from the French *genièvre*, meaning juniper, a plant whose berries were used by compound distillers to flavour the raw spirit supplied by the large distilling companies; in London it was known as geneva and then as gin. The drinking of spirits had become widespread in mid-seventeenth-century Europe and in London by then a large number of outlets and public houses were beginning to sell brandy. The political economist, Charles Davenant, in an essay which urged that excise duties was the proper way to sustain the government in the event of a long war, remarked that drinking brandy and 'strong waters' was 'a growing vice among the common people, and may in time prevail as much as opium with the turks, to which many attribute the scarcity of people in the East.'

The eighteenth-century phenomenon of dram-shops and gin-shops was the result of a number of factors. One was government encouragement to retailers of spirits outside the

Dram drinkers. The ease with which gin could be purchased, and its cheapness, changed London from a city of brandy, ale and wine drinkers into one overcrowded with cheap gin distillers. Gin was drunk from morning to night and was sometimes given instead of wages.

licensing structure that pertained to alehouses and taverns – it was the easiest thing in the world for any chandler, oilman or grocer to make up his own brand of spirits. Secondly, gin was cheap to make and cheap to buy, and therefore inexpensive, to get drunk on. Thirdly, the desperation of the day, the unremitting poverty that many in London encountered, made oblivion brought on by cheap gin the more desirable.

All this did not escape the notice of the magistrates who dealt with the sometimes tragic consequences of this growing obsession, but the cynical disregard and self-serving of the government allowed it to continue. While the Middlesex magistrates in 1721 roundly condemned the retailing of gin in shops as causing 'more mischief and inconveniences to this town [London] than all the other public houses joined together', the landowners' lobby in Parliament saw off any preventive measures. Those concerned about the epidemic were a mixed bag. They included social reformers such as Hogarth, whose *Gin Lane* print is synonymous with the period and the social conditions, the increasingly influential (and temperance minded) Methodists, the keepers of alehouses and taverns whose legitimate trade suffered, and the Excise Office, which raised relatively little money from the sales of gin because many of the outlets were informal and not registered for excise payment.

Official discouragement of gin retailing was slow to mature. An Act which imposed an excise duty of £20 on retailers was widely ignored and repealed at the instance of the landowning lobby, in 1733. In 1736 the government imposed a remarkable duty of a pound on each gallon sold and an annual licence fee of £50, but this was a travesty since in seven years only three licences were taken out while sales of gin still increased and neither the government or the hard-pressed Middlesex magistrates were able to do anything about it. An Act of 1743 finally recognized the reality of the situation and sought

*T*HE *Foundling Hospital, Guilford Street. The hospital was founded in 1742, the fruition of persistent efforts by Captain Thomas Coram to rescue unwanted babies and children from the streets. The view shows the hospital's second home in the fields of Bloomsbury.*

to channel the selling of gin into established public houses; gradually the duty on spirits was increased so as to make them prohibitive to drink in excess and in 1751 another Act was instrumental in gradually ending the epidemic.

Eighteenth-century Charity

In all this destitution, recklessness and lack of responsibility, children and infants were frequent victims. Many were left uncared for while their parents succumbed to stupor; others were abandoned on purpose rather than on whim, some murdered, others left home of their own accord in search of food. No well-meaning authority made it its business to pick up the unfortunates and no one kept count of the infanticides. It was a society brutalized not only by this and many other extravagances of human behaviour, but one which, unlike the Victorians, thought that solutions could not be imposed.

The parish authorities paid reluctant and inadequate attention to the numbers of abandoned children, and the Church was preoccupied at the time with building some rather fine churches in London. It was left to a former sea-captain to campaign for the infants. Thomas Coram (1668-1751) had retired about 1719 from a lifetime at sea and a passion for shipbuilding and colonial development, to live at Rotherhithe. The sight of abandoned babies by the roadside was distressing enough to him, but the waste of resources to one who wanted to people the colonies with English stock was also shocking. He may well have read Addison's article in the *Guardian* in 1713 in which the author urged a

> *provision for foundlings, or for those children who, through want of such a provision, are exposed to the barbarity of cruel and unnatural parents. One does not know how to speak on such a subject without horror; but what multitude of infants have been made away with by those who brought them into the world and were afterwards either ashamed, or unable to provide for them!*

Addison here, of course, was referring to children born to poor women out of wedlock. The plight of such women was emphasized by a later historian of the Foundling Hospital: 'Neither she nor the offspring of her guilt appear to have been admitted within the pale of human compassion; her false step was her final doom, without even the chance, however desirous, of returning to the road of rectitude.' If they were not abandoned in the streets, unwanted children were simply starved or farmed out to wet-nurses, which amounted to the same thing mostly. A Dr Cadogan, writing in 1750, remarked that 'the ancient Custom of exposing them to Wild Beasts or drowning them would certainly be a much quicker way of dispatching them' than the lingering deaths they had in the eighteenth century at the hands of nurses. Certainly there was infanticide: 10 per cent of the women hanged at Tyburn during this period (including one that already had ten children) were found guilty of that offence.

Though the problem of illegitimate children worsened as the gin epidemic took hold, Coram's petition to King George II in 1737 discreetly avoided mentioning it and concentrated on the plight of those children abandoned, neglected or abused by parents or wet-nurses. On 'Innocents' Day' that year the captain attended St James's Palace to present a similar petition to the Princess Amelia but, as Coram noted, the Lady-in-waiting, Lady Isabella Finch, 'gave me very rough words, and bid me begone with my Petition, which I did, without presenting it.'

Despite Lady Isabella's only claim to fame, Coram's Foundling Hospital received its Royal Charter in 1739 at a gathering which included six dukes, eleven earls, numerous other landowners, City worthies and William Hogarth: the seventy-year-old sea captain, still fit enough to walk ten or twelve miles a day, had carried through his obsession.

The Hospital opened in a house in Hatton Garden in March 1741. Of the 136 children received in the first year, 56 died – a rather better survival rate than in central London workhouses. Though Coram's enterprise was generally welcomed, the governors received a representation from the Vestry of St Andrew's, Holborn, in whose parish the Hospital stood, complaining that mothers who had had their child refused by the Hospital officers for whatever reason had often just abandoned it in the locality instead. This meant, under the Poor Law, that St Andrew's became responsible not just for the care of the infant until it either died or grew up to employable age, but liable for any future costs of workhouse accommodation should he or she fall again on hard times.

Minutes of the Hospital for 1741 are a strong comment on the times:

> *The Expressions of Grief of the Women whose Children could not be admitted were Scarcely more observable than those of some of the Women who parted with their Children...*
>
> *All the Children who were received (Except Three) were dressed very clean from whence and other Circumstances they appeared not to have been under the care of Parish officers, nevertheless many of them appeared as if Stupifyed with some Opiate, and some of them almost Starved, One as in the Agonies of Death thro' want of Food, too weak to Suck, or to receive Nourishment.*

The Foundling Hospital soon looked for expansion and at about the same time as the opening in Hatton Garden 56 acres were bought north of Lamb's Conduit Street. It was a rather isolated spot, open to countryside on three sides and with a burial ground just to the north of it; furthermore, if the Hospital wished to develop its surplus land, there were difficulties about access. The residents of Queen Square and Great Ormond Street were hostile to development anyway. Acclimatized to their uninterrupted views of Highgate and Hampstead, it was inevitable that they should protest and suggest that building on the Foundling Estate would take away the fresh air that the children required. As a result of these problems early development on the estate was slow and of indifferent quality, consisting for the most part of terraces along what became Guilford Street. It was not until the nineteenth century that the grander Brunswick and Mecklenburgh Squares were built.

The Hospital became a fashionable cause, taken up by nobility whose names – Bedford, Richmond and Pembroke – were given to previously unidentified children at their christenings. Other heroes' names were chosen: there are people today who have surnames such as Chaucer, Shakespeare, Bacon, Drake, Cromwell and Hogarth, and who derive them not from famous ancestors but from these hastily arranged ceremonies at the Foundling Hospital. Handel donated an organ to the Chapel and, giving performances there of his *Messiah*, he raised some £7,000 for the Hospital. Hogarth presented a handsome portrait of Coram and it became the custom for other artists to donate pictures, so that on certain days of the year the courtroom of the Hospital was thrown open as an art gallery. The first register of governors is a roll-call of London aristocracy supplemented by such luminaries as Thomas Archer the architect, politician John Hampden and Hogarth.

While Society appeared on decorous occasions, it was sometimes rather a scrum for those who had come to abandon children. Even by 1742 in the old house in Hatton Garden, the original method of first-come first-served had to be jettisoned because of unruly scenes. Instituted instead was a lottery of drawing coloured balls, but in 1756 a bizarre system was introduced of dropping a basket over the front wall in Guilford Street into which a mother could put her baby (two months was supposed to be the maximum age). On the first day 117 babies were deposited and by the end of the first month there were 425. This was, of course, more than the resources of the Hospital could cope with and a rule was swiftly introduced that children over the age of two months but below two years would also be received if accompanied by the sum of £100. This was no deterrent. Between June and December in 1756, when the new rule was in force, 1,783 children were admitted. Of nearly 15,000 children received in the first forty-six months of indiscriminate admission nearly two-thirds died in infancy, and it became clear that the open heartedness of the Hospital was being abused and that workhouse officers in London and the provinces were dumping unwanted and probably sickly children into its hands. A woman who lived three hundred miles away from London wrote:

> There is set up in our corporation a new and uncommon trade, namely, the conveying of children to the Foundling Hospital. The person employed in this trade is a woman of notoriously bad character. She undertakes the carrying of these children at so much a head. She has, I am told, made one trip already; and is now set upon her journey with two of her daughters, each with a child on her back.

An historian of the Hospital noted an incident in which a man accosted at Highgate had four children in panniers which he was taking from Yorkshire to the Hospital.

Jonas Hanway, a reformer and strong supporter of the Hospital (but better remembered for his popularization of the umbrella), also had his scheme for rescuing young boys. In 1756 he founded the Marine Society, which had two aims: the training of young boys for naval service and, as a consequence, the end of press-ganging. This organization often found its charitable aims thwarted in peace-time when the demand for seamen, especially ill-trained boys, reduced dramatically, but the description of their advertisements attracting 'three hundred friendless boys and distressed boys who flocked from brickfields, bulks, coal-wharfs, glass-houses and other places of shelter' indicates the sorry deficiencies of the time.

The endeavours of Coram and Hanway are the best-known charities of the period, but there were other, smaller, ventures such as the Orphan Working School, founded in 1758 by fourteen men whose intention was not so much the education of poor orphans but the teaching of a trade. For eight hours a day they learned shoemaking, or made netting, and only after several years at the school were they taught reading and religion. Sir John Fielding, the Bow Street magistrate, was instrumental in founding the Orphan Asylum for Deserted Girls which took girls who might otherwise be forced into prostitution. He revealed in a report that on a typical night when the constables arrested about forty prostitutes, most of them were under eighteen and some as young as twelve. Sir John's Asylum was but a minor impediment to the vast increase in prostitution which was to continue well into the nineteenth century. Relatively dormant since the halcyon days of the South Bank, prostitution surfaced again in Southwark when the Astley circus brought crowds to St George's Fields. By then the parish authorities both there and elsewhere had given up the unequal struggle to suppress it, but a 1751 law which enabled two parishioners to submit evidence and receive £10 each as a reward, provided a good income for those who took the pursuit seriously.

Chimney-sweep climbing boys became a celebrated cause of Hanway's. Generally these unfortunate children were supplied as 'apprentices' by parish authorities, keen to be rid of their upkeep. Hanway was appalled by this and the lack of washing the children got, and the few clothes they were given. He said, indignantly, that 'Chimney-sweepers ought to breed their own children to the business, then perhaps they will wash, clothe and feed them. As it is, they do neither, and these poor black urchins have no protectors and are

*B*OY *crossing-sweepers illustrated in Henry Mayhew's* London Labour and the London Poor.
The crossing-sweepers, whose function was to sweep away mud, dust and horse dung from
roads at usual crossing points, were often homeless and parentless children. Although very
poor indeed, they escaped the more awful life led by chimney-sweep boys.

treated worse than a humane person would treat a dog. . .' A Parliamentary committee in
1788 was informed of boys as young as four being bound to chimney-sweep masters, of
boys who had not washed for four or five years, and of masters who took far more boys
than they needed so that the surplus could beg in the streets.

Only a fraction of those in trouble were scooped up in charitable nets. For the rest they
lived rough, either working at menial tasks or else resorting to petty crime; when it
was absolutely necessary the parish took the youngest into workhouses and hoped to
extract some labour from them. A grim story in a newspaper report of 1784 told the
story of lodgers in a slum house near Fleet Market who burst open the door of an upstairs room and there found the putrefying corpse of a woman in bed, and four children
naked and almost starved to death, three of them so weak from want of food they could
not stand. The eldest boy, who could just speak, said that their mother had died some
days before and that their father left them soon after. The children were removed to
the workhouse, there to take their chances. Resort to the workhouse seems to have been
the last option on both sides – the poor were as reluctant to enter as the masters were to
have them there.

THE 'TIME OF TERROR'

A S THE CENTURY PROGRESSED the stability of working-class society in London became
ever more fragile. There were highpoints of social unrest, bad enough for the
authorities to fear revolution. Some stemmed from poverty, others from religious beliefs.
After Dr Henry Sacheverell preached sermons in London in 1709-10 berating tolerance
of non-conformists, his arrest and trial excited riots in his support. The 1780 riots,
whipped up by Lord George Gordon in London at the passing of the Roman Catholic
Relief Act, were very serious indeed. A Catholic chapel at Moorfields was gutted, the Bow

Street magistrate's court was attacked, Newgate and Clink prisons were destroyed and the prisoners released, as they were at the Fleet. During this 'time of terror' over 450 people were killed or wounded, a figure excluding the 35 executed for their part in the carnage.

There were political riots in 1715 when Jacobites gathered in Snow Hill and drank loyal toasts to the late James II and stripped any passers-by who refused to join in. In the 1760s and 1770s London witnessed many demonstrations and riots in support of John Wilkes, banned from his seat in Parliament and threatened with prison for an alleged libel against the King. The weavers of Spitalfields, including many Huguenots, were a constant threat to the parish authorities during the eighteenth century. In 1719 four thousand of them paraded through the City attacking women wearing Indian calicoes and linens the import of which, they said, was ruining their livelihoods. In 1763 'several thousand' weavers assembled in Spitalfields and proceeded to break up labour-saving looms. Two years later the Duke of Bedford's opposition to the levying of increased customs duties on imported silks was the cause of an attack on his house in Bloomsbury Square: the weavers were to celebrate the banning of such imports in 1766 but it was a respite only, because their livelihoods were gradually obliterated altogether by the increasing use of machinery. When they rioted again in 1769 and destroyed 150 looms their ringleaders were hanged at Bethnal Green.

THE BEGINNINGS OF THE POLICE

THE PRESERVATION OF PUBLIC ORDER on such occasions was a cumbersome matter – no police force existed and troops had to be called in if things got out of control. It was Thomas de Veil, son of a Huguenot cleric, who unwittingly set in motion the events which led to the foundation of the Metropolitan Police in 1829. De Veil was a 'trading justice', though more honest than most in the sense that he took only enough bribes, it is said, to keep him and his office going. De Veil made himself unpopular in the early days of his magisterial career when he was active in the censorship of a satire by the young Henry Fielding .

The government itself took charge of the opening night and de Veil, with a copy of the Riot Act in his pocket as a last resort, and some Grenadier Guards on stage to keep order, was met by a storm of abuse from the spectators. 'Missiles were hurled about the theatre' and, outside, the mob attacked the coaches of some of the audience while the parish watchmen and constables discreetly kept their distance. De Veil also supported heavy-handed government measures regulating the sale of gin, which so enraged the population that a mob besieged his former residence in Frith Street to protest against them and him.

However, de Veil did set up a magistrate's office when he moved to Bow Street in 1739. This became renowned for its efficiency and comparative honesty and it was this that ironically Henry Fielding was appointed to in 1748, just before completing *Tom Jones*. He was an inappropriate choice on the face of it since he was usually involved in some political controversy, but he took his duties seriously and established Bow Street not only as the most important court in Westminster but in the city as a whole; his work, a twentieth-century historian of the police has remarked, was the 'foundation stone of all subsequent legal and police reform'. Fielding's industry is not in doubt, but much credit should go to his clerk, Joseph Brogden, who was paid out of the income from fines, and Saunders Welch who helped to organize constables while at the same time running a grocery shop in Museum Street.

Fielding created a force of public-spirited constables which took the job of thief-taking seriously. 'Mr Fielding's People' became known as the 'Bow Street Runners'; they wore no uniform and were unpaid other than a share of the rewards for apprehension. This was no mean innovation – the reputation for corruption on the part of parish constables was famous. As recently as 1742, the constables appointed by the parish of St Martin-in-the Fields had been involved in a scandalous affair. Horace Walpole described the events at length:

> There has lately been the most horrible scene of murder imaginable; a party of drunken constables took it into their heads to put the laws in execution against disorderly persons, and so took up every woman they met, until they had collected five or six and twenty, all of whom they thrust into St Martin's Round House, where they kept them all night with doors and windows closed. The poor creatures, who could neither stir nor breathe, screamed as long as they had any breath left, begging at least for water, one poor creature said she was worth eighteen pence and would gladly give it for a draft of water, but in vain! So well did they keep them there that in the morning four were found stifled to death, two died soon after, and a dozen more are in a shocking way. . . ..several of them were beggars, who from having no lodging were necessarily found in the street, and others honest labouring women. One of the dead was a poor washerwoman, big with child, who was returning home late from washing. One of the constables is taken, and others absconded, but I question if any of them will suffer death.

Angry local people tore down the watch house and the chief constable was tried for the murder of the women; he was transported to America and there worked as a slave in the tobacco fields.

John Fielding, Henry Fielding's half-brother, blind since about the age of nineteen, succeeded him after his death and was in charge of Bow Street from 1754 to 1779. In 1762 he published a plan for the comprehensive policing of the metropolis which anticipated the creation of the Metropolitan Police by over fifty years, and spent his long years as magistrate conscientiously trying to rid London of some of its evils. Fielding was particularly keen on public street-lighting so as to make darkness safer, and appears to have been the first to suggest that lamps be mounted on posts on the footway, rather than attached to houses. His horse and foot patrols in Westminster were copied by many London parishes, such as Hampstead, Camberwell and Stoke Newington, who obtained their own Acts of Parliament permitting them to raise a local rate to pay for lighting and foot guards to improve safety.

John Fielding presided at Bow Street at a time of an alarming increase in crime. Robbery, and in particular highway robbery, seemed the inevitable fate of anyone foolish enough to venture into rougher areas or to travel unarmed across the heathlands outside London. The Lord Mayor himself was robbed in 1776, in his own chaise and in sight of his retinue, in Chiswick by a single highwayman.

Public Executions

Henry fielding, though dedicated to catching rogues, inveighed against the barbaric spectacle of Tyburn. The executions there, he contended, did not reform those with criminal tendencies but only provided public entertainment. And yet he thought that *public* executions were preferred by the victims themselves. In his *Inquiry into the Late Increase of Robbers* he remarked:

> The day appointed by law for the thief's shame is the day of glory in his own opinion. His procession to Tyburn and his last moments there are all triumphant; attended with the compassion of the weak and tender hearted, and with the applause, admiration and envy of all the bold and hardened. His behaviour in his present condition, not the crimes, how atrocious soever, which brought him to it, is the subject of contemplation. And if he hath sense enough to temper his boldness with any degree of decency, his death is spoken of by many with honour, by most with pity, and by all with approbation.

Bernard Mandeville, who published a pamphlet on Tyburn hangings in 1725, was also sceptical of the deterrent value of Tyburn executions. They were occasions so ribald and commonplace, he complained, that the poor believed that there was nothing to a hanging but 'an awry neck and a wet pair of breeches.' The hangings, or 'legal massacres' as Dr Johnson called them, took place about every six weeks and were mainly festive occasions beginning at Newgate prison in the City and ending at Tyburn gallows just north of today's Marble Arch. Around the gallows the paraphernalia of public events was present – food and drink stalls, entertainers and broadsheet sellers. A special stand, called Mother Proctor's Pews, was erected and was said to be one of the most valuable properties in the neighbourhood – £500 was taken for seats at the execution of Earl Ferrers in 1760. Criminals, officials and public all took part in expected customs and rituals. The prisoner was permitted to spend the few days between sentence and execution in a state of intoxication if he wished and he could see as many friends and visitors as the turnkey would take money from. The famous Jack Sheppard, hero of spectacular escapes if not crimes, made his gaolers a good deal of money as numerous people wanted to see him in his last confinement. His visitors included James Figg, the prize-fighter, who supplied Sheppard and his guardians with drinks en route to Tyburn, and court painter Sir James Thornhill who painted a portrait of him in his cell. On the eve of execution day a bell was rung at nearby St Sepulchre's, courtesy of an old bequest, and the last sacrament was offered at Newgate by a chaplain anxious to incorporate any last confessions or words, either actual or purported, in a pamphlet for sale on the streets, especially if the prisoner had some notoriety. One such amanuensis, on a salary of £180, left an estate of over £5,000.

Most prisoners were conveyed in open carts along Holborn and then Oxford Street where the dreaded gallows at the western end at the junction with the 'road to Edgware' would have been visible long before they were reached. But it was possible, if the money was right, to choose a different conveyance. Earl Ferrers, hanged in 1760 for the murder of his steward (he was the last peer to be hanged for crime in England) used his own landau drawn by six horses from, in his case, the Tower to Tyburn; he wore a suit of light clothes embroidered with silver for the occasion. On the other hand, Jenny Diver, a notorious pickpocket who had returned illegally from transportation, went to the gallows in a 'mourning coach veiled and strongly guarded, there being a design formed to rescue her.' James Boswell, who enjoyed executions, travelled in the mourning coach of a clergyman sentenced to death for the murder of the woman he loved.

Tyburn gallows consisted of three posts, eighteen feet high, placed in a triangular fashion and connected by long cross beams, each capable of accommodating eight victims. At first, before the business of hanging became more sophisticated with drop platforms, the prisoner might be invited to climb a ladder, put his head in a noose which was then tightened, and then jump off the ladder of his own accord; failing that he would be pushed or 'turned off'. Another common method was for the victim to stand on the tail of a cart with his head in a noose and then the horses would be lashed forward to leave the poor man hanging. Death was not necessarily instantaneous and there are many accounts of the hangman or friends hanging on to the feet of a victim to hasten death. Hangmen were notoriously unpopular, drunk or incompetent, though they needed their wits about them to commandeer and barter the body and its clothes afterwards to the highest bidders; they were household names if they retained the position for any length of time but they were often styled 'Jack Ketch' after the seventeenth-century hangman who executed many followers of the Duke of Monmouth. In 1752 there were angry scenes when the relatives of John Thrift, a former executioner, attempted to have his body buried in the churchyard of St Paul's Covent Garden, and it was only towards the evening that they were able to do so. Calcraft, who was hangman for forty-five years in the nineteenth century, was consistently inefficient, to the distress of the crowd, not to say victims; many reports have him hanging on to the shoulders of the prisoner so as to quicken the strangulation which his own miscalculation had prolonged.

The hanging of women was even more ghoulish since, at least in the case of murder, it was often required that they first be strangled and then burnt. Catherine Hayes, strangled at Tyburn in 1726 for the murder of her husband, was still conscious when left to the flames because the executioner mismanaged the affair. A similar fate befell Mary Herring in 1773 and it was not until 1788 that the last woman – Margaret Sullivan, whose crime had been to colour copper coin so that it appeared to be silver – was dealt with in this fashion. The hanging of women drew in the crowds – enormous numbers gathered to watch, with much satisfaction, the execution of Mrs Elizabeth Brownrigg in 1767, found guilty of the murder of one of her apprentice girls, and in the following year Sarah Meteyard and her daughter (the latter unconscious) were on the scaffold for the death, by starvation and beating, of an apprentice girl in their milliner's shop in Bruton Street.

The death sentence was exacted, it seems, for almost any crime from murder to familiarity with gypsies. The Waltham Black Act of 1722, intended as a temporary measure to stem the tide of criminal activity, made numerous petty crimes liable to capital punishment, so that eventually more than two hundred offences were included. Many people were indeed hanged for trivial matters but it seems that juries quite often acquitted minor offenders because of the harshness of the law or else transportation was ordered rather than execution. Pardons were common, so that by 1810, when Samuel Romilly published a book on the criminal law in England, he was able to reveal that of the 1,872 people sent to Newgate between 1803 and 1810 for larceny in either a shop or residence, only one was eventually executed.

In 1817, the artist George Cruikshank, moved by the execution of a woman for passing a forged pound note, began his own campaign to have the laws relaxed – no other crime, except for murder, resulted in so many executions as forgery. In 1830, even Sir Robert Peel had to confess that:

It is impossible to conceal from ourselves that capital punishments are more frequent and the criminal law more severe on the whole in this country than in any country in the world.

PRISONS

Aconsequence of this obsession with execution for virtually any offence was that prisons were not, in the eighteenth century, usually instruments of punishment. A large number of debtors were incarcerated for years at a time, particularly in City and Southwark prisons, as an encouragement to pay off their creditors, but the prisons were

Newgate prison by Thomas Shepherd, 1829. Newgate was one of the oldest of London's prisons, having been established in the gatehouse by the 12th century. By 1724 it was 'a terrible stinking dark' place. A new building in 1778 was destroyed by the Gordon Rioters.

informal and convivial compared with the 'improved' gaols devised by well-intentioned Victorians. Families often lodged with the prisoners, together with pets and livestock, so that it was possible for children to know no other home. One man, Joseph Bernardi, who was gaoled at Newgate in 1689 for political offences, died there forty-seven years later, during which time his wife bore him ten children. There is clear evidence that the debtor prisons, in which inmates could be held for many years, were substantially run by the prisoners themselves with the tacit approval of bribed turnkeys. At the same time the London gaols were notoriously crowded, brutal, corrupt and unhygienic – conditions that could not have been unknown to either the City Corporation or the government. As early as 1691 Moses Pitt had published his revelations of the Fleet Prison, while incarcerated there for debt, in *The Cry of the Oppressed*. In 1719 Newgate Prison was described as a 'place of calamity' and a 'habitation of misery': the authorities were to pay for their neglect because in 1750 gaol fever swept the prison and in its wake took the lives of over fifty dignitaries and officials at the Old Bailey. This incident gave rise not to improvement, but to a custom for judges to carry posies in front of them at Sessions in the hope that they would ward off infection an affectation still paraded on today in May and September.

A Parliamentary Committee in 1726 found gross extortion and corruption at the Fleet (the management of which was farmed out by the City). The warden refused to surrender the bodies of deceased prisoners without payment and inmates unable to line his pockets were treated infamously. One Jacob Solas, a Portuguese, was kept in irons for two months in a room above the common sewer, adjoining a refuse heap. When he was released from this hole he was in bad mental shape:

> Though his chains were taken off, his terror still remained, and the unhappy man was prevailed upon by that terror not only to labour gratis for the deputy, but to swear also at random all that he hath required of him.

It was found that many prisoners were able to live outside the walls of the prison provided that they had paid the appropriate sum to the warden.

Clerkenwell House of Detention, off Clerkenwell Green, was described as 'a great brothel, kept under the protection of the law for the emolument of its ministers'; the Fleet Prison was thought to be the largest brothel in London, since not only were prostitutes allowed access but women prisoners, facing execution, courted pregnancy in the hope that this would bring commutation. In 1728 the Marshalsea prison in Southwark was contracted out to a local butcher who, in an attempt to retrieve the £400 fee he paid to the authorities, went to inordinate lengths to make a profit out of the running of it:

> To raise this rent oppression, extortion, cruelty and even torture were exercised, the prisoners being kept in close, crowded rooms, from thirty to fifty being placed in an apartment not sixteen feet square, and three persons being allotted to each bed, each paying 2s 6d per week.

The tendency of courts to sentence prisoners to transportation rather than execution (in the late 1760s the courts sentenced 70 per cent of prisoners to transportation) was an embarrassment to the authorities in 1776 when the American War of Independence prevented its implementation. Prisoners were therefore housed in hulks lying in the Thames and from these fetid ships went out each day to do hard labour on public works. It was not until 1787 that the first convicts were sent off to Australia, there to work in unbearable conditions.

The end of the eighteenth century and the early part of the nineteenth century witnessed attempts to 'reform' as well as to punish prisoners. In 1794 building began on the Coldbath Fields Prison for the county of Middlesex, on the site of today's Mount Pleasant Post Office. At first it resembled in its operation the very worst of City prisons:

> Men, women, and boys were indiscriminately herded together in this chief county prison, without employment or wholesome control; while smoking gaming, singing, and every species of brutalizing conversation, tended to the unlimited advancement of crime and pollution.

An inmate complained that:

> *These charitable dungeons, founded for the reformation of the vicious, are composed of bricks and stones, without fire or any furniture but straw, and no other barrier against the weather than iron grates.*

Gradually the nature of this prison changed so that it functioned, with the approval of prison reformers such as Jeremy Bentham and John Howard, in a way that kept prisoners isolated and, above all, silent:

> *All had to work for ten hours daily. For the first month or so they worked in solitude; afterwards they laboured twenty or thirty together, but were not allowed to speak to each other. The ordinary employment was oakum picking, but skilled hands are employed in matmaking, shoemaking, carpentry and joinery.*

The Millbank Penitentiary 1827. Millbank Prison, roughly on the site of today's Tate Gallery, was a very large building, its blocks radiating like wheel spokes from a central observation block. In theory it was possible to keep watch on all prisoners with the least effort of manpower.

The first major experiment in prison reform took place in the Millbank Penitentiary, a giant fortress of a building opened in 1816 on the site of today's Tate Gallery. It was built, in theory, on principles laid down by Bentham. Remorselessly unattractive blocks stretched out like wheel spokes from a central observation tower, and these were surrounded by a high octagonal-shaped wall and a moat. The policy of separating the prisoners in silence, combined with heavy doses of religion, sent many of the inmates mad but the Rev. Daniel Nihil, appointed as chaplain-governor in 1837, was even more zealous in these matters and thought that the previous regime had been too lax. It was revealed that under Nihil's administration three girls, two of them aged ten and a third aged seven, had been kept in solitary confinement for twelve months with the prospect of two more years.

Millbank was a failure both as an institution and a building and it was supplanted by

Pentonville 'Model Prison' in Islington, which opened in 1842. Here indeed was a prison which met the ambitions of reformers and salved the consciences of the élite. The monotonous regime of the prisoners, as detailed by Henry Mayhew, was regarded as conducive to reform. Solitary confinement was at first compulsory for eighteen months, until it was realized that insanity could result. Work on six days of the week began at six in the morning and continued for 8½ hours punctuated by solitary meals, exercise and worship; for the visit to the chapel the inmates were obliged to wear masks so that neither they nor their friends could be recognizable and they were, in any case, put into separate boxed pews precluding contact with others. These masks were also worn during exercise. Mayhew described this mask, basically a cap pulled down, with eye holes, as like 'the outward vestment to some wandering soul rather than that of a human being; for the eyes, glistening through the apertures in the mask, give one the notion of a spirit peeping out behind it.' These victims of good intentions were allowed one visitor each six months and the one letter they were permitted to write and receive in the same time had to meet certain standards:

> *All letters of an improper or idle tendency either to or from convicts or containing slang or objectionable expressions will be suppressed. The permission to write and receive letters is given to the convicts for the purpose of enabling them to keep up a connection with their respectable friends and not that they may hear the news of the day.*

This prohibition on written affection and news sprang logically from the main purpose of Pentonville – the reform and discipline of prisoners before they were sent away, usually for ever, to Australia or other colonies. The Home Secretary just before the opening of the prison spelled it out:

> *I propose therefore, that no prisoners shall be admitted into Pentonville without the knowledge that it is the portal to the penal colony, and without the certainty that he bids adieu to his connections in England, and that he must henceforth look forward to a life of labour in another hemisphere.*

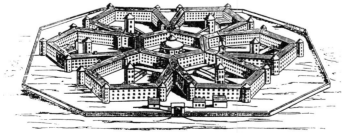

BIRD'S-EYE VIEW OF MILLBANK PRISON.
(Copied from a Model by the Clerk of the Works.)

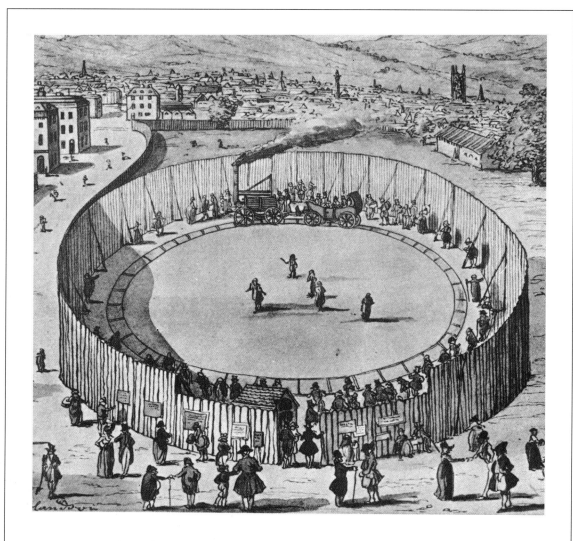

Richard Trevithick's 'Catch-me-if-you-can' demonstration railway at the northern end of Gower Street in 1802. Trevithick, whose work previously had been in the transportation of mining material and in steam carriages, built this circular track which could be described as a first passenger railway long before the establishment of the first proper railway. It was, however, neither a technical or financial success, and he turned to other fields of invention instead, leaving the field clear for George Stephenson. On Trevithick's railway rides were offered at one shilling each in the months of July and August, but the sideshow was spoilt by a rail track which broke, and by an engine which overturned.

CHAPTER XIII

A CITY IN MOTION

I N JULY 1808 PASSERS-BY AT THE NORTHERN END OF GOWER STREET WOULD HAVE NOTICED THE temporary appearance there of a small, circular railway track. On this a Mr Richard Trevithick was exhibiting a steam engine that pulled a diminutive carriage in which, for the price of one shilling, anyone could ride. Those bystanders and those passengers were witnesses to a revolution, but one that took a long time coming. In fact, this premature birth of the railway age went largely unnoticed and, discouraged by technical problems and a poor financial return on his sideshow, Trevithick diverted into other aspects of steam power, leaving railway engines to George Stephenson. It was to be another twenty-eight years before Londoners saw a sequel.

The need for better transportation of both freight and people was met by innovations in the nineteenth century which changed habits, commerce and landscape irrevocably. While London had been entertained since 1784 by the occasional manned balloon flight above its astonished gaze (such flights, like Trevithick's railway, oddly out of sequence in the history of transportation), travel on the ground had hardly improved since medieval times. In the City and in Westminster congestion prevailed and for the most part road surfaces in town and suburbs were both ill-made and perilous. In November 1736 Lord Hervey, in his *Memoirs of the Court of George II*, remarked that the Court at Kensington Palace was isolated from London by 'a great impassable gulf of mud'. As we have seen, the care of the major roads in the earlier part of the eighteenth century was firmly and unwisely in the hands of the parishes and improvement came only when their management was hived off to private turnpike trusts. Even then road surfaces were poor and it was not until the 1820s that the techniques introduced by John McAdam transformed the road traveller's lot. For example, the road which is now Archway Road, blasted through a ridge in 1813 so that an easier way to the north could be made, was at first a financial disappointment. There was not only a reluctance to pay the toll but there was justifiable comment that the road surface was hardly an improvement on the traditional highway that went steeply up to Highgate village.

By the early eighteenth century coaches were more comfortable but, whether they were hackneys in town or stage coaches for longer journeys, the cost of such travel was geared to the economics of keeping a horse and the amount of weight the beast could pull singly

A STAGE *coach, by William Hogarth, 1747. The 'Old Angle Inn' is crowded with life on its open galleries around the courtyard.*

or in harness with others. Travel at speed and in comfort was therefore still beyond the pockets of most and, worse, there were few economies to be gained in travelling a distance – a post chaise journey from London to Manchester could cost over £10. Travelling by the post method, whereby fresh horses were attached at frequent intervals, was by far the fastest form of transport – as the system developed the London to Birmingham time was reduced from eighteen hours to twelve and by 1836 it was possible to travel from London to Bristol in eleven hours, but the cost of this speed was a change of horses every hour, and a horse working-life of only three years.

THE CANALS

LONDONERS' FIRST EXPERIENCE OF BULK INLAND TRANSPORTATION did not affect their own mobility: the canals moved freight, not people. The early canals were built with an assured market and function; they had specific tasks, such as the movement of coal to feed mills, the carriage of bricks so as to turn villages into industrial towns, the bringing in of raw cotton from ports and its return in manufactured form to those same ports for export. Like the railways after them, the canals were a product of and a stimulant to the Industrial Revolution, but sadly for the canals the output of industry could not eventually be satisfied by the speed of waterway transport.

Canals were mostly peripheral to London and were constructed so close to the railway age that they were superfluous before they could significantly impinge on the capital's life and trade. The Grand Junction Canal from the Midlands came initially no nearer than Brentford where, from 1794, its cargoes were off-loaded for transmission on the Thames to the London docks. It was the rapid expansion of those docks in the early part of the nineteenth century that made it necessary and financially attractive to construct a direct canal link to reach them. The West India Docks, the London Docks, the East India Docks, which all opened between 1802 and 1806, transformed the appearance and working lives of the East End, but they were hampered by the lack of a bulk carrying route to the Midlands and the industrial north.

The Grand Junction Canal Company was best placed to exploit the situation since in 1801 it had constructed a branch canal to the village of Paddington, where it built a basin containing a lucrative settlement of wharves and warehouses. To this previously quiet area hundreds of delivery carts converged daily, and then re-emerged along the New Road down to City warehouses or else on to the significantly named Commercial Road which had, in 1803, been constructed to serve the docks. Paddington became a market, its rural nature destroyed, and when the railways eventually intruded their unquiet enterprise into London, the canal basin there was a logical place near which to build a railway terminus.

View of the proposed St Katharine's Docks to the east of the Tower of London, published in The Gentleman's Magazine *in 1826. Designed by Thomas Telford and Philip Hardwick, the docks were erected on a site from which were displaced, over eleven thousand people.*

In 1801 railways were not yet on the horizon and a canal link from Paddington to the London docks was confidently mooted and must have seemed, as the docks expanded, the surest financial investment to be had. As it turned out it was, like Hugh Myddelton's New River in the seventeenth century, a disappointing venture. Also, as it turned out, the project was carried through not by the Grand Junction but by the separate Regent's Canal Company, which obtained its own Act of Parliament.

The route of this waterway from Paddington to Limehouse, called the Regent's Canal, is circuitous. Cutting directly through London was too expensive even then, and would have involved the company in troublesome negotiations with landholders who had more to lose than some hayfields. Furthermore, the essential hinterland of warehouses to handle canal traffic would be difficult to carve out of built-up areas. Fortuitously, Regent's Park, with its terraces, villas and landscaped areas, was being formed at the time and its architect, John Nash, was imaginative enough to see a canal through its grounds as an adornment rather than as a lower-class intrusion, though the canal was kept to the outer edges of the park with a secure fence between the two. However the route eventually excavated was nearly its undoing. It faced hostility, many technical problems, high legal costs and delays. It took a long time to build, from 1812, when the Act was obtained, until 1820 when state barges followed by others 'laden with Manufactured Goods' glided in the triumph of the day down to the Thames. In contrast, the Grand Junction from Northamptonshire to Brentford was begun in 1793 and was in operation by November 1794, albeit using part of the Oxford Canal and the river Brent for some of its way.

The Regent's Canal, despite its traffic to the docks, was never particularly profitable and inevitably lost out to the railways when they came. Yet it had the effect of creating employment in new areas of London. The Imperial Gas Works, reliant on coal, set up

The Basin of the Grand Junction Canal at Paddington, published in 1801. Eventually, buildings were to surround this stretch of water, especially when it was connected to the Regent's Canal which led to the docks. The basin may still be seen from the high vantage point of Westway.

various manufacturing plants along its banks, particularly at St Pancras where the Victorian gasholders survive today. Here the company could take in vast quantities of coal, mainly from Staffordshire, which supplemented supplies from the north-east coalfields that were shipped via the North Sea and the London docks. The handling of coal was one of the tougher jobs on the canal. In almost all cases the holds were emptied by hand and shovel in hot and dusty conditions. It was then carried down a narrow gang-plank to the quay. According to one man:

> The dust gets into the throat, and very nearly suffocates you. You can scrape the coal-dust off the tongue with the teeth, and do what you will it is impossible to get the least spittle into the mouth. I have known the coal dust to be that thick in a ship's hold, that I have been unable to see my mate, though he was only two feet from me.

Working on the coal ships was not a job that you could continue into middle age.

The Independent Gas Light and Coke Company built its own branch from the canal at Haggerston and the Gas Light and Coke Company had works at Curtain Road and Old Street. The furniture industry centred on Shoreditch had easier access to timber which could be offloaded at the City Road Basin or else at any factory along the way. This facility was timely, for the great increase in demand for furniture that occurred in Victorian times required it. At the Cumberland Basin east of Albany Street building materials were brought in to construct the Regent's Park terraces. The carriers, Pickford, established a vast enterprise at the City Road Basin and in so doing confirmed the worst fears of the warehouse owners at Paddington Basin who had predicted that the Regent's Canal would ruin their trade.

The adjacency of the canal must have encouraged numerous entrepreneurs to take advantage of it. The Gardner family for example, dairy farmers of Mile End, had the canal cut through their land. Assisted by this fortuitous stretch of bankside they built up a fleet of sailing barges that was usually employed in bringing bricks from the Medway to supply the legion of builders erecting houses on the fields of Hackney, Stoke Newington and Camden Town. The sailing barges were offloaded at the Regent's Canal Dock on the Thames on to the narrower barges of the canal.

The role of canals, at least in London, was the conveyance in bulk of heavy goods, such as timber, grain, stone and metals, and they did not, due to their slowness, have an effect on the transportation of perishable foods. Also, they were not, as railways became, part of London life in general – indeed the men, women and children who worked the waterways, and who led necessarily mobile, compact lives, reminded wary Londoners of gypsies in their caravans.

Moving *people* about London was a harder problem to solve. Some were rich enough to own a horse, which also implied that they could afford stabling at both ends of their journeys. A census taken at Temple Bar in 1850 counted 5,000 men on horseback during the day: by the 1880s a man on horseback in town was a rarity. There was a profusion of private coaches housed in the mews premises of Marylebone and Mayfair, which added to congestion in town. There were gigs – the least stylish of the vehicles – dog-carts (though the use of dogs was prohibited in 1839), the chaise for older people, and landaus, victorias, phaetons and broughams.

In town there were hackney cabs – by mid-century more usually cabriolets drawn by a single horse – but they were expensive to use and therefore the transport of a minority. Hundreds of short-stage coaches came in from the villages around London, such as Richmond, Camberwell, Kensington, Ealing and Hampstead. It was estimated in 1825 that there were about six hundred such coaches serving the City and West End; of those which went to the City about one-third carried passengers from south of the river. Generally a seat had to be booked in advance at one of the inns which served as ticket offices en route, but the drivers were permitted to pick up casual passengers on the way until, that is, he reached inner London, where he was barred from plying for hire and had to go straight to his terminus.

The commonest way to travel to business, to friends, or to entertainment was simply to walk. A young man called John Thomas Pocock, who lived impecuniously in Kilburn, walked virtually everywhere. His diary of the years 1826–30 treats lightly of daily expeditions which nowadays would not even be contemplated:

11 Aug 1828: To Paddington [from Kilburn] before breakfast, with my father as far as Soho, when I pursued my way to Limehouse. Called at Yates as I passed, Fred had just returned; then went to Mr Holmes with whom I did not stay 10 minutes, but came back to my uncle's. Had tea and came home wet through and very tired, having walked nearly 20 miles to-day.

31 Aug 1828: Left Bishopsgate early, went first to Bromley in Kent, 10 miles from his house, then across the fields to Beckenham – afterwards to the pretty little town of Sydenham – next Croydon – through shady Camberwell to Brixton where we had tea with the Underwoods and recounted our day's adventure. On coming back we found we had walked 25 miles 'for pleasure'. What would your milksop cockney apprentices say to this?

At the end of November in 1829 young Pocock travelled part of his way home on 'a Paddington omnibus'. In July that year George Shillibeer had introduced the omnibus into London, or at least on to the New Road, from Paddington all the way down the City Road to the Bank of England. A French invention, it was a high-sprung, single-deck vehicle that could seat about twenty passengers and which was drawn by three horses abreast. Its true innovation lay not so much in its construction, but in the fact that it plied for hire along a set route, and took up and set down passengers wherever required, unlike the short-stage coaches, which only set down and took up passengers at stages (usually inns).

The advent of the omnibus was heralded by an announcement:

G. Shillibeer, induced by the universal admiration the above Vehicles called forth at Paris, has commenced running one upon the Parisian mode, from PADDINGTON to the BANK. The superiority of this Carriage over the ordinary Stage Coaches, for comfort and safety, must be obvious, all the Passengers being Inside, and the Fare charged from Paddington to the Bank being One Shilling, and from Islington to the Bank or Paddington, only sixpence. The Proprietor begs to add, that a person of great respectability attends his Vehicle as Conductor; and every possible attention will be paid to the accommodation of Ladies and Children.

The *Morning Post* described it as a 'handsome machine, in the shape of a van, with windows on each side, and one at the end.' There were similar vehicles already in existence. Young Pocock himself records in December the same year that he rode to Greenwich in 'the four-horse white omnibus'.

Despite the fact that omnibuses were not allowed at first into the centre of London, Shillibeer's enterprise was successful and much copied. Soon there were numerous omnibus companies, each sporting a distinctive livery, plying the most profitable roads outside the centre, aggressively racing or blocking each other in the quest for passengers. It was common, unless a recognized stopping place was reached, to set down or gather up fares in the centre of the road so that a rival behind could not pass and take up those waiting at the next stop. The business was soon so competitive that the owners found that uncontrolled operations were driving them all out of business. As a result they divided the day up between them and their drivers combined together to ensure that any pirate bus was deprived of passengers along the route. In 1855 an amalgamation of bus companies took place when the Compagnie Generale des Omnibus de Londres, registered in Paris, set about buying up many of the companies. By that time London was becoming

A horse-bus serving Upper Clapton and Hackney, c.1845, by James Pollard. Horse-buses, as distinct from stage carriages, began with Shillibeer's 'omnibus' in 1829. They appear not to have carried passengers on the roof, as shown in this picture, until the mid 1840s.

increasingly horse-bound – Wilson's, a bus company near what is now Highbury Corner, had 500 horses to service their 50 buses.

The resistance of the hackney-cab drivers in town to the introduction of buses there was quickly broken. The need for omnibuses was evident to all and in any case the cab drivers, renowned for their rudeness and inconsiderate driving, had few admirers despite their grand top hats and overlapping capes that kept them warm and dry. Shillibeer summed it up:

> *middling classes of tradespeople whose finances cannot admit of the accommodation of a hackney coach and therefore necessitate to lose that time in walking which might be beneficially devoted to business*

would gain enormously from the use of buses in town. This was true as far as east-west transport was concerned. London had grown parallel to the Thames (on which steamboats were plentiful when Victoria came to the throne in 1837) and its main highways were on the same axis, but the north-south roads were less amenable to buses. Regent Street was only just built; Charing Cross Road, Shaftesbury Avenue and Victoria Street were yet to come; and Southampton Row and Kingsway were not built until the twentieth century. In the mid nineteenth century these latter routes, if they existed at all, were no more than narrow lanes that had to be negotiated with much difficulty. Even so, in 1832, three years after Mr Shillibeer began his service, the hackney-cab monopoly was abandoned and buses, though controlled in number, were allowed into the centre.

THE COMING OF THE RAILWAYS

THE FIRST RAILWAY TO REACH LONDON, in 1836, was hardly a threat to road transport, though it was the first in the country to carry only passengers. It was on the south bank, running from Deptford originally (by 1838 it extended to Greenwich) to the south side of London Bridge; it ran on a twin-track viaduct which for the most part crossed open fields, with hardly a disturbance of the agriculture and market gardens beneath, until it reached and straddled the Bermondsey slums. So unsure of its profitability was it that the Company included by its track a footpath and charged a toll of one penny for its use to those who preferred a pedestrian trip to work.

The London to Greenwich railway was only moderately successful because its passenger base was small: it was only really profitable once other railways, intent also on reaching the City, used its track and terminus. Efforts were made by the railway company

The London and Birmingham Railroad station at Euston Square, 1837. This illustration, made soon after the railway opened, depicts a train of open carriages and a track leading up to the cutting through Camden Town.

to obtain other passengers than those going to work. It popularized the line as convenient for day-trips to Greenwich and, once the London to Croydon railway had joined it, as an easy way to reach the beautiful countryside around such places as Anerley.

The next railway to reach London, the London & Birmingham, built a terminus at Euston and was of no use to suburban commuters at all, and nor was it intended to be: its line from Euston to Boxmoor was opened in July 1837, with Harrow the first stop outside the capital. The daily service consisted of three trains in each direction, sometimes made up of forty 4-wheel carriages, many of them simply open trucks without seats in which passengers took their chances against the weather or the red-hot cinders spewing out of the locomotive. The early prints of these trains and engines, reminiscent now of toy train sets, give no warning of the awesome fiery monsters that were to come, spreading black detritus over adjacent areas, but the careful administrators of the Eton

College estate at Belsize Park were far-sighted enough to insist that the railway went into a tunnel beneath its land. This tunnel, an engineering triumph of the first degree, and the construction of the line in a cutting down to Euston, brought to London's acquaintance men known as navvies. These were the direct descendants of the 'navigators' who built the canal system, and whose lives were hard, brutish, isolated and so intolerable that only drink could blur their discomforts. These men, who could lift about twenty tons of earth a day, were a different breed from the gangs of agricultural workers who came at harvest time to the fields around London, and constituted a source of worry to authorities and vicars alike.

The actual size of the construction work of the London & Birmingham line near London was a marvel in itself, larger even than the building of the east London docks which were, in any case, too far away to be familiar to most Londoners. Charles Dickens had witnessed the work at Camden Town and described it graphically in *Dombey and Son*:

> *The first shock of a great earthquake had, just at that period, rent the whole neighbourhood to its centre. Traces of its course were visible on every side. Houses were knocked down; streets broken through and stopped; deep pits and trenches dug in the ground; enormous heaps of earth and clay thrown up; buildings that were undermined and shaking, propped by great beams of wood. Here, a chaos of carts, overthrown and jumbled together, lay topsy-turvy at the bottom of a steep, unnatural hill; there confused treasures of iron soaked and rusted in something that had accidentally become a pond. Everywhere were bridges that led nowhere; thoroughfares that were wholly impassable; Babel towers of chimneys, wanting half their height; temporary wooden houses and enclosures, in the most unlikely situations; carcasses of ragged tenements, and fragments of unfinished walls and arches, and piles of scaffolding, and wildernesses of bricks, and giant forms of cranes, and tripods straddling above nothing.*

Dickens conveys well the impact that railways had on the fringes of London and the impotence of those most affected to prevent their excesses. The legislative process by which railway companies obtained permission to build paid little regard to householders or tenants who lived near or on the line route itself – the land taken was generally part of estates owned by men who were either in Parliament themselves or had strong allies there. Parish vestries were confined to haggling with the railway companies over the rateable values lost once premises were demolished. St Pancras Vestry, which was the most involved in this since Euston, St Pancras and King's Cross were all built on its territory, seems not to have objected to the railway lines themselves but only to the loss of rates that followed. Nowhere in the minutes of this vestry which cover the period of the great railway building boom, is there any complaint about the upheaval, noise, smoke and uncaring displacement caused by railways. The fact is that such social concerns were lost in the rush to establish the mechanical age.

Other railways followed the London & Birmingham in quick succession. In 1838 the Great Western opened from a station near today's Paddington, with a service to Bristol of eight trains a day. In 1839 the Eastern Counties Railway came into Shoreditch and the following year the London to Blackwall line began operation. The latter two were typical of the disregard shown to tightly packed neighbourhoods of poorer people, built, as they were, mostly on rooftop-level viaducts which punched their way either over or through streets of run-down houses. The Eastern Counties line displaced several streets at

Shoreditch and nine hundred working-class dwellings were lost. The London to Blackwall line (now used by the Docklands Light Railway), was built to entice passengers disembarking at Blackwall from ferries and steamers from Gravesend, and generally to service the docks; this last function was the reason behind the City's opposition to its construction, because any facilities for the private docks were against the interests of the London Dock in which the City had a financial investment. This line, estimated to have either displaced or blighted 2,850 dwellings, was originally rope-drawn because the promoters were worried that cinders from the railway would set the roofs of the houses or the rigging of ships on fire, but even this precaution was abandoned after a few years. When the companies running their trains into London Bridge established a West End terminus at Charing Cross they simply carried their trains, again at rooftop level, from one terminus to another thereby blighting that part of south London with myriad bridges and viaducts.

Some railways serviced existing settlements outside central London, others promoted a population increase. Surbiton, for example, was very much a railway creation, sitting on the London & Southampton line, and it came about because Kingston vestry declined to have a railway in its town centre. The line was therefore diverted with a stop at first called Kingston-on-Railway, and soon speculative builders erected eight hundred 'desirable residences' nearby. The growth of Ealing was marked after the coming of the Great Western, and the Great Northern opened up Bowes Park, Hornsey and Wood Green. The railways had to make precise calculations. It was all very well to open up new territory but return on capital invested was entirely dependent upon peak-hour traffic twice a day: as a rule women did not come into town during the day. This dilemma was still to be faced in the 1920s when the District Line was reluctant to extend to the Becontree Estate for the same reason, despite the most attractive of terms offered by the LCC. The companies also had to provide special trains each day for 'workmen' travelling at much reduced rates. These were heavily used, and not only by manual workers, since poorer office workers were happy to take advantage of them and arrive at their offices before they opened.

Workmen's fares were not a voluntary concession or a marketing ploy on the part of the railway companies. They were forced on them by legislation, partly as compensation for the fact that they were able to displace residents almost at will. When the North London Railway, which ran circuitously from Camden Town to the London docks, wanted to form a passenger branch from Dalston down to Broad Street in the City, permission was granted only if the company ran a train each weekday convenient 'for the labouring classes at or beyond Kingsland and having business in London, at fares not exceeding 1d'. The Great Eastern, seeking to extend its line from the Shoreditch terminus to the more convenient Liverpool Street, was obliged to run a train from Edmonton and Walthamstow each day before 7 a.m. and another back at 6 p.m. convenient for 'artisans, mechanics and labourers'. Tottenham, Edmonton and Walthamstow, previously delightful villages, were built up very quickly indeed with depressingly similar streets of small houses and by the end of the century were so well served by surface trains that they were ignored when the Underground system was constructed – an omission only remedied when the Victoria Line was constructed in 1968.

Despite the availability of trains, there were still 'walking suburbs' such as Islington, Camden Town and Holloway, which were then regarded as close enough to the City and the West End for commuting on foot. The Thames Tunnel – that heroic enterprise of the Brunels which finally opened in 1843 – had 17,000 toll-payers a week, mainly workers walking from the south to the north and back. The Eastern Counties line had only two trains a day stopping at Mile End, whereas seven went to Stratford and Tottenham, indicating that Mile End people walked to the City as a matter of course. This walking invasion was a feature of London until the advent of trams in the 1870s.

With one exception, no new railway reached London in the 1840s when railway stocks, after the heady hopes of the 1830s, were low. That exception, the West London Railway, was a financial disaster. It was built on the bed of the Counters Creek waterway, west of Holland Park, itself an unprofitable venture. This line, which earned the nickname 'Punch's Railway' from the constant derision published in that journal, sometimes took only £15 per month. In the 1850s, as confidence returned so did railway

Finchley road station on the North London line; from the Illustrated London News, *1860. The view is from the west and we are looking towards Frognal and Hampstead under which the railway was constructed in a long tunnel.*

proposals. Those that were built included the North London Railway, the Great Northern, which reached a terminus at York Way before King's Cross station was erected in 1851, and the very successful London, Tilbury & Southend Railway. In the 1860s the main activity in London centred around Charing Cross, Victoria and Waterloo and in 1868 the Midland Railway got to St Pancras where it built its famous hotel, which was opened in 1873.

The Great Exhibition of 1851 brought thousands of visitors to London. It was a bonus to cabbies, bus conductors and railways alike, but in the long-term it encouraged visits to London by rail. There were not, however, many hotels to suit small pockets. There were coaching inns but these, perversely, were often not in the right locations for tourists – places like La Belle Sauvage on Ludgate Hill and the Bull and Mouth in St Martin-le-Grand, which had underground stabling for 400 horses, were beyond the railway traveller's radius. Indeed, as the railways stole the coach traffic the coaching inns gave up their role of providing rooms. The London & Birmingham (renamed the London & North Western) railway began a new trend in 1839 when it established a railway hotel on each side of its terminus building at Euston, one being a straightforward hotel, the other intended for the cheaper end of the market, providing dormitories rather than private rooms. As each new railway reached London it enhanced its station with a hotel. Those at Paddington, London Bridge, Cannon Street, Charing Cross, Victoria, King's Cross and St Pancras all offered a standard of accommodation previously the reward of the rich in places like Pulteney's in Piccadilly, and Clarendon and Long's in New Bond Street. This entirely new service industry in London enticed even more cheap labour to the capital.

Railways moved people but they also moved freight. They transformed the diet of London by bringing in cheap fresh food in abundance. Potatoes, root vegetables, milk and

KING'S CROSS Station. The terminus for the Great Northern Railway was designed by Lewis Cubitt and completed in 1852. Its architecture is much admired, but unfortunately its façade has been obscured for much of its existence.

above all, fish, poured into the goods yards. Special warehouses for potatoes were established near railway stations, but fish by tradition and influence still went on to Billingsgate in the City, there to be bought by middle-men before retailers could bid for it. This was not a convenient arrangement as trade developed, since Billingsgate was remote from the principal railway stations and was surrounded by narrow City lanes. The City may be excused for rebuilding the fish market there in 1850 when railway trade was still less than the river-borne trade, but in 1874 they rebuilt the market again even though it was patently absurd to do so on that same site. The answer to this apparent short-sightedness lay in both the Corporation's thrift and its fear that moving the fish market outside the City boundaries might lose its monopoly of the London fish trade.

The Corporation had also been blatantly inefficient in providing dock mooring space on the Thames in the eighteenth century and then doggedly opposed the creation of docks beyond its control. It was also slow to relocate Smithfield to the cattle market in the open fields of Islington in 1855. The urgency of this move is reflected in the average figures for 1852–4 which show that on the two main days of the cattle market at Smithfield, nearly 5,000 cattle, about 30,000 sheep and 2,000 pigs went under the hammer there. These animals, unless they were penned outside London and their quality taken on trust, were herded through the congested streets of London for sale.

TRAMS

TRAMWAYS CONSOLIDATED THE GROWTH OF INNER SUBURBIA. From Clapham to Holloway, from Bow to Fulham, the comforting clank of iron wheels on iron rails could be heard, encouraging both an exodus of town residents and an influx of provincials to settle

SMITHFIELD CATTLE MARKET, c.1829. By the time of this illustration by Thomas Shepherd, the absurdity of having the premier cattle market so close to London was apparent. Herds of cattle and flocks of poultry were driven through the inner city and back out again to abattoirs.

in areas close to London that were difficult or uneconomic for railways. Omnibuses were French and it was the American, George Francis Train, who first introduced horse-drawn trams to the the streets of London in 1861. He was permitted three experimental tracks – Bayswater Road, Victoria Street and Westminster Bridge to Kennington – but the authorities were not enthusiastic. Part of the trouble was that the rails protruded slightly above the road surface, making them dangerous for other traffic. In Bayswater Road it was regarded anyway as a noisy intrusion, and it is notable that when the first three tramway lines were sanctioned in 1869 they were all in areas where the population was less influential. Reintroduction of horse-drawn trams came about with the invention of a different track which did not obtrude above the surface. They were immensely popular, and cheap, and within six years were carrying almost as much traffic as horse-buses, despite being barred the centre of London and the bridges across the Thames. In Highgate a cable tramway was laid so that trams might be winched up the steep hill to the village. Though invented by a Scot, the cable tramway had been developed in San Francisco. It was not a mechanical success in Highgate and was frequently out of action and for long periods, but it seems to have been fondly regarded. In 1909, when the last cable cars went up and down the route, they were seen off in style by a large crowd:

> *Popular airs led by a man playing a cornet were also sung, each car as it went off the service being greeted by singing Auld Lang Syne. The climax was reached when the last car started on its journey down the hill. People fought to get on. Everyone seemed to possess coloured lights, crackers, fireworks and sticks. The conductor made a brave attempt to collect fares, but so great was the crush that he was unable to get beyond the top of the staircase.*

A HORSE tram in Upper Clapton. The introduction of 'street railways' revolutionized transport in London – wheels on metal rails met less rolling resistance than those on the crude road surfaces of the day, and horses could therefore pull more people.

Tramways became very political. When the London County Council came into existence in 1889, the majority party, the Progressives – a mix of Liberals and Socialists – was dissatisfied with the performance of the tramway companies and was anxious to buy them out and amalgamate them into a public service. Proposals to this effect were impeded by the 'Moderates' (Conservatives) who merely stayed away from meetings in which purchase of lines was considered, thereby reducing those left voting to numbers below the legal requirement. It was not until 1 January 1899 that the first municipal tram in London set off accompanied by widely pessimistic forecasts, the Council having first of all reduced the working hours of the tramworkers to sixty hours a week. In fact, a profit was made in the first year and tramways were revolutionized in 1903 when the first electric tram ran from Westminster Bridge to the Council's new housing estate in Tooting.

THE UNDERGROUND

THE MOST IMPORTANT INNOVATION in transporting Londoners was also the slowest to develop. The Underground was the brainchild of a successful solicitor and an unsuccessful politician, Charles Pearson, who as early as 1843 was advocating to the electors of Lambeth 'a line. . .beneath the surface of the roadway through a spacious archway'. He was not elected and it was not until twenty years later, soon after his death, that the Metropolitan Railway from Paddington to Farringdon opened. Pearson's problems were manifold. First he had to persuade the local authorities through which the line passed that he might dig up the road, lay the railway, build the tunnel itself and then cover over again – much of this work was done on the Marylebone and Euston Roads, by then busy with horse-drawn traffic. South of King's Cross the line swept through the difficult terrain of the Fleet valley where uncharted streams could cost a fortune to divert or circumnavigate. The writer Arnold Bennett was on hand to describe the dramatic burst of the Fleet sewer into the railway workings in 1862:

> The terrific scaffolding of beams was flung like firewood into the air and fell with awful crashes. The populace screamed at the thought of workmen entombed and massacred. A silence!. . .The whole bottom of the excavation moved in one mass. The crown of the arch of the mighty Fleet Sewer had broken.

The work was enormously destructive in this area. George Godwin in *The Builder* estimated in 1864 that the cutting through the Fleet valley lost 1,000 dwellings housing 12,000 people, but then again there were plans for extensive demolition and improvements in this area, particularly on the part of the City. John Hollingshead, proprietor of the Gaiety Theatre, described the early building work in 1860:

> A few wooden houses on wheels first make their appearance and squat like Punch and Judy shows at the side of the gutter. A few wagons next arrive, well loaded with timber and planks, and accompanied by a number of gravel-coloured men with pickaxes and shovels. In a day and a night, or a little more, a few hundred yards of roadway are enclosed, and a strange quiet reigns for a time, in consequence of the carriage traffic being diverted. . . The calm of the main thoroughfare is soon disturbed by the arrival of steam engines, horses, carpenters and troops of navvies within the enclosure. The sound of pickaxes, spades and hammers, puffing of steam, and murmur of voices begin: never to cease, day or night.
>
> Huge timber structures spring up at intervals along the centre of the road, where spots for opening shaft holes are marked out, and it is not many hours before iron buckets are at work, dragging up the heart of the roadway. This rubbish is carted off on a tramway as quickly as possible and tilted down a gaping pit, with a noise like distant thunder, to be carried away into the country along the underground branch railway already completed.

Pearson also had to find an engine to pull the carriages. In an age of steam traction this was no easy matter, since the smoke and steam from the engine in a tunnel could easily suffocate both crew and passengers. An engine was devised whereby the smoke and steam were ducted into a tank behind the engine and the contents released into the atmosphere when the train was outside a tunnel. Quaint reminders of this are nos. 23 and 24 Leinster Gardens, near Paddington, which are merely dummy houses, complete with windows: behind their façades the Metropolitan trains once let off steam. There were also ventilating shafts along the middle of the Euston Road which improved the atmosphere below ground.

A trial run was completed, using open wagons and coaches, in 1862. Numerous dignitaries were carried, including Liberal politician William Gladstone, and the formal opening took place on 9 January 1863, although the Prime Minister, Mr Palmerston, declined to attend as he 'wished to remain above ground for as long as possible'. The precautions to prevent suffocation or choking seem to have worked, for there were no problems for passengers up to the time the line was electrified. Sir William Hardman noted in his diary a journey made on the line soon after it opened:

> Mary Anne and I made our first trip down the 'Drain'. We walked to the Edgware Road and took first class tickets for King's Cross. We experienced no disagreeable odour, beyond the smell common to tunnels. The carriages hold ten persons, with divided seats, and are lighted by gas; they are also so lofty that a six footer may stand erect with his hat on.

The Metropolitan was immensely successful. Not only was the public enthusiastic but it opened at a time of renewed speculation in railway building. In 1864 Parliament had before it 259 different projects which proposed three hundred miles of railways in or about London. One of these was to make an inner underground railway circle in London and to this end the Metropolitan was permitted to extend in both directions, and a new company, the Metropolitan District Railway, in many ways related to the Metropolitan, began work on a parallel route to the south, with the intention that they join up at the east and the west to form a circle around the centre of London. At first the two companies co-operated, but as the years went by their relationship deteriorated – their managers detested each other anyway – and Londoners became increasingly irritated at the time it was all taking. Delays occurred particularly on the District Line where the original plan had been to build it at the same time as the construction of the Embankment and Embankment Gardens. The latter was a vast project initiated by the Metropolitan Board of Works, under the supervision of their engineer, Joseph Bazalgette. Such were the delays, however, that Bazalgette in disgust had to proceed with his new road by the Thames and see it torn up later to lay the railway beneath. By 1871 the District Line had reached Mansion House, but the Metropolitan was then only at Moorgate and there had stopped. It was another thirteen years before the two routes joined.

On these trains, as with surface railways, there were three classes of carriages, but still the Underground was a curiously classless form of transport, possibly because whatever fare was paid the passengers had to endure the same drawbacks of sudden darkness when the gaslighting failed and the smokey conditions of the stations.

Neither the Metropolitan or the District went through the West End or the centre of the City since the method of construction meant that any building over the route would have to be demolished. It needed a breakthrough in tunnel engineering to burrow economically through London, and its discovery coincided with the development and adoption of electric traction, which eliminated the steam and dirt of conventional engines. The world's first electric tube railway opened in 1890 on a line running from King William Street in the City to Stockwell, a curious route on the face of it, but one that sought to attract the large number of people who came north from places like Kennington and Clapham into London each day.

Between 1870 and 1890 there were numerous offshoots at ground, or just below surface level, of the District and Metropolitan lines, but the most important tube lines built were those which at last went through the centre of London. The Central Line (1900), the Piccadilly (1906), the Bakerloo (1906) and the Northern (much of it in 1907) opened up the shops and entertainments of the West End to a very wide public. This massive expansion was mostly the work of the remarkable Charles Yerkes, an unscrupulous and fraudulent American made rich by Chicago street-cars. He gained control of the District Railway in 1901 and after building his own power station at Lots Road by the Thames at Chelsea, electrified the line. He then bought up the powers already granted to build what became the Piccadilly Line (the initials of the original title – the Great Northern Piccadilly & Brompton Railway may still be seen in the red tiles that decorate some of the first stations), and those that pertained to the 'Hampstead tube', which is now one arm of the Northern Line; to this he added the partly constructed Baker

A TRIAL trip of wagons on the first London Underground in August 1862. In wagon 23 is Mr Gladstone, then Chancellor of the Exchequer. The railway officially opened the following year.

Street & Waterloo line (Bakerloo for short) and then merged them into one company, leaving the Metropolitan outside of the system – a parting of the ways that even today is recognizable in the layout of a number of the interchange stations. In five or six years three tube lines were built.

The schematic map we now see of the Underground system implies an orderly and planned progression, but as we have seen it came about intermittently, leaving some considerable gaps to be filled, most notably in south and north-east London, and leaving some oddities, such as Aldwych station, which was originally intended to be the terminus of the Great Northern & Strand line that became submerged into the Piccadilly line. Generally, these early tube railways went to places already built up, but their many tentacles, extended in the twentieth century to the outskirts of Greater London, were to be instrumental in the transformation of the capital and the depopulation of central London.

ANGELA BURDETT-COUTTS (top left) (1814–1906), wealthy philanthropist. William Anthony, (top right) for fifty years nightwatchman in Spitalfields. A destitute child, (bottom left) photographed by the Barnardo Home. Dr Thomas Barnardo (bottom right) (1845–1905), at the age of sixty .

CHAPTER XIV

CLEANING UP THE CAPITAL

WHEN THE MUNICIPAL CORPORATIONS ACT OF 1835 REORGANIZED LOCAL authorities to cope with the realities of the nineteenth century, London was excluded. Yet of all the cities and towns that needed reform none was more wanting than the metropolis itself where authority was in the hands of the City Corporation, seven boards of Commissioners of Sewers, well above a hundred paving, lighting and cleansing boards, over one hundred vestries, many of them self-perpetuating, diverse liberties and other arcane authorities, numerous boards of guardians, three police authorities and some turnpike trusts. In the mismanaged parish of St Pancras alone there were twenty-five paving boards responsible for the maintenance of pavements and roads, on which sat nine hundred commissioners each drawing a fee, and even then the parish was devoid of paving in some areas. Absurdities abounded: Oxford Street was divided between four parishes, and the Strand was the responsibility of seven different paving boards. At parish boundaries a main road was divided down the middle so that maintenance or cleansing was rarely co-ordinated.

This chaos of control was the inevitable result of government lethargy and the influence of the City of London, anxious to retain its privilege and powers. There had already been proposals for an overall London authority to hold sway over the City, Westminster and the numerous parishes within the area of the Bills of Mortality, accompanied by a general reform of those parishes, but the City had effectively prevented such schemes. Yet at the same time the City was unwilling to enlarge its own borders for fear of its power being overwhelmed by representatives from other metropolitan areas.

Change simply had to come, if only to solve the chronic deficiencies of the London sewage system. This was the prime task of the Metropolitan Board of Works (MBW), formed in 1855, the first authority to have a remit over a number of aspects of metropolitan life. It was, however, indirectly elected, its members nominated by the City, parishes and district boards and therefore without a democratic base. The Board's influence over London was limited, extending to not much more than the creation of new thoroughfares such as Charing Cross Road and Queen Victoria Street, the numbering of streets, the enforcement of general building rules, the construction of a new sewage system for London – its main achievement – and, as time went on, the acquisition and management of open spaces. It was not the most appealing form of London government or one that unified its citizens, and once corruption amongst its officers and members was revealed its standing was further undermined.

The MBW did not even have powers to enforce sanitary regulations, a serious omission at a time when some vestries were intentionally neglecting them. The Public Health Act of 1848 permitted local authorities to employ medical officers of health: some immediately took advantage of this – the City, intent on forestalling government interference in its affairs, quickly secured the talented services of sanitary reformer and pathologist, Sir John Simon; but others were reluctant to spend their ratepayers' money. Only by 1858 were there forty-eight medical officers at work in the London parishes, some with genuine support from their paymasters, others resented. A few vestries found that they had employed medical officers keener on their work than they wanted them to be. The vestry of St James in Westminster cut the salary of its medical officer to discourage his reforming zeal as did St Pancras, and in St George the Martyr in Southwark the medical officer resigned in protest at the restraint put on his activities. The St Pancras vestry, in a long-running victimization of its medical officer, even disallowed him a locked drawer in his desk for confidential papers. This particular vestry had its own secrets to hide, which were publicly revealed when the Poor Law Commissioners noted that at St Pancras Workhouse an open cesspool existed in the yard there, and that inmates sleeping two or three to a bed in dormitories relied on pails for much of the day and night. Elsewhere, as well as in St Pancras, medical officers had great difficulty in persuading their masters to appoint an adequate number of 'Inspectors of Nuisances' (sanitary inspectors). Bethnal Green, notorious for its corruption at the beginning of the century and for its slums, had one inspector for 15,000 houses and Shoreditch had one for 17,000 houses. Bethnal Green's condition was minutely recorded in 1848 by a Dr Gavin in a book with the rather ambiguous title of *Sanitary Ramblings*. Gavin, a crusading public-health man and lecturer in forensic medicine at Charing Cross Hospital, found more than enough evidence in the East End of London to support his views. He estimated that in Bethnal Green the average life expectancy among the labouring class was a mere sixteen years, with 22 per cent of all children dying within the first year of birth. He found standpipes with 'highly coloured deposits', which was hardly surprising given the general state of the area:

> *Parallel to, and north of, Arch 81 of the Railway, and abutting on the lane, is a small pool of pasty putrescent filth, and a collection of garbage. On the south side of the same arch is an open black filthy ditch, which is from eight to ten feet wide, and from three to four hundred feet long. The uncovered privies at the back of North Street drain their soil into it; the soil has accumulated, and with decomposing cats and dogs, and refuse, which are now thrown into it, since Lambs Fields have been occupied, produce an odour of the most abominable character.*

Insanitary slums were not just an inner London problem: salubrious suburbs like Hampstead had them as well. That parish had the good fortune to employ a conscientious doctor, trained at Guy's and St Thomas's hospitals, and a founder of the Metropolitan Association of Medical Officers of Health. He was particularly concerned about Crockett's Court, some small houses at the lower end of Heath Street, where 117 people crowded into eighteen dwellings. He noted that in this area 'the very ground is saturated with the faeculence of ages. Not only is the atmosphere contaminated in courts and alleys by this cause, but the water also becomes impure as it percolates to our springs and wells'.

Typically, the lessons of three cholera epidemics which swept London were ignored. The disease came to London in 1832, beginning in Rotherhithe and then flourishing because it was not understood that it was carried in the water systems. Sewers were scoured, slaughterhouses cleansed and cesspools closed, but the disease continued unchecked. It returned with greater force in 1849 when 800 people died in the City alone. Despite the efforts of the General Board of Health, whose instructions could with impunity be disregarded by local Poor Law Guardians, it lasted for about four months. In London as a whole there were 30,000 cases, of which 14,000 were fatal. In 1854 another epidemic seized Soho, Southwark and Vauxhall and it was in Soho that a local obstetrician, John Snow, produced evidence of the connection between the disease and

Model dwellings erected near King's Cross in 1844. These houses were an early group specifically built for poorer people, but most charitable housing built in this period was in blocks of flats, which had shared water and water closet facilities on communal landings.

the local water supply. However, his conclusions were slow to find support among medical officers. (Snow's other claim to fame is that he administered chloroform to Queen Victoria during the birth of her eighth child, thereby establishing confidence in its medical use.)

HOUSING

Private endeavours were responsible for a number of reforms. Local authorities were powerless, even if they had the will, to provide sanitary housing, and it was the Metropolitan Association for Improving the Dwellings of the Industrious Classes, formed in 1841, which was first to take the initiative. Its object, succinctly put, was 'The purchase and construction of dwelling-houses, to be let to the poorer classes of persons, so as to remove the evils arising from the construction and arrangement of such dwellings, more especially in densely-populated districts'.

The title of the Association is significant in itself. 'Metropolitan' is appropriated, and proclaims not only a London wider than the small concerns of parishes but a body of people looking at the condition of the whole capital. The paternalism of the Victorian age, which came hand-in-hand with religious fervour and cant, is there too in the singling out of the 'Industrious Classes': among the plethora of such societies that followed only a few ventured into housing for the unskilled and, by implication, lazy and improvident.

Three distinct forms of housing for poorer families developed. One came from the renovation of existing properties, which was spasmodically attempted until social reformer Octavia Hill made it work on a larger scale; the second was the erection of blocks of flats in inner London; the third was the creation of large estates of artisans' houses in outer London, usually dependent for their survival and prosperity on the nearness of a railway station and the provision of workmen's trains.

Equally necessary in some parts of London was the provision of better lodging hostels for a transient population. This was especially so in Whitechapel and Spitalfields, where the creation of Commercial Street in 1848 and the general tidying up of the Aldgate area had destroyed numerous poor lodging houses that only the desperate resorted to. Henry Mayhew, one of the founders of *Punch*, is best known for his meticulous investigations into the conditions endured by the poorer classes of London, entitled *London Labour and London Poor*, published in 1851. This remarkably detailed survey has enriched many a social history. It revealed to those who were interested the appalling overcrowding and decadence of private lodging houses, where it was not unusual to find 18 to 20 people to a room. Mayhew described the arrangements at a place in Whitechapel:

> *I knew two brothers (Birmingham nailers) who each brought a young woman out of service from the country. After a while each became dissatisfied with his partner. The mistress of the house (an old procuress from Portsmouth) proposed that they should change their wives. They did so, to the amusement of nine other couples sleeping on the same floor, and some of whom followed the example, and more than once during the night.*

A block for '300 Bachelor Mechanics' was erected in Spicer Street, Spitalfields in 1848–9 by the Metropolitan Association, with at least some attention to architectural style so that the Association could 'exert the beneficial influence of art, even in Spitalfields'. In the block, where each sleeping cubicle had a window, were facilities for washing, a reading room, and a cook-shop. On the other hand, residents were obliged to endure the attentions of a preacher each Sunday.

The Society also turned its attention to renovation and conversion of existing slum property, such as tenements in Wild Court off Drury Lane and Tyndall's Buildings off Gray's Inn Road. In these the object was to provide a habitable room, with shared water supply and lavatory accommodation. It was not until 1892 that Lord Rowton began his scheme to build hostels for men. These red-brick, many-windowed but still gaunt buildings (the largest, Arlington House, survives in Camden Town) came to typify hostel accommodation for impoverished men; but they were held in high esteem, not the least because each resident had his own cubicle. 'The men strive to maintain their position by coming in to our houses and take a pride in living in them and it is our duty to make it as desirable a residence for them as possible', proclaimed one annual report.

Mayhew was just one observer who noticed that the earlier 'Model' lodging houses were rarely popular and remarked, after an interview with one who used them:

The Model lodgers are kept, as it were, in leading strings, and triumphed over by lords and ladies, masters and matrons, who, while they pique themselves on the efforts they are making to 'better the condition of the poor', are making them their slaves, and driving them into unreasonable thraldom; while the rich and noble managers, reckless of their own professed benevolence, are making the poor poorer, by adding insult to wretchedness.

The Metropolitan Association was not a charity, though it needed to be philanthropic. Investors expected a 5 per cent return on their money, this to be obtained from economies in building and management and the rents paid by tenants. It was not until 1847 that the Association's first family dwellings were built, when 110 families moved into

MODEL houses designed by Henry Roberts, with the approval of the Prince Consort, as shown at the Great Exhibition in 1851. They were later transferred to a park at Kennington and used by park staff.

Metropolitan Buildings opposite Old St Pancras church: these five-storey dwellings were also the first purpose-built flats in London. *The Times* opined that 'an Oxford student might find himself at home in any one of the bedrooms and parlours', and there was much comment that each flat had a kitchen range and its own piped water, serving a water closet. *The Times* might also have noted that here were probably the first sanitary dwellings in London built specifically for working class families, who had before put up with the subdivided hand-me-down houses left behind by better-off people. This acknowledgement that the poor needed (and merited) sanitary and more spacious accommodation which suited their financial circumstances was, perhaps, the most significant revolution in this field.

The architect Henry Roberts designed fourteen dwellings around a courtyard near King's Cross in 1845 for the Society for Improving the Condition of the Labouring

Classes, which attracted some criticism for their meanness. However, Roberts was taken up by Prince Albert, and he displayed some 'model' cottages for the Great Exhibition of 1851, which are still at large in Kennington Park being used by the ground staff. Though they received a good deal of publicity because of their royal patronage, model cottages were not taken up by societies and developers, who were more interested in large block schemes in towns, or else estates of quite alien dimensions just out of town.

The 1860s saw the building of many more tenement blocks, which had higher density figures than the slum houses they replaced. Numerous philanthropists were at work in the field. The Improved Industrial Dwellings Company concentrated at first on the King's Cross area – Stanley Buildings in Pancras Road may still be seen; the Central London Dwellings Improvement Company converted slums in Covent Garden; and the Baroness Angela Burdett-Coutts built Columbia Square in Bethnal Green, overlooking her

PEABODY SQUARE, off Essex Road, Islington, from the Illustrated London News *in 1866. The Peabody estates provided low-cost housing to poor working people, but they were built economically and with a depressing uniformity.*

hopelessly underused market building. She and her architect, H.A. Darbishire, could not resist (as with her market, which had moral admonitions around the walls) imposing their sanctimonious views on the tenants of the flats. Darbishire told the Architectural Association in 1863 that the aim was to design a block of flats so as to 'oblige the Poor, willy nilly, to live in a sanitary state'. Permanently open windows on the corridors ensured a brisk supply of fresh air and in the apartments themselves doors and windows were made deliberately ill-fitting so that draughts abounded. This concern with ventilation of poor homes is evident in many schemes that followed. In Columbia Square plaster and paper were not allowed on the walls, the bricks of which had to be whitewashed. On the other hand, Darbishire, as befitted the architect of Holly Village in Highgate, could not resist Gothic touches: in the quadrangle formed by the Columbia Square blocks an Eleanor Cross clock tower was built.

The efforts of home-grown societies were dwarfed by the formation of the Peabody Trust based on a massive donation from the American, George Peabody; their first dwellings were opened in Spitalfields in 1864 and others followed in many areas of London. It cannot be said that they had architectural distinction as had some of the model dwellings, nor were they spacious compared with those lovingly designed for the Baroness Burdett-Coutts, but they came at an opportune time and thousands had good reason to be grateful, even if they left them with some relief. Even meaner in architecture and proportions were those built by the Improved Industrial Dwellings Company, an organization founded by Sir Sydney Waterlow, Lord Mayor of London.

When the newly married Rev. Samuel and Henrietta Barnett moved into the impoverished parish of St Jude's, Whitechapel in 1873 they sought to improve the working-class lot with opera, flower shows and lectures on Socrates and Milton. It was some time before this somewhat priggish, evangelizing couple could offer much else to this desperate area of London. It was they who, with others, formed the East End Dwellings Company following the passing of the Artizans and Labourers Dwellings Act of 1875, which permitted compulsory purchase of slum areas. But the Rev. Barnett had more to say about the outward appearance of housing schemes than was to be uttered by other societies and borough councils in later years:

> It is, I believe, false economy, as it is false benevolence, which provides for fellow-creatures things acknowledged to be ugly. In the long run such things will be rejected and although it is too early to form conclusions, there is evidence that repulsive-looking buildings repel tenants.

Octavia Hill, whose reputation is now rather saintly, worked enthusiastically with the Charity Organization Society in converting buildings for accommodation. She was also involved with the East End Dwellings Company in designing tenement blocks, some of which shocked the young and earnest Beatrice Webb, who acted as a rent collector. Describing one of the Hill developments near the Mint at Tower Hill she said:

> Right along the whole length of the building confronting the blank wall ran four open galleries, out of which led narrow passages, each passage to five rooms, identical in size and shape, except that the one at the end of the passage was much smaller than the others. All the rooms were 'decorated' in the same dull, dead-red distemper, unpleasantly reminiscent of a butcher's shop. Within these uniform, cell-like apartments there were no labour-saving appliances, not even a sink and water tap! Three narrow stone staircases led from the yard to the topmost gallery; on the landings between the galleries and the stairs were sinks and taps (three sinks and six taps to about sixty rooms): behind a tall wooden screen were placed sets of six closets on the trough system, sluiced every three hours. . .used in common by a miscellaneous crowd of men, women and children, [which] became the obtrusively dominant feature of the several staircases, up and down which trooped, morning, noon and night the 600 or more inhabitants of the buildings.

As Octavia Hill commented to a Parliamentary Committee on Housing: 'If you have water on every floor that is quite sufficient for working people.'

Most tenement schemes replaced crowded courtyards and alleys in inner London and made no dent on the slums of outer suburbia which had been created in the earlier part of the century. These were described in the *Architectural Magazine* in 1834:

The smallest of these are built, principally for the occupation of the poor, in the suburbs of London, in inferior situations. These houses consist of two rooms; they have generally from 12ft to 14ft frontage, and are from 12ft to 14ft deep, having an access on the ground floor in front into the lower room, and steps outside at the back leading into the upper room. Three, four, or more have a yard and other conveniences in common.

These hasty developments were mostly in the East End where speculators kept pace with the spread of docks and factories along the marshy north bank of the Thames. Dickens summed up their deficiency and social disadvantage when writing to the Baroness Burdett-Coutts in 1852. He said that if only housing for the working-class had been built in blocks of high density then London would have been spared so many acres of 'walnut shell' houses, and it would still be possible for the poor to leave their front doors and go

THE wryly named Paradise Row in Agar Town. These houses were part of a settlement of slums north of St Pancras Station built on very short leases, so that there was no incentive to provide services or drainage. They were mainly inhabited by poor Irish people.

for a walk in the country. Dickens made famous the shortest-lived of these developments, Agar Town, just north of St Pancras Old Church. Here plots had been let out on 21-year leases with the inevitable consequence that any house built was a hovel. This predominantly Irish settlement, lacking drainage, sewers, pavements, surfaced roads, and dust and rubbish collection, was described by Dickens as 'A Suburban Connemara'. Another remarkable slum was in Rotherhithe, south of the river, an estate of tiny and primitive houses called St Helena erected on land surplus to the requirements of the East London Railway Company; its 600 houses were so lacking in substance and amenities that they were all built within about a year.

The forerunners of council housing estates were cottage estates in what was then suburban London, mostly pioneered by the Artizans, Labourers and General Dwellings Company, formed in 1867. The word 'Park' was used in the name of most of them, just as

'Court' (which had bad connotations in Victorian times) has been taken over by borough councils since the 1960s to enhance the status of council blocks. Loughborough Park near Coldharbour Lane, Shaftesbury Park near Lavender Hill, Queen's Park off Harrow Road, and Noel Park at Wood Green are all survivors of these early garden suburbs built for working-class tenants. They were not approved of by Octavia Hill who was against the segregation of the working classes, and many others pointed out that the artisans were at some distance from their jobs with all the expense that that involved. The question as to the desirability of mixing working and residential areas presented itself for the first time to the Victorians, and solutions have varied with sociological fashion ever since.

THE WORKHOUSE

IT WAS ONLY IN REAL DESPERATION that anyone threw themselves on the mercy of a workhouse, an institution whose reputation had deteriorated since the eighteenth century when most were established, and whose terrors had worsened since the reorganization of poor relief in 1834. The dilemma for the Victorians (and for authorities before and after) was how to shelter the homeless in relatively humane conditions but at the same time make the experience a deterrent. The conditions thought necessary by the authorities to give incentive to the workshy might well have been approved of by the public, but they were also shared willy-nilly by those, perhaps infirm and handicapped, who had no hope of ever being self-reliant. Gradually, as public opinion and local authority experience matured, 'deserving' poor were removed from the workhouse rigours into other regimes: children into vast schools, the sick into infirmaries, the slightly eccentric and the insane into asylums.

It had been thought during the drastic 1834 shake-up of the workhouse system that the buildings might be self-supporting and that the labour of the inmates would pay for their upkeep. At the end of the eighteenth century Jeremy Bentham had proposed grotesque workhouses in which 2,000 paupers slept in cells within observation from a central tower. Fortunately, his plans were not adopted for workhouses, but his similar proposal for prison buildings found fateful reality in the Millbank Penitentiary.

Reform of the workhouses was made necessary by the larger numbers of destitute people flooding into cities and the indifferent and haphazard performance of parish authorities in dealing with them. There were no overall standards to be met in the level of expenditure on buildings or inmates and no routine inspections of establishments. Several well-publicized scandals highlighted the need for change but there had been, in any case, a growing concern since the middle of the eighteenth century at the treatment of the poor. The social reformer, Jonas Hanway, had pressed in 1766 for the removal from workhouses of children under six – in one parish he found that of fifty-four children either born in or taken into the workhouse in one year, none had survived. It was the custom to send infant orphans into 'the country', which could be no further than Highgate or Fulham, to be wet-nursed or fostered and there they still died in great numbers. Greater care was taken by parishes to make sure that children were apprenticed properly instead of being sold, in effect, to whichever tradesman had the money. But vestries were still able, as happened in St Pancras, to send children of seven and upwards to work at a cotton manufactory in Hampstead Road, where they worked from six in the

St James's Westminster parish workhouse, by Pugin and Rowlandson, 1809. The site of this workhouse was between Poland Street and Marshall Street and is now occupied by a large public garage. The building portrayed here was opened in 1727.

morning till six at night. Even in the comparatively well-run parish of St Marylebone there were abuses of power. Idleness was punished by a diet of bread and water, or a 'strait-waistcoat' was made obligatory at dinner time; persistent offenders were sent to a Mr Rocket at Bethnal Green who, it seemed, had a good track record in dealing with refractory inmates.

The various reforms, however, led inexorably to a situation in which 'outdoor relief' – the doling out of money to the destitute while they remained in whatever homes they had, was extinguished. The Victorian zeal for 'improving' the poor, for controlling their existence in their darkest hours so that they might, with the guidance of authority and religion, eventually take their place again in society, albeit in its lower echelons, was nowhere more evident than in the workhouse system after 1834.

The new Poor Law was the work of the sanitary reformer, Edwin Chadwick, who has fallen badly from grace as modern historians have examined his irrascible and egotistical career in public health, particularly in his role as Secretary to the Poor Law Commission, which supervised the implementation of the new Act. Succinctly, the law prohibited outdoor relief to able-bodied people and their families, and created a uniform system of administration through Boards of Guardians supervised by a strong central body. Inevitably, this aroused the opposition of local vestries who saw their own independence whittled away. St Pancras vestry, a body not given to moderation, fought a long and acrimonious campaign against the jurisdiction of the Poor Law Commissioners. Many people objected to the new workhouses, not because of the abuses constantly revealed in *The Times*, but because they did not reduce the Poor Rate as had been confidently suggested. This was hardly surprising, since the gathering under one roof of those who had previously stayed in their own dwellings, and the decision to abolish the use of inmate labour to run the workhouses inevitably led to increased expenditure. And if ratepayers were dissatisfied their discontent was nothing to the misery of the inmates themselves who were subject to stringent rules that satisfied the ideological obsessions of Chadwick.

A consequence of housing the poor together in one building was the breaking-up of families. Economy dictated that the workhouse should be built as a series of single-sex dormitories and cohabitation between married couples was not permitted. It was thought by the authorities that children should be further separated so that they were not subject to the influences of adult inmates. To this end a number of large schools were built in London's suburbs, in which children spent much of their abbreviated childhoods. One such building, the Central London District School, was erected in 1857 by the City of London and two east London workhouse unions at Hanwell; the boys were taught agriculture and manual trades (Charlie Chaplin became its most famous ex-pupil) and the girls, inevitably, endured domestic work (which doubled up as free labour for the School itself) in the hope that they might be placed as low-paid live-in servants as soon as they were old enough.

EMIGRATION

THE PROLIFERATION OF THE POOR IN LONDON taxed both authorities and the general public, who were stirred by a series of government reports, heart-rending descriptions by commentators like Mayhew and Dickens, and the scarcely veiled rivalry between the Established Church and the evangelists in doing good works. What was to be done with the poor? How best to reduce their numbers?

One answer was emigration. The British Empire needed labour and, not to put too fine a point upon it, needed women for propagation. The Female Emigrants' Home in Hatton Garden sent off its first consignment, consisting of '38 women of excellent character' to Port Phillip, Australia in 1850. But many women, especially those of the 'governess class' who went to New Zealand and Australia, found that they were expected to work in the house or the fields, which in the immutable class structure of England would have been unthinkable.

Workhouses sent children, many of whom merely transferred their pauper status to another country. Dr Barnardo favoured Canada in particular and sent thousands of children there in the 1880s, but at least he attempted to supervise their welfare once they had arrived in a country increasingly uneasy at the influx of cheap and quite often inexperienced labour.

From being a panacea in the 1850s emigration became the wrong answer by the end of the 1890s. The 800 non-conformists who set out for New Zealand from the London Docks in 1862 and the 850 Poplar residents who had gone off to Canada after the bad winter of 1866–7, went at the right time and were, no doubt, among those in their new countries who were resentful twenty years later when the tide of British immigrants had grown enormously. Organizations such as the Workman's Emigration Society for the Consolidation of the British Empire and the Deptford Relief Society which helped discharged dockhands to emigrate, were both formed in 1870 – probably the last decade when mass emigration was beneficial to both countries involved.

SANITATION

THE POOR LAW ACT OF 1834 with all its faults and dreadful consequences was, at least, no half-measure, which is more than can be said about the various enactments designed to bring better sanitation and purer water supplies to London. Chadwick, in publishing his famous report on the sanitary conditions of the labouring population in

An abrasive portrayal of the quality of water supply provided by London water companies, by William Heath, 1828. It was not until 1852 that the companies were prohibited from taking water from the polluted Thames below Teddington.

1842, declared that cholera, a frequent scourge, was a consequence of bad drainage, inadequate ventilation and indifferent water supply. In this last conclusion Chadwick encouraged even more enemies than he already had, for the water companies were a powerful lobby. Pursuing his views still further in 1850 Chadwick proposed that the companies stop drawing their water from the polluted Thames and take it instead from other sources; even worse, he thought that water supply should be taken away from private companies and put in the hands of a metropolitan body. Controversy went on for years. The water companies and vestries, usually at war over the cost and infrequency of water supplies, found common cause in opposing a metropolitan body, and in a Parliament which contained at least one hundred water company shareholders legislation was bound to fall substantially short of Chadwick's proposals. The Metropolitan Water Act of 1852 prohibited companies from taking water from the Thames below Teddington and insisted that whatever was supplied from elsewhere should be filtered, but it was only in 1857 that reservoirs in and out of London were covered. Meanwhile, the 1854 cholera epidemic claimed hundreds of lives and in 1866 over 4,000 deaths occurred in Stratford and West Ham, served by the East London Water Company which had, with impunity, failed to filter its supplies. It was not until 1871 that the government appointed an official Water Examiner.

The state of drinking water was of major concern to Victorian Londoners. Its topicality was enhanced by various epidemics and the growing evangelism of temperance societies – the moral superiority enjoyed by those who preferred to drink water is emphasized in biblical quotations often to be found carved in public fountains that from 1859 were to be seen around London. And not before time, for it was well known that the pumps and wells available to the public were a hazard rather than a benefit – even in the better

ALDGATE PUMP, watercolour by Thomas Shepherd. This pump drew its supply from a fresh spring and its water was healthier than most. Two pre-Fire buildings in Leadenhall Street are seen in the centre.

regulated City it was recommended by the Medical Officer in 1866 that none of them should be used for drinking purposes. Prominent among those who urged the provision of free public drinking fountains was the Quaker banker Samuel Gurney, and it was he who paid for the erection of the first public fountain in London in 1859, when an elaborately sculpted edifice was unveiled in Newgate Street.

In that same year what became the Metropolitan Drinking Fountain and Cattle Trough Association was formed with the ambition to provide many more in co-operation with parish authorities who, it was hoped, would pay for the water if the Association supplied the fountain. This was not always possible since some local authorities refused to have the cost on the rates and the Association had to pay for the water as well. This parsimonious attitude on the part of some parishes was put to shame by the numerous benefactors who paid for the erection of fountains which were no mere faucets but were often works of art in themselves. The so-called Buxton fountain now south of today's Houses of Parliament and the one erected by Angela Burdett-Coutts in Victoria Park (unveiled, according to the *Illustrated London News*, in front of ten thousand spectators) are first-class if extravagant examples of the genre, but many more besides still exist, a mixture of competent sculpture and good intentions, usually neglected by the later twentieth-century authorities who have them in their care.

Nor was outer cleanliness neglected as the movement to erect public baths and washhouses gathered momentum. In London the Association for Promoting Cleanliness Among the Poor opened some baths in East Smithfield in 1844, at which the customers could also apply for whitewash and pails to paint their homes. In its first year it had 35,000 customers for the baths and nearly 50,000 used the washing and ironing facilities. The Association's work was supplemented after an Act of 1846 permitted local authorities

THE Baths and Washhouses, Endell Street, administered by the parishes of St Giles-in-the-Fields and St George Bloomsbury. These have since been superseded by the Oasis leisure complex, which includes a swimming pool.

to erect baths and washhouses. St Martin-in-the Fields appears to have been the first parish to take advantage, when in 1849 premises were opened in Orange Street. Swimming pools were a slightly later development and were often private ventures. The Metropolitan Tepid and Cold Swimming Bath was in the City Road by 1860 and in 1875 a large pontoon was tied up by Charing Cross Railway Bridge, where the Floating Swimming Pool Company promised filtered water from the Thames and room for several hundred swimmers within the tethered structure.

The provision of public lavatories was a problem for the vestries. Residents disliked their location anywhere near their homes, and even when underground lavatories became usual they were almost invariably placed at transport interchanges. The introduction of public lavatories for ladies was strongly resisted. When, in 1880, a Mr Alfred Watkyns of Paris proposed erecting a '*chalet de toilette et de nécessité*' in Camden Town, complete with billboards and shoeblacks outside, the local residents presented a petition to the Vestry which claimed that the chalet 'would have a tendency to diminish that innate sense of modesty so much admired in our countrywomen'.

By 1860, the Thames had become very polluted because of the gradual eradication of cesspits, and the widespread use of water closets and sewers which drained into the river. Additionally, water supplies were contaminated in some areas by the excessive use of burial grounds where already fetid ground was used time and again for new burials. The state of these churchyards had been a scandal since Dr George Walker, a surgeon in the Drury Lane area, had warned of the incidence of disease, particularly typhus, in neighbourhoods adjacent to overcrowded burial grounds. In Drury Lane itself was a ground of only 400 square yards which was thought to contain the remains of about 20,000 bodies. In describing the ground attached to St Anne's, Soho, Walker noted that rotten coffin wood and bones were scattered about and that the ground was very full and considerably raised above its orginal level – it still is and on sunny days now is adorned with people eating their lunchtime sandwiches. Of the burial ground attached to St Giles-in-the Fields, Walker noted that 'Here in this place of "Christian burial", you may see human heads, covered with hair; and, here, in this "consecrated ground", are human bones with flesh still adhering to them.' It was shown that in the burial ground at Spa Fields the judicious use of quicklime had facilitated the burial of 80,000 bodies in an area meant to hold 1,000. *The Builder* proclaimed in 1843 that:

> *This London, the centre of civilization, this condensation of wisdom and intelligence, this huge wedge and conglomerate of pride, buries – no it does not bury – but stores and piles up 50,000 of its dead to putrefy, to rot, to give out exhalations, to darken the air with vapours, faugh! it is loathsome to think of it; but it is strictly true, 50,000 desecrated corpses are every year stacked in some 150 limited pits of churchyards, burial grounds they are called.*

The most infamous was that attached to Enon Chapel, Clements Lane, a place for dissenters opened in 1823, which derived much of its income from cheap burials directly beneath its wooden floor. Walker described it:

> *Soon after interments were made a peculiarly long narrow black fly was observed to crawl out of many of the coffins; this insect, a product of the putrefaction of the bodies, was observed on the following season to be succeeded by another, which had the appearance of a common bug with wings.*

The children attending the Sunday School, held in this chapel in which these insects were seen to be crawling and flying in vast numbers during the summer months, called them 'body bugs'. Between 1823 and 1847, when the chapel became a dance hall, over 12,000 bodies were put to moulder there. Other descriptions were published of remains unceremoniously taken up to make way for new bodies, of grave diggers who had to be drunk to do the job, of stenches that made people ill. A Society for the Abolition of Burials in Towns was formed but by the time Walker published a book on the matter in 1839 radical change was occurring, for London at last was permitted to have cemeteries.

In 1830 the London Cemetery Company was formed at the instigation of a barrister, George Carden. Helped by the panic that ensued during the 1832 cholera epidemic, the Company obtained permission to build London's first cemetery at Kensal Green; this was such a resounding success that others followed at Norwood, Highgate, Brompton, Nunhead and Abney by 1840.

All of these cemeteries were private in the sense that the burial plots were more expensive than the working classes could afford. This exclusivity, together with the lavish landscaping and architectural touches that decorated them, made affluent Victorians think again about the nature of funerals. Gone was the sordid churchyard and all its connotations of disease, desecration and body-snatching; here instead were places in which dignity and pomp were encouraged and appropriate, and it was possible to mix with a better class of mourners. So popular were these new cemeteries that by 1841 Jay's Mourning House in Regent Street had opened, selling nothing but a wide range of accoutrements felt necessary to celebrate death. In eight years an entirely new retail trade developed and it was not long before any sizeable draper's had a mourning section – the

A STOCK blank invitation to a funeral, published in 1809 but using a drawing by Hogarth. These were, most probably, ordered in bulk by the undertaker, Humphrey Drew of King Street, Westminster, and sold retail as part of his services.

business of Courtauld's was to thrive on the weaving of black crape. Undertakers, once jacks-of-several trades, piled the business of burial high with nuances and arcane heraldic symbolism so that a funeral became a visual statement of social standing.

Ostentation was not the sole province of the middle classes. Where possible, a working-class funeral displayed the same badges of substance and at times was just as bizarre. Mary Robinson, the self-styled 'Queen of the Costermongers', was buried at Finchley Cemetery in 1884 in sumptuous style. She had amassed a fortune (rumoured at £50,000) from lending money to other costermongers in Somers Town where she lived, but her usual activity was the sale of cats' meat. For the funeral she had arranged that the coffin should be carried by four men wearing white smocks, followed by twenty-four women wearing violet dresses and white aprons with feathers. At the funeral of boxing hero, Tom Sayers, in 1865, a procession estimated at ten thousand accompanied the hearse through Camden Town up to Highgate Cemetery; the crowd, we are told, contained many costermongers, dog fanciers, fighters and thieves.

The provision of private cemeteries diminished, but did not solve, the problem of overcrowded churchyards and it was not until after a succession of Acts, beginning in 1850, that public cemeteries were permitted. In 1854 St Pancras Vestry, so backward in other things, opened London's first municipal cemetery, albeit in Finchley.

VICTORIAN PHILANTHROPY

By THE 1870s LONDON WAS AWASH WITH CHARITIES. It was an age innocent of acronyms or euphemistic titles, and charitable organizations rejoiced often in very long and, to modern ears, embarrassingly precise names. The St Marylebone Home for Incurable Young and Middle-aged Women, the Strangers Home for Asiatics, Africans and South Sea Islanders, the School of Discipline for Girls, the Operative Jewish Converts' Institution for teaching printing and bookbinding to Jews 'who in consequence of their conversion to Christianity, have lost friends and occupation', did not dither around the point of their existence. Nor did the Home for Female Inebriates in Kennington, the Destitute Children's Dinners Society, the various Homes for Penitent Prostitutes or the Blind Man's Friend Charity disguise their functions in neutral or ambivalent names. Inherent in this blunt approach was the reality that charity was not given discreetly and recipients were forcibly reminded of their good fortune. Deference was both a virtue and a necessity.

This was particularly true in the case of dispensaries – organizations established to provide health care, or at least the services of a doctor, for those too poor to afford a doctor's fee. The usual procedure was for the patient to secure first a letter of recommendation from one of the dispensary's benefactors. The rules of the Highgate Dispensary, begun in 1787, were typical enough:

> *The patients are to provide all necessary phials etc., they are to behave themselves decently and soberly and are to conform strictly to such rules as are given to them. . .or they will be immediately dismissed. They are to keep their letters of recommendation clean under cover, they are to deliver the same when cured, at the Dispensary and are immediately thereupon to return a letter of thanks to the governor who recommended them, on pain of not being admitted to any future benefit.*

The first dispensary appears to have been that founded in Red Lion Square in 1769; they were in places as diverse as Brentford and Tower Hamlets, and one was established by Nathan Rothschild for Stamford Hill and Stoke Newington in 1825, indicating the spread of Jews to those areas. Some dispensaries grew into hospitals – University College, Charing Cross, the Elizabeth Garrett Anderson in Euston Road, Moorfields, the Royal Northern and the West London hospitals all began this way.

There had been a steady addition to the number of hospitals available to Londoners. To the medieval St Bartholomew's and St Thomas's had been added, between 1720 and 1745, Westminster, subscribed by the public, Guy's, St George's, the London and the Middlesex. The major foundations of the nineteenth century tended to be more specialist

WESTMINSTER HOSPITAL, Broad Sanctuary, Westminster; an undated photograph. In the foreground is the monument commemorating ex-Westminster School pupils killed in the Crimean War.

– several eye hospitals, including Moorfields, began in response to the number of soldiers returning from the Nile campaign in the early 1800s with blindness caused by a disease caught in Egypt; consumption was prevalent, leading to the founding of the Brompton Consumption Hospital and the City of London Hospital for Diseases of the Chest; the Royal Dental Hospital began in Soho in 1858; the Hospital for Sick Children in Great Ormond Street was founded in 1852. The so-called Lock hospitals dealt with venereal disease: one was established in 1746 specifically for the treatment of women and children who had caught the disease by being raped – it was a popular belief that venereal disease could be cured by sexual intercourse with a child. There were also some large infirmaries built specifically for workhouse inmates and a substantial number of major London hospitals, such as the Whittington in Highgate (which was an amalgam of three workhouse infirmaries), St Mary Abbots in Kensington, St Stephen's in Fulham Road, King's College in Denmark Hill, Oldchurch in Romford and the West Middlesex, all began this way.

Gradually it was accepted that more should be done specifically for women, and not just in childbirth. A Dr Protheroe Smith founded the Hospital for Women in Red Lion Square in 1843 for the 'treatment of those maladies which neither rank, wealth nor character can avert from the female sex'.

Maternity provision in hospitals began, rather belatedly compared with France, when two wards of St James's Infirmary in Westminster were set aside in 1739 for the use of poor women. This was no ordinary act of philanthropy for the man who began it, Sir

THE London Female Penitentiary in Pentonville Road, depicted in an appeal brochure for funds to pay for an extension. The word Penitentiary is now so commonly associated with prisons that its old meaning, a place for the penitent, is almost ignored.

Richard Manningham, aimed to give potential midwives proper training there. More lying-in hospitals followed, but were usually available only to married women. It was the Westminster Hospital and the General Lying-in Hospital which first admitted single women having their *first* child.

A moral point is made with this regulation, for having children out of wedlock had to be discouraged. In this period, when it is estimated that there were up to 80,000 women and children working either full time or occasionally as prostitutes in London, the authorities were alarmed at the increase in illegitimate births and infanticide. The coroner for north London in 1866 remarked that in that one year he had held inquests on 80 children found dead in the streets and suspected that as many more young corpses remained undiscovered.

In this period, prostitution was so commonplace in London that it linked the underworld with good society. Institutions for 'fallen women' were established, almost invariably with the word 'penitent' or 'preventive' (of disease) in their titles. A typical house was the London Female Penitentiary in Pentonville Road in which the inmates had to exhibit a genuine desire to reform and to show no 'refractory disposition or unmanageable temper'. By 1863 it was estimated that 4,172 women had stayed there, and of these 1,400 had been placed in domestic service, some 900 had been reconciled to friends or families, over 600 had left at their own request and 31 had died. In Fulham a 'Refuge' for 'young females' was opened in what is now Rigault Road. This was later converted to a prison and what survives has become a complex of studio apartments. In 1885, what had been an Asylum for Idiots in Highgate was taken for a penitentiary whose inmates did local laundry and wedding trousseaux.

Prostitutes were remarkably visible both in the streets and in public buildings. In the evenings, when primitive street-lighting made the scene even more lurid, they crowded the main thoroughfares of the West End, especially near theatres in which some were tacitly permitted to solicit in the lounges. (It was, in any case, the common belief that most actresses were prostitutes as well.) Mayhew was not alone among contemporary commentators to perceive that prostitutes permeated society openly at all levels. He observed:

> Not to speak of the first class of kept women, who are supported by men of opulence and rank in the privacy of their own dwellings, the whole of the other classes are to be found in the Haymarket, from the beautiful girl with fresh blooming cheek, newly arrived from the provinces, and the pale, elegant, young lady from a milliner's shop in the aristocratic West End, to the old, bloated women who have grown grey in prostitution, or become invalid through venereal disease.

The women also frequented cafés called 'night-houses', rather seedy establishments which sold a mixture of food, drink and sexual introductions, or else casinos where gambling and dancing were also attractions. That the West End was a magnet for thousands of girls is emphasized in editions of the *Camden and Kentish Towns Gazette*. Editorials of 1867 rail against feckless and overdressed servant-girls heading for the Haymarket on Sundays. These were the casual participants. There was a wide diversity in those for whom the income was their livelihood. At the top end of the scale they could be seen riding in Hyde Park to the prurient interest of men and the disdain of other women; at the bottom of the profession they were syphilitic and pathetic women eking out a living in the slums of dockland.

Mayhew and others believed that the principal cause of prostitution was poverty and went to some trouble to interview many of the girls involved. They were not only poor girls unable to survive on the wages of a sweated trade, but widows struggling to maintain a family on women's wages and unwilling to go into a workhouse where they would be irrevocably separated from their children. Even the most courageous and hard-working among them was caught in the nineteenth-century poverty trap: if she was employed, even on a pitiful wage, parishes were reluctant to give her additional relief; if she had an illegitimate child its maintenance was entirely hers and she would find it difficult to find anything but the most menial employment. Sometimes the prostitutes were children whose home had disappeared with their parents, or else that stock character in novels, the seduced maidservant.

LONDON'S GREEN SPACES

THE VICTORIANS ATTEMPTED SIGNIFICANT CHANGES in many areas of London's social life. To them technical advance and religious belief were likely bedfellows and it must have seemed that many problems could be solved by their dual application. Of their reforms one comes down to us virtually intact – the rescue and provision of open spaces in and around the metropolis. We must be grateful for their obsession with 'fresh air', and the persistence and ingenuity with which campaigners used the primitive legal framework to obtain their prizes. There were, however, several strands in this accumulation of open spaces unrivalled by any other city.

Before the nineteenth century London was already blessed with large parks, in each case the result of kings appropriating land. Hyde Park, formerly belonging to the monks

THE Holme, Regent's Park, by Thomas Shepherd, 1827. This magnificent house was built c.1819 by the 19-year-old Decimus Burton for his father, James Burton, who was himself an architect and builder. Burton senior developed much of Brunswick Square.

of Westminster Abbey, was taken by Henry VIII at the Dissolution of the Monasteries and opened to the public by the beginning of the seventeenth century; Green Park was enclosed by Henry VIII and made into a royal park by Charles II; nearby St James's Park was originally attached to the hospital for leprous women on the site of St James's Palace; Richmond Park was for long used by the public with partial freedom until it was officially opened to the public, and Greenwich Park, in royal hands since the fifteenth century, was in public use by the eighteenth century. This collection was enlarged in 1812 when Marylebone Fields, another of Henry VIII's acquisitions, was transformed into Regent's Park and in 1841 the Crown Commissioners were persuaded to buy up the Eton College interest in adjoining Primrose Hill. Thus, what were for the most part hunting grounds for Tudor and Stuart monarchs all became landscaped parks for the people without the intervention of philanthropy.

More ancient in origin were the commons and public greens to be found around the metropolis and it was to these that the general public went for Bank Holiday fairs and sunny Sunday afternoons. There are many accounts of entertainments for visitors on Hampstead Heath, donkey rides and cream teas, all of which did very good business once the railway had reached the area.

During the eighteenth and early nineteenth centuries commons were being enclosed as private freehold property by lords of the manor as and when they could get an Act of Parliament to do so. Sometimes this was because the lord of the manor was anxious to turn the common land to agricultural account, or else he had his eye on future building development. His right to do so was questionable in English law, because those who held land of him in the vicinity also had rights of pasturage on the common. Dulwich College was permitted by an Act in 1805 to take 130 acres of the common there, Finchley Common was enclosed in 1816, Rush Common at Brixton disappeared after 1810 and also that year an Act permitted the enclosure of all the Lewisham commons other than Blackheath.

By far the most notorious cause was Hampstead Heath, subject of an acrimonious dispute that went on for forty years. It began when the only issue at stake was the rights of the commoners, but it lasted well into the period when it was loftily considered that the general public's need for large open spaces transcended the right, supposed or actual, of a ground landlord to develop for profit. Though the matter engrossed Parliament, lawyers and the public for so many years, it began as a minor affair in 1829 and if handled differently then would have been over quickly. The lord of Hampstead manor, Thomas Maryon Wilson, asked Parliament to allow him to vary his father's will so that he could develop his estates on either side of the newly constructed Finchley Road and sixty acres of park land virtually enclosed by Hampstead Heath. None of this land was subject to commoners' rights. Parliament, packed with landowners like himself, would normally have made no difficulty, but Wilson unwisely asked for permission to build on heath land as well, land which belonged in that grey area of English law where common rights intruded. This was trouble enough since the Hampstead copyholders were an articulate and influential body, but to complicate matters, Hampstead Heath was already more than a local consideration. This was indicated in a supporting speech in Parliament by Sir Charles Burrell, a Sussex landowner, who opined that 'the Lord of the Manor of Hampstead ought not to be precluded from improving his property with the consent of the copyholders, because the tradesmen of the Metropolis chose to make it a place of recreation for themselves, their wives, children and friends.'

Parliament was persuaded otherwise, however, and when a chastened Maryon Wilson returned to the fray fourteen years later after a building recession he excised the heath land from his application. It is a measure of how public opinion about open space had changed by 1843 that opposition to his new plan was based on the *desirability* of retaining the sixty acres contiguous to the heath as open park land: development on those acres, it was claimed, would negate the beneficial value of the nearby heath.

The campaign against Sir Thomas's plans did not finally succeed until his death in 1869, by which time the local residents, whose altruistic fight was no doubt bolstered by a shrewd assessment of the value of their own properties adjacent to open heath, were aided by the Commons Preservation Society, formed in 1865 for the urgent task of saving commons all over the country.

It is from this period that we find the Metropolitan Board of Works and the City of London playing the principal roles of saviours. The MBW's status was straightforward insofar as it was the only body enabled to perform such a task (sometimes with reluctance) within its boundaries. In general, its policy was to buy off the lords of the manors rather than take the more difficult, but cheaper, way of using the Metropolitan Commons Act of 1866 to bypass them altogether. The Metropolitan Board of Works took into its hands commons in Streatham, Clapham, Tooting, Plumstead and Wandsworth as the building boom in south London gathered pace, and numerous smaller spaces such as Stoke Newington Green; it took over Hackney Downs where local men had torn down, with the tacit connivance of the police, all of the enclosure fences erected by the lord of the manor.

The City of London's part in this was more unorthodox since the City had, strictly speaking, no jurisdiction outside its own borders nor any apparent political need to exert one. And yet the City gathered into its portfolio some large chunks of land on the outskirts of London which the MBW was unable to buy because of its territorial terms of reference, and which were beyond the means and perhaps the powers of local vestries. A case could be made for the Corporation's purchase in 1886 of Highgate Wood – the railway now made it easier for City residents, starved of green spaces, to travel out for the day to Highgate. But the City also took over Epping Forest in 1878, Burnham Beeches (1879), Coulsdon Commons (1883), Queen's Park, Kilburn (1887) and West Wickham Common. Clearly there was a substantial lobby influencing the Corporation in its decisions to make these purchases which inherently entailed a continuous and indefinite expenditure; they were far beyond the perceived needs of the dwindling City population. In effect the City was buying on behalf of metropolitan London.

This generosity on the part of the City came, too, after the creation of two parks specifically for Londoners in the crowded slums around the City, Victoria and Finsbury parks. Victoria Park was opened in 1845 between the expanding villages of Bethnal Green and Hackney but still in a location, as *The Builder* complained, 'shut off from general knowledge'. It was a legitimate point, because the new park was at some distance from the teeming alleys of Mile End, Whitechapel and Wapping. However, the original purpose of the park (which therefore influenced the site chosen), was to be a focus of good middle-class houses. It was also part of a government plan to create large open spaces, in the style of Regent's Park, to the north, east and south of the centre of London – Finsbury, Victoria and Battersea parks are the somewhat truncated results.

The architect for Victoria Park was James Pennethorne, whose enthusiasm for slum clearance had led to the construction of New Oxford Street and Commercial Street. The original scheme was for grand carriageways, ornamental waters and landscaped lawns, the sort of features that would attract the would-be fashionable to this unfashionable area of London. However, the plots of land in the grand approach roads he planned found few buyers and, in the end, the park became more recreational than ornamental and more suited to the thousands of local people who needed it. It was left to Angela Burdett-Coutts to provide the money for a new approach road (Burdett Road) across Poplar to make the park more accessible to the riverside parishes.

In 1924 an LCC handbook described the sports facilities, lakes and swimming pools. The Park, it proclaimed, 'is the playground, the garden, and the forum of the East End'. George Bernard Shaw described it in *Candida*:

A lake for bathers, flower beds which are triumphs of the admired cockney art of carpet gardening, and a sandpit, originally imported from the seaside for the delight of children, but speedily deserted on its becoming a natural vermin preserve for all the petty fauna of Kingsland, Hackney and Hoxton. A bandstand, an unfurnished forum for religious, anti-religious, and political orators, cricket pitches, a gymnasium, and an old-fashioned stone kiosk are among its attractions.

Finsbury Park began as a municipal venture in 1850 when a meeting of Finsbury residents resolved to look for some open space for a parish of half a million people which had hardly any at all. The scheme attracted government support but it was not until 1869 that it was formed out of part of the old Hornsey Wood. It was not one of the MBW's more notable successes, since the original plan to buy 250 acres was whittled down by a pennypinching Board to 120 acres and even then vestries such as Kensington, Woolwich, St Marylebone and St Pancras (all of whom had royal parks in or near their borders) were opposed to the whole thing. On the other hand Islington, a parish adjacent to the land in question and without open space of its own, was enthusiastic and, no doubt with calculated generosity, proposed that another park should be formed for the residents of Bermondsey and Rotherhithe. Herein lay a weakness in the MBW's make-up in that localized schemes could run foul of the representatives of vestries that had no pertinent interest in them.

Eventually the battle to save open spaces was mostly won but the results were scarcely even-handed. Hampstead and Highgate, which had the heath and Highgate Wood already, were subsequently blessed with Parliament Hill, Kenwood, Golders Hill, Queen's Wood and the privately donated Waterlow Park, whereas Islington had Highbury Fields and very little else and even areas such as Notting Hill, developing while the cause was at its brightest, had little open space until Holland Park became available in the 1950s; the people of Greenwich, who already had the park gained unrestricted use of Blackheath.

There were numerous small spaces to be worried about. Leicester Square was a rubbish tip and eyesore once the Great Globe (erected in 1851, the year of the Great Exhibition) had gone. Its land title was the cause of much dispute and it was suggested that the MBW should let it go for redevelopment. It was saved, eventually, by a generous donation from financier-cum-MP Albert Grant who some have likened to the ill-fated financier in Trollope's *The Way We Live Now*: certainly he went bankrupt as spectacularly as the fictional character did. And while the owners of estates resolutely excluded the public from the gardens in the many London squares, other village greens, such as Shepherds Bush and Camberwell Green, were brought back into use.

There was another group of open spaces in London – old burial grounds, which after closing orders were put on them deteriorated for want of care and purpose. There were, fortunately, other campaigners who saw their potential and formed the Metropolitan Public Gardens Association in 1882. By 1895 some thirty graveyards had been transformed into gardens.

THE POLICE

POLICING WAS ANOTHER ASPECT OF METROPOLITAN LIFE attended to in the nineteenth century. Though improvements had been effected in the watching system of the capital, mainly through innovations at the Bow Street magistrate's office, London was still largely unpoliced. A Parliamentary Committee in 1770 had met to inquire into the increase of robberies in the City and Westminster, though the City managed to get itself excluded from the investigation. As is the way with most Parliamentary Inquiry reports, nothing was done despite an increase in crime and the apparent inability of the authorities to cope with civil disorders – the anti-Catholic Gordon Riots of 1780 kept London in thrall for about a week. During these, as in any serious affair, the authorities were obliged to bring out troops because the parish watchmen and constables were incapable of deterring a mob, and in any case they were not co-ordinated or trained to do so. The Bow Street office, with a force of about seventy men armed with cutlasses, continued to act as the central crime detection and policing force for that large part of Middlesex near to the City, while the City itself strengthened its own old arrangements. Six more magistrates' offices were created by the end of the century – the one at Great Marlborough Street still exists – but successive governments were still reluctant to proceed with wholesale reform, partly because Londoners and many members of Parliament were highly suspicious of a new force which might in its nature be military. There was a further flurry of speculation as to what might be done at the time of the sensational and grisly murders at Ratcliff Highway in 1811, when in two incidents a few days apart seven people were gruesomely murdered in their houses in this desperately poor part of London. A lodger in a local public house was eventually arrested (he committed suicide before his trial), but this occurred only after forty false arrests had been made, which served to confirm to the general public the ineptitude of the policing system and the incompetence of its officers.

The first police force in London was actually the Marine Police Institution, now known as the River Police, formed in 1798 at the instigation of Middlesex magistrates Patrick Colquhoun and John Harriot. Colquhoun had brought to the public's attention the large-scale pilfering that occurred in the crowded docks of London, quite often with the connivance of ship staff and dock officials. He noted in his *Treatise on the Commerce and Police of the River Thames* (1796) that ship's mates and revenue officers were bribed 20 to 30 guineas a night to hear nothing, leaving organized gangs 'completely prepared with iron crows, adzes, and other utensils, to open and again head-up the casks – with shovels to take out the sugar, and a number of bags made to contain 100lb each.' Or else the stevedores had special clothing with pouches concealed and 'By these means they were enabled to carry off sugars, coffee, cocoa, ginger, pimento and every other article which could be obtained by pillage.' Even the rat-catchers, brought on board to deal with infestation, were part of the system of pillage, as were young boys called mudlarks, who normally searched the Thames mud at low tide for lost or discarded articles: these were organized to wait beneath the ship's sides to receive packages thrown down to them by thieves. This vast loss of merchandise was helped by the the City's insistence, once again based on a fear of lost privileges, that almost every ship had to come to an inadequate Pool of London for offloading and there they had to wait, sometimes for weeks, in the confusion. The West India Company largely financed the creation of a police force on the lines suggested by Colquhoun, much of which was recruited from seamen and watermen familiar with the river and the docks, but their work was made difficult until the high walls that were to distinguish London's dockland were built around each dock complex.

It was Home Secretary Sir Robert Peel who had the patience to steer a Bill through Parliament which created a metropolitan police force in 1829. After all the disagreements on the matter there was a certain weariness in the opposition or perhaps the public was now more receptive. Londoners felt that they were unprotected and a mock advertisement published in 1821 sums up the prevailing view of the public watchmen:

> *Wanted, a hundred thousand men for London watchmen. None need apply for this lucrative situation without being the age of sixty, seventy, eighty, or ninety years; blind with one eye and seeing very little with the other; crippled in one or both legs, deaf as a post; with an asthmatical cough that tears them to pieces; whose speed will keep pace with a snail, and the strength of whose arm would not be able to arrest an old washerwoman of fourscore returned from a hard day's fag at the washtub.*

The City was excluded from any plan to police the metropolitan area. Peel did not want to take the Corporation on, for it could easily scupper his Bill, and the City was happy to

An unidentified force of 'Peelers', thought to be from a south London station.

retain its old ways. Under Peel's plan the metropolitan area as then defined was divided into seventeen districts with a force of about three thousand men, whose central headquarters was at 4 Whitehall Place. Despite a low-key presence – much thought was given to their uniform so as not to antagonize London – it was some time before the force was accepted without hostility. The City, which already had a well-organized day and night watch, established its own police force ten years later.

THE BEGINNINGS OF THE FIRE BRIGADE

ANY PROGRESS IN FIRE-FIGHTING depended upon innovations and private enterprise at first. With pressured water difficult to come by until the nineteenth century, the facilities to limit a fire were necessarily inadequate. Chimneys caught fire if they were not swept regularly and sparks could ignite a thatched roof; the extensive use of candles was logistically certain to cause fires – Whitehall Palace was lost in this way – and if the embers of fires or ovens were not doused properly, as with the Great Fire of 1666, then there was always the possibility of a piece of wood or coal rolling out into a room. The temptation, however, was to keep a fire in all night because before the advent of matches the business of lighting a new one with flint and tinder (paper was scarce and expensive) was time consuming.

Bellmen patrolled London streets at night from 1556 urging residents to take care of fire and candle; many houses had ladders and barrels of water outside, plus grappling hooks for pulling down thatch if necessary. Additionally, parishes in and out of the City had places where ladders and water squirts on wheels were stored, though the gathering together of a volunteer fire brigade usually took too much time.

Finchley Fire Brigade in the 1870s.

The control of a fire on a high building was very difficult indeed. When the fine steeple of old St Paul's was struck by lightning in 1561 (a sign of displeasure from God at the accession of Elizabeth I, it was thought by those in the know), fire-fighting was directed by the Bishop of London and the Lord Keeper of the Great Seal, among others. It was suggested that the blazing steeple should be shot down by cannon, a dangerous exercise in itself, but before anything could be decided the cross and eagle fell down and set the south aisle alight. The blaze was put out eventually by carving a fire-break in the roof, and by enlisting a human chain of five hundred water-carriers.

In 1676, ten years after the Great Fire had destroyed most of the City, six hundred houses in Southwark were burnt down, and in 1682 a blaze in Wapping, despite the adjacency of water, destroyed 'one thousand' houses – probably an exaggeration, but indicative of its scale. At the end of the seventeenth century fire insurance was on offer, and each company formed its own brigade that would attend to fires in buildings they insured, though their job was to save property, not lives. The custom of fixing fire-marks to houses, to indicate which insurance company was responsible, began in that period. This was an improvement but still not satisfactory, for if two adjoining houses were on fire and they were with different insurance companies, then the nearest water facilities were fought and squabbled over, and often monopolized by the first brigade to reach the scene. Even so, the relative efficiency of the insurance brigades encouraged a laxity on the part of the City wards in the matter and the civic brigades turned out only to claim the reward usually given for engines which arrived at a fire, however late.

Inevitably the fire insurance brigades operated within the populous areas of the City and Westminster. In the villages outside where it would not have been feasible or economic to pledge assistance, households were dependent upon parish facilities and the volunteer brigades. By the mid-nineteenth century, however, some of these villages had become towns as populous as the City, but still with rudimentary fire-fighting provision. In 1840 St Pancras Vestry reported that there were four stations in the parish, each with three ladders that would reach an ordinary house, but they were heavy and cumbersome and 'little known to the public'. There was even doubt about whether they had ever been used. There were four fire engines, but one had scarcely been used because no one knew how to operate it. Another engine was surrounded by heaps of stones and impossible to bring out quickly. If St Pancras was derelict in its duty at least in Hackney and St Marylebone the vestries had set up their own brigades of paid, but part-time members under a permanent engineer. In addition, the Royal Society for the Protection of Life from Fire, a voluntary society, had ten stations in the metropolis which appeared to function well and were first to experiment with any new escape apparatus.

The first fire engine with a steam-driven pump was used in the spectacular fire which destroyed the Argyll Rooms near Oxford Circus in 1830. It was a triumphant debut, because the manual fire pumps there froze up in the cold night and only the steam pump kept going.

Competition between insurance brigades was an unnecessary and uneconomic consequence of the system. This led to the companies combining and to the establishment of the London Fire Engine Establishment in 1833, under the command of James Braidwood, with a full-time force of eighty firemen based in nineteen fire stations around central London. It was formed in time to attend to the fire which destroyed most of the Houses of Parliament in 1834, though it saved Westminster Hall. Brave and spectacular effort though it was, the fire insurance companies were obliged to impress upon the government that Parliament had not been insured at all, and that the expense of fighting the blaze had fallen on them; the government was unimpressed by this nudge towards subsidy.

Though the insurance brigade was more professional it was still reliant on local supervision of fire regulations and the indifferent service provided by water companies – quite often it would arrive at a fire to find the man responsible for turning on the watercock unavailable, or the water pressure too low to be serviceable. These deficiencies came home to roost in the Tooley Street fire of 1861. In a warehouse containing saltpetre, tallow and sugar a stock of hemp had apparently ignited by internal combustion; the fire spread through the building because fire doors were open and then moved on to adjacent buildings. Braidwood himself was killed by a collapsing wall and it took two days to

UNTIL the insurance companies combined to form a single fire brigade, there was rivalry between the individual company brigades to be first at a fire which involved properties insured by several companies. The first on the scene gained access to the best and nearest supply of water, leaving other brigades to find alternative sources or else to wait until the only one was available.

control the blaze. The Tooley Street fire cost the insurance companies about £2 million and though they savagely increased premiums the following year they decided to tell the government that they were unable any more to fund a fire brigade.

By then, London was a considerable fire hazard. The laying of gas mains alone presented an incalculable danger and the existing fire fighting system simply had to be replaced. In 1865, after the usual tussle with the City of London, which declined to have a fire service under the control of the Metropolitan Police, a Metropolitan Fire Brigade was formed under the aupices of the Metropolitan Board of Works. The new organization had an area far larger than the old insurance brigade. It stretched from Hampstead to Crystal Palace, and from Wormwood Scrubs to Plumstead, and it was some time before it could build stations and recruit sufficient staff to perform its obligations.

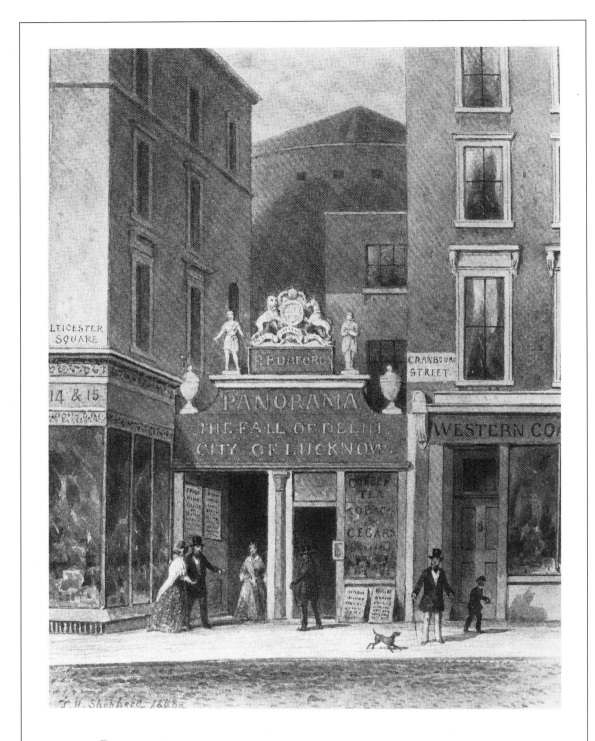

BURFORD'S PANORAMA in Cranbourn Street, Leicester Square, by Thomas Shepherd. This immensely popular form of entertainment was begun by Thomas Barker who, in 1793, leased these premises and erected three circular galleries to display his new art form. His pupil, John Burford, carried on the business. The present Notre Dame de France church in Leicester Place now occupies the old premises.

CHAPTER XV

MOVING SCENES, BRIGHT LIGHTS AND OTHER PLEASURES

IN THE NINETEENTH CENTURY, THE EYE AND THE EAR WERE DELIGHTED WITH INCREASING sophistication. Complicated dioramas, spectacular exhibitions, floridly designed theatres, people's palaces and gin palaces, concert halls and amusement parks, all had their day until in 1896 a display in London of 'moving pictures' foreshadowed their demise or diminishment.

Earlier pleasures were still available; it was not until 1859 that the last of seven 'farewell' evenings was staged at Vauxhall Gardens. It was a protracted end to a long era, and no doubt the management hoped that the threat of closure each time would bring the faithful back to the gas-lit gardens on the south bank. But open-air entertainment, always at the mercy of the elements, could not now match, except with fireworks and balloonists, the scenic and architectural effects contrived elsewhere. Receipts were as unpredictable as the weather, and the location of Vauxhall, once a magical and sparkling jewel on the south shore of the Thames, became a disadvantage as 'the West End', in its entertainment sense, developed.

Three more pleasure gardens of significant size were established before this form of entertainment ran its course. Cremorne Gardens, Chelsea, on the banks of the Thames (the site mostly now covered by Lots Road Power Station) was the largest and most spectacular. Public entertainment here had begun in 1832 when the owner of Cremorne House arranged its grounds so that members could shoot and play golf and every now and then be regaled with fireworks, outdoor entertainments and balloon ascents, one of which featured the intrepid Charles Green accompanied by a leopard. Under the management of a former waiter, the Cremorne in 1846 was transformed into another Vauxhall, adding to the latter's difficulties. It had numerous attractions, including a large orchestra and dancing platform, an immense pagoda, a banqueting hall, concert-room, playhouse and lake. In 1861 a lady of the name of Selina Young, known as 'the female Blondin', attempted to cross the Thames from there by tightrope, only to allow herself to be rescued when a vandal cut the guy-ropes (she was subsequently crippled for life after a fall at Highbury Barn).

A list of attractions over the years at Cremorne reveals a great deal of ingenuity and imagination, but it gradually fell into disrepute. In 1874 a man was killed when his flying-machine, attached to a balloon, fell onto Sydney Street, Chelsea, and there were numerous incidents of bad behaviour at the grounds, especially on Boat Race days. In 1877 the proprietor of Cremorne, short of money and in bad health, gave up the struggle and closed the grounds.

The chief attraction of some pleasure gardens at Kentish Town appears to have been the gaslights – 100,000 of them, according to the publicity. This was the venture of Charles Weston, who was also proprietor of the Holborn Empire theatre. The gardens were developed on seven acres of land attached to his house in Highgate Road in 1863, but by 1868 he was bankrupt and the land became railway sidings.

The third pleasure gardens were in North Woolwich (that part of Woolwich north of the Thames), an area developed from about 1850 on open, low-lying land by the river. The owner of the Pavilion Hotel converted his grounds into ornamental gardens in 1851 and gradually, with the aid of steamboat trips and the new railway, business expanded so that it was possible to stage the full gamut of entertainments, such as balloon ascents, fireworks and concerts. Charles Morton, who we shall encounter later as one of the pioneers of music hall, was for a short time manager here, but decided that it was too much at the mercy of the climate to warrant investment. A later owner devised a baby show in 1869, which drew mothers and babies from all over the country. *The Illustrated Times* described the unusual affair:

> *The youngest mother in the show was fifteen and a few months and the youngest child was six weeks, except in the notable case of a triplet of babies who were but eighteen days old, and whose mother nursed one at a time, while a friend held the other two. In wretched contrast to a baby giant, who looked like a living copy of the Infant Samuel Johnson as Hercules strangling the snakes in Sir Joshua's famous canvas, those puny three called forth pity more than curious interest. They were very odd-looking – one in particular resembling a piece of antique ugliness in a picture of Holbein's. They were also very small, their poor little arms and legs being no bigger than a man's finger.*

The pleasure gardens at North Woolwich appear to have been the last of their kind in London and did not disappear until the 1880s, when much of that area became a public open space.

PANORAMAS AND DIORAMAS

A NEW ATTRACTION HAD BEEN BROUGHT TO LONDON in 1789 by an Irish artist, Robert Barker. He had invented a way of painting on a canvas stretched around the inside of a large cylinder so that, for someone standing in the middle of the drum, it was possible to feel part of the scene represented and to obtain a remarkable degree of perspective. This trick of the eye (another was to be cinema) was called a 'panorama', a word that then entered the English language. Barker was astute enough to patent his idea and by 1793 had improved his technical presentation so that the illusion was more convincing. He opened a new building off Leicester Square, which consisted of a rotunda 90 feet in diameter, with two viewing galleries, one above the other. The remains of this structure survive in the French church which succeeded it in Leicester Place.

This attempt to free landscape painting from its two dimensional form received the approbation even of Sir Joshua Reynolds, who came to see Barker's view of London, as portrayed from the roof of Albion Flour Mills in Southwark. He said to Barker: 'I find I was in error in supposing your invention could never succeed, for the present exhibition proves it is capable of producing effects, and representing nature in a manner far superior to the limited scale of pictures in general.' This was praise indeed but even then not as extravagant as the opinion of painter Benjamin West that this was the greatest improvement in the history of painting.

Such accolades did not, however, ensure a long life for this sort of entertaining art and although there were numerous imitators once Barker's patent ran out in 1801, it was an attraction that was fading by the 1830s. For a time, though, it was popular enough to warrant serious investment and as the novelty wore off special effects of 'movement' were

THE Colosseum, Regent's Park; engraving by W. Radcliff after Thomas Shepherd. The Colosseum opened in 1829 featuring an enormous panorama of London which had origi-nally been drawn by Thomas Hornor, perched precariously in a cabin on top of the dome of St Paul's Cathedral. The enterprise was not a financial success and the building, designed by Decimus Burton, was demolished in 1875; Colosseum Terrace is on its site.

devised, thereby further side-lining the panorama as an entertainment rather than as an art.

Two buildings within a stone's throw of each other became the main rivals to Barker's. The largest was the Colosseum in Regent's Park, a project devised by a land surveyor, Thomas Hornor, who had already turned the skill of cartography into a 'bird's eye' art form. In the summer of 1820 he installed himself very early each morning, complete with cooking facilities, on a platform at the top of the dome of St Paul's Cathedral, and there composed a 360 degree drawing for a panorama of London. Surprisingly, Hornor received a number of visitors to watch him at work, once they had braved the vertiginous perpendicular climb required after the inbuilt staircase had been left behind. The panorama, however, needed a gallery and a rotunda; this was designed by Decimus Burton and erected between Regent's Park and Albany Street. For several years, numerous artists with a head for heights painted the detail of Hornor's sketches on the canvas already in place, and on the dome of the building. Unfortunately, the project, which opened in 1829, was dogged by financial troubles and was to worry Hornor to death. A succession of owners managed to keep it open, introducing new attractions such as *London by Night* and *Paris by Night*, and by adding a new building, the Royal Cyclorama, which showed Lisbon before and after its famous earthquake.

Dioramas attempted to make up for the static and silent drawbacks of panoramas. This invention, brought to a fine art by Louis Daguerre, was presented at the Diorama at Park Square East, Regent's Park, in a building designed by the young Augustus Charles Pugin. The illusion of movement and change was achieved by exposing an image painted on both sides of a transparent material to various lighting effects so that, for example, a Parisian scene could change from daylight to dusk, from sunny to overcast. The spectators watched this transition through a tunnel-like aperture and after its completion the auditorium, including walls and ceiling, moved so that the spectators looked through another tunnel at a different object. The more obvious solution of actually moving the exhibits rather than the spectators was realized in the British Diorama which functioned at 73 Oxford Street in 1828, though its reputation for illusion was inferior to that of the Diorama in Regent's Park.

In this spate of visual innovations the Cosmorama came to London, like the Diorama, from the Continent. The spectator viewed images in a dimly lit room through a series of lenses which gave the illusion of perspective and panorama, and noise and smoke could also be contrived: in effect it was a peepshow. A temporary Cosmorama was opened in St James's Street in 1821 and then in a proper building, again designed by Pugin, in Oxford Street, where it was a modest diversion, just as the later newsreel cinemas were, from a serious bout of shopping.

There were also numerous moving panoramas, consisting of very long paintings on a reel which were unwound gradually before the spectators – the scene might be a journey along a river or a road and could be accompanied by a spoken commentary, while special effects simulated waves or thunderstorms. This early form of virtual reality had the advantage of being more portable than those in the special buildings erected in Regent's Park and Leicester Place. On the continent moving panoramas were developed with great sophistication so that it was possible to sit in a stationary railway carriage while scenery on a roller flashed by, or else the audience might go up and down as on a boat while the scenery was viewed.

Dioramas and panoramas in one form or other survived up to the age of the cinema. It is claimed that a diorama, lit by electricity and depicting a journey from Niagara to London, was seen by over a million people in a year at its building in Westminster.

The Great Globe erected by James Wyld in Leicester Square in 1851 to take advantage of the crowds in London visiting the Great Exhibition was a more complex series of panoramas. It was a globe-shaped rotunda and with the aid of four flights of stairs inside the spectators could see different parts of the world painted on the surfaces around them which 'delineated the physical features of the earth, the horizontal surface being on the scale of an inch to ten miles, and mountains shown by mechanical devices, on thrice that scale'. Snow, enhanced by gaslight, was on top of mountains, and volcanoes erupted in a red glow. Wyld's venture was an enormous success (he also did well selling atlases there) and it was not until 1862 that the Globe was closed.

On a grand scale too, but without panoramas, was the Egyptian Hall in Piccadilly, opened in 1812 to house the collection of showman William Bullock. This consisted of 'upwards of Fifteen Thousand Natural and Foreign Curiosities, Antiques, and Productions of the Fine Arts'. The building, enriched with carved figures and hieroglyphics on its exterior, contained a hall measuring 60 × 40 feet in which the main exhibition was displayed, and also another in Italian style. However, Mr Bullock's collection did not draw the crowds and the building was used thereafter for miscellaneous shows, some of them artistic – Benjamin West exhibited one of his large paintings here and made a considerable sum of money – and some educational. Other shows were merely sensational – Siamese twins attracted the crowds in 1829 as did 'General' Tom Thumb when he arrived to exhibit himself in 1844, brought to the door by a miniature coach and four.

The Egyptian Hall, Piccadilly, 1827, by Thomas Shepherd. The Egyptian Hall was opened in 1812 for the display of curiosities, antiques and works of art belonging to a showman, William Bullock. The then fashionable interest in things Egyptian was the result of the war with Napoleon.

THE GREAT EXHIBITION

IT IS POSSIBLE TO DETECT in all these contrivances and buildings a thread of serious curiosity on the part of the spectators. Londoners of the nineteenth century, although they still liked the freak shows that their ancestors delighted in, were flocking to peepshows and panoramas which had an educative element. An increasingly literate population, stimulated by numerous cheap publications, had become entranced by travel in particular, and by scenic delights in general and they were not so easily fobbed off with entertainments of a purely frivolous nature. The immense pride that Londoners took in the 1851 Great Exhibition stemmed not just from its success nationally and internationally, but from its combination of entertainment and serious endeavour at a time when public opinion was receptive to that apparent contradiction. Prince Albert, whose patronage of and enthusiasm for the Exhibition overcame much political opposition, may well have been too earnest for many people's tastes (and too overpraised by the Queen to endear him to her listeners), but his ambitions for his adopted nation, as crystallized in the Exhibition, were in sympathy with its new-found mood.

The Great Exhibition was, first of all, a triumph of organization made possible by the abilities of Henry Cole, a civil servant in general charge of the project, and Dr Lyon Playfair who arranged the exhibits. Serious work did not begin until the appointment in January 1850 of twenty-seven Commissioners who were, among other duties, available for fund-raising. A Building Committee, which included such names as Robert Stephenson, Isambard Brunel, Charles Barry and William Cubitt, turned down each of the 245 building designs submitted to them but then distinguished themselves by preparing their own plan which, apart from requiring 15 million bricks and a dome larger than that

VIEW of the south side of the Crystal Palace in Hyde Park, near Princes Gate. The original design by Paxton envisaged one without the central atrium – this was added to accommodate some trees on the site.

of St Peter's in Rome, would take too long to build and was ridiculed by their peers and the public. In the ensuing confusion and recriminations Joseph Paxton, a self-taught architect hitherto known for his glass structures in aristocratic gardens, drew a sketch for a 'Crystal Palace' on blotting paper while on a visit to London. In nine days he returned with full plans, in which he had been helped by William Barlow, the engineer of the Midland Railway (and later to design St Pancras station), that envisaged not a brick building but one made mostly of glass and iron, which could be taken out of Hyde Park once the Exhibition was over. As his plans went backwards and forwards between interested parties the concept was improved with the introduction of a transept; this relieved the uniformity of the original elevation and enclosed some large trees on the site.

The final plan was accepted in July 1850 and the Exhibition opened on 1 May 1851, evidence again of the remarkable speed with which the Victorians completed building projects (the present Covent Garden opera house, opened in 1858, took eight months to build). Construction of the Crystal Palace involved the use of standard and interchangeable components which, being mainly glass panes, iron girders and pipes, were made off site. Upon concrete foundations, 34 miles of iron pipes were laid through base plates to take the hollow iron columns which supported the building. Despite the fact that scaffolding was not used in the construction of the building, Paxton himself noted that three columns and two girders were being erected in only sixteen minutes and eighteen thousand panes of glass were inserted in a week. This output depended upon the regular supply of components from one ironworks and one glass manufacturer – a reliance that could not have been well-founded before the age of railways. Even so, it was a gamble, as Dickens emphasized:

> Two parties in London relying on the accuracy and goodwill of a single ironmaster, the owners of a single glass-works in Birmingham and of one master-carpenter in London, bound themselves for a certain sum of money, and in a few months, to cover eighteen acres with a building upwards of a third of a mile long.

The actual construction was almost as absorbing as the exhibition itself: while political criticism in press and Parliament raged and then lessened, Londoners came to look at this new wonder growing in their midst and it became something of a national challenge to finish the building in time. The contractors charged onlookers five shillings for a close view of work in progress – the Duke of Wellington at nearby Apsley House let children watch it free on occasions.

It is a measure of the national self-confidence of that period that half the display space was allocated to 'foreign countries' – those that weren't in the British Empire. In all, there were about 14,000 exhibitors, each with their complement of staff to be accommodated, and there were over 100,000 items on show in the eleven miles of stalls.

Queen Victoria confided in her diary that the opening of the Exhibition on 1 May was 'the greatest day in our history'. In some ways it was. Thousands camped in the park overnight and by the time of the ceremony it was thought that over half a million people were there to witness the comings and goings. All roads were packed with vehicles, all cabs were taken, all hotel rooms were occupied. London was *en fête* for weeks, and it is doubtful if any other event in London's history has involved so many people. One thousand carriages of state arrived, together with numerous other vehicles, to convey the 30,000 guests privileged enough to be inside. And once the formal speeches had been made the 'Hallelujah Chorus', sung by massed choirs of six hundred voices in this modern cathedral, confirmed as no words could that London, for all its faults, was the capital of Europe. It was an awesome occasion. *The Times* recorded:

> There was yesterday witnessed a sight the like of which has never happened before and which in the nature of things can never be repeated. They who were so fortunate as to see it hardly knew what most to admire, or in what form to clothe the sense of wonder and even of mystery which struggled within them. The edifice, the treasures of art collected therein, the assemblage and the solemnity of the occasion, all conspired to suggest something even more than sense could scan or imagination attain.

The Exhibition was no one-day wonder. Over the 140 days it was open over 6 million visitors were recorded and on days when admission was only a shilling crowds of 70,000 were common. And just as the availability of railways had made the building's construction possible so they ensured that millions of provincial people came. The Victorians, with their love of statistics, delighted in being told that over 934,000 Bath buns were sold, and over 1 million bottles of non-alcoholic drink were consumed (anything stronger was banned along with smoking and dogs).

MUSEUMS

THE LEGACY OF THE EXHIBITION was not one of better design in British industry where it has traditionally been ignored. The most visible consequences of the 1851 outpouring of patriotism, pride and innovation are the museums at Brompton on land bought by the profits made by the Exhibition. In 1852 Marlborough House was used to contain a Museum of Manufactures, a project dear to the heart of the Prince Consort. In this unsuitable space many of the exhibits from the Crystal Palace were housed as was also a School of Art and Design which had been previously at Somerset House. Here the ideals of the Great Exhibition were carried forward, and the exhibits included a 'Chamber of Horrors' in which a collection of *badly* designed commonplace articles were shown.

Purchase of land at Brompton was pushed through with great determination by Prince Albert, but did not immediately result in buildings, partly because a grandiose plan to move the National Gallery to a prime position (where the Natural History and Science Museums now are), fell through after a great deal of shilly-shallying. The restless Prince was therefore left with the construction of a small museum on a detached portion of the estate which became the South Kensington Museum and, in time, the Victoria & Albert. Ironically, for a venture that propounded good design as a way of life, the building itself was excoriated in the press. It was an iron structure which owed more to an engineer than an architect. *The Builder* blasted: 'Its ugliness is unmitigated: never was a beautiful sward, where daisies blossom and trees and shrubs put forth their leaves and branches and flowers in forms of beauty unapproachable by man, so vilely disfigured.' It went on: the building 'is in three equal spans, all at the same height from the ground, like huge boilers placed side by side', and it is from this description that the epithet for this museum, the Brompton Boilers, derived. Few dissented from these opinions and it was also found that the building had severe condensation problems.

Fortunately for the development of London, the commitment to transform these flowered acres into a centre for museums did not waver, despite this early fiasco. The Natural History Museum, designed by Waterhouse, was able to display in some magnificence treasures that had accumulated in the British Museum, unseen by the general public. The Science Museum was formed from a variety of small collections but did not materialize until before the First World War.

In the sixty-odd years of Victoria's reign there was a remarkable and sustained development of public buildings which aimed to educate and fascinate the curious. London was pre-eminent in this, though most buildings came about, in the absence of an effective London authority, from sometimes generous but usually muddled government intervention. By contrast, in provincial towns museums, libraries, concert halls and assembly halls appeared in plenty, often the gift of self-made industrialists anxious to have their names in stone or terracotta, or else they were the products of civic pride paid for by corporations able to raise the money to build them. In London, the National Gallery began with the purchase by the government of the picture collection of the late John Julius Angerstein in 1824, and was supplemented by a donation of other works by Sir George Beaumont. These were kept, at first, in Angerstein's house in Pall Mall, until the new building designed by William Wilkins in Trafalgar Square was opened. Here, the Gallery and the Royal Academy unharmoniously shared the accommodation until the latter went off to Burlington House. The National Portrait Gallery began modestly in Great George Street with only fifty-six paintings forming the basis of what was to be a 'Gallery of the Portraits of the most Eminent Persons in British History', viewed only on two days a week.

Two businessmen were responsible for another two galleries. The tea-merchant, Frederick Horniman, amassed a large collection of curios in his house in London Road, Forest Hill, which were occasionally on view to the public. Later this was rehoused in a splendid art nouveau museum built on the site of the house. On Millbank, a reluctant government accepted the gift of sugar-refiner Sir Henry Tate of a building and sixty-seven contemporary paintings, which was to develop into London's museum of modern art.

These attractions were in areas of London already favoured, but there were also two developments in the East End. The first was the Bethnal Green Museum, at that time administered by the local authority. The much criticised iron building of the South Kensington Museum (see p. 216), nicknamed the 'Brompton Boilers', was at that time on the point of demolition to make way for the present Victoria & Albert Museum. The structure was instead transported eastwards, re-erected in 1872 with a brickwork exterior and opened as the Bethnal Green Museum. The first exhibition there was of remarkable quality, being much of the Wallace Collection, which had been left to the public and was awaiting the conversion of Hertford House in Manchester Square. *The People's Magazine* was pleased to report, nine months after the opening in 1872:

> *The people in whose interest this noble undertaking was started, have proved themselves able to appreciate their privileges. The galleries have been thronged by eager visitors who show by their quiet demeanour and intelligent remarks, that the labouring classes of this country are amenable to the refining influences of the arts.*

THE PEOPLE'S PALACES

REFINING INFLUENCES WERE ALSO AT WORK in the Mile End Road. Here, the People's Palace, opened in 1887, was, however, a quite different establishment, providing entertainment of a populist nature, together with educational facilities. One root of it was the New Philosophical Institute, founded by Barber Beaumont in Mile End Road fifty years previously. This was in effect a mechanics' institute which atttempted to give 'persons in the neighbourhood. . .the means of meeting together for mental and moral improvement and amusement in their intervals of business freed from the baneful excitement of intoxicating liquors.' In 1884 its trustees joined forces with the Drapers' Company, which ran the nearby Bancroft Almshouses and School, to create a place of recreation and education for the East End. Two years earlier, Walter Besant, a prodigious

THE People's Palace in Mile End Road, as proposed by its architect E. R. Robson. The first part to be opened was the Queen's Hall in 1887. The remaining buildings are now part of Queen Mary College.

writer of books about London, had published a novel called *All Sorts and Conditions of Men*, in which a young man of Stepney birth and Mayfair adoption, and a young woman of affluent birth and a passion for lawn tennis, discover that in the East End there was little but misery to be found. The East End was portrayed as having 'no institutions of their own to speak of, no public buildings of any importance, no municipality, no gentry, no carriages, no soldiers, no picture-galleries, no theatres, no opera – they have nothing.' The young couple introduced, as is the way with reformers, their own values into what was to them an alien society, and built on land that belonged to them a 'Palace of Delights' in which East Enders could relax, learn and acquire some delicacy. Despite such nonsense the novel was a great success and within five years of publication the Queen herself made one of her rare visits to the East End to open an actual People's Palace. The main feature of the building was the Queen's Hall, which was used mainly for concerts and other entertainments, but gradually the educational work of the Palace, centred around the Technical College on the same site (Hilaire Belloc was an early lecturer), predominated – the surviving buildings are now part of Queen Mary College.

Another 'Palace' – the Great Exhibition had made the word almost obligatory – was Alexandra Palace in Hornsey. With the Crystal Palace itself now re-erected and thriving on the southern heights of London at Sydenham, this was north London's counterpart. A private company converted some open farmland into a park on this site overlooking London and on its summit they re-erected the buildings used to house the 1862 International Exhibition held in South Kensington. However, the company went into liquidation and the empty Palace lay dormant until May 1873 when it was opened to the public, only to burn down sixteen days later. Its successor, largely the building that we see today, was erected within two years and its history up to the present time has been one of grand plans and bankruptcies. There were remarkable firework displays on the slopes, particularly that of 1888 when the 'Last Days of Pompeii' were re-enacted, using the boating lake as the Bay of Naples. Two hundred people dressed as officials, soldiers and slaves took part in this extravaganza, which ended with the spectacular eruption of Mount Vesuvius. Such events were hugely popular but they did not help the financial problems of the Palace itself, which was too large and too inaccessible ever to be viable.

Glass and iron, so handsomely demonstrated by Paxton in his Crystal Palace, were now *de rigueur* in many a large building in London. It was an obvious form of construction for railway stations, but elsewhere it was used to great effect. The Agricultural Hall in Islington was opened in 1862 by the Smithfield Club for occasional agricultural and livestock shows and the rest of the time was let for miscellaneous events, such as military tournaments, circuses, indoor races and dog shows. It was not, in truth, a particularly handsome building, and neither was Olympia in Hammersmith Road, opened originally as the National Agricultural Hall in 1884, but given its more attractive name in 1886 when it staged the 'Paris Hippodrome', a circus-cum-spectacular which included a chariot race, numerous animals and a stag hunt.

The Royal Aquarium in Westminster was a pseudo-classical building with a glass and iron nave. Its name, intended to cash in on the Victorians' appetite for peering at exotic fish, belied its many attractions. It was opened in 1876 and was soon to sport a winter garden, exhibitions, musical entertainments, lectures, roller skating, billiards and performing animals. The promoters' intellectual ambitions for the building were not realized however, and the building's attractions became a hotch-potch of quick-fashion entertainments that occasionally made money, but mostly did not. This elaborate venture died an early death and the site was sold to the Methodists in 1903 for the erection of their Central Hall.

All of these 'palaces', just like the panoramas, began with some educational pretensions, or at least they were added in much the same way as the busy developers of London planted a church in their streets to give them cachet and respectability. Their multifarious and temporary shows could not, by their nature, secure a stable and regular audience, and the struggle to fill seats was a constant one they were no match for the quite remarkable explosion in the number of theatres and music halls which characterized the last half of the nineteenth century.

THEATRE

At the beginning of Victoria's reign theatre had atrophied. The two 'patent' theatres, the Theatre Royal Drury Lane and Covent Garden, still guarded their privilege so that, in theory and mostly in practice, drama could not be presented elsewhere in the London area. It was possible to stage opera, musical entertainments and other forms of musical drama, but not plays; even 'penny gaffs' – temporary small theatres set up in any cheap premises – were pursued by the full rigour of the law if they dared to feature drama without music. Echoes of this absurd prohibition could be observed as late as 1911, long after the patent theatres had lost out, when the Palladium, licensed as a music hall, was fined for including an unmusical excerpt from Shakespeare's *Julius Caesar* in its bill. The reluctance of successive governments to allow more freedom in presenting drama was

Covent garden Theatre, 1810. This was the second theatre on the site (the present building is the third). It was built in 1809 to the designs of Robert Smirke, who modelled it on the Temple of Minerva in Athens.

related to their fear that sedition could be a consequence, despite the fact that the Lord Chamberlain could censor any play. Several entrepreneurs in the East End resented the application of the law to that part of London, and Sam Lane who ran the Union Saloon in Shoreditch, a small theatre and music room attached to his public house, led a march to Westminster which urged the case of East End workers who were entitled to theatre but were denied it because West End prices precluded them. He himself had been prosecuted for presenting Jerrold's *Black Eyed Susan* in his premises.

The Theatre Regulation Act of 1843 abolished the patent theatres but, as luck would have it, because of the depressed economy, no new theatres were opened until 1866. However, the intepretation of this Act by the Lord Chamberlain resulted in some confusion. On his insistence it became usual for managements to seek either a music and dancing licence which permitted the sale of food and drink within the auditorium, or else a licence to stage dramatic productions where food and drink were consigned to anterooms. They were not permitted to obtain both and, by implication, dramatic productions could not take place if refreshments were sold in the auditorium. This was not always a clear division since the intrepid Sam Lane, who later managed the immensely successful Britannia Theatre at Hoxton (it was larger than either Drury Lane or Covent Garden), sold food to his audiences during dramatic performances, seemingly without prosecution. But Lane appears to have been an exception and those who had music rooms or small theatres attached to their public houses – the usual arrangement at the time of the Act – generally could ill afford to pass up the income from selling refreshments during performances and opted for the licence that allowed it. From this legal technicality music hall, as the Victorians came to know it, developed.

MUSIC HALL

MUSIC HALL HAD HAD SOME DECOROUS BEGINNINGS, much more serious than its boisterous descendant. Concerts were given in rooms attached to public houses, part of a process of transforming pubs into places where people were entertained as they drank. The best-known early music hall was part of a hotel. It was run by W.C. Evans, a former actor and chorister, who converted the basement of his Grand Hotel at 43 King Street, Covent Garden into a song-and-supper room in the early 1840s. It was a late-night affair with only men allowed in, since some of the songs were risqué as indeed were the versions supplied by the audience. But a later proprietor constructed an airier auditorium in the yard at the back in 1855, complete with classical columns and gaslight, and introduced opera selections and madrigals instead. Here, women were allowed to watch the proceedings from a gallery, but strict watch was kept to deter the numerous prostitutes in the area.

Blanchard Jerrold, in his *London – A Pilgrimage* (1872) was to reminisce about Evans's Music Hall: 'Any night, you could at once tell by a sudden influx that the House was up.' He remembered in particular a later proprietor called Paddy Green, who 'tapped his snuff box to only the discreetest and sweetest of tunes. . .at the head of a long table, and you could hardly catch the sharp features of the noble earl opposite to you, for the tobacco clouds.'

Mr Evans's establishment was not the only music hall in the area: the well-known Cyder Cellars in Maiden Lane, and the Coal Hole in the Strand, had reputations nearly as famous and a clientele which also excluded the working man, and there was also the Mogul, attached to a public house in Drury Lane, which was later replaced by the Middlesex Music Hall.

The entertainment at Charles Morton's Canterbury Hall in Westminster Bridge Road included opera, the first performances in this country of Offenbach, and the premiere of Gounod's *Faust*. But Morton was the shrewdest operator in the music-hall scene and was credited as being its foremost entrepreneur. He was well aware of the swell of appetite for more populist fare among the working and lower middle classes and he built a new music hall over the skittle ground attached to the Canterbury Arms and then rebuilt it to accommodate 1,500 people. It was, judging by an illustration of its interior, remarkably palatial. A contemporary visitor noted:

At the opposite end to that at which we enter is the platform, on which are placed a grand piano and a harmonium on which the performers play in the intervals when the previous singers have left the stage. The chairman sits just beneath them. It is dull work to him, but there he must sit drinking and smoking cigars from seven to twelve o'clock. The room is crowded, and almost every gentleman has a pipe or cigar in his mouth. Evidently the majority present are respectable mechanics or small tradesmen with their wives.

It was said of Morton that he presented an entertainment of contrasts – comic and sentimental, gymnasts, step-dancers and comedians. He was later to be found managing the Oxford Music Hall, near the junction of Oxford Street and Tottenham Court Road, when music hall in London was entering its heyday. The *National Review* in 1861 noted that:

The Canterbury Music Hall in Westminster Bridge Road; from The Builder, *1876. This building, erected on the skittle ground of the adjacent pub, was one of the most palatial of the early music halls.*

The decay of the street ballad singer we attribute more to the establishment of such places of entertainment as Canterbury Hall and the Oxford, and the sale [there] of penny song books, than to the advance of education or the interference of the police. . .we do not pretend that they will be any great loss.

Typical of substantial music halls that developed from public houses were those of Islington which was regarded, along with the East End, as a centre for them. Collins' Music Hall on Islington Green developed from the Lansdowne Arms; the diet was mainly comic songs, for which the founder, Samuel Collins, was known, but it attracted well-known artists such as George Robey, Marie Lloyd and Harry Lauder. Deacon's Music Hall near Sadler's Wells is remembered in reminiscences of a performer who worked there – even the wage of the 'Chairman' (£5 a week all found) is noted. Music hall was also produced at the Eagle in the City Road, where the artists vied for popularity with renowned doorstep sandwiches and pork pies. Adjoining this was a 'Grecian' Pavilion complete with organ and pianola, where vocalists, including blacked-up minstrels – often called Ethiopians – appeared.

In 1878 there were 57 theatres and 414 music halls licensed by the Middlesex, Surrey and City authorities. Not all of these necessarily were functioning but the impact of music halls may be imagined from these statistics. The top-class entertainers were much in demand in and out of London. Jingoist acts usually did well and stereotypes were appreciated and expected: George Leybourne invented the 'swell' down on his luck – *Champagne Charlie* was his most famous song; Little Tich was the most famous 'dwarf' performer, though *The Spectator* critic said fastidiously, as early as 1893, that 'Personally I do not take much pleasure in the contortions of this grotesque homuncule, this footlight Quasimodo'; Harry Lauder represented a mean and a drinking Scotsman; Vesta Tilley was by far the best male impersonator, famous for her *Burlington Bertie* song; Albert Chevalier typified the coster; and cockney entertainer Marie Lloyd perfected innuendo in her songs; George Robey was a sophisticated comedian and G.H. Elliott, billed as 'the Chocolate Coloured Coon' perpetuated the early 'nigger minstrel' routine well into the 1960s, when the absurd *Black and White Minstrel Show was* on television.

VARIETY THEATRE

FROM MUSIC HALL DEVELOPED THE VARIETY THEATRE – it would be a brave person to define precisely the difference in performance terms, but the new buildings it produced were in an entirely different league to those of the music halls. In the two decades before and after the turn of the century two architects, Frank Matcham and William Sprague, between them built at least thirty-two theatres (not all of them for variety) in London and its suburbs, from the Shepherds Bush Empire to the Rotherhithe Hippodrome, and from the Camden Theatre to the Brixton Empire. Of these about half survive, almost all of them in the inner London area, evidence itself of the decline of theatres outside the West End.

Variety theatre was family theatre; it was music hall made respectable and, indeed, music-hall artists went from one to the other; it was also opulence beyond the experience of many – deep-pile carpets, bright lights, courteous service, gold paint and mouldings; and it was entertainment and spectacle skilfully adapted to contemporary taste and expectations. It was also a tale of rivalry between two theatre empires, one created by Edward Moss and the other by Oswald Stoll.

The London Hippodrome, designed by Matcham in 1900, at the corner of Cranbourn Street and Charing Cross Road, was a spectacular Moss venture. It was at first a circus with a large pool of water as a stage feature fed, it seems, from one of London's underground streams. Lupino Lane, appearing in a farrago called *Zuyder Zee*, nearly lost his life when an unanticipated torrent of water swept him into the auditorium. Water shows were popular, though circus did not draw the crowds sufficiently, and in 1909 the latter was gone, to be replaced by operetta, ballet and then one-act plays once they were allowed in theatres holding music hall licences. Variety theatre then became its stock fare, though revues and musical comedies were more common up to the Second World War.

Stoll, meanwhile, was building a vast variety theatre in St Martin's Lane which he called the Coliseum. It was an enterprise that deserved its superlatives. It was the largest theatre in London, and it had (and still has) a revolving stage in three sections. An advertising sign in the globe on the roof also revolved, and for the first time in a theatre there were lifts to take people to the upper floors. There was an enclosed royal lounge which could be electrically moved to the reception foyer to receive the weary royal guests, and then be withdrawn, complete with the party, away from the public gaze. Telephones for the use of customers were installed and doctors in the audience could be located, if they wished, in their seats if any emergency was notified them. Unfortunately, the moving lounge did not work very well, and the London County Council objected to the advertising sign, so that it was replaced by intermittent lights that gave the illusion of a moving globe. Despite all this the Coliseum, again by Matcham, was a remarkable

A PROGRAMME for the Bedford Palace of Varieties in Camden Town, early 1900s. The Bedford was one of the better-known music halls of north London and was still presenting conventional drama in the 1950s.

building, but as a variety theatre it was a flop and it was closed in two years. It reopened the following year and became a 'regular' theatre in 1931.

The Granville Theatre of Varieties at Walham Green and the Bedford Palace of Varieties in Camden Town were more typical of this new breed of theatre. The Granville, another Matcham building, was opened in 1898 in a newly thriving part of London which had superseded Fulham High Street as the commercial centre of Fulham. It was on a very good site and, founded by music-hall star Dan Leno, it did very good business. Stoll was quick to recognize this area's potential and tried unsuccessfully for years to obtain permission to open another theatre nearby, but he was always refused on the grounds that 'a sufficient number of these establishments already drew crowds of undesirables to the area'. Oswald Stoll Mansions, originally built for disabled ex-servicemen in the First World War, now cover the site he had in mind.

The Bedford has left more memorabilia than most other theatres now remembered only by older generations. This is partly because Belle Elmore, the ill-fated wife of the murderer Dr Crippen, worked here and indeed went through the picket line that included Marie Lloyd during the 1907 strike by music-hall artists. The great lady said that it was best to let Elmore through as she would soon empty the house. The Bedford's fame also rests on the many pictures that Walter Sickert made not only of the sumptuous Bertie Crewe building in the High Street, but of its predecessor, the old music hall to its rear, which had been built on to the Bedford Arms.

In 1884 a brave enterprise was begun in Stratford, east London: the Theatre Royal was a straight theatre, not a music hall, and with an audience unaccustomed to the discipline then common in West End theatres. In the opening production of a play called *Richelieu* the leading man won much applause but, as *The Stage* reported:

*T*HE *Britannia Theatre, Hoxton; from* The Builder, *1858. This illustration was made after the enlargement of the theatre, owned by Sam Lane, to accommodate 3000 people. His widow, Sarah, also acted here and appeared as principal boy in pantomime in her seventies.*

He worked under difficulties and in one important scene had to interrupt the action of the play in order to reprove some inattentive gods who were appeasing their appetites. At the end of the act Mr Dillon very properly delivered the dwellers on high a lecture on the sin of cracking nuts, and it is to be hoped they will profit by his very earnest reproof.

This was not the only difficulty, for while the local press welcomed the theatre for its repertoire, which included plays that did not have a murder every twenty minutes, the local vicar emerged with a petition, signed by other clergy, opposing it because it 'would not tend to the moral elevation of the people of the neighbourhood'.

The best-known theatres in east London were the Britannia at Hoxton, where pantomime reigned supreme and the Whitechapel Pavilion Theatre, a strongly Jewish establishment. Performances at the Britannia could last for five hours without interval.

COFFEE TAVERNS

THE UNINHIBITED PLEASURE THAT THE WORKING AND LOWER MIDDLE CLASSES found in music hall and variety had not gone unnoticed by those who felt that they were getting into bad habits. Prominent among them was Emma Cons, who in 1880 took over the Royal Victoria Hall near Waterloo Station, which in due course became the famous Old Vic Theatre. Miss Cons and others, including Thomas Hughes, author of *Tom Brown's Schooldays*, and Joseph Fry, chocolate manufacturer, had in 1876 formed the Coffee Taverns Company. The aim was to counter the drinking attractions of pubs and music halls by providing non-alcoholic recreations. To this end Miss Cons was responsible for the conversion of the Walmer Castle public house in Marylebone into a coffee tavern where the old beer cellar was made into a gymnasium in which men and boys were

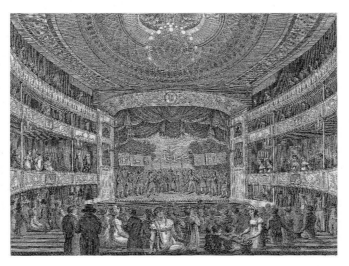

THE Royal Coburg Theatre soon after its opening in 1818. The theatre, now the Old Vic, had mixed fortunes in its early days. It was taken over by Emma Cons, who turned it into an alcohol-free music hall.

segregated. She was able to report a year later: 'Many [customers] are now leading sober and good lives who a year ago were a source of expense to the community and. . .are now hard-working respectable people, emancipated from the enslaving vices into which they were falling.'

It was John Hollingshead, proprietor of the hugely successful Gaiety Theatre in the Strand, who made the suggestion that the Coffee Taverns Company turn the Victoria Hall in Lambeth into a coffee music hall. This opened in 1880, but even with an admission price of only one penny, respectable audiences for this homogenized music hall, bereft of innuendo and alcohol, were to be found only on Saturdays. But Emma Cons persisted with the scheme and was fortunate to attract the financial backing of a wealthy but reformist MP, Samuel Morley, whose hopes for the future of mankind, like those of Miss Cons, rested firmly on education backed up by temperance. As a result the theatre mounted a continuous educational programme of lectures and classes which were better attended than the stage productions and were to lead to the establishment of Morley College, at first in a building at the rear of the theatre. The theatre side of the place was of secondary importance until the arrival of Lilian Baylis, a niece of Emma Cons, who took over management in 1912, and from her time the theatrical reputation of the Old Vic evolved.

THE ADVENT OF THE TEASHOP

BY THE TIME OF MISS BAYLIS the temperance movement had passed its heyday, though it certainly survived as an adjunct of religion for many years to come. It did not, of course, have the good tunes that the devil had, but more importantly its demise was hastened when the provision of food and drink became more respectable. In particular, public houses were rebuilt in opulent style, with electric light, moulded ceilings, etched mirrors and windows, and comfortable seating. Bars were segregated so that in the saloon the clerical classes, at lunchtime or on their way home to the suburbs, would feel comfortable and respectable at the same time. The success of the new pubs coincided with the spread of teashops. The Aerated Bread Company, based in Camden Town, diversified into teashops in 1880, at the same time as the British Tea Table Company began in the City. The ABC chain was regarded as being well managed, for when the company run by Salmon and Gluckstein, tobacconists, wished to open a Lyons teashop in Piccadilly in 1894, their first, they were permitted to on condition that it was run on the same principles as the ABC. Though latecomers to the scene Lyons became the most successful, opening their first 'corner house' in Coventry Street in 1907, which when extended could seat over four thousand people. Soon a Lyons teashop, with its elegant gilt fascia lettering, and its marble tables inside, was in every high street – cheap, pleasant, with standardized food, much of it centrally prepared at Cadby Hall in Hammersmith Road.

Two other catering innovators were Felix Spiers and Christopher Ponds, who in the 1870s opened restaurants attached to railway stations, or else in places like the Agricultural Hall in Islington, which were distinctly above the common standard. Their star establishment was the Criterion in Piccadilly Circus, a beautifully tiled building designed by Verity, which opened on two floors in 1873; it was joined later by the Criterion Theatre in the basement, the first theatre to be built entirely underground. The Trocadero Restaurant across the road began life as a music hall called the Trocadero Palace, but when Shaftesbury Avenue was built the whole place was altered to accommodate the line of the road. The lease of the building was taken up by J. Lyons and here was opened the famous Long Bar, a place of ornate decor and variegated marbles.

LONDON ZOO

SPECTACLE AND EDUCATION WERE INTERTWINED at the new Zoological Gardens in Regent's Park, a circumstance that was to give rise (and still does) to sometimes intractable problems. The Zoological Society of London had been formed in 1826 at the instigation of Sir Stamford Raffles, retired founder and governor of Singapore. Raffles, a man of indefatigable energy, died on his birthday at the age of only forty-five, worn out by a life of strenuous work in hot climates and a scholastic career whose written labours were lost when the ship carrying them sank as he returned to England. He had been active, with Wilberforce, in the suppression of the slave trade and because of this the vicar of Hendon, where Raffles was living at the time of his death, declined to officiate at the funeral service since he himself derived much of his extra-stipendiary income from slave plantations.

The main intention in establishing a collection of animals in Regent's Park was to allow their study by zoologists, but income to help pay for this was raised by permitting members of the public – but not at first the general public – to visit the grounds. Decimus Burton was employed to build a series of what were, in effect, follies to house the animals, but unfortunately the habitual needs of the animals were not known and were certainly

THE giraffes at London Zoo and the Arabs who brought them over to England. The collection of animals here was begun in 1828, augmented in 1830 with those housed at Windsor Castle, and in 1832-4 with the remaining animals at the Tower of London.

not provided for in their design. This elegant and worthy enterprise was in stark contrast to the cramped menagerie then existing at Exeter Change in the Strand where quite large animals owned by Edward Cross were corralled in accommodation even smaller than that provided at Regent's Park. As we have seen (page 139) an elephant went mad there in 1826 and had to be shot by a company of soldiers. Cross eventually sold his collection to the Surrey Literary, Scientific and Zoological Institution, which he himself founded, to form the basis of the Surrey Zoological Gardens, on a 13-acre site east of Vauxhall Gardens.

This zoo, despite its academic parents, appears to have been a showplace pure and simple and was for a long time more popular than its north London counterpart. Rides on giant tortoises, balloon ascents and fireworks, which must have frightened the animals, were frequent attractions, and on one occasion, when a balloon ascent failed to

An elephant and its cub outside King's Cross station; date unknown. The animals were unloaded at London Docks and are on their way to the Zoological Gardens in Regent's Park, with a minimum of fuss and without what would now be an obligatory police escort.

materialize, a mob threw stones at the officials and the balloon, shattering glass in the Lion House, and were only quietened when the pyrotechnic version of the eruption of Mount Vesuvius began.

A cycling race at Alexandra Palace; watercolour by C. A. Fesch, 1886. Cycling as a sport was popular, but it had important social consequences – it enabled thousands of men to cycle to work from the outer limits of London, and it also became an acceptable means of transport for women.

CHAPTER XVI

A SPORTING LIFE

RACING

THE CHURCH OF ST JOHN, LADBROKE GROVE STANDS PROMINENTLY TODAY ON THE SITE of the spectators' viewpoint as they watched horse-racing on the slopes below in 1837. That year, with building development in the doldrums, James Weller Ladbroke leased out some acres to John Whyte who established three courses here at the 'Hippodrome' – one for racing, one for gentlemen who wished to exercise their horses, and one for ladies, children and invalids who could hire traps and ponies.

Described in an advertisement in *Sporting Magazine* as an 'emporium even more extensive and attractive than Ascot or Epsom', it was the nearest racecourse to London and its main course ran in an oval beneath the mound on which the paying customers gathered. It was also adjacent to one of the more notorious slum areas of outer London whose residents, by virtue of a public path that crossed the course, were able to mix at will with the quality of spectators that the proprietor hoped to encourage. As the *Sunday Times* complained: 'A more filthy or disgusting crew than that which entered, we have seldom had the misfortune to encounter.' As they strayed from the path permitted them:

> *Relying upon their numbers, they spread themselves over the whole of the ground, defiling the atmosphere as they go, and carrying into the neighbourhood of stands and carriages, where the ladies are most assembled, a coarseness and obscenity of language as repulsive to every feeling of manhood as to every sense of common decency.*

The standard of racing was also poor. 'Save Hokey Pokey, there was nothing that could climb, or hobble, much more leap over a hedge, and as to a hurdle, it was absurd to attempt one.'

Mr Whyte had other problems. The local residents who had bought houses nearby on the assumption that the development would have some prestige were now obliged to have a racecourse as a local attraction and a racecrowd for company and it was maintained that 'the scum and offal of London assembled in the peaceful hamlet of Notting Hill'. This opposition was never to go away; nor did the impermeable nature of the soil on which the course was laid – a heavy clay that leading jockeys refused to ride on. All in all Mr Whyte's venture was a débâcle and the local residents heaved a sigh of relief when he closed the place in 1842 after suffering heavy losses.

A racecourse was opened on the fields beneath Alexandra Palace in 1868, although the Palace had not yet opened. It was never a distinguished course, but it managed to struggle on until 1970, when the Jockey Club withdrew its licence. Jockeys as famous as Fred Archer, Steve Donoghue and Gordon Richards were to be seen there but too many building and development inhibitions prevented the proprietors from turning the course into a profitable one.

Horse-racing was and still is today in the hands of an upper middle class and aristocratic élite; with leisure on hand and the facility to travel, there was no particular need for them to have courses nearer to London than Windsor or Epsom; and by the time the working class had the leisure to attend race meetings the spread of London had made land too expensive for the establishment of any reasonably large course. Greyhound racing, which became immensely popular in the later 1920s, was slow to start, although

*T*HE *Hippodrome racecourse, Ladbroke Grove, c.1839. The racecourse, around the high land where St John's, Ladbroke Grove, now stands, had a less than glorious existence. It opened in 1837, to the dismay of local residents, who feared not only the crowds but an influx of undesirable people on race days. The soil was too wet for racing and hardly a good horse was to be seen there. The construction of this short-lived enterprise was permitted by the landlords when development of the estate foundered in a property recession. The course closed in 1842 after heavy losses.*

as early as 1876 a mechanical hare which 'so closely resembles the running of a living animal as to be eagerly pursued by greyhounds' was exhibited at the Welsh Harp reservoir in Willesden.

CRICKET

CRICKET, TOO, WAS A SPORT RUN BY GENTLEMEN, but outside London and Middlesex it had become a working-class sport as well, especially in Nottingham where William Clarke, a bricklayer turned cricket organizer, and good underarm bowler, was turning the game upside down by forming All-England teams under the nose of the Marylebone Cricket Club, which regarded itself as the arbiter of English cricket. Clarke, without a private income, played and promoted cricket for money, which offended many in the MCC who regarded professionals as second-class players and northern professionals as infinitely worse, as Harold Larwood was to discover in later years. Northern professionals continued to cause trouble for the guardians of Lord's and went so far as to challenge the MCC's ruling on bowling law. *The Times* thundered:

> *The cause of this unfortunate position of things is to be found in the too prosperous conditions of the players. So long as they can earn more money by playing matches against twenty-twos than by appearing at Lord's – so long as they can be 'mistered' in public houses, and stared at at railway stations, they will care very little for being absent from the Metropolitan Ground, but they are wrong. They may be certain that the 'Gentlemen' will not give way in the struggle.*

MIDDLESEX vs *Surrey at Lords in 1895. The pavilion in the background was opened in 1891. This is the third of Thomas Lord's cricket grounds. On each move Lord transferred the original turf to the new ground.*

Cricket retained its two roots – public school and working class – as it became widespread. Typical of a gentry-cum-aristocratic team was Blackheath Dartmouth Cricket Club, which played on the Earl of Dartmouth's land, but which had no hesitation in hiring an occasional professional if high wagers were in the air. Catering for both classes was a club in Hampstead which ran two pitches, one for 'subscribers' and another for tradesmen.

Enormous wagers rested on the outcome of matches. The game became more competitive and more organized, and in 1864 the Middlesex County Cricket Club was formed by the Walker family of seven cricketing brothers, who lived in a house called Arnos Grove, and whose Southgate team successfully challenged the United All England team for several years. The county club developed out of this Southgate nucleus and often played at a disused cattle market in Islington.

SKATING

A NEW CRAZE BEGAN IN 1875 which involved an entirely new public in physical recreation. This was roller skating – an import from America where the problem of a guidable roller skate had been solved and patented. The first rink in England was opened with great success in Brighton in 1874, where the charge was one shilling for the skating and sixpence to hire the skates. In London the first franchise to develop the invention was bought by a Mr Prince, who owned a sports club in Belgravia; he was careful to ensure that the better-off classes took up the activity and it was not long before the Prince of Wales was a skater. The number of women to gain entry into Mr Prince's exclusive rink was limited to those who had been presented at Court, and those that did gain entry skated in the voluminous dresses of the period while their male partners were to be found in suits and stiff wing collars.

Sadler's Wells Theatre and the Royal Standard Theatre in Shoreditch were gutted so as to lay down rinks, though the one at Sadler's Wells failed in a month; by 1876 it was estimated that about fifty skating rinks existed in London. At the Oxford Circus rink, on which the present Salvation Army hall stands, the Coldstream Guards were enlisted to provide background music, and at the Duke's Theatre a burlesque with performers on skates pre-dated Lloyd Webber's *Starlight Express* by a hundred years.

At the same time ice skating became the rage. There was a 'Glaciarium' at the Old Clock House in the King's Road, Chelsea, and the Victoria Rink in Cambridge Heath Road boasted 30,000 square feet of ice.

TENNIS

T HE ALL ENGLAND CROQUET CLUB was formed in 1869, added Lawn Tennis to its title in 1877 and then, recognizing the latter game's greater popularity, renamed itself the All England Lawn Tennis and Croquet Club five years later; the first Wimbledon tennis championships were played on the Club's lawns in 1877. For the middle classes tennis was an improvement on skating – a court could be established in many of the large gardens of suburban houses, or else exclusive tennis clubs permitted the apparent quest for exercise to disguise a search for a marital partner.

The Queen's Club in Fulham developed to cater for the tennis craze. It was laid out as a general sports club when the Princes Rackets and Tennis Club closed in 1887, and by 1900 there were thirty grass courts, surrounded by indoor courts, a cricket pitch and a rink which could be used either for roller skating or ice skating simply by flooding the asphalt in winter in the hope that it froze. Nearby in Fulham the élite Hurlingham Club began soon after 1867 to cater for pigeon shooters – in those days real pigeons were set loose from traps to the accompaniment of great excitement and heavy bets. Polo was introduced here in 1874 from India and it was so successful with the aristocratic classes that Hurlingham became the most important venue for this expensive pursuit. At a gala match to celebrate the Queen's Jubilee in 1887, no fewer than thirty royals were present. By the time that pigeon-shooting had been banned, other sports were added, including tennis, archery, croquet and golf.

FOOTBALL

TENNIS, DESPITE THE INTRODUCTION OF HARD COURTS in municipal parks in the twentieth century, remained mainly a middle-class game, but football, which was briefly given society status by public schools in the nineteenth century, was reclaimed by the working classes, whose undisciplined and roisterous enthusiasm for it is noted since at least the sixteenth century.

The Football Association (FA) was formed in 1863 to regularize the rules of the sport and encourage its development. Clubs from the London area at the first assembly of the Association were Barnes, Blackheath Proprietary School, Blackheath Crusaders, Crystal Palace (a forerunner of the present club), Forest (Leytonstone), Kensington School, No Names (Kilburn), Perceval House (Blackheath), Surbiton and the War Office. Blackheath Proprietary School was unhappy with a new rule that the ball should *not* be carried by players other than by the goalkeeper, and the school also declined to accept rules which prohibited holding, pushing, tripping and hacking of shins which would 'utterly destroy their game and take away all interest'. This aggressive team left the Association and continued to play their own brand of football which, some say, developed into rugby.

The FA Trophy (Cup) was first played for in 1871, but it was not until 1883 that the stranglehold of teams from southern public schools, the universities and the Army was broken, when Blackburn Olympic defeated the Old Etonians at the Oval. The formation of the Football League in 1888 emphasized the shift of proficiency in the game from amateurs in the south to professionals in the north, to such an extent that when the team based on Woolwich Arsenal applied for membership of the League after their formation in 1886, their nearest geographical opponents were in Birmingham which meant, of course, a good deal of expensive and time-consuming travel to matches.

Most of the London clubs had modest and uncontrived origins. Arsenal were, as their old name denotes, made up of workers at the Woolwich Arsenal in south London, and it was not until 1913, seeking larger attendances, that they moved to Highbury in north London. Conversely, Millwall descend from Millwall Rovers, a team made up of workers from Morton's jam factory in West Ferry Road in the Isle of Dogs, and they later migrated to the other side of the river. Tottenham Hotspur were an offspin of Hotspur Cricket Club, formed in the Northumberland Park area of Tottenham, and which used the nickname of that early member of the Percy family in their title; a meeting of the cricket members underneath a street gaslamp in 1882 is said to have formed the football club so that they had something to do during the winter. A club called Upton Park in east London became the rather prosaic Thames Ironworks in 1895, before changing to West Ham in 1900. Two youth clubs, Christchurch Rangers and St Jude's Institute, came together in 1886 to form Queen's Park Rangers, and the lads of a Sunday School at St Andrew's church in Greyhound Road founded Fulham St Andrew's in 1879 – seventeen years later they acquired the derelict house and grounds called Craven Cottage. Crystal Palace may claim seniority as a club, but though founded in 1861 for members of the staff at the building, the club went into abeyance for a time and was refounded in 1905. The only club formed with commerce in mind appears to have been Chelsea after a local businessman, H.A. Mears, conceived the idea of turning Stamford Bridge Athletics Ground into a football stadium, and when Fulham declined to take up residence he formed his own team.

Caricature of John Henry Newman by 'Spy', published in Vanity Fair. *Newman (1801-90), was a leader of the Oxford Movement which sought to uphold the integrity of the Prayer Book and defend the doctrine of the apostolic succession. In 1841 he argued in a tract that the Protestant articles did not disavow Catholicism. He himself was received into the Catholic church in 1845, founded Brompton Oratory in 1850 and in 1879 was created a cardinal.*

CHAPTER XVII

A MISSION TO SAVE

THE NINETEENTH CENTURY WAS REMARKABLE FOR ITS RENEWED PREOCCUPATION WITH religion, a vast proliferation of churches and chapels, and the evangelical nature of its religious activity. This came intertwined with political reform, Sabbatarianism, temperance, charity work and education, so that in the end saving souls was a rampant business.

This was a far cry from the late eighteenth century when religion, by comparison, was in the doldrums. Over the previous hundred years the Test and Corporation Acts of the seventeenth century had helped the Church of England see off Dissent. Those Acts had precluded non-conformists from taking part in national or municipal life either as representatives or paid officials, from going to Oxford or Cambridge, or from obtaining a commission in the Army or Navy. Though the Church in theory required conformity to its doctrines, it was extremely tolerant in how those doctrines might be interpreted, and almost anyone, unless Jewish, Catholic or devoutly non-conformist, could be accommodated within it. And why not, if a professional career or a place in local society was at stake? Even the surge of Methodism was not, in the lifetime of its founder, a threat, for it was regarded by many, including Wesley himself, as an adjunct of the Church of England. Financially, the Church was in good heart, even if its revenues were inequitably distributed, and it retained its power to levy a Church Rate across the board, to be paid by believers or non-believers regardless.

It was hardly surprising then that the Church of England began the century in complacent mood, and yet within thirty or forty years it was consumed by controversy and factions and was in direct rivalry with both the State and non-conformist sects.

EVANGELICAL CHRISTIANITY

THE RELIGIOUS REVIVAL OF VICTORIAN TIMES may be summed up in the word 'evangelical'. The flowering of the Methodist church, the repeal in 1828 of restrictions on non-conformists, the need of the Church of England to respond to social problems, and the influence of new thought about its own nature, all shook the Church's complacency.

The most public shock were the publications of the so-called Oxford Movement, a group of Oxford University scholars, including Newman, Pusey, W.G. Ward and Hurrell Froude. In *Tracts for the Times*, published from 1833, they sought to re-locate the Church of England in the Holy Catholic Church and to contrive for it an apostolic descent. Coming from such learned pens these publications provoked a storm of outrage from those who smelled a whiff of incense and candles behind them. Newman emphasized that his definition of the Holy Catholic Church did not necessarily mean the Roman Catholic Church, but even so he was himself to go over to Rome in 1845. There were, however, many within the Church of England who sympathized with the Oxford Movement's view that the Church should consider its nature. The Church had, after all, descended into not much more than a social appendage and a complex of pluralisms. Closely allied countrywide to the squirearchy, it was seen as no friend

The Rev. Charles Spurgeon (1834-92), one of the most famous evangelical preachers of his time. The Metropolitan Tabernacle near the Elephant and Castle, which could seat six thousand people, was built especially for him.

to the growing swarms of destitute and desperate. The vicars in their pulpits compiled their thematic and sometimes closely argued and delicately phrased sermons for the approval of those in the front pews, leaving the servants, charity children and almspeople in the galleries yawning from incomprehension or boredom. The unmarried clergy were useful additions to make up a dinner table at the larger houses or to take an interest in the less attractive daughters, but they were rarely regarded as social workers among those who had no dinner table. In short the parish priest may have been a stable influence in the social fabric but he was hardly a religious influence. Among many lay people, a closer involvement of the Church in social problems was anathema anyway. Lord Melbourne, who found himself listening to a sermon advocating such a course, remonstrated afterwards that 'things have come to a pretty pass when religion is allowed to invade the sphere of private life.'

The Oxford Movement preached a return to that paternalistic age, pre-Reformation, when the clergy and monasteries supposedly cared for the community. This matched quite well the growing enthusiasm for Gothic architecture and the rejection of 'heathen' architecture for church buildings in particular. When University College in Gower Street opened in 1828 to give university education to those who might be excluded by religion or the lack of it from Oxford or Cambridge, the use of Classical architecture instead of Gothic confirmed many prejudices. A measure of the controversy which the Oxford Movement provoked were the so-called 'surplice riots' which took place at St Barnabas Pimlico in 1850, a new church built to incorporate the ritualistic ideas of the Movement, and at St George-in-the-East, off Ratcliff Highway, where the rector and curate introduced similar practices, regarded as Roman Catholic, in 1859. The St George-in-the-East Vestry circularized other London vestries asking for their support in banning these 'innovations' and the Bishop of London was persuaded to appoint a Low Church afternoon lecturer there; outraged parishioners fearing a return to Catholicism, entered the church with their hats on, smoking pipes and leading dogs.

The decision of the Pope to revive the Catholic hierarchy in England did not quieten matters. So worried were Catholics at violence against their persons that when the Passionist Fathers were looking for a new home in north London in 1858, they disguised themselves so as not to be recognized as priests before they took a lease on the Black Dog public house at Highgate, which became in time part of the church of St Joseph's.

Whatever else it did the Oxford Movement helped to divide an increasingly thoughtful Church of England into three factions: the High Church, which sympathized with the Oxford Movement and in some cases adopted rituals which outraged anti-Rome Christians; the Broad Church which hoped that the Church would contain all sorts of inclinations from Methodism to Christian Socialism; and the Low Church, an evangelical wing which would have been equally at home, even if it disliked the architecture, in a Methodist hall. And while the High Church was inclined to immerse itself in theology, the Broad and the Low Church went actively into the minefield of social problems.

As for the Dissenters, they themselves had fragmented. The Methodists, Independents and Quakers of the eighteenth century were joined by new factions. There were Primitive, Calvinist, Wesleyan and Whitfield Methodists; Baptists, General Baptists and Particular Baptists; Presbyterians, Scotch Calvanists and Calvanists; Unitarians, Freethinkers, Irvingites, Huntingdon Connectionites, Moravians, Sandemanians and followers of Joanna Southcott – a bewildering selection, but most of them propounding an uncompromising fire and brimstone message. The Purgatory of the Catholics, and the priest's ability to ameliorate it, might have been sniffed at, but the evangelicals were quite certain about Hell's revenge and their own ability to avoid it. None however were so gloomy or masochistic as the Plymouth Brethren. Poor Edmund Gosse, the poet, was brought up by a decidedly austere father who was a member of the Brethren, and had a childhood devoid of pleasure and diversion.

Preachers attracted enormous crowds unthinkable in modern times and they sold vast quantities of sermons. None was so popular as Charles Spurgeon, who was 'called' to the pulpit of a baptist congregation in Southwark in 1854 and who in a year or two was hiring the Surrey Gardens music hall because those attending numbered ten thousand. At the age of twenty-two he was the most popular preacher in London and by 1861 the Metropolitan Tabernacle was built for him at Newington Butts (part still survives) which could and often did accommodate six thousand people. One of his sermons, dealing with baptismal regeneration, sold 200,000 copies. Another meteor was the Rev. Edward Irving who took over the almost deserted Caledonian Church near Hatton Garden in 1822. In a few months attendances were at least 1,500, including nobility, the Duke of York and the prime minister. His sermon for the London Missionary Society at the Whitfield Chapel in Tottenham Court Road in 1824 was so long that it had two intervals of hymn singing: it was dedicated, with some aptness, to the poet Coleridge, who himself could hardly bear to be interrupted.

CHURCH BUILDINGS

A GREAT MANY CHURCHES WERE PLANNED and built to adorn the new housing developments of London – these were always Church of England, and the Dissenters had to shift for themselves in finding sites to rival them. Most of these churches were, in effect, a selling point, intended to impress on the middle classes, who bought the terrace houses of mid-nineteenth-century London, that they were buying into respectability. Not all of these new buildings were cynical ploys of developers. The easily led Rev. Samuel Walker, a devout man with good financial reserves, lovingly built a church in Notting Hill on which he proposed to erect a spire taller than that of Salisbury Cathedral, but alas his investment in the surrounding estate crashed due to the activities of the developer, and he was left with an incomplete church that was spireless for the rest of its existence.

By the time the Church of England realized that it had not enough churches to accommodate the vastly increased population of London, the Dissenting sects had taken advantage. Chapels and mission halls by the hundreds were built and their ministers entered the homes of the deprived with the same eagerness (and bearing the same gifts) as missionaries to the Congo. The Church of England responded with more and more buildings, together with church halls and Sunday Schools, but it was through its funding of day schools that it made a comeback amongst the poorer classes. Many Church of England clergy, however, did not have either the inclination or the panache to proselytize among the working classes. The Rev. Pratt who worked from Christ Church in Deptford was so much a failure that his funding was withdrawn because no one came to his church. He was, he said, 'always about among the people' but 'he couldn't get at 'em.'

CHARITY

N O POLITICAL REFORM MAY BE DISCERNED in the evangelizing activities of either the Church of England or the Dissenting sects. They seem to have accepted that God had ordained that some were poor and some were rich and that a person's place in life could not be radically altered in this respect: they might all be equal in death, but that would have to wait a while. From this stemmed the admonition that the poor must be sober, industrious and obedient and there is good reason to believe, as many have suggested, that England escaped a political revolution of the kind that engulfed the Continent because of the number of religious organizations repeating such admonitions at a crucial period.

But the churches did unleash an enormous wave of charitable funds, even if the money was often misdirected, and they were doing what the State and the municipalities declined to do. In this they were at one with the views of the Oxford Movement in reclaiming the function of charity for the Church so that the State was not involved. It was this perceived role of the Church that was also at stake in the long and acrimonious debates that preceded the passing of the Elementary Education Act of 1870 which enabled School Boards to provide education in competition with those schools run by Church and non-conformist bodies.

The number of missions which existed in London at the height of this outpouring of zeal will probably never be known. Some were in temporary accommodation; the buildings of others have long since gone or else have been transformed into factories or warehouses, though the larger ones quite often remain, used now by sects of other names.

Outdoor preaching at the People's Mission Hall, Whitechapel, in 1870 (left). Rev. William Booth (1829–1912), who founded the Salvation Army in 1878 (right). The wearing of a uniform meant the presence of the Army among the poor was immediately recognizable.

Typical of these was the one erected in Kentish Town to hear the message of William Gittens. He first began in a little room, and so naturally did sermonizing become him that within years he had his own 'Ebenezer' chapel. A witness wrote that 'While discoursing on the love of God as exhibited to a sinful world by the gift of His beloved Son, he has occasionally been overcome by his emotions, and tears have rolled down his face, and the congregation could not fail to be deeply impressed by his theme.' John Ruskin in his *Praeterita* describes a chapel in the Walworth Road as:

> *An oblong, flat-ceiled barn, lighted by windows with semi-circular heads, brick-arched, filled by small-paned glass held by iron bars [and with] galleries propped on iron pipes, up both sides; pews filling the barn floor, all but its two lateral, straw-matted passages; pulpit, sublimely isolated, central from sides, and clear of altar-rails.*

Ploughing the hardest ground was the Salvation Army. Margaret Harkness (under the pseudonym of John Law) in her book *In Darkest London* (1889) notes the reception given to clergymen and Salvation Army at a place in the East End:

> *They were a savage looking set of men. No policeman ever entered alone into their kitchen. A clergyman found his way in one Sunday evening. He was stripped, in order that the men might see if he was a detective. Finding all his linen marked with the same name, and nothing in his pockets, they kicked him out, advising him never to come there again unless he was plentifully supplied with soup tickets.*

Things were different when the Salvation Army women clutching bundles of *War Cry* visited:

> *There they sat, doing nothing, when the slum saviours opened the door. Bits of pipe, ginger-beer bottles, pots and refuse lay upon the earthen floor. A lamp hung from the ceiling. They were glad to have a War Cry to break the monotony of their Sunday afternoon, and they greeted the slum saviours. They sang a hymn and the thieves joined in the chorus!*

The Salvationists did not approve of workhouses and nor were they allowed in by the authorities – only Church of England and Roman Catholic ministers had right of entry into the bastilles of the nineteenth century. Margaret Harkness is again our observer:

> *General Booth has stormed many places, but he has not gained admittance for his red vests and poke bonnets into the metropolitan workhouses. These places remain closed to him. The Salvationists hold meetings and sing hymns at the gates, and they seem to think the time is coming when their drums will be heard even in the Bastille. But at present workhouse religion is carried on to order, and pauper souls are as strictly watched as pauper bodies.*

TEMPERANCE

ALL THE EVANGELICALS WERE AGREED ON ONE THING – that alcohol led downwards. So impressive was their lobbying on this subject that by the 1880s no politician could afford to shy away from support for the Temperance movement. It was *the* politically correct campaign of the century. The success of the Temperance movement may be seen in the lack of public houses in housing developments of the 1870s to 1890s – on both sides of the Finchley Road, for example or in Muswell Hill. On outlying estates, such as those of the Artizans, Labourers and General Dwellings Company at Wood Green, Queen's Park and Shaftesbury Park, pubs were excluded – an absence thought both morally right and attractive. The London County Council either suppressed pub licences in areas which it redeveloped or else as a matter of social policy included as few as possible in new estates, separating them as far as possible from residential areas. The owners of large London estates gradually reduced, by opposing licence renewals, the number of outlets on their estates. The Bedford Estate tally was reduced by at least twenty by the end of the century, and the Duke of Westminster pursued a similar policy on his Grosvenor Estate. They were responding to many accusations that the aristocracy with its vested interests in the manufacture of beer and spirits was happy enough to encourage retail outlets on their own lands.

It was a campaign that bit deep long after it had lost its momentum. The Progressives on the LCC were accused with purposely reducing the number of public houses whenever they could, and there is no doubt that they did. Even as late as the 1920s Ramsay MacDonald proclaimed that:

Everyone admits that the drink problem is pressing both from a moral and an economic point of view; that the Trade has become a menace to the public life of the country, and that it corrupts politics; that a temperate democracy is required to shoulder the responsibilities of popular Government.

The Independent Labour Party passed a resolution in 1923 which said, 'This Conference declares its antagonism to the drink traffic as an insidious factor in social degradation, and affirms its belief in the public ownership and control of the liquor traffic.'

SABBATARIANISM

TEMPERANCE IMPINGED UPON THE RELAXATION of the very classes that the evangelicals were trying to convert to their religious views. So did Sabbatarianism. This was not a new fixation, for it already bedevilled the family life of millions by the beginning of the century. There was, though, a paternalism within it that was never quite eradicated. In 1844 William Gladstone, in pushing through an Act which obliged railway companies to run third-class carriages that had protection from the weather, was not prepared to have these carriages available on Sundays, though he had no objection to carriages being used by first- and second-class passengers. In his view 'the working respectable mechanic would not choose the Lord's day for travelling, and were it otherwise it would be bad policy in government to encourage such a system. The observance of the Sabbath is the main support of religion.' In social reformer John Ruskin's home only the Bible was read on Sundays and the pictures on the wall were either screened off or turned around so as not to distract.

As many things as possible were closed on Sundays, although in working-class areas the ban on street markets was often ignored, since it was the only full day that people could shop. Baroness Burdett-Coutts's Columbia Market in the East End did not open on a Sunday, which did not endear it to the local population, which included many Jews for whom Sunday was an important shopping day. The LCC, prompted by a mixture of low-church radicals and Fabians banned music in their parks on Sundays, and the playing of games until 1922.

Beer is—
Best Left Alone

THE library of the Highgate Literary and Scientific Institution in 1895. This Institution was founded in 1839, in a period of intense activity in the promotion of knowledge to all classes of society. Many such institutions were opened throughout the country but that at Highgate is one of the few which survive today and it is, remarkably, very much unchanged in its nature. It remains the centre of Highgate Village life, with a flourishing library and programme of talks on literary and scientific subjects.

CHAPTER XVIII

A BIT OF LEARNING

THE LITERARY DUSTMAN AT HOME

SCHOOLS FOR THE POOR

WHEN THE LONDON SCHOOL BOARD (LSB) OPENED ITS FIRST PURPOSE-BUILT school in 1873, in Old Castle Street, Whitechapel, there was no great fuss. It was, however, a significant event in the history of London's education, for it marked the beginning, not only of compulsory education between the ages of 5 and 13, but of the division which exists today between local authority and voluntary (mainly church) schools.

The passing of Forster's Education Act of 1870, which set up school boards throughout England, was perceived correctly as affecting only working-class children; and in many people's minds it applied only to children too poor or too godless to attend National or British schools. The question of whether God should appear in the curriculum was, in fact, one which stirred up much argument and in the end the LSB settled for a compromise which allowed for Bible readings in schools, but of an undenominational nature. This did not, however, satisfy the many Jewish parents of the pupils at Old Castle Street, but trouble was averted by the appointment of a Jewish headmaster.

There were other opponents to Board schools. First were those who thought that they were a threat to the British and National schools and all the other schools administered by philanthropic, religious and parochial bodies. Second were the ratepayers who suspected that they would be an expense over which they had no control, since the Board would precept the local authority for the money needed. Although illiteracy was rife in London (a correspondent to *The Times* in 1868 noted that of 54 children between the ages of 8 and 16 he examined, only 19 could read well), it was only an amendment to the Act which brought about London's inclusion. If the vested interests had had their way, the provision of education in the capital might have continued, like the administration of the London parishes themselves, in the same way for quite a while longer.

Research by the LSB established that about 575,000 children in the metropolitan area fell within its remit, of which about 400,000 went to some sort of low-grade school and the rest to none at all. That London had got into this abysmal state was partly due to the remarkable increase of population which had swamped the resources that vestries and charities could muster, and partly to the reluctance of the churches, Established and non-conformist, to look beyond their own concerns and interests.

For at least forty years debate had raged as to the desirability of government intervention in education, or indeed in any local facility. The grant for school building made in 1834 to the National and British Schools was seen by many to be the thin end of an expensive wedge even though state provision of education was not really a prospect at the time. But during the nineteenth century governments looked more closely and legislated more particularly so that the wide variety of educational establishments on offer were no longer as unsupervised as a hundred years earlier. It was obvious, for example, that in many places the endowments for school provision, made perhaps centuries before, were not being used to great effect. A merger with another charity might well produce a school that was of significance rather than continuing with two indifferent institutions.

Putting aside the problems of the poorest in society, nineteenth-century London inherited a robust assembly of schools. Endowed schools, a good many of ancient

A CARPENTRY class at the Kilburn Lane Higher Grade School in the 1890s. Board schools taught working-class children and manual skills were an important part of the curriculum.

foundation, existed around the City and in the suburbs; some had developed, by the standards of the day, into adequate grammar schools and others had lagged, for want of money or initiative, so that they offered hardly more than very elementary education passed on by scarcely educated tutors – Highgate School was an example of the latter, intended for poor pupils and virtually ignored by the priest who was supposed to teach them. The Endowed schools were sometimes called Free schools, but they were not necessarily available to the poor since some had admission fees, and boys had often to supply their own books and other equipment, quite beyond a poor family's resources.

There were numerous 'academies', of which a number were founded in the latter part of the seventeenth century by non-conformist clergymen dispossessed of their livings by intolerant Acts of Parliament, and by the eighteenth-century non-conformist academies existed in probably every village around London outside of the proscribed 5-mile radius.

Other schools were founded simply to give employment to younger sons of middle-class families unable to exist on whatever private income came their way; or else governesses, with some inherited money, escaped the social limbo of giving private tuition to children of better-off families and set up on their own. Charity schools without any endowments at all struggled to educate poor children in reading at least, and from the Bible in most cases. There were schools run by City livery companies such as Merchant Taylors', others attached to ecclesiastical bodies such as St Paul's or Westminster Abbey, and there were modest schools funded by parish authorities or churches such as Clerkenwell Parochial School, which is now in Amwell Street. The Sunday School movement began in the later part of the eighteenth century as non-conformist churches expanded their activities and the established church sought for ways to match their conversion rates. At the lower end of the scale were Dame schools, often little more than child-minding facilities in crowded

A DAME school in Camden Town; date unknown. The illustration hits hard at the inadequacy of such schools but for some parents they were, despite their shortcomings, socially preferable to Board schools.

rooms managed by women with hardly any education at all. It was considered by the Duke of Newcastle's Commission in 1859 that generally Dame schools taught nothing but reading and sewing; but nevertheless some did have educated and conscientious women in charge and the social status of these modest establishments was preferred to that of the later National Schools by many parents.

The local religious schools, as numbers rose and resources were at a premium, were to be the scene of experiments in tuition in the nineteenth century. In 1808 what was to become the British and Foreign School Society was established to promote the educational methods of the Quaker, Joseph Lancaster. He had begun a school for very poor children at his family home in south London and in 1801 took a room in Borough Road to expand his activities. Over the door he inscribed: 'All who will may send their children and have them educated freely, and those who do not wish to have education for nothing may pay for it if they please.' Lancaster had little money himself – even less with which to pay tutors – and was obliged to devise a way in which the more advanced pupils could teach the others. His school was thus divided into small units each under the charge of a pupil-monitor, and gradually a smattering of education was passed on to everyone at a remarkably small cost. In a pamphlet Lancaster issued in 1803 he described how flat tables covered with a fine layer of sand served as writing tablets; spelling sheets were placed in front of each unit of pupils and from them they traced words in the sand until they remembered their formation: after that the pupils went on to memorizing passages from the Bible. Discipline was instilled, not by corporal punishment, of which Lancaster disapproved, but by a combination of merit marks, shackles and cages, and even tying to a pillar.

The financial advantages of this system were self-evident and it was to be adopted in hundreds of new schools. The British schools were, in theory, nondenominational and their popularity and cheapness alarmed the Established church as it saw its virtual monopoly in the field of mass education under threat. The result was the establishment in 1811 of the National Society for Promoting the Education of the Poor in the Principles of the Established Church, whose similar teaching method (the 'Madras' system) devised by an Anglican priest, Andrew Bell, led to another expansion of schools. The National Society, however, had the advantage of the co-operation of parish churches in taking over the existing church schools. The first National school was opened soon after the formation of the Society in Holborn Hill, and by 1815 more than five hundred were in existence throughout the country.

Though they dealt in large numbers the British and National schools still did not enrol the poorest children, who were often too dirty and too dishevelled to be admitted. Their tuition was taken up by the Ragged School Union, under the aegis of Lord Shaftesbury, which bound together many individual efforts to alleviate the problem. The best known of these Ragged schools in London, probably because it has a modern successor, is that in Field Lane near Saffron Hill. That area was one of the poorest in London, overcrowded, lacking in elementary sanitation, full of fetid lodging houses used around the clock, and with a reputation for criminal activity. In 1841 a small, unfurnished back room was taken

RAGGED SCHOOLS.—FIELD-LANE SAB-BATH SCHOOL. 65, West-street, Saffron-hill.—A room has been opened and supported in this wretched neighbourhood for upwards of 12 months, and religious instruction imparted to the poor by a few laymen of the churches of England and Scotland and Protestant Dissenters. Their benevolent endeavours have been greatly blessed : about 50 (adults and children) assemble on the Sundays, likewise on Monday and Thursday evenings. The application for admission far exceeds the room engaged, and the teachers are desirous of taking another adjoining, but are necessitated to APPEAL to the Christian public for pecuniary assistance to carry out their designs. Donations will be thankfully received by the Rev. P. Lorimer, 12, Colebrooke-row, Islington ; W. D. Owen, Esq., 43, Great Coram-street ; Mr. P. M'Donald, Secretary, 30, Great Sutton-street, Clerkenwell ; or by the Treasurer, Mr. S. R. Starey, 17, Ampton-street, Gray's-inn-road. Left-off garments sent to the schools will be carefully distributed.

An advertisement for the Field Lane School in The Times *in 1843, which caught the eye of Lord Ashley (subsequently Earl of Shaftesbury). He became associated with it until his death.*

for the Field Lane Sabbath School and in it forty-five boys and girls crowded to listen to gospel stories. An early assistant teacher at the Field Lane school records his first impressions:

> I was led to visit the Field Lane Sabbath School, then lately commenced, where I witnessed a scene so foreign to anything I had ever before experienced or heard of that it made an impression on my mind never to be effaced. On opening the door of the school, then held up a miserable court in Saffron Hill, Clerkenwell, a motley group of half-clad youths rushed up the rickety staircase into a small apartment, some ten feet square, and commenced leaping upon and overturning the forms which stood in their way; others showed their daring agility by descending from the first floor window into the yard beneath, whilst the remainder evinced their love of fun and mischief by blowing out the lights . . . when, however, some order was obtained and the two teachers present endeavoured to impart instruction with candle in hand, they were obliged to keep on their hats for protection from the rotten vegetables and animal refuse which the rebels without were continually throwing through the broken windows.

Dickens came across the school in later years:

> I found my first ragged school in an obscene place called West Street, Saffron Hill, pitifully struggling for life under every disadvantage. It had no means; it had no suitable rooms; it derived no power or protection from being recognized by any authority; it attracted within its walls a fluctating swarm of faces – young in years, but youthful in nothing else – that scowled Hope out of countenance.

The British, National and Ragged schools dispensed very basic learning indeed, as did the later workhouse schools which taught children between bouts of labour. They had no wider aspirations, nor could they have for attendance, before Forster's Act, was not compulsory and in many cases secondary to the business of making money to help keep the household afloat. Even as late as 1899 the London School Board, in a sample survey of 112 schools, discovered that 1,143 children worked 19–29 hours a week, 729 worked 30–39 hours and 285 more than 40 hours – all in addition to the time they were required to be at school.

British and National schools had much to fear from the emergence of Board schools, to the extent that sometimes clergymen who were members of the London School Board voted against improvements in standards in case the church schools were obliged to follow suit.

One member of the Board, Canon Cronwell, was later to declare, 'I thank God I have never entered a Board school', so presumably his presence on the Board was a spoiling tactic. Given this sort of member it is surprising to find that the calibre of the first London School Board was exceptionally high. It was elected – for the first time in local elections – by secret ballot; in addition voters choosing, say, four candidates in any one district were permitted to put all their four votes behind one candidate. This may explain the fact that two women were elected, Emily Davies, a pioneer in the enfranchisement and education of women, and Dr Elizabeth Garrett, the first woman doctor in England, who gained more votes than any other candidate throughout London.

SCHOOLS FOR THE MONEYED CLASSES

THE BACKBONE OF SERIOUS EDUCATION in the nineteenth century was the academy, many of which were founded at the end of the seventeenth century. They ranged considerably in status and standard. Some hoped to entice sons of the upper reaches of Society. One such was Hackney School, formerly known as Newcome's Academy, which was begun in 1685 and catered for 'noblemen's and gentlemen's sons': this was no trumped-up advertising claim because sons of the Essex, Grafton and Devonshire families did attend and its most famous pupil was the natural philosopher, Henry Cavendish, who was in attendance in 1742. The village of Hackney was also renowned for its girls' schools, rare establishments at a time when the education of girls was considered unimportant and if it existed at all took place at home in the care of a governess. The libidinous Pepys

BURLINGTON HOUSE ACADEMY, Fulham; lithograph by C. Hawkins. The school began under Lewis Vaslet, a Frenchman, in 1728. A later owner, who had previously run an academy in Old Burlington Street, Piccadilly, took over the premises and renamed it Burlington House. The school and its three acres of ground were taken over by the government in 1855 for the erection of a women's reformatory.

records that on the pretext of visiting Hackney church in 1667 he was actually there to see 'the young ladies of the schools, whereof there is great store, very pretty'; and the scurrilous biographer John Aubrey cautioned that at Hackney the girls learned 'pride and wantonness'.

The Burlington House Academy in Fulham attracted pupils of status. The young Lord Compton was a pupil in the 1730s when the school was run by Nicholas Guillibeau, who often wrote to the Countess Compton on her son's progress: 'His Lordship continues in very good health only his hollow tooth has felt a little discomfort these four or five days but since I have stopped the hole with a grain of mastick it has been easier'. And later: 'His Lordship drinks no malt drink, the beer here being newer than he is used to at home makes him dislike it, so I thought I would mention this to your Ladyship because this is about the time Your Ladyship used to order wine for his Lordship's use.'

Great Ealing School had standing among the middle classes. Thought to have been founded in 1698, it was taken over by a clergyman in 1791, and was run on lines similar to Eton. By 1820 it had 365 pupils. An observer wrote of it in the 1830s:

> *The school being almost considered a public one, the fagging system was regularly carried out. . .the education was first-rate (particularly in the classics) and as the time was judiciously divided, and there was no alternative to learn, the boys progressed rapidly, and the school turned out some bright fellows.*

The bright fellows included writer and publisher Charles Knight, Cardinal Newman, T.H. Huxley and W.S. Gilbert.

Marylebone School began in 1703 under the headmastership of a Huguenot, Dennis de la Place. The dramatist, George Colman the younger, was a pupil here and recollects that

THE playground and building of Great Ealing School. The school was founded at the end of the 17th century in the rectory of Ealing church. Pupils included Thomas Huxley and the future Cardinal Newman.

though the school made much of its ability in progressing boys to Westminster School, its main specialization was French.

Highgate was particularly favoured by schools because of its many large and adaptable houses, its middle-class residents and its rural scenery and clean air. The number of private schools here actually increased after the passing of the 1870 Education Act. Dr Benjamin Duncan's Commercial Academy, here from 1813, was run on Pestalozzian lines, so that learning by rote was abandoned; the curriculum also included astronomy, architecture, logic and elocution. In the village too was one of possibly only two Jewish academies in the country. Hyman Hurwitz, a distinguished scholar and friend of Coleridge, founded his school for Jewish boys and girls in 1802, but unfortunately his successor became involved in a minor scandal related to a missing emerald, and went bankrupt in 1843. A Unitarian school was founded in Highgate in 1885 – Channing

School still flourishes – by two devout ladies and a Unitarian minister. The wary ladies insisted that only males under eight and over eighty were permitted at school functions and parties, and even gentlemen lecturers were chaperoned in the building.

There were also academies which specialized in teaching the children of colonial servants or else sons destined for the army. One ambitious academy was at Norland House in Holland Park Road, for the 'civil or military education of sons of the gentry'. The curriculum included 'Fortification, Navigation, Fencing and Riding' and had facilities for horse riding at the rear. In Powis Square in Notting Hill, six houses were used by Wren College, where young men, many of them Indian or Eurasian, were coached for entry into the Indian Civil Service.

A good number of the orphanage schools attained 'academy' standard. The Licensed Victuallers' School in Kennington was highly regarded, as was the Royal Soldiers' and

*P*UPILS *of University College School, Gower Street, at play in 1833; by George Scharf. The school acted as a 'feeder' to University College itself, and was therefore extensively patronized by Nonconformists, Catholics and Jews.*

Sailors' Daughters Home in Hampstead, established originally for children orphaned in the Crimean War, but which gradually took as pupils the children of servicemen in general.

University College School was founded in Gower Street as part of the enthusiasm which surrounded the establishment of University College itself and a general feeling amongst the radical middle classes that the public schools inculcated useless and sometimes brutal habits. Like its parent, UCS was without religious teaching or bars to admission, and it was a flourishing concern until the parents of its most likely pupils moved out of central London, whereupon the school moved to Hampstead. Another secular school was established by the Hill family who took the old Bruce Castle in Tottenham in 1822 so as to open a London branch of their Birmingham School. One of the Hill sons involved in the venture was Rowland, the future inventor of the Penny Post.

The stated aims of the enterprise were to further moral principles and habits among the pupils, to develop the powers of mind and body, and only thirdly to dispense knowledge. Also encouraged was the administration of discipline by the boys themselves.

All of the above were, in contemporary terms, substantial enterprises, but most academies were quite small, usually in a terrace house that would otherwise house one or two families. The one that Dickens attended, Wellington House Academy by Mornington Crescent, was typical of its kind. He learned 'Latin, mathematics, history and the hornpipe' and 'occasionally issued a small morning newspaper containing comic advertisements and scraps of news'. Frances Mary Buss, who opened her North London Collegiate School for Ladies in 1850, was in a similar house in Camden Street, Camden Town. The location was chosen because of the number of 'professional men' in the neighbourhood, and because she sensed that the old indifference to the education of

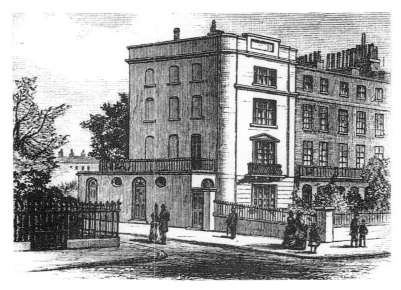

WELLINGTON HOUSE ACADEMY near the junction of Hampstead Road and Mornington Crescent. It was here that Charles Dickens received some schooling. The Academy consisted of one large room in which several classes worked at the same time.

daughters was fading and that inexpensive schools for middle-class and lower middle-class girls were wanted. There were, she realized, numerous girls whose parents could not afford governesses or the more select academies, but whose position in life prohibited them from sending their children to the socially inferior National or British schools; in this void their daughters received very little education at all. It is interesting to note that in the very year that Miss Buss's school opened on her own initiative and at her own expense, the North London Collegiate School for Boys was established by St Pancras Vestry for precisely the same social strata of boys. The difference was, of course, that the Vestry was prepared to support education for boys at this level but not for girls. The North London Collegiate was by no means the first school for girls but its quality guarantees it a place in the history of London education. Frances Buss had attended the newly opened Queen's College in Harley Street in 1848, which began teacher-training courses for women, and the skills she learnt there, together with her previous knowledge and practice of the Pestalozzian method of teaching, produced a school which was to be a model for many more.

The training of teachers was now being taken seriously. With the government taking ever more interest in the quality of private schools, and the burgeoning middle classes demanding better teaching and better results, this was bound to come. The government even funded a short-lived experiment in training teachers who were to look after pauper and criminal children. This took place in Kneller Hall, Whitton, where a crumbling mansion was host to a gathering of students instructed by Dr Frederick Temple and Francis Turner Palgrave.

UNIVERSITIES

At THE BEGINNING OF THE NINETEENTH CENTURY London was almost the only European capital that did not possess a university. Moreover, many young men of perfectly good education, but who just happened to be from Dissenting, Roman Catholic, Jewish or agnostic families, were precluded from attending Oxford or Cambridge. There were also criticisms of the absurd and destructive class distinctions in those places and of the restricted curriculum which had hardly expanded since the eighteenth century. Medical practice was not taught there and was centred mainly on the teaching hospitals of London; law, of course, was mostly taught north and south of Fleet Street.

Daniel Defoe had urged the formation of a university of colleges spread around London in the 1720s but it was Scots poet Thomas Campbell who appears to have given the nudge which set the project in motion. He had returned enthused from Bonn University where he was impressed by the way in which religious toleration was embedded. He proposed a 'great London University' for 'effectively and multifariously teaching, examining, exercising and rewarding with honours, in the liberal arts and sciences, the youth of our middling rich people.' His cause was taken up by Henry Brougham and George Birkbeck, who had both been instrumental in the development of mechanics' institutes and the founding of the Society for the Diffusion of Useful Knowledge. Soon other, quite powerful, allies were found, particularly those representing sections of the community debarred from Oxford and Cambridge. It is a measure of the maturity of those involved, many of them deeply religious, that it was agreed at the outset that religion should be neither a bar to entry nor taught in the new university.

By 1826 a limited liability company was formed to create the university and shares were issued in the normal way. Almost immediately, with the land already bought by enthusiastic backers, work on the 'Godless College' at the top of Gower Street began. William Wilkins designed the building in neo-Grecian style; it was briefly fashionable then, but it incurred the inevitable comment that a pagan style suited a pagan institution. Despite the numerous interested parties, the shortage of money and the hostility of the press in general, University College was opened in 1828, just two years after the first formal meeting which established it.

University College had thrown down the gauntlet to the Establishment. Before it had even opened the Duke of Wellington had chaired the first meeting of a committee which, with three archbishops, seven bishops and some nobility around the table, decided that a college for 'general education' should be founded in London that would 'immure the minds of youth with a knowledge of the doctrines and duties of Christianity as inculcated by the United Church of England and Ireland.' From this emerged King's College in the Strand, opened in 1831.

London thus had two establishments each claiming either in name or practice to be a 'university', but only King's College, with the ear of the Tories and the Church, was chartered, and University College, run by a limited company, had to wait for a Whig administration before attempting to be equal in this respect. University College was also challenged by the Oxford and Cambridge universities in its ambition to grant degrees, and by the medical schools who resented an upstart in their own speciality. The Whigs when they came to power were not as co-operative as was hoped and in the end engineered a compromise that established a body called the University of London, which

Drawn by Tho. H. Shepherd.   Engraved by W. Wallis.

University College London, in Gower Street, 1827. Originally a private enterprise that sought to provide university education in London without the religious prohibitions of Oxford and Cambridge, the College eventually became part of the federal University of London.

could issue degrees to students at both University College and King's College, and in time this federal arrangement has been extended to include numerous educational institutions in the capital.

LIBRARIES

THIS PERIOD IS REMARKABLE FOR VENTURES promoting further and adult education, of which University College and King's College were but two. Science, and not literature, was to the fore, represented by the enthusiasm for mechanics' institutes and the middle-class Literary & Scientific Institutions. The London Mechanics' Institution was founded in 1823 and its constitution underlines this commitment to science, one that would not have been made at the beginning of the century:

Among the objects which the London Institution shall have especially in view shall be the establishment of lectureships on the different arts and sciences, a library of reference and circulation, a reading room, a museum of models, a school of design and an experimental workshop and laboratory.

Only one Literary & Scientific Institution now survives in London, so far as is known, and that is at Highgate, where a combination of factors has combined to keep it flourishing despite many desperate periods. Its first rules declared that it was in existence to 'create and foster a taste for reading and a taste for intellectual pursuits – to bring within reach of Artisan and Mechanic those mental enjoyments which next to the consolations of religion and the blessings of natural affection are the best friends to Virtue and Happiness'. No present-day society on its formation would dare to express such sentiments for all sorts of politically correct reasons, but few would secretly condemn such aspirations. In truth, however, the Highgate Institution did not do very well when it came to Artisans and Mechanics and for most of its history it has been supported by middle-class residents; yet to this day about half of the regular lectures given there are related to science, even in an era when science has lost its popular fascination. Not all such institutions, however, embraced science. In both Blackheath and Greenwich, for example, the institutions were literary only and provided, certainly in Blackheath, a lending library and reading room that opened at 8 a.m. (early enough for the commuter to read *The Times* and board the train at the adjacent railway station).

These institutions were, until the advent of public libraries towards the end of the nineteenth century, almost the only libraries available in most areas of London. There were also subscription libraries, such as the one in Hampstead, established in 1833 with such luminaries as Lucy Aikin, John Constable, Samuel Rogers and Joanna Baillie among subscribers, and the publishers John Murray and Longman as active supporters. Later the library was to offer free facilities to people too poor to pay the subscription and even provided a side door so that they might enter and depart without being seen to accept charity. Mudie's Circulating Library, founded in 1842 in New Oxford Street, was for publishers the most influential of the subscription libraries because it could make or break a title by the number of copies it ordered. The most learned subscription library was and still is the London Library in St James's Square, floated at a meeting in 1840, and opened in May 1841, at the instigation of the newly famous and lionized essayist and historian Thomas Carlyle. Legend has it that the prickly Carlyle pursued this project after failing to persuade the equally prickly Panizzi, Principal Librarian at the British Museum, that he warranted a private room for study there. But Carlyle was right in one lament – there was not a good library from which he could *borrow*. The London Library was pushed forward by aristocracy, scholars, clerics, bibliophiles, writers and politicians, the sort of mixture that has prevailed for much of its history, and which T.S. Eliot, without any deference to egalitarianism, described as 'the élite of culture'. The institution has survived a number of crises, not the least being an unanticipated demand for rates in 1957, but it has retained its nineteenth-century interior atmosphere and book arrangement so that any visit is still a challenge to all but the really initiated.

The first free municipal library in London appears to have been that established by the Vestry of St Marylebone in Gloucester Place in 1854. It was primarily a reading room since, when it reported in 1856, it had only 1,000 volumes in its lending section which

PLATE IX

*T*wo well-known London charities are shown in this print. In the centre an obelisk at St George's Fields overlooks the School for the Indigent Blind, a charity established in 1799 for the moral, mental, and industrial training of poor blind children. This building was erected in the 1830s. In the distance is the Royal Bethlehem Hospital – known popularly as Bedlam the principal lunatic asylum for London, which had begun in medieval times on a site now covered by Liverpool Street station. The building shown here, was finished c.1815 and is now used by the Imperial War Museum.

A Parliamentary Enquiry into conditions at some lunatic asylums, established in 1815, drew on the services an artist when it went to the Royal Bethlehem Hospital. Thousands of engravings of this patient tied to a post were printed and helped to fan the campaign for reform of treatment of the insane.

Plate X

T*he Pantheon, Oxford Street. The interior of the Pantheon, an assembly house in Oxford Street, was designed by James Wyatt in the style of St Sophia, Constantinople. It opened in 1772, when 1500 guests attended the ceremony. Despite its initial popularity its attractions soon palled and a disastrous fire in 1792 destroyed much of the building. Its successor, not nearly so ornate, was never successful. The site is today covered by a Marks & Spencer store.*

T*he success of the Pantheon helped to diminish the attractions of the assemblies at the house of Mrs Cornelys in Soho Square. She is pictured here in a grotesque caricature.*

Plate XI

Covent Garden Market, early 19th century, by Pugin and Rowlandson. The market then was an accumulation of old shacks and later purpose-built sheds, inadequate for the amount of business that took place. The present market building (restored in the 1970s) was built c.1829 to the designs of Charles Fowler, although the present roof was added later.

The fruit and vegetable market gradually dominated the streets around the Piazza where many premises were turned into warehouses. Of the businesses it spawned, one was the making of barrows. The best-known was that of Ellen Keeley in Neal Street, which remained here until the market closed in 1974.

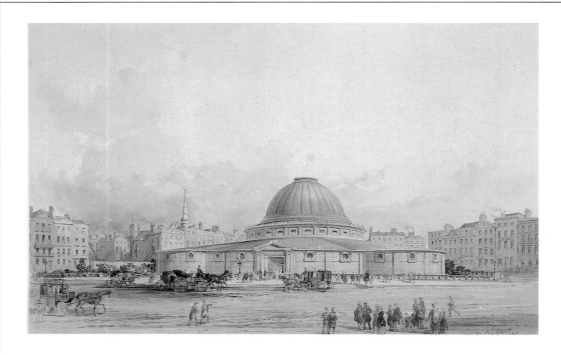

PLATE XII

*T*HE *Great Globe, Leicester Square, watercolour by E. Walker, 1851. James Wyld, geographer and showman, took advantage of the crowds visiting London to see the Great Exhibition, to construct a building which neatly combined enthusiasm for knowledge and spectacle. The globe, which was 40ft in diameter, showed the features of the earth on different levels, and could be viewed by a series of catwalks and staircases. It was not demolished until 1862.*

*T*HE *interior of James Wyld's Great Globe in 1851.*

PLATE XIII

THE Surrey Zoological Gardens in 1851. While the Zoological Gardens in Regent's Park, opened in 1827, were primarily a facility for zoological study, the zoo begun near the Elephant and Castle in 1831 was a place for entertainment. It began seriously enough when Edward Cross, the proprietor of a menagerie in Exeter Change in the Strand, persuaded the Surrey Literary, Scientific and Zoological Society (which he had himself founded) to buy his collection and open it to the public.

THE Zoological Gardens at Regent's Park continued to thrive long after the Surrey Gardens closed. Not only did it have a larger array of animals and a grounding in serious zoological research, but it had social cachét as well. Its attendances were very much increased once the underground railway reached Camden Town.

Plate XIV

Shillibeer's omnibus. Mr Shillibeer's omnibus was instrumental in changing the way people travelled in London. He introduced a vehicle which was relatively economic to run and which went along a set route, stopping at known halts. The first service began in July 1829 when buses ran between Paddington and the Bank along what are now the Marylebone-Euston-Pentonville Roads. The original fare was 1/6d for the whole journey.

A London bus conveying stockbrokers to the City during the Railway mania in November 1845.

Plate XV

The construction of St Pancras station and hotel. St Pancras station, the terminus of the Midland Railway, now covers the site of a large assembly of low-grade streets and alleys. The station, the roof of which may be seen, was designed by W. H. Barlow and opened in 1868; the hotel, opened five years later, is the work of George Gilbert Scott. Because the line had to cross the Regent's Canal the decision was taken to go above it, with the consequence that the station and hotel are well above street level. This provided a vast quantity of storage beneath the station which was built to precise measurements so as to accommodate beer barrels from the midlands.

The grand staircase of the Midland Grand hotel at St Pancras Station.

Plate XVI

HAMPSTEAD *Heath was a popular place for celebrating Bank Holiday. In particular, it was a favourite with east Londoners, especially when the North London line provided a service from Dalston to Hampstead. This Phil May cartoon sums up the exuberance of the occasions.*

by then recorded withdrawals of about 5,700 volumes 'with no loss'. However, the residents of St Marylebone decided in 1857 that they could not afford the expense and the library was closed. William Ewart's Act allowing local authorities to open free libraries was largely ignored in central London. It was a permissive Act and the procedure of calling public meetings of ratepayers to decide if the Act should be adopted was both cumbersome and at the mercy of those determined to resist further expenditure of ratepayers' money. Moreover, the ratepayers entitled to be present were at that time by no means the majority of the population: those with most to gain from free libraries were the very ones who had no vote in the matter. The City of London voted against adoption in 1855, although they made the previously private Guildhall Library open to the public the following year, and Paddington ratepayers voted the same way in 1856. But generally, the question was not put until the 1870s when parishes such as St Pancras, Islington and

In the surge of enthusiasm for education that characterized the 1830s and 1840s, the City of Westminster Literary, Scientific and Mechanics Institution was one of many to be founded. This building, shown here c.1840, was on the east side of Great Smith Street.

Bethnal Green resisted the blandishments of radicals to adopt the Act. Westminster opened their first library in 1857, but it was then a long gap until the outer London areas of Richmond, Ealing, Fulham and Hammersmith followed suit. In some intractable parishes it was necessary for rich men to help them along. Sir Henry Tate, the sugar refiner, Andrew Carnegie, the Scots American businessman, and Passmore Edwards, a publisher, were all active in this field. Tate's buildings were to be found at Brixton and South Lambeth Road, Carnegie's in many areas of London, and Edwards, who founded about seventy institutions with his donations, provided the money for libraries in Shoreditch, Whitechapel, Hoxton and Poplar, among many others.

It could not be said, though, that London's local authorities were particularly enthusiastic about public libraries – it was only in 1890 that Finsbury became the first library in Britain to allow readers open access to the lending shelves.

*T*HE *opening of the Totterdown estate in Tooting in 1903. Totterdown was the first of the LCC's 'cottage' estates, so far removed from employment opportunities that the council was obliged to open its first electric tramway to serve it. The estate consisted of 1300 houses but only four shops. It was calculated that, including the acquisition of land, each three-room cottage cost about £263 to build and was let at 7/6d per week. The monotonous straight roads were not landscaped.*

CHAPTER XIX
STRIVING FOR UTOPIAS

The Birth of the Council Estate

IN 1919, WITH THE PHRASE 'HOMES FIT FOR HEROES' STILL POTENT, THE LONDON COUNTY Council began buying acres of marshy land in Barking, Dagenham and Ilford that stretched south to the Tilbury road, with the Thames in the further distance. On this unattractive tract of Essex was created the Becontree housing estate, thought to be the largest in the world. This civic philanthropy on a drawing board resulted in homes for over 100,000 people, arranged geometrically in roads, streets, crescents and avenues, almost all two-storey, mostly red-brick, some carefully varied, some carefully similar. Interspersed were shopping parades of identical units, clinics, libraries, and barn-like public houses at a walking distance and in a ratio to population that deterred the drinking classes. There were and are no vistas save long straight streets with sensible trees; there were and are no surprises of detail or structure to encounter; and the parks are as predictable and calculated as the built environment. There is no room for eccentricity, except nowadays some of these modest 'cottage' houses, bought privately in recent years, sport stone cladding or 'Tudor' decor. There are no minute and adventurous side-turnings and no stairways ending in unseen destinations; there are no places which invite genuine mischief, and appetite, for want of this, often turns to destruction.

Becontree was planned, with good intentions, for people whose aspirations had been dulled, who came from overcrowded houses, mainly in the East End, where gas stoves were on landings, shared lavatories were outside, and where damp affected walls and belongings. For many the cultivation of a garden, the novelty of extra bedrooms, a bathroom, indoor toilets and kitchens without bugs, represented release from squalor and were sufficient consummation of expectations. No matter that so much had been left behind: the corner shops, street markets, the local bookie, the small and friendly pub, the itinerant tradesmen, the gregarious street life, the family relationships, and the close proximity of employment and pleasures. All these were foregone in exchange for decent accommodation designed by men for whom tidiness and temperance were writ large.

Other planned working-class areas have since far surpassed Becontree in awfulness, but not in its overall sterility. Yet these developments stem not from the sort of paternalism displayed by model-dwelling builders, who housed tenants in barrack-like blocks that announced their status in life, but from presumptuous notions of Utopia, or at least a version of Utopia that was consigned to working-class people. Nor were local authorities alone in these notions – they merely inherited them from garden-suburb planners who enticed the middle classes out of London's teeming centre.

Becontree, which seems to epitomize municipal housing and Socialist experiment between the two World Wars, was actually built by the Conservatives (then called Municipal Reformers) who controlled the LCC (the Labour Party did not gain a majority until 1934, which it maintained until the Council's abolition in 1965). But it was the 'Progressives', a coalition of Liberals, Radicals and Socialists, who were in the majority in 1903 when the LCC first began its cottage-estate programme. This was at Totterdown in Tooting where about 1,300 modest, large-gabled houses and four shops were erected in a dispiriting grid scheme whose main advantage was that the LCC built its first electric tramway to service it. The rents and tram fares were cheap and Totterdown soon filled up.

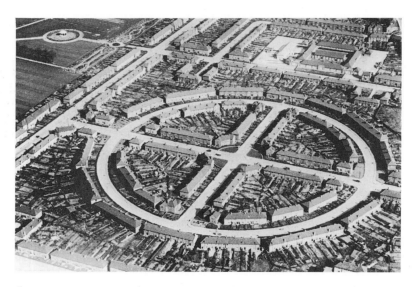

An aerial view of the Becontree estate in Essex, reputed to be the largest housing estate in the world. The temperance minded LCC kept public houses to an absolute minimum, and the numbers of shops was severely restricted, thereby limiting consumer choice.

More architecturally promising was the Old Oak Lane scheme at Acton (c.1912–13), where an attempt to embody the garden-suburb ideals of Ebenezer Howard was made. Large cottage-estates outside the central area were a controversial solution to London's housing problems and not necessarily suited to everyone. Generally the rents could be afforded only by families whose wage-earner was in reliable employment, and even then the availability of workmen's fares was the only way in which living so far away from employment could be economic.

The LCC had built flats at first. In the flush of election and power following the formation of the LCC in 1889 the Progressives planned the pioneering estate of flats in Boundary Street, Shoreditch, where Tony Benn's grandfather, John Benn, had been prominent in drawing attention to the many slums. In these 15 acres of derelict houses there was a death rate of 42 per 1,000, and the life expectancy of twenty-five years was

THE Boundary Street estate in Shoreditch, a large development which replaced a concentration of slum buildings. Its construction involved the rehousing of 5,700 people elsewhere, very few of whom were rehoused in the new scheme.

similar to that of Calcutta residents. The new estate, however, raised innumerable problems, not the least being the displacement of so many people without alternative accommodation. Over 5,700 people were moved out and the new dwellings housed 5,500 – a nett loss. Furthermore, hardly any of those who had left the original slums were rehoused in the new scheme. The LCC, if it were to do anything that was at all significant in rehousing, had to buy and build on land outside of the central area so that displaced tenants could be settled there before redevelopment.

It was a dilemma for the LCC. Writing in 1901, A.H. Beavan in his *Imperial London* noted:

> *The overcrowding of the Metropolis is perhaps the most pressing social problem of the day, and the most difficult to cope with. The poorer classes must live near their place of employment, being unable to afford even the smallest and cheapest of railway-fare; while the value of land anywhere near the centres of business is so great, and the demolition of small houses thereon to make room for big warehouses so continuous; that the filthiest and most meagre lodgings are filled to overflowing, though let for rents that absorb nearly all the scanty earnings of the tenants.*

Inevitably, therefore, the LCC often had to buy cheap land outside its own boundaries. This was a policy of necessity, but it was one that did not endear the LCC to rural boroughs and other county councils, who found themselves overwhelmed by a single-class intake of people for whom schools, clinics and services had to be provided. A gentleman giving evidence to a Royal Commission in 1938 accused the LCC of being 'a colonizing power, like ancient Rome, pouring out the treasure and labour of her citizens in order to make new homes for them in foreign lands.' Middle-class people who had moved out to these rural parts, where their own vision of Utopia beckoned, found to their horror that working-class estates were envisaged in their adopted neighbourhoods. Just as much to the point, industry tended, but not always, to follow these new settlements, so that those already in their Dunroamins had to start again elsewhere to avoid being near an industrial estate. This was not the case in Becontree, since it was not an area the middle-classes had gone to in the first place, and its overwhelmingly working-class residents were for many years without local jobs until Ford's shifted car production to Dagenham; in the meantime transport facilities to take them to their old jobs in London were very poor indeed.

Another early LCC estate, begun before the First World War, was that at White Hart Lane at Tottenham: it was halted while the war raged. The earlier development period displays houses closely packed in a grid layout and the post-war part, with the garden-suburb vogue in full swing, has more space and variety in its road layout.

THE GARDEN SUBURBS

LONDON'S FIRST GARDEN SUBURB was Bedford Park at Chiswick. Built between 1875 and 1881 on the grounds of a mansion called Bedford House, it was essentially a commuting village dependent upon the railway opened at Turnham Green. Designed by Norman Shaw and others to be a middle-class community, it acquired an 'arty' reputation as well. The houses were built when domestic servants were still cheap and so therefore rooms for them were included. But compared with the Victorian terrace house of central London the drudgery was lessened: the kitchen was at ground floor level and the houses were convenient enough, when servants became scarce, to be run by their owners.

Shaw's architectural ideas may also be seen in Hampstead Garden Suburb, where its founder, Henrietta Barnett, who had helped form the East End Dwellings Company (see page 185), envisaged an integration of working and middle classes in a leafy suburb a distance from Hampstead. This venture arose inadvertently out of the plan to construct the 'Hampstead tube' to Golders Green, then a completely rural area, with a station between Hampstead and Golders Green near the delightful Wyldes farm. Mrs Barnett, who with her clergyman husband was still working in the dismal environment of Whitechapel, had a house near here for a retreat, and she determined to buy the heathland in this area to prevent the station being constructed and the development which would inevitably occur around it. (The underground platforms were actually built and may be seen in the darkness on the way to Golders Green). Mrs Barnett was forceful enough to cajole the money together from a number of benefactors and she then went on to buy on her own behalf the rest of the Wyldes estate of 240 acres on which to build the Suburb. She was much influenced by Ebenezer Howard's Garden City movement but she also had first-hand experience of just how brutalizing an environment could be. The Bishop of

London was later to say that 'the Garden Suburb was intended to be an exact contrast and antidote to all Mrs Barnett had seen and known in Whitechapel'. She may not have romanticized to the extent of Alfred Lyttleton, who thought of the Suburb as a place where 'the poor shall teach the rich, and in which the rich, let us hope, shall help the poor to help themselves', but certainly her Utopia was indeed a place where artisans and intellectuals mixed and exchanged their knowledge without embarrassment; it was one in which

> *We who live in peace and comfort [should not forget] the sad, the poor and the bereft. . . .the wicked, the naughty, the sick, the demented, the sorrowful, the blind, the halt, the maimed, the old, the handicapped and children are facts – facts which have to be faced, facts which demand thought, facts which should be reckoned with in town planning.*

A GROUP of houses on the Hampstead Garden Suburb. The Suburb was built during the fashion for garden cities. The first houses were opened in 1907 soon after the Underground railway reached its terminus at Golders Green.

Noble words but, unfortunately, this mixing of the classes, this contrived tryst of fortunate and deprived, was the least realized of her hopes. The early plans which showed a hostel for working lads and 'barns' to house tools and costermonger barrows were abandoned and there were not many takers for the cheaper accommodation. A similar disappointment occurred at the prestige Highpoint flats (1935) in nearby Highgate where the architect, Lubetkin, persuaded the developer, Zigismund Gestetner, to let some flats to tenants of modest means so that there should be a mix of classes, but it was found that the working-class tenants, for one reason or another, moved out.

The overall architect for Hampstead Garden Suburb was Raymond Unwin. His estate, begun in 1907, was inward looking, its focus a community centre, two churches and two schools, impeccably designed but too large in scale against the two-storey houses. But the whole thing is without life as though Unwin was afraid to introduce anything that might cause controversy. There are no shops, no restaurants, no pubs, no places of seditious amusement. In these respects it is Becontree without the working classes. There is a story that Unwin, before he became an architect, wanted to enter the Church and did, as a young man, consult Henrietta Barnett's clergyman husband in the matter. Asked if he were more concerned about Man's unhappiness than his wickedness, Unwin replied the former, and was promptly advised not to go into the Church. Instead he became an architect and planner sometimes involved in schemes which aimed, by environmental and architectural means, to change lives for the better. He was not the first and certainly not the last architect in the twentieth century to believe that this was possible.

In Ealing a different experiment was in progress. In 1891, Ebenezer Howard had formed a company called General Builders, basically a self-help house-building movement, of which there was a branch in Ealing. In 1901 this became Ealing Tenants

Brentham village, Ealing, during construction. The village derived from the Garden City movement and the self-help ethic. The prospective tenants would themselves help to build the houses, which were then rented. All houses had baths but not necessarily bathrooms.

Ltd which, with the participation of local MP Henry Vivian, raised sufficient money to build its first houses – the Brentham Garden Village – and by 1905 fifty terraced houses were up and running. In 1907, with another 30 acres in prospect, Unwin was distracted from Hampstead to advise on garden city layouts at Ealing. Central to the policy of the development were communal facilities – a hall, allotments, playing fields, tennis courts and an Institute in which theatricals and dances were staged. A more straightforward scheme was built in 1906 on the slopes of Muswell Hill, where a local businessman turned 23 acres into the Rookfield garden estate with Arts and Crafts houses around informal but private roads which remained under the control of the residents. It was a middle-class enclave in a middle-class area, near to transport and good shopping.

Another garden suburb in the area, isolated from such amenities, attempted a mix of classes which, by an historical quirk, pertains today. In 1923 Alderman Abraham Davis JP bought up the 55 acres of the Burdett-Coutts Holly Lodge estate on Highgate West Hill. It was reported at the time that Mr Davis intended to build 'a garden suburb to include 500 houses for middle-class residents', although the first plan published indicated about half that number. In the event Davis changed his mind and allocated a good chunk of the grounds for the building of mock Tudor flats for Lady Workers' Homes Ltd which sought to provide good accommodation for the many single women now working in London as shorthand-typists and telephonists. Many of these flats have in modern times been bought up by the local authority for single-person occupancy, while the rest of the estate, mainly mock-Tudor semi-detached and detached houses, remains privately owned and usually much sought-after. In Gidea Park, Essex, the grounds of Gidea Hall were used in 1910 to construct a superior garden suburb, which was designed by leading architects of the day.

Makepeace Mansions on the Holly Lodge Estate, Highgate. These 'Tudorized' apartment blocks were specifically built for 'women office workers' in the 1920s. A communal restaurant and social club were also provided for this new class of London worker.

THE PRIVATE DEVELOPERS

For most, utopian dreams lay not in garden suburbs and council estates. They lay instead in uninhibited, unplanned speculative developments, with or without amenities, built around inner London before the Second World War. At first, these estates owed their fortunes to the surface railways, but then they rode on the actual or hoped-for extension of tube or tram lines, along the main roads out of London. Young married couples who had, as children, visited the nearby countryside, found their houses in the fields they had played and picnicked in. These developments were cut-throat businesses, with many houses selling for as little as £300 but more usually from £500 to £1,000; but even with very low mortgage rates some builders found that they had overstretched their resources.

Merton and Morden, served by the London & South Western Railway main line, was popular and heavily developed in the first decade of the century, at least fifteen years before the Underground railway arrived in the vicinity. West Ham was already built up by the turn of the century and East Enders seeking cheap houses were already buying further out in East Ham and Ilford. The prize in the north was Golders Green, a place of scattered dwellings in the early 1900s, and peopled only by estate agents in temporary huts well before the Hampstead tube had reached its isolated terminus in 1907. Over 4,000 houses were built in the next eight years in the half-timbered, rough cast, gabled, tudorized style that was to typify the area, and the developers then moved on to Hendon to repeat the process. In the first decade of the twentieth century most of the small townships around London increased their population dramatically – for example, Acton by 52 per cent, Barnes by 71 per cent and Chingford by 86 per cent. In this plethora of building, and in that after the First World War, 'modern' architecture was virtually ignored. People did not aspire to the smooth lines, concrete shapes, flat roofs and balconies of the modern movement – these were almost exclusively the preserve of commercial buildings. The developers rightly judged that what their clients wanted was the semblance of a cottage or a country house near to a tube station, not a machine for living in. As a result the developers, like many of their eighteenth- and nineteenth-century predecessors, did not for the most part use architects at all, and their builders were equipped not with a rolled drawing but with a good pattern book. The speculators had, it seems, complete freedom except for their obligations under various Health Regulation Acts. Just as two developers, W. Peter Griggs and Archibald Corbett, created Ilford, so George Cross set the scene for Edgware: 'In moulding that slice of the suburbs of London in any way I pleased; planning roads as I would; naming them as I fancied.'

Inside the 'cottages' were other things to entice. Electricity, at least for lighting; gas ovens were installed as a substitute for the ubiquitous, time-consuming, range – heat was manageable at last; fitted bathrooms, with baths next to tiled walls, and fixed washbasins seemed more hygienic, although they lacked the colour and individuality of Victorian bathrooms which were usually adaptations of dressing rooms, complete with fireplaces, occasional furniture and carpets; hallways were semi-baronial, no longer a passageway but a squarish shape from which other rooms led; windows were larger and tended to be landscape rather than portrait in shape; dust-gathering mouldings were much reduced and at a time when most houses still burnt coal this was welcomed; from about 1910 the larger houses had garages attached with access direct from the house itself.

To complete the package was the garden. It is doubtful if many of those who moved out of inner London to buy their first house in places like Hendon or Sidcup had had a garden before – a small patch, perhaps, which only flowers enlivened, but in suburbia there was room for vegetables, greenhouses, lawns, trees and even playhouses. There was also a quite new social obligation to keep up a front garden so that the status of the street should not be diminished. For some time the social advantages of gardening had been somehow interwoven with the merits of temperance and in inner London the provision of allotments for the poorer classes was a common one: it was thought that they might keep working men out of the pubs. A typical scheme was begun in Highgate in 1847 for landless tradesmen and workers and the first list of allotment holders included six shoemakers, nineteen farmhands, an omnibus driver, a washerwoman, a deaf mute, a lunatic's attendant and a rate collector. Some objected to the scheme on the grounds that the poor would be rendered unfit for labour after their exertions growing vegetables, or else would simply sit on their plots smoking and drinking.

Suburban gardeners inherited no rules from previous occupants. Classical and formal Victorian gardens could be dispensed with and 'natural' gardens created. Paths meandered, lawns were shaped in quite unclassical proportions, topiary and ponds were dug, box hedges and a wild assortment of flowers from suburban nurseries were introduced, different kinds of paving were tried, simple wooden garden furniture replaced the much more expensive ornate Victorian items; and statuettes, both classical and grossly sentimental faced each other across rockeries.

All sorts of factors were behind this rush to suburbia. By the 1920s London was dirty, smoky, congested and run-down and had few attractions for anyone with the money to leave it; and when trains and trams made flight possible it became inevitable as well. Some

The transformed Southgate village in the 1930s. The delicately designed yet prominent Underground station stands in the centre of a replanned neighbourhood as developers build semi-detached houses on the fields beyond.

of the dreams did not materialize. Families, and particularly women, found themselves isolated on estates a very long walk from neighbourhood shops, and they found new relationships difficult to form; contacts and friends came from structured arrangements, such as clubs and societies. And the countryside that had seemed so near was lost under an outer suburbia that seemed to have no limits. For many, especially those without cars, the country was realised in their own gardens.

THE NEW TOWNS

ONE MORE UTOPIAN SOLUTION REMAINED – New Towns. The reduction of London's population by its dispersal into the countryside was close to the heart of Patrick

Abercrombie, who in 1943 and 1944 produced plans for the futures of London and Greater London. He advocated not an unplanned, unpredictable enlargement of small towns and villages near to London, but a jump across a Green Belt that would circle London to self-reliant, self-contained new towns in which residence and employment could be balanced. This plan took some time to realize and in the meantime the LCC pursued its old policy of outer estates such as Borehamwood, Oxhey and Harold Hill which only added to urban sprawl and the intensity of commuting because, on the whole, employment was not provided.

Stevenage, first occupied in 1952, was the first of the new towns for Londoners; Crawley, Harlow, Hemel Hempstead, Basildon, Bracknell and Hatfield were others. But the peopling of these towns caused serious problems in London itself, for it was rapidly discovered that only skilled workers and their families were likely to be accepted by the public corporations that managed them. The unskilled, and almost inevitably the low-paid, were left in the sub-standard accommodation that was common all over inner London, and their only hope of better living conditions was to join the vast waiting-lists for local authority housing. In addition, the discouragement by London councils of local manufacturers – a policy that had its genesis in the garden-city ideals of separating residencies and industries – persuaded employers to follow their skilled workers to accommodation provided by new town corporations at bargain prices. Just as skilled workers and their workshops and small factories were moving out so commerce was moving in. This again, was no help to the unskilled worker – a complaint echoed in the later Docklands development where the tenants of the factories and offices wanted skills that hardly existed in the indigenous population. In the East End unemployment was rising quickly anyway with the gradual removal of the docks to Tilbury, which had a disastrous knock-on effect in the closure of those businesses that serviced or relied on the dock facilities.

HIGH-RISE HOUSING

TOWER BLOCKS WERE NOT, PERHAPS, PERCEIVED AS UTOPIAN, but they were certainly recommended as a new way of life. In fact, they stemmed from necessity. Urged on by the long and apparently intractable waiting-lists, government exhortations, the shortage of sites, and the cost of laying out low-rise developments such as the Lansbury Estate in the East End, local authorities discovered the supposed financial virtues of high-rise blocks, using components pre-made off site. The borough of Newham alone built 125 of them and the LCC was active all over London in their construction, especially in the south. The financial advantages were found in the end to be illusory since, built cheaply, the flats were expensive and difficult to maintain and the difficulties of housing families on upper floors, a drawback which must have seemed obvious even if ignored, were incurable. Parents found that they had to confine their children to playing within the flats since the balconies were after all too small and too dangerous, and it was impossible to oversee them playing on the common ground that surrounded the blocks. This in turn created noise for residents above and below and claustrophobia for the parents and children alike. The worst ordeals occurred when the lifts either broke down or were vandalized. People, old or with children in prams, were stranded and sometimes in

RONAN POINT, Newham. On 16 May 1968 a gas explosion on the 18th floor caused the collapse of one corner of the building, resulting in the deaths of five people. More than all the evidence then available as to the unsuitability of tower blocks, this disaster was responsible for an abrupt change of direction by council planning authorities to low-rise developments.

despair. Despite the brave efforts of many tenants' associations, tower blocks were regarded as the least desirable housing to be had and the occupiers became increasingly transient. In 1968 a gas explosion in an upper flat of Ronan Point, a block in Newham, caused the collapse of flats above and below it, and five people were killed in this vertiginous disaster. It was to end the tower-block solution, though there were enough other problems to have hastened its demise.

Interior of the Coal Exchange, Lower Thames Street. A fine cast-iron building torn down by the City of London for road widening. It was designed by J. B. Bunning and opened by Prince Albert on the last occasion on which the state barge was used.

CHAPTER XX

AROUSAL OF A MULTITUDE

Out With the Old

THE VICTORIANS DIDN'T MUCH CARE FOR OLD ARCHITECTURE AND DIDN'T HESITATE TO tear it down where it suited them to do so. Until the 1890s 'preservation' battles took place politely in the columns of *The Times* or else in scholarly and antiquarian journals, but the sum total of deterrence was the public hostility that could be mustered, for there were no planning laws to prevent demolition. The Ancient Monuments Act of 1882 incorporated the first expression of preserving old buildings in the interests of present and future generations, but it had a tight brief, confining itself to buildings without occupants, such as Stonehenge, and because of this was not relevant to London.

By the 1890s much of the old City of London had been rebuilt with the Victorian office blocks that later generations have sought to save, and there was no let up in this transformation until the 1930s. The dilemma for the Victorians was exactly the same as for modern developers: potential tenants wanted offices more suited to the nature of their global trade and the volume of their staff, and small units of accommodation based on the old site width of City properties were no longer useful. In the West End, Regent Street fell into the same category: its shops, which once served the fashionable carriage trade of London, became inadequate to deal with trainloads of customers from the provinces, whose purchases came out of smaller incomes. The *Daily Telegraph* noted that the customers from the suburbs and country were:

> *A most valuable class of customer. . ..but in the main they are ladies who want things in quite the most up-to-date style at a very moderate outlay. That means just two important factors to the shopkeeper. In the first place, he must use a cheaper kind of material, on which there is only a small margin of profit, and secondly he is unable to recoup himself on the cost of making up. . ..one has to do at least five times the volume of business to get the same returns, and even then the net profits are less.*

Regent Street's demolition did not occur until the 1920s when the majority of leases expired, and when replanned it was with an eye to what had happened in Oxford Street, where many of the small shop units had been demolished and in their place larger stores erected in which goods could be properly displayed.

There was, too, legitimate concern that traffic congestion was hindering the development of the capital. As early as 1846 the *Illustrated London News* pointed out that:

> *The streets of London are choked by their ordinary traffic, and the life blood of the huge giant is compelled to run through veins and arteries that have never expanded since the days and dimensions of its infancy. . . .The real remedy is the opening of entirely new routes through the whole mass. The streams of traffic would then be diverted into parallel lines, and it would be possible to pass through the metropolis in which time is more valuable than any other in the world, at something above the pace of a funeral.*

New roads such as Queen Victoria Street, New Oxford Street, the Embankment, Farringdon Street and Clerkenwell Road, were attempts to address the problem and for the most part went through areas so awful that few opposed their wholesale demolition.

THE Ironmongers' Almshouses in Kingsland Road, Hoxton. The almshouses were built in 1715, the bequest of Sir Robert Geffrye, Lord Mayor of London and Master of the Ironmongers' Company. They were sympathetically converted into the Geffrye Museum of Furniture.

The story of London's increasing preoccupation with preservation is essentially a twentieth-century tale and it became in the end not just a matter for antiquarians and architectural historians, but a cause taken up by the least articulate of people. It had wide repercussions. By the 1960s it was expressing itself in the renovation of late Georgian and early Victorian houses in the inner suburbs of London, and by the 1970s in the formation of numerous neighbourhood groups, each fighting for amenities, or for the retention of buildings, or against proposals for new ones. Preservation became no longer just the field of those who could adequately describe a building, but was also close to the hearts of non–architectural people who felt that a building's worth was more than an assessment of its suitability for an old function. The protesters were a mixed bag, and against them was a variety of bedfellows. The latter consisted of the pragmatic who simply thought that buildings in each generation should relate to the uses expected of them; the new profession of planners anxious to make their marks; commercial interests with valuable plots to develop; those from Patrick Abercrombie onwards who thought that new wide roads slicing their way through London suburbs were beneficent as well as necessary; and borough councillors who saw in the grim statistics of outside lavatories and non-existent bathrooms a challenge that could be met only by comprehensive development.

Concern at demolitions had been voiced in the 1850s, especially after 1854 when the Bishop of London, faced with so many empty churches in the City, listed twenty-nine of them for demolition, including some of Wren's finest buildings and others which had escaped the Great Fire. Despite a public outcry, at least fourteen of them had gone by the 1890s, including St Mary Magdalene in Old Fish Street, St Mildred Poultry and St Matthew Friday Street. In 1875 the Society for Photographing Relics of Old London was formed – its 120 photographs are mostly of seventeenth-century houses and inns which were judged the least likely buildings to escape redevelopment. But properly, the preservation movement began with the demolition by the London School Board in 1893 of the Old Palace, Bromley-by-Bow, to make way for a new school. The Palace was in essence a Jacobean building with Tudor beneath, and though the defence was mounted that the LSB did not know what they were taking down, there was sufficient information at the time to have given them pause for thought. Most noise was made by the architect, C.R. Ashbee, who made the point that:

> We now have on the site of King James' Palace a well-built Board School. . . ..sanitary, solid, grey, grim and commonplace. What we might have had with a little thought, and with no extra expense. . . ..would have been an ideal Board School with a record of every period of English history from the time of Henry VIII, as a daily object lesson for the little citizens of Bromley, a school-house that contained panelling of James, I, carving of William III. . . ..rooms all the more gracious for the sumptuous additions of the later Stuarts. . . ..a school-house to be proud of.

Out of this débâcle the privately funded London Survey Committee was formed to record significant buildings in London so that there should never again be ignorance, real or supposed, as to the merit of what was taken down. Ashbee, who edited the first volume on, appropriately, the parish of Bromley-by-Bow, said in his introduction:

> Nothing is done to protect the open spaces, the trees or gardens, that might with proper planning be preserved; if there is any beautiful object of the past, some house, perhaps, that could be utilized for library, club, museum, school or parish purposes, it is torn down and sold to the wreckers for its value in old materials.

Eventually the work of the Committee was absorbed into the scholarly *Survey of London* volumes and funded by the LCC who, in 1898, obtained powers to spend money on the preservation of buildings and places of architectural or historical interest.

There were some early and disparate triumphs in the suburbs. Marble Hill, Twickenham, a delightful Palladian house which had been empty for years, was rescued by the LCC in 1901; in the same year Dollis Hill House, one-time residence of Lord Aberdeen and Mark Twain, was saved by the local authority and, with its grounds, formed into Gladstone Park. On the other hand, Cranbrook in Ilford was needlessly lost in the tide of development that swamped that suburb. In 1902 William Hogarth's house at Chiswick, a 'little box of a house', was in decay and was bought by a Colonel Shipway who restored it and presented it to the Middlesex County Council. But the most astonishing coup was the removal of what was left of the fifteenth-century mansion of Sir John Crosby, in Bishopsgate, which was transported and re-erected in Chelsea. Crosby Place was a building of immense importance but even so this transposition, this saving of it at all costs, was a significant advance.

Ashbee's plea to find new uses for good old buildings was realized in the 1914 adaptation by the LCC of the Ironmongers' Company almshouses in Kingsland Road, Hackney, to form the Geffrye Museum of furniture, thereby simultaneously saving a building and provoking interest in the furniture district of London. Rich benefactors saved other buildings. Lord Iveagh bought Kenwood House in Highgate and eventually donated it to the LCC; Lord Rothermere stepped in and purchased the Bethlehem Royal Hospital in Lambeth, designed by Robert Smirke – the building, minus its wings, became the Imperial War Museum and the grounds a park to be administered by the LCC.

Commercial necessity, however, usually prevailed. Before and after the First World War mansions disappeared seemingly without much of a fight. Park Lane had the most casualties, where the houses of the wealthy and the elegant Regency terrace houses disappeared to be replaced by flats and hotels. They included Camelford House (1912), Grosvenor House (1926), Dorchester House (1929), and Brooke House (1933). In Piccadilly, Devonshire House was replaced with flats and showrooms after 1924; south of the Strand the picturesque Adelphi Terrace was lost.

Up to the Second World War the cause of preservation depended entirely upon middle-class energy, the occasional gesture by a rich person, or the activities of the LCC. But it was the LCC which found itself branded as philistine when it proposed the demolition of Sir John Rennie's Waterloo Bridge, a structure universally admitted attractive but inadequate for its needs. The bridge became as famous a cause as did the Euston Doric Arch in the 1960s, and in its support a 'conference of societies' was formed in 1925 to urge its retention. In all, the LCC voted five times to demolish the bridge, but the Council's resolve was persistently distracted by an alternative scheme to construct a new bridge at Charing Cross, which would have the advantage of replacing what was regarded as a true eyesore, the Charing Cross railway bridge. Why demolish a thing of beauty – the Waterloo Bridge – when you could relieve traffic congestion *and* get rid of one that was ugly? But alternatively, as John Gatti, Chairman of the LCC's Finance Committee eloquently put it, if the

> *only function of the bridge is to be beautiful, or that if it is beautiful it can dispense with performing other functions, I have nothing more to say; but if you hold that the first function of Art is to add beauty to utility, and that utility must come first, and that a growing city with growing demands must perforce sometimes have to let things go.*

This reasoning was to emerge time and time again, less elegantly put, in the next fifty or sixty years.

A Royal Commission suggested a comprehensive rebuilding of the bridge, to which the LCC agreed, but only on condition that the government pay three-quarters of the cost of building a new bridge at Charing Cross. The government declined to fund either project and soon the LCC and the government were at loggerheads, a situation which the return of a majority Labour Party at County Hall in 1934 did nothing to assuage. The LCC decided to pay for the demolition and construction of a new Waterloo Bridge out of the rates but Parliament denied them the powers to borrow the money; the matter drifted on acrimoniously until the government, in a weak position since it declined to put up any money at all, had to give in. Though there was an unattractive display of petulance and aggression on the part of Herbert Morrison, Leader of the LCC, when he ceremoniously dismantled the first stone on the old bridge, the blame for this demolition may be firmly placed at the door of Parliament, rather than that of the LCC.

Meanwhile, notable successes such as the rescue of Charlton House, Swakeleys, Boston Manor, Chiswick House and Valence House in Dagenham were notched up, all bought up by borough or county councils with the exception of Swakeleys, a private donation. But it could not be said that the desire to preserve was yet particularly strong; even in Hampstead the campaign to save the house lived in briefly by John Keats was successful only from the energies of American enthusiasts.

VALENCE HOUSE, Dagenham, a manor house once owned by the Dean and canons of Windsor. The building now houses a library and a local history centre.

The battleground thus far had been one of fine and important buildings, the participants generally the great and the good in voluntary societies, the borough and county councils, the government, landowners and developers. The main losses in London were the spectacular mansions of Park Lane and Mayfair, but even the most militant of preservationists could devise no way or purpose whereby these extravaganzas of a past lifestyle could be economically viable in the depressed decade that led up to the Second World War.

The contest, however, was properly joined towards the end of the 1950s when developers were wriggling from their post–war shackles and there was in the LCC, the City and ambitious borough councils a desire to change the capital in a radical fashion. In the face of this, preservation, though still a middle–class cry, began to gather other converts. Three buildings brought the issue of demolition firmly into focus.

The first was the destruction of St James's Theatre in King Street, St James's. Rumours began to circulate in 1954 that speculators had obtained the permission of the LCC to demolish the theatre and build an office block on the site, and despite denials the plan was officially announced in 1957. Famous names, including Winston Churchill, made their opinions and cheque-books public and in the House of Lords, to the delight of newspapers, Vivien Leigh stood in the visitors' gallery and called out 'My Lords! I wish to protest against the St James's Theatre being demolished!' Laurence Olivier and Leigh led a march of actors against the proposed plan, and Lord Silkin successfully steered a motion through the Lords opposing demolition, but it was to no avail. On the last night John Gregson declared that the closure of the theatre should never have been allowed to happen and that the audience should make a resolution that such a thing should never happen again.

St James's theatre, *King Street, St James's, c.1896. Designed by Samuel Beazley, the theatre opened in 1835. Here was staged for the first time Wilde's* Lady Windermere's Fan *and* The Importance of Being Earnest.

Gregson, especially on that night, was preaching to the converted, but there were, as yet, not enough converted. St James's Theatre was certainly not the last fine building to fall with the connivance of planning authorities. Another was the Coal Exchange in Lower Thames Street, an amazing cast-iron rotunda of galleries and trading floor which, by the 1960s, no longer had a function and stood resolutely in the way of road widening along the Thames. The City of London was responsible for this loss: it was the City which initiated its destruction, provided the reason for it, carried it out with undue haste and then justified the deed. And throughout the years of discussion the City showed an alarming unawareness of the nature of its own territory, as though the City could and ought to be transformed into another Manhattan without regard to what had gone before. One City alderman, then Chairman of its Streets Committee, described the Coal Exchange as a dingy place without paintings or other objects of artistic beauty and whose ironwork was bettered in the boarding houses of Ramsgate and Hastings, unacceptable even for public lavatories. It is doubtful if the alderman's colleagues had a sufficiently intimate acquaintance with those boarding houses, or indeed public lavatories, to follow his comparison, but it was a depressing reaction in an authority which had inherited, despite the awful ravages of war, many fine buildings and a street pattern that still held mysteries.

The LCC was hardly less to blame for the destruction of the Euston Arch, a Doric ornament which bestrode the avenue leading to the old Euston Station. In 1960 the LCC accepted the view of the British Transport Commission (BTC) that the Great Hall could not sensibly be retained in any overall rebuilding of the station but suggested that the Arch should be re-erected somewhere else. The matter of its preservation, now very much the concern of the Fine Art Commission, the Society for the Protection of Ancient

THE Doric arch at Euston Station, c.1895. Euston was the first London terminus of any pretensions and a great deal of fine architecture was lost when the present station was built. The arch itself was needlessly destroyed.

Buildings, the Victorian Society and numerous individuals, was then shuttled about between the BTC, the LCC and the government to the effect that nothing was done and the Arch was taken down.

THE DRIVE FOR PRESERVATION

IT WAS THE WANTON DESTRUCTION OF THE EUSTON ARCH which was responsible, at least it seems so in hindsight, for the coming together of various strands of preservationist enthusiasm. The interested societies learned from this experience how to combine for significant campaigns, and British Rail came to grief against well-mounted opposition when they later proposed the demolition of King's Cross and St Pancras stations. The

Euston Arch saga and the misery caused to local residents during the construction of Westway through north Kensington helped to bring about a general reflection on what was happening, a doubt, perhaps, that change was necessarily progress. Those two very public schemes were mirrored by countless others all over London; radical changes were made without consultation or imagination and the general public began to tire of them. Committees and associations were formed to reclaim their own neighbourhoods, and planning officers with tidy visions found them disputed. Partly this was due to the nature of the replacements offered – the chillingly unfriendly buildings of the 1960s, the unsuitable environment offered by tower blocks of cheap construction, the wider roads and the demeaning and planned segregation of council tenants from London's general life. Unfortunately, such things have a gestation period of at least ten years and it was to be well into the 1970s before those responsible could display a change of heart.

As the proportion of working-class councillors on many Labour borough councils grew smaller after the late 1950s to be replaced by first-generation middle-class men and women with university educations, enthusiasm for comprehensive replanning became more ambivalent and less forthright. The drive to erase statistically unhygienic houses was tempered by a new sympathy for renovating old terraces. This was hardly surprising since this new breed of Labour councillors were often themselves people who had taken on an older property and brought it up to a standard well beyond that achieved in the tower blocks that they were nodding through at meetings. A further complication then set in: conservation became identified with private ownership and, inevitably, was branded a middle-class fetish. 'Gentrification' became a pejorative term that encompassed not only a veiled criticism for taking over formerly working-class houses, but of having the income to do so. In recent years this has expressed itself in vandalistic attacks on such properties, especially in Hackney where the contrasts in income are at their most extreme. This would have been hard to avoid, since borough council planning officers and architects reap few gold stars in the architectural press for renovating old houses, and did not press for such a policy; and their departments necessarily lacked the commitment, imagination and patience of house owners. Councils did, of course, renovate and convert some terrace housing, but on the whole it was the private owner who rescued huge tracts of inner London from their slum condition.

Preservation of whole environments, much more difficult to specify and thus justify, became as newsworthy as fights for individual buildings. First there was the plan by the British Library to demolish the area south of Great Russell Street for a new building. There are, indeed, buildings of significance in this area, but the case for the area's retention was based on its unique character rather than its architectural merits, and it was the residents, as much a mixture of classes as London is likely to possess nowadays, that won the battle. In 1972 grand plans were announced for Covent Garden once the fruit and vegetable market moved out to Nine Elms. The issue here was not so much the market building itself, whose demolition was not contemplated, but the numerous premises around which not only contained the very neglected buldings left by market traders, but those of other trades – craftsmen of all kinds, printers, publishers, costumiers, art supply shops and the like. And though the planners recognized that there were many buildings which gave the area a visual variety, it seemed to them that Covent Garden was an unusual, possibly the last, opportunity to plan anew a central area of London. A four-acre open space was proposed by Long Acre, hotels, conference centres and a sports centre were envisaged;

and two important roads at sunken level, one on the route of Shorts Gardens, the other on that of Maiden Lane, were to be constructed. This transformation was approved by the GLC, the City of Westminster and the London Borough of Camden.

The reaction of press and public was uniformly hostile, and a very well-organized residents' association was able to harness a feeling among the general public that the planners had at last gone mad. In July 1972, Lady Dartmouth resigned as Chair of the Covent Garden Committee of the GLC, stating that 'No individuals or bodies who represent the general public have supported us, and I have felt increasingly that our proposals are out of tune with public opinion which fears that the area will become a faceless, concrete jungle.' With the Barbican rebuilding already visible and lamented, the public had indeed imagined what was in store. Technically the grand scheme was scuppered by the announcement of the Secretary of State for the Environment in 1973

COVENT GARDEN market building during renovation in 1979. This building was not at risk in the proposed redevelopment of the area, although a serious suggestion was made to strip it of its roof, which was a later addition. It is now home to boutiques and food shops.

that while he endorsed the proposal for a Comprehensive Development he did, in addition, list another 245 properties. This, in effect, precluded anything comprehensive at all, as the Minister well knew, and ushered in the birth of a Covent Garden which owes more to the spending power of tourists than the original wishes of the local residents. The commercial forces set loose when Covent Garden was saved and the relaxation of letting guidelines were, in the end, too powerful to be withstood.

Part of the Ossulston Street estate, Somers Town begun in 1927. Designed by the LCC's architects' department, it was much influenced by local authority housing in Vienna. It was begun in 1927 and when it was finished ten years later, it consisted of over 500 dwellings arranged in a series of polygonal courts.

CHAPTER XXI

POLITICAL DIVIDES

POLITICS IN TWENTIETH-CENTURY LONDON HAVE ESSENTIALLY BEEN ABOUT MUNICIPAL activity and influence. As we saw in Chapter 14 local authorities in the inner London area had been left to their own devices for much of the nineteenth century, restricted in their governing powers, limited in their rate-raising capability, parsimonious in their outlook and jealous of their narrow autonomy. They opposed the activities of the Metropolitan Board of Works and the London School Board, not only because the concept of a governed metropolis was alien to them, but because by tradition expenditure on anything but the very basic necessities – and especially by outside bodies able to precept them – was regarded as unjustifiable. Civic dignity in the vestries rested upon how much could be done on how little, whereas in provincial cities with populations smaller than some of the London vestries municipal pride had gone beyond such calculations.

THE LONDON COUNTY COUNCIL

THE CREATION OF THE LONDON COUNTY COUNCIL (LCC) in 1889, and its politicization, changed things irrevocably. From the beginning most LCC councillors were elected on party tickets, though this did not preclude cross-voting if a candidate had sufficient charisma. Lord Rosebery, a prominent Liberal and later Prime Minister, was elected from the Conservative City of Westminster, and John Burns, a prominent Socialist, won his seat with Liberal backing in Battersea.

From the beginning the LCC attracted candidates of affluence and much ability. Of those elected in 1889, 103 were professionals, managers or employers, three could be found in *Debrett's Peerage* and only two were manual workers: this mix, with the exception of a growing number of women who claimed no paid employment, was to be much the same until the end of the LCC in 1965.

The party which took power at the beginning, the Progressives, was a coalition of Liberals, Radicals and Socialists that was mutually advantageous. The Liberals were in decline nationally and needed to prop up their muncipal power base, and the Radicals and the Socialists were too weak in numbers to hope for a majority on their own. The components did, in any case, have policies in common such as local authority control of public utilities and transport, but most importantly they were behind Lord Rosebery (their first chairman) in his vision of London's government having an active and promotional role. London the metropolis, at long last, was to have a voice, a unity and a policy. Their Conservative opponents, called the Moderates, saw London government, at least at the beginning, much as many vestries saw parish government, as a carefully restricted entity which would rarely exceed the minimum obligations it was charged with.

This difference of outlook as to the level of LCC intervention in people's lives and the scope of services it provided continued throughout the life of the LCC and its successor the Greater London Council, and it was mirrored in the borough councils which made up its area.

The mission to reform and transform was the LCC's strength but as an authority it was undermined by severe weaknesses. It did not, as with other cities, have control of public utilities, nor of transport, police, markets nor even of its life blood, the Port of London. It also had several natural enemies: the parish vestries (later the boroughs) jealous of their powers; the City of London which for most purposes had evaded the LCC's clutches; and Parliament itself, suspicious from the beginning of the upstart it had itself created. When the Conservative Lord Salisbury became Prime Minister he upgraded the London parishes into borough councils (in 1899) so that they could if they chose act as twenty-eight brakes on the activities of the LCC. Thus the interests ranged against this ambitious metropolitan authority were powerful ones, and the more political the LCC was obliged to get, the less the co-operation of Parliament could be expected, especially as for much of its life the political complexion of the LCC differed from that of the government of the day.

With the exception of tramways the LCC did not remedy any of the deficiencies listed above. The water companies were absorbed beyond its control into the Metropolitan Water Board in 1902, and the other utilities retained their independence until nationalization after the Second World War; the police remained under the control of the Home Office – a unique situation – while the City Police survived intact under their old masters; the markets remained the property of the City and the Duke of Bedford, and the Port of London Authority survived the decline of the docks. Short of money and wary of the accusations of extravagance levelled against their predecessors the Metropolitan Board of Works, the Progressives did not press ahead with any major road schemes to relieve London's congestion and slums, with the very large exception of Kingsway and Aldwych. They did, however, embark on an era of municipal housing which, when the Moderates gained power in 1907, was expanded, and they did buy up and electrify tramways within London's boundaries as private operating leases expired.

It was a frustrating time for the Fabians in the Progressives' ranks. This earnest, middle-class, sometimes naïve and romantic group of activists and intellectuals had already had some success in propounding their social reformist ideas when in 1888 three of their members were elected to the London School Board. They hoped for a great deal more from the LCC, for their most cogent policies proposed municipal ownership of many of the services the LCC were excluded from.

The 1880s was a decade of political ferment in London. In 1881 the Marxist, Henry Hyndman, had formed what became the Social Democratic Federation (without the blessing of Marx who did not care for its founder) an organization which alarmed the authorities since it was in favour of revolution. Hyndman and his Federation took part in the 1886 march to the West End to protest against unemployment; this ended in riots and looting and the arrest of Hyndman and John Burns. Engels had no great opinion of either Hyndman or the march. He noted in a letter that:

The unemployed who followed [Hyndman and the SDF] in order to hold a fresh meeting in Hyde Park, were mostly the types who do not want to work anyhow, hawkers, loafers, police spies, pickpockets. When the aristocrats at the club window sneered at them they broke the said windows, ditto the shop windows; they looted the wine dealers' shops and immediately set up a consumers' association for the contents in the streets, so that in Hyde Park Hyndman and Co. had hastily to pocket their blood–thirsty phrases and go in for pacification.

In November 1887, despite an official ban, a demonstration marched to Trafalgar Square on what became known as 'Bloody Sunday'. It was organized by the Metropolitan Radical Federation to protest against the imprisonment of an Irish Nationalist, William O'Brien. Needless to say the SDF, the Socialist League and other Radical groups took part and the day ended in serious disorder. John Burns and a Scottish laird turned Radical, R.B. Cunninghame Graham, were badly beaten up by the police and the marchers were forced back by batons. A month later at another demonstration a workman was clubbed to death by police. At his funeral William Morris gave the oration:

Our friend who lies here has had a hard life and met with a hard death; and if society had been differently constituted his life might have been a delightful, a beautiful and a happy one. It is our business to begin to organise for the pupose of seeing that such things shall not happen; to try to make this earth a beautiful and happy place.

Hyndman's revolutionary zeal did not appeal to many. William Morris left his Federation in 1884 and began his own anti-political Socialist League; the Fabians, founded in Hampstead, also in 1884, believed that sure political change came gradually. Eminent members like Webb and Shaw saw it coming with the capture of the Liberal Party by the Radicals already within. Hyndman's organization was to lose out eventually to the Independent Labour Party and was later to merge into the Communist Party.

Following these street demonstrations, which put the London authorities in a jittery condition, two famous occasions of industrial action and the publication of a survey of London's labour conditions were again to ignite the East End; they were also to create new and militant trade unions and gain the active interest of many comfortably off and influential Liberals and Radicals.

The first industrial action was the Match Girls' Strike of 1888. The unlikely and quite unexpected strike of women working at the Bryant & May match factory at Bow captured the notice of the nation and was to give heart to many. It began with a crusading article by Annie Besant entitled 'White Slavery in London', published in June 1888. She described the dangerous conditions in which the women worked, risking phosphorous poisoning and skin cancer; they worked from 6.30 a.m. to 6 p.m. in the summer, and were also subject to a system of fines for minor offences such as talking, dropping matches etc. Bryant sacked Besant's informants, and a strike by this previously unorganized and powerless workforce began. It was to last three weeks, attract the passion of the nation's press for and against, and in the end was mostly successful. It was an object lesson for their male counterparts in the area.

The match girls were considered unskilled workers as indeed were the many thousands who scraped a living in sweat shops in the East End or as casual workers in the docks. Ninety per cent of British workers were then unorganized and most worked in sweated industries. Trade unions that existed in London were mostly descendants of old craft guilds and in effect were Friendly Societies. They had no interest in the majority of workers who were either unskilled or partly skilled. Ben Tillett, a diminutive but powerful agitator, had unsuccessfully tried to form a union of general dockers in 1887, but in March 1889 Will Thorne, an illiterate gas worker, addressed a meeting of men mainly from the Beckton Gas Works in Barking to propose the formation of a union which would fight for shorter hours. He declared to them:

The strike committee of the Matchgirls' Strike of 1888. Standing, at the top of the picture, is Annie Besant, theosophist and social reformer; to her right is Herbert Burrows, a campaigner for better factory conditions.

The way you have been treated at your work for many years is scandalous, brutal, and inhuman. I pledge my word that, if you will stand firm and don't waver, within six months we will claim and win the eight-hour day, a six-day week, and the abolition of the present slave-driving methods in vogue not only at the Beckton Gas Works, but all over the country.

The Union signed up thousands of members and won their eight-hour day without a strike, the Gas Light and Coke Company acceding to the bargain proposed. Helping Thorne in all this was Eleanor Marx, daughter of Karl Marx, who did the clerical work that Thorne couldn't, and who addressed meetings of workers in the Barking Road.

The 1889 Dock Strike reminded Londoners again of the horrors and squalor of working conditions in the East End. Since it paralyzed the London docks it had to be taken seriously by many who stood to lose money, and it had an even higher profile in the press than the Match Girls' Strike. Ostensibly it arose out of a minor dispute relating to payment for the unloading of a ship, but as with so many dock strikes that followed it was to do with larger issues and the way in which dockers were expected to work and somehow exist. The men went on strike for sixpence instead of fivepence per hour, a guarantee that no man should be taken on for less than four hours' labour, and a demand that piecework should be abolished. At the same time the nation was made well aware of the appallingly hard conditions the men suffered and the indignities suffered in the system of casual labour in the docks.

Ben Tillett, the strike leader, found to his surprise a great deal of solidarity and was able to form at his second attempt a general docks union; he was encouraged in the strike by the mainly Irish stevedores and of labour luminaries such as Will Thorne, John Burns and Tom Mann. It was an orderly four-week affair, supported by the local population, and it

Ben Tillett, leader of the dockers (left), a mild-mannered but effective labour leader. The more charismatic John Burns is seen on the right addressing a meeting of striking dockers.

took the form of frequent marches from the Wades Arms pub in Poplar to Tower Hill that impressed onlookers and press alike. John Burns, in a distinctive white boater, led many of the processions and his clearly argued, non-revolutionary speeches described the conditions at the docks and the demeaning system whereby each morning men had to fight for work at the whim of an overseer; he maintained that the wages for such strenuous work were insufficient to keep a man strong enough to do it. Ben Tillett later described the degradation of the morning 'call-ons' for work:

> *Coats, flesh and even ears were torn off, men were crushed to death in the struggle, helpless if fallen. The strong literally threw themselves over the heads of their fellows and battled with kick and curse, through the kicking, punching, cursing crowd to the rails of the 'cage' which held them like rats – mad, human rats who saw food in the ticket.*

W.J. Fishman in his book *East End 1888* quotes some moving descriptions of conditions in the docks, one of which was originally in the campaigning *Lancet*.

> *Competition, the desire for cheapness, the struggle for profits, seem to have wrought their worst in the docks. Here men have been known to work for 2½d an hour. Here men faint from over-exhaustion and want of food. Here lives are needlessly squandered; men are ruptured, their spines injured, their bones broken, and their skulls fractured, so as to get ships loaded and unloaded a little quicker and a little cheaper.*

Towards the end of the strike it seemed as if it would falter, but with unexpected donations from Australian unionists, support from the Salvation Army, and with Cardinal Manning as a mediator, the dockers won their sixpence per hour after negotiations at the Mansion House.

Also in 1889, Londoners were shocked by the publication of the first part of Charles Booth's *Life and Labour of the People in London*, a dry, statistical, comprehensive and shaming account of the extent of poverty in London. Booth was a wealthy Liverpool shipowner who took an interest in social matters. Though a Radical he was not enthusiastic at the idea of trade union militancy and he feared Socialism as he thought that business would no longer 'be tried in the court of profit and loss'. Booth attempted to provide incontrovertible evidence on which sound and lasting reforms could be based. Inevitably, the worst excesses of exploitation were in the East End, but he found pockets of extreme poverty all over central London from which Londoners had previously averted their eyes.

With the exception of Hyndman, who briefly had influence with East End Radical clubs middle-class political reformers were mainly on the sidelines in this growth of new trade unions; furthermore, the close relationships that many of them enjoyed with the Liberal Party were a cause of suspicion to trade union activists. When Keir Hardie, representing the miners, attended a Trades Union Congress in London in 1887, he made a scathing attack on Henry Broadhurst, secretary of the TUC, for his Liberal connections and strongly criticized the Liberal Party for condoning 'sweating' employers among their own MPs. Likewise, at the formation meeting of the Independent Labour Party in 1893, it was only by two votes that the Fabian Society, whose hopes for the conversion of the Liberal Party were well known, was permitted to attend.

In the election of 1892 Keir Hardie was returned as an independent Labour MP for West Ham and John Burns was voted in for Battersea: Socialism had arrived in Parliament, although Burns was later to veer back to the Liberals. An astonishing scene took place in the House in June when the House voted a message of condolence to the French on the assassination of their President, and a message of congratulation to the Queen on the birth of a granddaughter. Keir Hardie rose to ask if a message of condolence was to be sent to the relatives of the 260 men and boys recently lost in a mining disaster in south Wales. The Prime Minister declined to send such an official message and when the vote was taken on the message to the Queen, Hardie moved an amendment that the Queen should send a message to the miners' families. The house erupted in a royalist scream and Hardie was ostracized by most of the other members.

Eight years later in February 1900, at a meeting held at the Memorial Hall, Farringdon Street, the formation of the Labour Party was proposed and agreed with the most prosaic wording that it was possible to construct and garner support for.

Socialism was not the only political movement worrying the authorities. In 1883 and 1884 there were further Fenian bombings; buildings damaged included the offices of *The Times* and Victoria Station. A bomb left on the Metropolitan Line at Paddington injured sixty-two people.

In 1885 police raided the International Anarchist Club in Stephen Mews, near Fitzroy Square, after bomb explosions at the House of Commons and the Tower of London; an hysterical mob later stripped the premises bare. The following year the Club Autonomie, another anarchist group, was established in Charlotte Street. The International Club, which was frequented by European emigrés, was connected with William Morris's Socialist League. The anarchists were few in number and their activities spasmodic. In 1893 a young tailor set out for Greenwich with the idea of blowing up the Observatory, but the bomb went off prematurely, killing him. This incident formed the basis of Joseph Conrad's novel, *The Secret Agent*. In 1897 there was an explosion on an Underground train, which killed one person, and this too was attributed to anarchists. Even more gruesomely, in December 1910 a group of Russian-speaking anarchists (probably from Latvia) were disturbed robbing a jeweller's shop in Houndsditch and three policemen were shot while attempting to arrest them. It was not until early January 1911 that police tracked down the men (or at least they thought they had) to 100 Sidney Street in the East End. A force of four hundred armed police, together with several regiments of soldiers, under the supervision of Winston Churchill, besieged the house in an operation that cost the lives of one policeman and one fireman – the house was set on fire and two men inside were found dead.

There were many Europeans in exile in London in this period, and it was in a chapel in Southgate Road, Hackney, in 1907, that a Congress of exiled Russian Social Democrats was held. Those attending included Lenin, Stalin, Trotsky, Rosa Luxemburg and Maxim Gorky.

It will be seen from these events that the formation of the LCC took place in momentous times in London. The public, alarmed by unemployment, poverty, exploitation and social unrest, were in a mood for change and the Progessives, who seemed to offer a new vision, were elected.

When it came to implementing their programme the Progessives achieved more controversy than anything else. A weakened Liberal government declined to help them purchase the water and electricity authorities, and the cost of replacing housing in the inner areas became so expensive that the Council was forced to buy cheap land outside its own area. Spectacular open spaces in the London area had already been acquired by the old MBW and the LCC's acquisitions were neighbourhood parks which were relatively expensive to run but without the political kudos that, say, a Hampstead Heath would have brought them.

However, the Progressives spent whatever good will they obtained from opening small parks by banning the playing of games in them on Sundays, usually the day on which parents and children could use them together. This Sabbatarianism was seen as an unwarranted intrusion into people's lives and so was the Council's supervision and suppression of music halls and, where possible, public houses. There was, particularly among the Radicals and Socialists, a strong temperance lobby and more than a dash of puritanism – Emma Cons, whom we have noted earlier for her work with the Coffee House Taverns (page 226), was an alderman in the first Council, and Sidney Webb, who chaired the LCC's Technical Education Committee, was a strong advocate of public libraries in the hope that they would 'go far to cut out the tavern as the poor man's club'. The Labour leaders Will Crooks, John Burns, Keir Hardie and J. Ramsay MacDonald held similar views.

In 1889, the LCC was given powers to license theatres and music halls at a time when moral crusaders saw the latter as a corrupting influence over the working-classes. Armed with powers to insist on stringent building standards, the LCC was able to suppress many halls, particularly in poorer districts. The Council also appointed numerous inspectors to attend performances and report on the behaviour of both players and audience before any licence renewal.

These activities created dissension in the ranks of the Fabian Society, from where much of this paternal puritanism emanated. A prominent member and Christan Socialist, Steward Headlam, formed an Anti-Puritan League for the Defence of the People's Pleasure in 1904 which inveighed against the inspectorate, Sabbatarianism and the systematic non-renewal of public house licences.

Perversely, while the Progressives pursued these policies in the face of working-class hostility, they were politically dependent on the votes of that class to return to power. In 1907 they were shunted from office, never to return.

There were no surprises to come from the Municipal Reform Party (MRP) that took over and no landmarks that need assessing. The Moderates, as a name, had been dropped, and the Conservatives emerged on the LCC as the MRP dedicated to rolling back, or at least abandoning, the tide of wished-for municipalization that had caused so much worry to vested interests and so much frustration to its perpetrators. The MRP concentrated instead on running housing and education efficiently and reducing the county rate in an undistinguished reign that covered the period of the First World War, the further decline of the Liberal Party and the dramatic rises and falls of the Labour Party.

The Municipal Reformers were also in power when that symbol of muncipal government, County Hall, was opened on the south bank. The construction of this building reflected the swings and roundabouts of opinion in the LCC and its relationship with central government. The LCC originally had offices in Spring Gardens off Trafalgar Square but soon outgrew them: by 1892, staff were working in six different buildings and by 1904 this had risen to twenty-five. The choice of a new site for offices was fraught with disagreement. Some, including Lord Rosebery, did not want a building physically near the Houses of Parliament, while others felt that this was an advantage. Other suggestions included space on the new Kingsway, where buildings were difficult to let, or else straddling a rebuilt Waterloo Bridge, or on the site of the Adelphi, but rarely was the undeveloped south side of the river contemplated. It was only in 1902 that the south bank was seriously proposed since the building of offices there could be part of a scheme to rescue the riverbank from dereliction. The Moderates, opposed to a headquarters in the centre of London because of the high cost of land and rates, were also against the south bank because of the extra cost needed to embank the shoreline and for the construction of foundations. John Burns, a south London councillor, was enthusiastic because he thought a south bank scheme would brighten up a poor part of London, but a member for Islington thought the area 'cheap and nasty'. Having obtained the necessary legislation in 1906 the Progressives then had a dilemma: should the building be grand to signify the importance of its occupants, and thereby risk accusations of wasting ratepayers' money, or should it be plain and thereby miss an architectural opportunity to rival other cities? The Progressives were spared the decision, for by the time a competition had been held and Ralph Knott's design chosen, the Municipal Reformers were in power. And by the time the building was opened in 1922, construction having been delayed during the war, County Hall was so familiar to Londoners that justification for its grandness was unnecessary. *The Times* hoped that the building of County Hall on the south bank might 'foretell the coming of a new and brighter era for the people of South London.'

It was during this era in metropolitan government that the Poplar affair occurred. It had been clear since the inception of the LCC that the rating system was iniquitous, and that it was illogical for the underprivileged residents of boroughs like Poplar to pay as much towards the LCC precept as those of affluent Westminster. This only compounded the poverty that existed in Poplar. But it was not a situation likely to change when the

COUNTY HALL, *the monumental building designed by Ralph Knott for the London County Council as its headquarters; drawing by Fed. Adcock. It replaced a cluster of untidy timber yards and wharves. Begun in 1909, it was not completed until 1933.*

government was a coalition run by Lloyd George, who needed the Conservative vote, and when the LCC was still in the hands of the Municipal Reform Party.

In 1921, the borough of Poplar, controlled by the Labour Party and led by George Lansbury, refused to pay their LCC and Metropolitan Police rates in protest at the unfairness of the system and their leaders were summoned to the High Court. Accompanied by two thousand people, they marched to the Law Courts and there were given time to reconsider their decision. Buoyed up by the support of those near and dear to them, the thirty rebel councillors expected assistance from Labour colleagues outside Poplar as well, but not much materialized. Most other Labour councils declined to follow their lead, and Herbert Morrison, secretary of the London Labour Party and mayor of Hackney (and who disliked Lansbury) said nothing in their favour and was worried that the behaviour of the Poplar group destroyed the credibility of the Labour Party at metropolitan and national levels as being fit to govern. But the councillors, male and female, went to prison in good heart and held council meetings in their cells. Eventually, worried that the revolt might spread, the LCC backed down and the councillors were freed.

VOTES FOR WOMEN

B Y 1925 THERE WERE TWENTY-FOUR WOMEN ON THE LCC. This was a surprising number given the Council's previous history in the matter. At the first LCC elections in 1889 two women, Lady Sandhurst and Jane Cobden, daughter of Richard Cobden, who had

THE Suffragettes commanded the headlines before the First World War with a series of demonstrations and, occasionally, outrages, that astounded press and public alike.

been leader of the successful campaign to abolish the Corn Laws in 1846, were voted in as Progressive councillors and Emma Cons was appointed an alderman. However, the defeated Moderate opponent of Lady Sandhurst went to court and won his case that the Act which set up the LCC did not actually specify that women councillors were permitted. It was not until 1907 that a general Act was passed to allow boroughs and county councils to have women councillors, although the London School Board and Poor Law Guardians already had women members. After this judgement Cobden and Cons abstained from Council duties for a year in which their election and appointment might be challenged, but when they resumed their activities a Moderate councillor successfully barred them, though oddly they still continued to attend meetings.

It was not until 1910 that women were able to sit in the LCC and it was in 1912 that the Suffragette movement, gathering strength for some years, firmly came to public notice. 'Votes for Women' had remained on the political agenda despite Gladstone's refusal to include such a measure in the Reform Bill of 1884. Emmeline Pankhurst and her husband, leaders of the Women's Suffrage movement, left the Liberal Party in protest and joined the Fabians instead – she was unable to impress the Independent Labour Party with her views either. From about 1905 Suffragettes switched from polite argument to hostile tactics, disturbing proceedings in Parliament and chaining themselves to railings, and a march to central London in 1913 ended in disarray and confrontation with the police and the arrest of Emmeline Pankhurst and others. The following year an unexploded bomb was found in St Paul's Cathedral and on Derby Day Emily Davidson threw herself to her death in front of a horse. Mrs Pankhurst was again arrested for incitement to violence and sentenced to three years penal servitude at Holloway Prison. Suffragettes were responsible for bomb explosions at St John the Evangelist church, Westminster, St Martin-in-the Fields church and at Westminster Abbey in 1914, and for the damage to two paintings at the Royal Academy. In the meantime the Women's Enfranchisement Bill was rejected by the Lords and the Suffragettes, once war was declared in August, put their energies into the war effort.

THE LABOUR LCC

THE HEYDAY OF THE LCC'S MUNICIPAL SOCIALISM was in the five years from 1934, when Labour took control under the leadership of Herbert Morrison. Though the same policies were resumed after the Second World War, municipalization was gradually more identified with Labour boroughs while the LCC seemed to many a rather remote ruling body. During the 1930s, however, the Labour LCC was to attract the support of all classes, even at times of their own party's national unpopularity. It ran a well-managed and humane policy of extensive health care, until the arrival of the National Health Service subsumed it, and created the best education system in the country. The hated workhouse hospitals were taken over in 1929 and made into general hospitals; health screening clinics were set up, particularly to combat tuberculosis; free milk was given to children to improve their diets; parks and playing fields were improved; well- designed swimming pools in which the materials of modern architecture could be used, were opened; and more and more housing was provided.

The architects' department at the LCC – inherited by Labour – was world renowned; talented anyway, it also looked outwards to Continental developments, the influence of which may still be seen clearly in blocks of flats in Ossulston Street, Somers Town.

FASCISM IN LONDON

THE CONVERSE OF COMFORTING MUNICIPAL SOCIALISM were the currents of strong right- and left-wing allegiances before the war. The conflicts between Fascists and left-wing groups which brought the East End back to prominence are more famous than the events deserve, since, despite the number of protagonists involved at times, they were apart from the mainstream of political life in London. The confrontations which took place were partly an extension of those in Italy, Spain and Germany, or else a despairing reaction to the malaise of the country's political and economic situation.

Fascists were not new in London – a number of street fights involving early Fascist organizations had taken place in London in 1925. They derived their enthusiasm from events in Italy where a disillusioned, fragmented, strike-torn country had been, it seemed to them, unified and made strong by Benito Mussolini, former Communist, but now a Fascist. If Italy could be rescued from its morass by a programme of strong leadership and strong discipline why should not the mess that was Britain? And if Italy under Mussolini could fight off the growing menace of Bolshevik revolution why not Britain? The knowledge that violence was used in large measure to subdue opponents, that Parliament in Italy was reduced to a rubber stamp, and that the military were the real rulers, was ignored or thought justified.

Fascism was not at that time overtly racist, nor was it when Sir Oswald Mosley left the Labour Party in 1930 after his proposals for state intervention in the economy and a massive public works programme to help relieve unemployment had been rejected. Convinced of his popular appeal to both middle and working classes, he formed what was called the New Party in 1931 and when a General Election was called in October it fielded twenty-four candidates, all of whom were heavily defeated. One of Mosley's most treasured spokesmen in the East End was the famous Jewish boxer 'Kid' Lewis, who stood confidently in Stepney but received only a derisory vote. From this time Mosley knew that the control of Parliament was beyond him, at least for the forseeable future, and after a visit to Italy he formed the British Union of Fascists in 1932. It was not until a large meeting at Olympia in 1934 that violence became common at their meetings and gatherings; with the rise to power of Hitler in Germany the British Union became increasingly military and militant, aping their German counterparts by parading in black shirts and producing blatantly anti-semitic propaganda. By 1936, when the famous battle in Cable Street, Whitechapel occurred, Mosley's party had lost its respectability and was obliged to find its converts among the rougher elements of the East End.

Anti-semitism already existed in the East End long before Mosley's supporters exploited it. The piecework wages paid in the garment industry, many of them in Jewish sweat shops, were a common target of resentment. In July 1936, Mosley, bedecked in uniform and jackboots, addressed a meeting of five thousand Fascists in Victoria Park, Hackney, which ended in serious disorder and injuries. He then announced that in October he would lead a large march throughout the East End. This should have been banned as it would almost certainly lead to civil disturbance but the Home Secretary declined to act. Instead, six thousand policemen were drafted in to ensure that the march proceeded without impediment, with the inevitable result that a battle ensued between the police and the Fascists on one hand and the thousands of people, not necessarily Communists or even left-wing, on the other. It is reported that by the afternoon about 100,000 anti-Fascists had massed at the junction of roads at Aldgate all the way down to Cable Street to prevent the march proceeding further. The police were so alarmed at the prospect that the Home Secretary was persuaded by telephone to order Mosley to cancel the march. It was a famous victory but it did not prevent further anti-Jewish attacks occurring, nor other confrontations, particularly in Dalston.

THE RENT RIOTS

THE DISPERSAL OF PEOPLE TO OUT-COUNTY ESTATES and New Towns between and after the war left inner London boroughs depopulated, though still with a massive housing shortage. To an extent this was a *perceived* shortage, a result of people's expectations being higher. Young families wanted self-contained accommodation, and they wanted to live apart from their parents. A startling illustration of the way in which family life had changed and overcrowding had been reduced is the old borough of St Pancras whose population in the 1870s was approximately the same as that for the whole of the borough of Camden into which it was incorporated in 1965. And that despite the intervening erection of flats. The housing shortage and the attempts to match it had political consequences. Those boroughs which could reasonably count on a Labour majority at elections invested in massive building programmes which in turn ensured that many areas would automatically return Labour candidates. This was particularly the case in the East End and inner south London. However, municipal housing incurred substantial losses from political decisions to keep rents well below an economic return. To balance this the local rate was pushed up and this gradually deterred businesses from staying in the area.

Rents for local authority accommodation became for a while a prominent political issue but as the realities of modern local authority financing have worsened they have inevitably risen whether an authority wants it or not. In the 1950s and 1960s local authorities did still have a choice – they could either keep council rents below an economic return and find the shortfall from ratepayers generally, or else they could raise them roughly to match what was required. If rents were raised there would as a consequence be families who could not pay them – how then to evolve a scheme in which those tenants paid less?

This dilemma was highlighted in the St Pancras Rent Riots of 1960. This borough, which had usually returned a Labour council, had a low-rent policy; furthermore the Labour administration up to the elections of 1959 was markedly left-wing, having distinguished itself, to the embarrassment of the Labour Party nationally, by flying the Red Flag from its Town Hall. The Conservatives were returned to power in 1959 and immediately set about introducing a rent scheme which involved differentials for people of different incomes. This was a return, the Labour Party councillors claimed, to the Means Test. These words had emotive value, for it was not so long from pre-war days when a test of means was taken before benefits for those unemployed could be paid. The indignity of those tests and more, perhaps, the desperation which led a family to apply for them in the first place, were still writ large in working-class memory. There is no doubt that Communist activists took leadership of the tenants out of the milder hands of the Labour councillors then in opposition. The dispute was turned into one of absurdly stark issues, but there was, nevertheless, a feeling even among moderate people involved that the departure from a civilized system of charging uniform rents was also a withdrawal from a municipal socialism that had so far pertained. No matter that opponents would jibe 'To each according to his means', differential rents meant that some people would *know* themselves to be poorer than the people next door.

The dispute went its inevitable course. A large number of tenants refused to pay their rents and eventually two leaders of the boycott were evicted from their flats in spite of neighbourly support. Also inevitably, the local Labour Party was unable to change the principle of the new rent system when it returned to power because the economics of local government precluded them from doing so.

DOCKLANDS

MORE COMPLEX POLITICS WERE IN PLAY in the redevelopment of Docklands. The use of containers and the location of facilities to handle them at Tilbury and Felixstowe hastened the demise of the already declining London docks and by the early 1970s large parts of them, north and south of the Thames, were closed and derelict. It was a catastrophe for those people who lived there, for most relied on the docks directly or indirectly for their incomes and relationships. Perhaps it was the high walls, which hid the extent of the retreat from industry, or the usual neglect of the East End, but it was some time before the general London public was aware of the enormous size of the vacuum left behind.

The very scale of the opportunity is almost certainly the cause of what some regard as a dreadful solution. In terms of both territory and resources what needed to be done was beyond the scope of any one of the borough authorities; they had not, in any case, so far distinguished themselves in the matter of their own public housing which was uniformly drab and uninspiring. However, they did have a serious claim to be intimately involved in the redevelopment, for it was their rateable income which was at stake. Equally, the Greater London Council (GLC), successor to the LCC after 1965, saw the matter as within its remit. For all intents and purposes Docklands was a New Town that could radically alter both the perception and the reality of East End London, and it could not be left to parochial interests. As Peter Walker, then Secretary of State for the Environment, said: 'There is no capital city of any magnitude anywhere in the world that probably will ever have the opportunity of a site of this size to develop in an imaginative way near its centre.' However, he went on to say: 'I do not think the format of the London boroughs – this is no criticism – for doing their normal work, likewise the GLC, is suited to that task.'

To the dismay of the local and county authorities the government commissioned a report on the future development of the area from an outside consultant. This led to a truce between the GLC and the five boroughs involved who then formed themselves into a Docklands Joint Committee. Their own plan for the area, however, was dispiriting, given the importance of the site – it was esssentially a housing estate with local amenities and some industry hopefully thrown in; and it did not propose that there should be a mix of social classes. In their disastrous scheme (disastrous, for it probably confirmed the government in its intention of hiving off Docklands to an unfettered corporation) municipal socialism probably made its last substantial appearance in London, but in this case the sums were wrong as well. Though needing considerable investment in roads and tube railways, the development proposed would never have had the income base to make them remotely economic. The GLC and the Labour boroughs had misjudged the opportunity and the times.

A hiatus then occurred with little agreement between any of the parties as to what was to be done. Tower Hamlets broke ranks and agreed to an important site at Wapping being taken by Rupert Murdoch's News International, but on the whole the prospects of renewing the docklands area with new investment, commerce and industry seemed remote. It was after the 1979 Election that the Conservative government took the decision to treat Docklands as a New Town, but instead of using the GLC (whose demise they planned anyway) to supervise its development they opted for a Development Corporation which was promptly boycotted by the frustrated GLC and given short shrift by the boroughs.

The London Docklands Development Corporation (LDDC) was able to forge ahead, if the progress that was made could be described thus, with a virtually unplanned New Town subject to few of the constraints that affected any other developer. To be profitable it set its sights on attracting commerce from an expensive and congested City of London, and on selling unusual residential properties to young professional people. For a brief period, during the boom years of the 1980s, it seemed as though it might partially succeed, but an economic recession, a lack of transport facilities and a fightback by the old forces of the City of London have made the future uncertain.

A New Authority for London?

POLITICS RATHER THAN IMPARTIAL JUDGEMENT have decided on the existence, status and size of any overall London authority. The Metropolitan Board of Works was reluctantly formed in 1855 and then only given limited powers; Progressives on the early LCC wanted a larger area to administer but governments declined to give more scope to a creature they were unsure of; as Tory voters drifted out of London in the 1930s it was the Conservatives who wanted to enlarge the LCC so that they could claw back some supporters and it was the Labour Party, afraid of losing control, which declined to press for expansion even though in planning terms it was desirable; it was a Conservative government which created the Greater London Council in 1965 in a bid to end Labour's hold on the capital, while at the same time increasing the powers of the boroughs; and it was the Conservatives under Mrs Thatcher, disappointed in their hope of control of the GLC and impatient of their confrontations with the GLC Leader, Ken Livingstone, that abolished it in 1986.

CHINATOWN in the East End in 1920; watercolour by William Monk. The first Chinatown in London developed in Limehouse where restaurants and lodgings catered for Chinese mariners.

CHAPTER XXII

STRANGERS TO OUR SHORES

THE PASSING OF THE COMMONWEALTH ACT OF 1948, UNDER WHICH CITIZENS OF Commonwealth countries were automatically granted citizenship of the United Kingdom, did not at first spark off a flood of immigration to this country. It was, for most Commonwealth countries, a period of relative peace, retrenchment or reorganization, and the social conditions which normally persuade people to settle in entirely foreign lands were not yet oppressive.

JEWS

REVOLUTION OR PERSECUTION HAD BEEN THE MOST COMMON CAUSE of immigration into England, as with the Huguenots and the Jews, and poverty brought the Irish. At first the Jews were an exception – they came freely and were affluent. Permitted back into the country by Cromwell (they had been expelled in 1290), there was a substantial community of Sephardic Jews from Spain and Portugal doing business in the City in the late Stuart period and some of them were wealthy enough to have houses in such suburbs as Highgate, Hackney and Clapton. The poorer Ashkenazi Jews from Germany, Poland and Holland arrived at the beginning of the eighteenth century and settled in Houndsditch, Spitalfields and Aldgate, where they joined the Huguenots already established there. The largest Jewish immigration came in the last twenty years of the nineteenth century when pogroms in Poland and Russia made flight necessary; once again they came to the Aldgate area.

Henry Mayhew was around to describe the Jewish quarter of *c.*1860, though he encountered a reluctance on the residents' part to give much information. The Jews traded, he said disapprovingly, in commodities for which there was no fixed price. They were wholesalers in all sorts of imported commodities, especially fruits, but also exotica such as ostrich feathers, parrots and cigars, and they were manufacturers of cheap clothes and furniture. Their fruit shops, he goes on, were in Duke's Place and Pudding Lane, but the superior ones were in Cheapside, Oxford Street, Piccadilly and Covent Garden market. Inferior Jewish jewellers were around Whitechapel, Bevis Marks and

Houndsditch, and the watchmakers were in Clerkenwell. Second-hand clothes were concentrated in Petticoat Lane, the manufacture of small items such as quills, pencils, cigars and sealing wax was in Mansell Street and Leman Street, and dealers in birds and shells lived in East Smithfield, Ratcliffe and Shadwell. Even the Jews, who lived in poor conditions and sold cheaply off barrows on the streets, were often undersold by Irish who could live on the smallest amount of money possible. There was, for the rest of the century, competition between the Irish and Jews for accommodation and trading pitches. Mayhew found the Jews rather noisy in their synagogues, without much interest in literature, fond of music and theatre; but their women were chaste. They did not, he noted approvingly, allow any of their number to live or die in a parish work-house and he admired their devotion to Jewish charities, an example to the rich Christians of London.

By the time of Charles Booth's inquiry into London labour in the 1880s there was a substantial increase in the number of poor Ashkenazi Jews in the Aldgate area, whose plight was to sorely try the generosity of the Sephardim. Booth in 1887 recorded nearly 29,000 Jews in Whitechapel, nearly 6,000 in St George's in the East, nearly 8,000 in Mile End and about 7,000 in Bethnal Green. In particular, the Jews replaced or displaced the Irish, many of whom were taking the opportunity to emigrate to colonies or else were moving to west and north-west London for employment on railway projects. And just as in modern times the Chinese in Soho broke through what were seen as limits of their area and then took over numerous properties outside, so did the Jews, according to Booth, turn Whitechapel and Spitalfields into a ghetto (though he also noted that different kinds and nationalities of Jews formed into separate ghettos within the whole area):

> The newcomers have gradually replaced the English population in whole districts which were formerly outside the Jewish quarter. Formerly in Whitechapel, Commercial Street roughly divided the Jewish haunts of Petticoat Lane and Goulston Street from the rougher English quarter lying in the East. Now the Jews have flowed across that line; Hanbury Street, Fashion Street, Pelham Street, Booth Street, Old Montague Street, and many streets and lanes and alleys have fallen before them; they fill whole blocks of model dwellings; they have introduced new trades as well as new habits and they live and crowd together and work and meet their fate independent of the great stream of London life surging around them.

By 1890, with the persecution of Polish Jews at its height, thousands were arriving in the Port of London, there to be met by the Poor Jews' Temporary Shelter organization, hard stretched to cope with the numbers; and in 1891 the Tzar ejected Jews from Russian cities.

This influx of poor Jews into the East End was as worrying to the Sephardim as to the government, for these more affluent and established immigrants found themselves identified in the press along with the rougher newcomers. Cultivated and urbane as many of them were, those who still operated their businesses from the East End were lumped in with the other Jews vilified in the press or else in such outpourings as those of the Fabian, Beatrice Webb. Though they might be rich enough to own mansions in Mayfair and Piccadilly they still encountered anti-semitism, fuelled by the perception of West End people that the East End ghetto – a foreign land indeed – would some day be a seat of sedition and civil unrest.

The Sephardic Jews were particularly concerned that the east European Jews spoke only Yiddish and did not make any attempts to assimilate themselves into the English community. It needed only the resentment of the poor indigenous classes of the East End, who found it difficult to compete in the manufacture of clothes and small items of furniture, to make the situation inflammable; it was no wonder that in the siege mentality induced by the Jack the Ripper murders, Jewish suspects were singled out by the mob.

By the turn of the century the area of Whitechapel, Goodman's Fields and Spitalfields and Houndsditch was overwhelmingly Jewish and yet, astonishingly, the community had been reduced to about 4,000 in the 1980s. The wealthier Askenazi went to Stamford Hill, Golders Green, Hackney and Norwood; the poorer to Tottenham, Edmonton, Ilford and Walthamstow; the Sephardim had already, by virtue of their earlier wealth, distributed themselves all over the capital.

NINETEENTH-CENTURY Irish immigrants to London settled in the poorer areas – St Giles-in-the-Fields and nearby Seven Dials, where there was casual work at Covent Garden. The whole St Giles rookery area was swept away with the construction of New Oxford Street.

THE IRISH

THE IRISH HAVE RARELY BEEN MASTERS of their own destinies in London. Their labour has usually been heavy but unskilled, wanted but casual. Mostly their's has been a male society, unlike that of the Jews who settled in family units, in the worst of accommodation and generally in solitary contemplation.

In numbers they settled around St Giles-in-the-Fields in the seventeenth century and comprised many of the victims of the Great Plague of 1665. In 1736 local men in Shoreditch rioted against the influx of the Irish who were prepared to do agricultural work cheaper than they, and in 1747 the writer Henry Fielding noted that in a lodging house he visited in Dyot Street, Bloomsbury, there were fifty-eight persons of both sexes, mostly Irish. In the nineteenth century the wretched area around Saffron Hill and the

Fleet valley was largely Irish and, as we have seen, they lived in much hardship in the East End, undercutting the Jews. Beatrice Webb, who was never short of a prejudice or two, noted in her book *My Apprenticeship*:

> *The worst scoundrel is the cockney-born Irishman. The woman is the Chinaman of the place: drudges as the women of savage races; she slaves all day and night. Describes the communism of this class. They do not migrate out of the district, but they are constantly changing their lodgings. . .they are like the circle of the suicides in Dante's Inferno: they go round and round within a certain area. They work for each other, hence the low ideal of work. They never leave the neighbourhood. From the dock gates they lounge back to the streets 'treating' and being 'treated', according to if they have earned a few pounds. . . .They never read. Except Catholics, they never go to church. On the Bank Holiday the whole family goes to Victoria Park.*

At Seven Dials the Irish ran the old clothes shops and junk stalls which made the area beyond visiting for many, and nearby they made a livelihood fetching and carrying in Covent Garden market. Here also were many Irish women, particularly those who carried loads of fruit on their heads. The Irish not only built the docks in the East End, but they manned them in all capacities and it was here, probably, as the docks expanded in the early nineteenth century, and the Thames Tunnel was built, that the first settled community of Irish resided. When New Oxford Street was cut through the rookeries of St Giles-in-the-Fields in the 1840s it is likely that many found their way to the appalling collection of hovels erected north of Old St Pancras church, called Agar Town. From here they were shunted out by the very Midland Railway and station that they had built and they probably moved on up to the small cottages of Gospel Oak, Camden Town and Kentish Town.

The railways, though built by itinerant gangs of mainly Irish labourers, also brought about permanent settlements, since the railway system needed labour in the goods yards, maintenance on the tracks, porters in the stations, drivers in the engines, delivery men for coal and potatoes, and others to drive cattle off trains. This kind of work provided regular income and men were able to bring over their families and take up proper residence. The large Irish contingents around King's Cross, Camden Town, Kentish Town, Holloway, Kilburn and Willesden are their descendants. They number now about 250,000 in London.

ITALIANS

ITALIANS SETTLED MAINLY IN THAT PART OF LONDON where Clerkenwell and Holborn join: some descendants of that community still live around St Peter's Italian church (1863) in Clerkenwell Road. They came from Piedmont and Lombardy at first and by the end of the nineteenth century there were several thousand residing in the streets around Hatton Garden, Saffron Hill and Leather Lane. So distinct an Italian enclave was it that Mazzini founded a short-lived school in Greville Street, Hatton Garden in 1841, and the Italian Benevolent Society was established in 1861 to help poor Italians. It was already an area of skilled craftsmen, particularly those making clocks, watches and measuring instruments; Italians were among them in the early nineteenth century and by the 1880s their numbers had grown considerably, augmented by others making picture frames. Italian street musicians, based on Clerkenwell, took the notice of Henry Mayhew. Poorly paid organ grinders, in the employ of *padroni*, set out from Clerkenwell on daily rounds of the streets of London to the not always receptive natives. The same employment system was later used for selling hot chestnuts in winter (the nuts supplied by family connections in northern Italy) and ice cream in the summer. Ice cream, in fact, seems to have appeared on the streets at the time Mayhew made his famous survey in the 1860s, and it was not long before *The Lancet* and local authorities began to be concerned at the unhygienic conditions in which it was prepared in Clerkenwell. It was estimated that about nine hundred highly decorative ice-cream barrows were based in the Italian quarter there. One man who did very well out of the business and whose interests bridged Clerkenwell and the West End, was the Swiss Italian, Carlo Gatti, who brought in bulk shipments of ice from Norway, kept it in pits in the East End and King's Cross (his old ice well is still there

DESPITE occasional scares as to the hygiene of its preparation, Italian ice cream was hugely popular in London – it was mainly sold off ice-cream vans mounted on cycles. This vendor, using a barrow, is operating in Greenwich in 1884.

in the Regent's Canal Museum in New Wharf Road) and was able to manufacture ice cream in large quantities.

Other migrants were *figurinai* – specialists in statuettes and ornamental plasterwork – who were also to be found in Soho and Fitzrovia. There were also itinerant knife grinders called *arrotini*, particularly active in the restaurant area of Soho where the kitchen and cutlery suppliers, Ferrari, are descendants of that trade.

The Soho Italians who settled in the 1890s seem not to have had close relationships with those in Clerkenwell. After first working in existing restaurants many graduated to opening their own distinctive café-restaurants so beloved by the Bohemians of London. Bertorelli's, the best-known of these, was established in Charlotte Street in 1912 by four brothers and was popular among the rackety and sometimes impecunious Fitzrovians for its cheap food.

Greek Cypriots

The greek cypriots first came to london for economic reasons in the 1930s, settling in Soho where they worked in hotels and restaurants, and in Camden Town, which was a convenient distance from the West End late at night. As with the Irish, it was mostly a male society, the immigrants sending money home and returning in the off-season. Political problems in Cyprus in the 1950s and 1960s prompted a larger exodus, but this time the migrants were families; they settled mostly in Camden Town with the existing community, diversifying into catering on their own behalf and into such trades as bakeries, shoe-repairing, dress-making; building on the popularity of their kebab bars they came to dominate, in London at least, the English fish and chip restaurants.

A Cypriot rag-trade developed around Finsbury Park; briefly, until the Asians arrived in large numbers, they took the trade over from the East End Jews who had by then moved up the economic scale. After the partition of Cyprus in 1974 a large number of immigrants went to Haringey and Hackney where the houses were cheaper than those in gentrified Camden Town.

West Indians

The first wave of black immigrants after the war encountered a colour bar (not then illegal) already in place. Even the famous West Indian cricketer, Learie Constantine, was asked to leave the Imperial Hotel in Russell Square in 1943, after making a previous booking for himself and his family, at a time when he was captain of the West Indies cricket team then playing England. The manageress repeatedly said that 'niggers' were not allowed there, but the hotel was successfully taken to court by Constantine for breach of contract. About five hundred Jamaicans arrived in force in 1948 on the SS *Empire Windrush* to a civic welcome and temporary shelter at Clapham and Brixton. This simple beginning, and the availability of rooming houses in the area, appears to be the reason for the later concentration of West Indians in Brixton. Peter Fryer, in his book *Staying Power*, notes that of these about 76 went into foundry work, 15 on to the railways, 15 were labourers, 15 went into agriculture and 10 were electricians. But they were by no means the beginning of an avalanche: immigration of West Indians was still below 2,000 a year in the early 1950s. In 1952 the US imposed restrictions on immigration from the West Indies and by 1957 West Indians were arriving in Britain at the rate of about 20,000 a year, encouraged by the prospect of jobs with London Transport and in the National Health Service (with the support of the Health Minister, Enoch Powell, who some years later was to make his infamous anti-immigration 'rivers of blood' speech). Trinidadians and Barbadians in particular went into London Transport and settled mainly in Notting Hill where, from 1957, a new Rent Act allowed greater latitude to private landlords. A Polish refugee called Perc Rachman built up an empire of high-rent flats let to blacks once white tenants had been bullied out, quite often by blacks employed by him. Trouble between whites and blacks had been brewing since as early as 1949, when an estimated one thousand white people besieged a hostel in Deptford in which blacks were staying. In 1958 gangs of whites persistently harassed blacks in Notting Hill. An open air meeting of Fascists there paved the way for the Notting Hill riots when whites launched an all-out attack on black homes in the streets around All Saints Road and rioted for three days with knock-on effects in Brixton.

ASIANS

IT IS SUGGESTED THAT THE SETTLEMENT OF ASIANS in Southall from the 1950s was begun by a particular employer who had experience of Punjabi labour, but almost certainly the vast enlargement of the Asian community here is related to the opportunities for light manufacture work in the west London industrial estates and the growth of Heathrow Airport with its need for labour at all hours. By 1958 there were already 55,000 Indians

THE Notting Hill Carnival, shown here in a photograph by David Ingham, began in 1965, at the instigation of a white social worker, Mrs Rhaune Laslett. It now takes place over an entire Bank Holiday weekend.

and Pakistanis in Britain, a figure which swelled to accommodate the flight of Asians from Uganda. Since then Asians (mostly Bengalis), and latterly Somalis also, have taken over the traditional area for first immigrants in London, the East End, and virtually monopolize the markets around Aldgate, though there had been a settlement of Indians related to the East India Company around Commercial Road and Cable Street since the nineteenth century. Using the family as a working unit, Asians now dominate those parts of the retail trade in London which demand long hours and a tolerance of low profit margins, such as newsagents and groceries. Asians have generally resisted the assimilation into English culture that politicians have assumed is desirable. The political decision to prevent the setting up of Moslem state schools, illogical as it seems given the freedom of Catholics and Jews in this field, is a consequence of a refusal to admit the defeat of this assimilation policy.

*F*EW *Chinese businesses were to be seen in the West End of London, even by the 1950s. Most Chinese residents were still involved with the East End dock trade. Above are Chinese sailors in 1877, at the East India Docks where a cargo of tea is being unloaded.*

THE CHINESE

CHINESE SETTLEMENT HAS BEEN IN TWO PHASES. The first Chinatown was at Limehouse in the nineteenth century and was composed almost entirely of Shanghai and Cantonese seamen or those who looked after the Chinese and Lascars (Indian seamen) that arrived at the docks. Many of the sailors worked on the ships of the East India Company, which established a vast barracks for the Chinese and Indians, according to the topographical historian, Daniel Lysons in 1811, in Shadwell. The author of a short history of Limehouse in 1930 noted:

> In Limehouse on any day in the week one may meet strangers whose home address is in any corner of the seven seas – Lascars with slipshod gait, Malays and Chinese, turbaned Indians, full-blooded negroes, Scandinavians and West Indians, and curious composite creatures in frock-coats and fezzes or dungarees and umbrellas, and every other incongruous combination.

The Victorians, aided by Conan Doyle, Oscar Wilde and Charles Dickens, were familiar with their opium dens. In *The Mystery of Edwin Drood* the hero finds himself in such a place in the care of a haggard woman who offers him opium pipes; Blanchard Jerrold in his *London – A Pilgrimage* described the 'tumble-down one storied houses, in which our old friend the Lascar opium smoker rolled upon his mattress, stirring his stifling narcotic over a lamp, and keeping his eyes – bright as burning coals – upon his latch.' Thomas Burke was even more imaginative and evocative:

The shuttered gloom of the quarter showed strangely menacing. Every whispering house seemed an abode of dreadful things, every window seemed filled with frightful eyes. Every corner half lit by the bleak light of a naked gas-jet seemed to harbour unholy things, and a sense of danger hung on every step.

These descriptions, of course, had the value of tabloid journalism and sensationalized the locality of a few hundred people who more than likely were absorbed by the hard work necessary in that part of London rather than in the pleasures of gambling or opium. The opening of the Strangers' Home for Asiatics, Africans and South Sea Islanders in West India Dock Road in 1857, which sought to care for the needs of sailors arriving in the area, is probably more indicative of the unromantic and prosaic nature of the area.

The modern Chinatown in Soho has been established with remarkable speed and seems to have been based entirely on restaurants. It is claimed that the impetus for this

CELEBRATING *the Chinese New Year in 1978, in Gerrard Street in the Chinatown quarter of Soho.*

was provided by Charlie Cheung, who already had a restaurant in the East End, opening another in Gerrard Street. Almost the whole area between Charing Cross Road, Shaftesbury Avenue, Leicester Square and Wardour Street is occupied by Chinese restaurants and shops, and there are many similar premises across Shaftesbury Avenue on either side of Old Compton Street.

Advertisement for Swan and Edgar at Piccadilly Circus in the early 1900s. This store, famous like the clock at Victoria Station as a meeting place, was subsequently rebuilt and survived until recent years when Tower Records replaced it.

CHAPTER XXIII

A CITY OF CONSUMERS

REGENT STREET

THE REBUILDING OF REGENT STREET FROM ABOUT 1905 UNTIL THE 1920S UNDERLINED THE retail revolution that had occurred in London from the mid nineteenth century. Nowadays, the demolition of Nash's elegant street would run the gamut of numerous and inconclusive planning inquiries (just as the future of Piccadilly Circus itself did in the 1970s); there were then many resentful voices raised against its destruction, but although the Commissioners of Woods and Forests, who managed the estate on behalf of the Crown, were anxious to obtain public approval of their plans for a new thoroughfare, there was never any doubt that the old street would come down. The buildings which then housed this centre of fashion were inadequate for their function, too small in many cases despite the knocking through of party walls, too dark to compete with the emporiums of Oxford Street, too overcrowded to be comfortable, and too reticent for modern window displays. Much of the curved stretch of road from Piccadilly to Oxford Circus, known as the Quadrant, had once been colonnaded so that 'those who have daily intercourse with the Public Establishments in Westminster, may go two-thirds of the way on foot under cover, and those who have nothing to do but walk about and amuse themselves may do so everyday in the week, instead of being frequently confined many days together to their Houses by rain.' Unfortunately for the shopkeepers, the colonnades became the haunt of people far from fashionable and made the interiors of their shops dark. They were taken down in 1848.

The matter of Regent Street's future was of some urgency by the early part of the century when original leases were due to expire and the owners of the site on which the Piccadilly Hotel now stands, with façades on both Piccadilly and Regent Street, wished to redevelop it. At the same time it was envisaged that Piccadilly Circus itself would be made into a more conspicuous landmark. Hardly anything was done before the outbreak of the First World War. Norman Shaw's designs were not liked by either the shopkeepers or the architectural press, since it was thought that they were too uniform, too expensive and the buildings too high. In the event Sir Reginald Blomfield was responsible for much of its rebuilding which although it is superficially uniform, is in fact based on uniformity within blocks. Thus accommodating the particular requirements of the larger retail stores already in existence and it was in larger stores that the future of retailing lay.

The Department Stores

By the beginning of the First World War virtually every high street in the metropolis had some kind of department store that was an enlargement of a draper's – their carcasses may still be seen today, picked over by developers and split into units as they went out of business, taking with them their eternally fascinating pneumatic cash cylinders that flew about the store at high speed to the delight of every child. Typical of these buildings which remain in their modern disguise is C & A Daniels in Kentish Town, a draper's that began in the late 1860s to serve a newly built area which needed all the cottons, linens, velvets, damasks and silks that fashion demanded and servants could cope with. It was founded by two brothers 'of farming stock' from Essex – quite a few of the emporiums of London were built up by previously inexperienced provincial men determined to do well in London – and developed into a large concern, with staff which lived on the premises under the watchful eye of a housekeeper. Staff still lived there during the Second World War, when an account of a bomb attack notes that the personnel in the building at the time were a restaurant cook, a manageress and a porter. The parents of author V.S. Pritchett first met in this store, where she was apprenticed in the millinery department and he was a floorwalker. Pritchett notes in his autobiography, *A Cab at the Door*, that the hours were 'eight to eight, weekdays, eleven o'clock Saturday nights. . . The poorly paid shop assistant fed in the basement, slept in the attics and went out to get drunk when the shop closed.' The staff also put up with 'cold draughts and the poisonous, headaching smell of gaslight'. It was, however, the invention of gaslight which made the long opening hours of stores possible.

Buildings that housed shops like Daniels' survive all over London from Brixton to Tottenham in high streets now battered by competition from out-of-town supermarkets. One such store and indeed one that claimed to be the first purpose-built 'department' store was Bon Marché in Brixton Road, opened in 1877. Begun by a man who had won a great deal of money in a betting coup, and modelled on the newly established store of the same name in Paris, it was described in *The Builder* as a 'novelty in market accommodation in the metropolis, embracing the sale of almost every imaginable article in food, furniture and dress, under one management, the whole of the employees residing on the premises'. The staff dining room could hold three hundred at one sitting. In the same year two other names to be famous in retailing opened new enterprises. In the Strand the Civil Service Association opened a new, rather grim-looking store which had its origins in a group of Post Office clerks combining in 1864 to buy a chest of tea for distribution among themselves. From this self-help enterprise membership was extended to other civil servants. In Chelsea Peter Jones, a draper who had begun business in Hackney twenty years earlier, acquired Nos 4–6 King's Road, after his first Chelsea premises nearby had collapsed, killing an apprentice. In the honoured tradition of the drapery trade he added and added until by 1905, the year of his death, he owned most of the block on which he had built a five-storey store lit by electricity.

The Victorian era was one of enormous expansion in the drapery trade and it saw the beginnings of some of the most famous names in West End retailing. These were, of course, the ones that did well and expanded, for the street directories of the Oxford Street area reveal dozens of drapers whose businesses did not extend beyond their one shop size and whose trading did not survive the retirement or death of their proprietors. As in all commerce, good opportunities have to be taken with some flair or else with considerable application, and it was particularly so in the drapery business where a shop succeeded by establishing a reputation for quality. These were days before branded goods carried their own guarantee of uniform quality and which, by advertising, sold themselves to a customer before she entered the shop. In the early Peter Jones or Peter Robinson the store managers or buyers commissioned their own goods and stood by their own judgements, or else bought in goods offered by small manufacturers. Thus it was common for an item to appear in only a single shop in Oxford Street and it required the assiduous skills of the sales assistant, almost invariably a man, to persuade a comfortably seated customer of its virtues. Though a sale lacked the hard bargaining and *frisson* of danger endured in a foreign street market, it went nevertheless by polite and established procedures in much the same way, as numerous samples were brought down from shelves, or out of packets for perusal. Selling was a leisurely affair involving a surfeit of deferential staff on the one hand and, on the other, women customers who, with the household food shopping delegated to servants, filled up a leisurely day: this riffling through of patterns, this fingering of silks and this assessment of brocades were, for these women, the extremities of an effortless lifestyle.

Some of the successful businesses were old-established even before the frantic expansion of Victorian times. Mr Swan and Mr Edgar had met and joined forces *c.*1812 and were in time to take up premises in the new Regent Street; William Debenham went into business with Thomas Clark in 1813 in a shop overlooking the fields of the Harley estate and in five years Debenham's daughter married Clement Freebody whose name was soon to be familiar when the store changed its title to 'Debenham & Freebody'; Dickins and his partner Smith opened a shop in Oxford Street before the end of the eighteenth century (it was not for another hundred years that John Pritchard Jones became a partner); the young Peter Robinson opened a draper's-cum-dressmaker's in 1833 between Oxford Circus and Great Portland Street, in time to take advantage of the new and lucrative market in mourning wear that accompanied the opening of private cemeteries around London. Mr James Marshall opened a shop in Vere Street in 1837, where he was joined by Mr John Snelgrove in 1848. Benjamin Harvey had a small draper's shop in the village of Knightsbridge in 1813 into which his daughter took a Colonel Nichols as partner, to create Harvey Nichols.

All of these businesses, founded on the growing demand for drapery and dressmaking, expanded by taking on shops nearby. They were matched in this by the extraordinary development of Whiteley's in Westbourne Grove, a street that had seen so many ups and downs that when William Whiteley arrived in 1863 it was already known as 'Bankrupt Avenue'. His potential customers came from the new estates of Notting Hill, Bayswater and Paddington and in view of the nearness of the West End, the poor reputation of Westbourne Grove and the vicissitudes of other traders, he might only have expected to make a respectable living here. However, Whiteley, a young man from Leeds who had learnt his trade in a draper's in the City, was as decisive as Gordon Selfridge was to be in breaking away from old retailing habits. He paid great attention to window dressing and to the clear marking of prices – then considered to be declassé; he used advertising to great effect and to the ire, and one suspects the physical malice, of his fellow traders, he introduced additional departments selling food, drink, furniture, hairdressing, books and even estate agency: when he opened a butchery local butchers demonstrated outside armed with marrow bones and cleavers. 'The Universal Provider' was his slogan – it was one which remained in people's memories. His shops were burned down by arsonists on several occasions; no-one was ever arrested, but it was strongly suspected that the culprits were local traders. The frequency of these blazes only added to his fame, since he always arose phoenix-like and seemingly wealthier each time, making money out of fire-sales on the way. By the time of his sensational death in 1907 – he was shot in his office by a man claiming to be his illegitimate son – he had fourteen shops in Westbourne Grove and another seven much larger units in Queensway, all of which were transformed after his death into a magnificent emporium that he would have cherished. Whiteley stirred up the retail trade like some showman emerging into a circus ring, changing for ever the quiet and deferential nests of the Marshalls, the Snelgroves, the Robinsons and the Debenhams.

WHITELEY'S store, Westbourne Grove earlier this century, still a collection of premises which had been patiently collected together by William Whiteley. After his death the store was rebuilt as a grand emporium in Queensway.

John Barker, a successful department manager for Whiteley, turned down the enormous salary of £1,000 per annum offered him at Westbourne Grove to go off and open his own shop in Kensington High Street in 1870, two years after the Underground railway had reached there. The street had recently been rebuilt, including the old 'Toy and Fancy Goods Repository' of Charles Derry and Joseph Toms, and what with the Underground, the nearness of Kensington Palace, the lavish developments north and south of the High Street and the adjacency of the Museum quarter, Barker was confident of his move there. The Ponting brothers went to both Westbourne Grove and Kensington High Street. One tried his luck, unsuccessfully, against Whiteley and another three began a shop for fancy goods, needlework supplies and silks which competed reasonably well against Barker who eventually took them over. Bourne & Hollingsworth also began in Westbourne Grove in 1894, but ten years later moved to Oxford Street where the premises they gradually acquired included a brothel, a cigarette manufacturers and 'a nest of Polish tailors'.

In Knightsbridge Harrod's established itself as a grocery before becoming a department store. In 1849, Henry Harrod, a tea merchant of Eastcheap, bought an existing shop, but it was his son, Charles Digby Harrod, who began to turn the business into the vast enterprise that it now is, for by then the area of Knightsbridge and Brompton was built up. In 1870 he had sixteen assistants and had extended the shop's scope to include stationery, perfume and pharmaceuticals, all squeezed into the original shop and a two storey extension at the rear. In 1883, when he had nearly a hundred staff, the premises burnt down and were rebuilt, but replaced from 1901 to 1905 by the present building.

Just as the Civil Service Stores was at first a private shop, so was the Army and Navy Stores in Victoria Street. It was begun in 1871 by army and navy officers who thought that

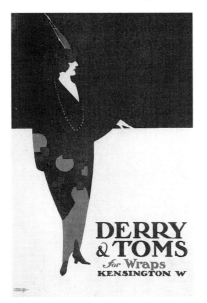 

An advertisement for Derry & Toms in Kensington High Street, early 20th century (left).
On the right is an advertisement for Selfridge's.

they were paying too much for their port and, as with the more abstemious post office clerks and their tea, ordered it wholesale and split the crates among themselves. The object of the enterprise when put on a more formal basis, was to 'supply the best articles of domestic use and general consumption at the lowest remunerative rates.' To this end they sold a wide variety of goods, including own-brand items, which could be delivered free to members in London and the suburbs. Their premises included a club room with notepaper, pens, and newspapers, and members might lunch there under the care of familiar waiters and order cabs through deferential doormen. The press was amused that dogs were not permitted in the place, and in 1876 there was controversy when a member's messenger was not allowed into the shop to buy something on his master's behalf because he was 'not a fit person to mingle in the crowd of members, including a large proportion of ladies', which was more to do with the poor man's class than with what he was wearing.

It was a remarkable enterprise founded on the pretensions and needs of Services personnel, active and pensioned off, in Britain and around the globe wherever the Empire hoisted a flag above its dubious title deeds. In 1922 membership was abolished and the store became a public one.

Just as Barker defected from Whiteley, so John Lewis left Peter Robinson, where he was a silk buyer. In 1864 he set up shop on part of the site of the present department store where his policy was cheapness combined with quality, one which has filtered down to the splendidly old-fashioned slogan still used of 'Never Knowingly Undersold'; it was not long before he occupied the whole block around his building and then set about acquiring the premises to the rear. In so doing he became unique among store owners in being imprisoned for three weeks for failing to accord by a court injunction not to spread into Cavendish Square. The autocratic and notoriously thrifty Lewis is said to have walked over to Sloane Square in 1905, with banknotes worth £22,500 in his pocket, which he paid to the widow of Peter Jones for the shop there which had fallen on hard times.

A director of John Barker's, John Barnes, was part of a triumvirate which established a new store to serve the middle-class area being built on both sides of the Finchley Road at Hampstead. This was a substantial gamble because the decision was made to construct a large store from the beginning, without the preliminary and patient gathering together of adjacent properties if trade permitted. Fourteen older shops were taken down to erect what was regarded in the trade as a very modern shop indeed with accommodation for four hundred staff, three dining rooms, and with the very latest of pneumatic-tube cash conveyors whizzing around the store. The *Draper's Record* was encouragingly optimistic at the time. There was, it thought, 'no reason why a big trading establishment should not be a mammoth establishment from the start, without undergoing the laborious and time-wasting process of the gradual addition of department on department.'

This period was also the heyday of Holloway Road, a reasonably fashionable shopping centre that attained success on the spending power of the numerous clerks and their families living there locally, and that of wealthier people in Highgate. So popular was this shopping centre, especially after the introduction of trams, that the principal traders in the road were of sufficient standing to finance the installation of gas-light along the main stretch. Of prime importance was the business established in 1867 by two Welsh brothers called Jones who gradually acquired properties along the main road until they were able to rebuild in style. The statistics of staff and equipment at Jones Brothers are quite astonishing. By 1892 they had over 500 employees many of whom lived in, 50 horses and 35 delivery vans, stabled and housed at the rear, and their printed catalogue ran to 1,400 pages with over 3,000 illustrations, bigger even than that issued by the Army and Navy Stores which did a large overseas trade. The deterioration of Holloway's reputation, which began at the beginning of the twentieth century, was echoed in the structure of the store, which featured a dome towards one end that was intended to sit centrally over a building twice the size. Those plans had to be abandoned, but the older part of the store remains, integrated into a Waitrose.

At Clapham Junction it was Arding & Hobbs, established in 1885, which catered for a new area; in Ealing Sayers & Son, drapers, had a thriving business both locally and abroad; in the Kilburn High Road, B.B. Evans dominated Kilburn and Willesden; in Kingston, Bentall's, which later bought up Sayers, was the chief drapery store; and in Richmond, Gosling's developed its ascendancy from the early nineteenth century.

An unusual development was a collection of shops run by Walter Gamage that owed nothing to new residential development but everything to the daily influx of office workers. Consequently, it catered mainly for men at first – their clothes, hobbies, sports, household tasks, suburban gardens, their children and their pets, and via its franchise to sell goods to boy scouts it sold camping gear and bicycles. Ever resourceful, Gamage sold motor-cycles and motoring equipment and after his death he lay in state in the motoring department, with members of his staff as guard of honour each day.

There were, however, disasters in this catalogue of store development. Gamage himself burnt his fingers very badly when he opened a new store on the north side of Oxford Street at the corner of Park Street (it is now a C&A store). It went bankrupt very quickly, his kind of retailing being out of kilter with the Oxford Street trade. Similarly, an attempt to extend the success of Oxford Street eastwards was a store erected between the wars in

The Selfridge building under construction in 1908. Its progress was followed avidly by Londoners and by architects, who were intrigued by its early use of a steel-framed structure.

New Oxford Street by Henry Glave, drapers, to replace a straggle of smaller buildings built up since the nineteenth century. It was a failure for by then trade had moved definitely westwards to where Selfridge's acted as a magnet.

It was Selfridge who personified the retailing revolution up to the Second World War. He came bursting in, pointing his American finger at the nub of things, an alien presence intervening in a polite commercial war in which casualties were unwanted and unlikely. He observed that 'they [the English] know how to make things. . .but not how to sell them'. In this he summed up the passivity of English retailing, the fear of actually creating a demand, the reticence in pushing a product so that it was impossible not to buy it. In Chicago he had risen from nowhere to be a junior partner (and the most successful employee) of Marshall Field, one of the most famous stores in America. Seeing no significant advancement for himself in Chicago he decided to take on London in a big way. His choice of what was regarded as the rather sluggish end of Oxford Street was an inspired one, for it was soon after the Central Line had been opened, giving three stations from which prospective customers might come, and the construction of the main part of the Northern Line which, via Tottenham Court Road station, could bring in customers from the affluent north of London. It was the era too of the motor bus, which swept aside the old and rather cumbersome horse-drawn vehicles. But the properties he wanted in Oxford Street were 'a crowded mass of ill-consorted shops and houses' locked in a tangle of ownerships, and his plans for the new store, prepared in Chicago, were hopelessly at variance with London planning laws. Selfridge's ideas for open-plan floors uninhibited by fire blocks were frowned upon and just as importantly, they involved the first use of a steel-frame construction in London, which gave the local authorities pause for thought.

Building, begun in 1908, became as with the Crystal Palace, a London tourist attraction. Immense girders manoeuvred by giant cranes, were sunk seventy feet below ground and soon the façade of enormous columns made their appearance in what was until then a nondescript part of the street; and when applications were invited for jobs in the 130 departments the public response was so great that nearly ten thousand people were interviewed. The opening of the store on a freezing cold day in March 1909 was as stage-managed as the pre-publicity. Selfridge himself unfurled the house flag from the roof as a trumpeter played; simultaneously the drapes covering the store windows were unfurled to reveal marvellous displays; there were flowers everywhere inside and somewhere there was an orchestra playing. It was an amazing day and the years that followed continued to be amazing.

CHAIN STORES

WHILE SELFRIDGE WAS INVENTING THE SUPER DEPARTMENT STORE, there were other retail forces at work: chain stores. The Co-operative movement probably invented multiple-branch stores and between the wars virtually every high street and many back streets had co-ops. They were slow to take root in London and did not command the same loyalty as those in the north of England. The most successful in London were attached to the Woolwich Arsenal Society, begun in 1868, but most in the metropolis came under the umbrella of the London Co-operative Society. This proved an unwieldy instrument when the pace of retailing speeded up after the last war. The cumbersome committee structure of management, the labour-consuming device of the 'dividend', the unimaginative products, the uninviting window displays and, overall, the lack of commercial commitment which successful entrepreneurs need, all contributed to its decline and, in many parts of London, its demise. Like Woolworth's after it, the Co-op's seemingly unassailable prominence was eroded as its own historical momentum prevented it from taking stock and changing shape in time.

We may contrast the Co-op's career with the firm that John James Sainsbury founded at about the same time. The young Sainsbury was in at the birth of grocery as we know it today; previously grocers had for the most part stocked only non-perishable foods, leaving the rest to street markets. As a boy in the early 1850s he lived near the New Cut market in Lambeth when the street market was the most important retail feature in working-class areas. Mayhew visited it and wrote:

> The street-sellers are to be seen in the greatest numbers at the London street markets on a Saturday night. Here, and in the shops immediately adjoining, the working-classes generally purchase their Sunday's dinner; and after pay-time on Saturday night, or early on Sunday morning, the crowd in the New Cut is almost impassable.
>
> The pavement and the road are crowded with purchasers and street-sellers. The housewife in her thick shawl, with the market-basket on her arm, walks slowly on, stopping now to look at the stall of caps, and now to cheapen a bunch of greens. Little boys, holding three or four onions in their hands, creep between the people, wriggling their way through every interstice, and asking for custom in whining tones.

Along this market, as with others, established shops both competed with and benefited from the market stalls. Sainsbury's first job was in a grocer's shop in the New Cut and it was here that he learned the appetites and shopping habits of working-class people that he was so ably to exploit. His first venture, in 1869, was a dairy in Drury Lane, where he sold butter, milk, eggs and cheese. Many dairies around London (usually Welsh-run) still had their own cows in-house, as it were, to the despair of sanitary inspectors; even worse, many premises were still used as slaughterhouses. An old Highgate resident remembered that at the beginning of the twentieth century the local pork butcher, Attkins, kept pigs near the shop and animals 'with their throats cut were still to be seen in brine tubs behind the shop'. The selling of milk was particularly competitive and another Highgate resident recalled that in the same period milk was delivered once in the morning and twice in the afternoon: it was not until 1932 that London milkmen were allowed a six-day week.

On the face of it there was nothing to distinguish Mr Sainsbury's dairy from so many others, but presumably he had flair, or a good business sense, for he was able to open a branch in 1876 in the unlikely area of Queen's Crescent, Kentish Town, a street which had its own street market and in which he had a stall as well. Even more unlikely, he opened a further branch at Croydon and it was here that he began experimenting in layout and style. His aim was to produce a shop which was both attractive and clean – he had an obsession with cleanliness at a time when shopkeepers weren't too fussy. Good-quality wood and marble counters abounded, the floor was tiled, and bentwood chairs were supplied for customers. From that time Sainsbury's developed at an astonishing rate, duplicating, with amendments, the Sainsbury style in each branch, with recognizable and dignified fascias; at the end of the 1880s he bought an old horse repository at Blackfriars to serve as a warehouse. Here he was emulating the co-ops – buying in bulk and selling cheap but, and this was the difference, in shops that were uniform as well as hygienic. The advance of food technology later in the century changed him from a dairy to a grocer; canned goods, packaged foods and frozen meats gradually favoured the shop rather than the market stall, especially with refrigeration available.

Sainsbury was not alone in pursuing a multiple-shop course – indeed, compared with some he was slow at it. Thomas Lipton, who opened his first shop in Glasgow in 1871 had five hundred by 1899. He used publicity extensively, driving pigs painted with his name through the streets and opening branches with the attendance of brass bands and elephants. Home and Colonial, begun in 1885, had four hundred shops by the end of the century, and Maypole Dairy, which began in Wolverhampton in 1887 had two hundred in the Midlands by 1900. David Greig, who began with a shop in Hornsey, had a similar swift rise to familiarity. Out of all these, though, it was Sainsbury who first adapted a shop (in Croydon) for self-service, although at the time, with rationing of many goods still in place, only part of the store could be conducted in this way.

Just as familiar in London high streets as these grocery multiples were clothing chain stores. Burton's were the top end of the market with ornate fascias, well-appointed shops, usually on corner sites, and beneath them were the Fifty Shilling Tailors. Dunn's, based in Camden Town, did good business when it was customary for every man to wear a hat and, of course, declined when it was not.

But the two names most earnestly desired by property developers were Woolworth's and Marks & Spencer's, both of whom represented at first a different kind of retailing –

An early Marks and Spencer store in the Edgware Road. This chain of stores began in the north of England as Penny Bazaars in which all goods were priced at one penny.

the bazaar. The latter were to be the first to make their presence felt. Michael Marks, formerly a street hawker of Russian-Polish birth, set up his first market stall in 1886 in a Leeds market. His selling message, 'Don't ask the price, its a Penny!', based on keen buying and small profit margin, was the basis for his expansion into permanent bazaar shops in which the merchandise – needles, buttons, handkerchiefs, soap etc. – was laid out in full view and was touchable. Like Whiteley, he believed in clear pricing and no haggling.

The first Marks & Spencer shop in London appears to have been in Brixton in 1907 where it occupied part of the Bon Marché store and by 1910 it had an annual turnover of over £9,000. Other branches were soon opened in Islington, Kilburn, Croydon and Tottenham. As with Sainsbury, the enterprise evolved a consistent typographical and display identity and in the 1930s its own style of architecture was to be seen – their stores are frequently the only distinguished buildings of that era now left in the high streets. And it was in the 1930s that Marks & Spencer's evolved a more distinct retailing image, away from the penny bazaar but still, as their expansion was in working-class areas, with items always under five shillings. Clothing was its main innovation and this gradually displaced the sort of items that Woolworth's, who were much later on the scene, sold.

Already an American institution, Woolworth's opened a shop in Liverpool in 1909, but by 1916 the only branches in London were those in Edgware Road and Deptford High Street. From that time, selling similar commodities to Marks & Spencer, they made far more progress than their rivals. Their approach was not to hassle the customer. Frank Woolworth wrote after a visit to England in 1900 that in an English shop, 'you are expected to buy, and to have made your choice from the window. They give you an icy stare if you follow the American custom of just going to look around.'

The Heal's furniture store in Tottenham Court Road before its rebuilding. The business began as an upholsterer's in 1818, but its fame rests on its development by Ambrose Heal, who took over its management in 1907.

FURNITURE STORES

WITH THE EXCEPTION OF WARING & GILLOW, furniture specialists stayed away from Oxford Street and were concentrated in Tottenham Court Road, which earlier had been a centre for upholsterers and the like: here, too, they were within easy distance of the piano industry around Camden and Kentish Towns whose products were essential to any Victorian home. A Robert Gillow, joiner, established a highly regarded business in Oxford Street (on part of the Selfridge site) c.1765, and in 1897 merged with the nearby cabinet-making firm of Waring. This firm designed the interiors and the furniture of many prestige buildings such as hotels and men's clubs. The most famous names in Tottenham Court Road were Heal's and Maple's, although there were in the nineteenth century about forty shops in the street devoted to furniture or furnishings, and in nearby Fitzrovia even more small companies acting as suppliers. Furniture shops such as

Gowns designed for Liberty's in 1887. Arthur Lazenby Liberty was the first to exploit the fashion in London for oriental art and style.

Catesby's (the same family as the Gunpowder Plot conspirator), Shoolbred's and Wolfe & Hollander now no longer exist, and Maple's is a shadow of its former self. The sweated labour of the furniture industry was the subject of a Parliamentary Inquiry in 1888 when a witness stated, 'I have worked for Messrs Maple; and they have always been, to my mind, the one firm for the cabinet trade who have been the pioneers in the sweating system.' The accusation was not proven but it was evident that Maple's, through their pre-eminent turnover in the business, were able to control the fortunes of many of the suppliers in the area and exact their own payment terms.

Whereas Maple's was a Victorian upstart, the business of Heal's began as a feather-bed maker in Rathbone Place *c.*1810. It was Ambrose Heal, patron of designers, who gave the company its unique reputation for stylish modern furniture in the twentieth century. Of that late nineteenth- to early twentieth-century flourish of furniture and design, Liberty's in Regent Street has survived with its scale intact. Arthur Lasenby Liberty, employed to import and sell Indian shawls at Farmer & Roger's 'Great Cloak and Shawl Emporium' in Regent Street, began his own business selling Oriental silks in the same street in 1875. Like the Oxford Street drapers, he acquired properties adjoining until, when the great rebuilding of Regent Street took place in the 1920s, he was able to rebuild; one part, confusingly, is in the Imperial mould to conform to the Crown estate's requirements in Regent Street, and another reflects his own predilections toward Tudor style in Great Marlborough Street, where the pseudo beams were taken from two men-o'-war.

CLOTHING

THE UNPREDICTABILITY OF RETAILING is nowhere more pronounced than in clothing. There can sometimes be a slow decline as in the case of Dunn's the hatters, or Burton's who were successful when every young man *wanted* to look like a bank clerk. But even with time to appreciate that changes are occuring it is often impossible for a business to change its style or at least change it satisfactorily. Or else, like some comet, a fashion will come and go. Such a phenomenon was Carnaby Street in the 1960s, when seemingly anything was possible. In this modest thoroughfare behind Regent Street a young man called John Stephen established some shops selling men's clothing, which were soon joined by others; so much of a tourist attraction did it become that Westminster Council was persuaded to treat it as a precinct, but by that time the street's pre-eminence in stylish clothing was lost to King's Road, Chelsea and its tourist trade later went on to Camden Lock instead. Barbara Hulanicki, who established a boutique in Chelsea, was famous by the time she opened Biba's in the old Derry & Toms building in Kensington High Street in 1974; it was a store loved by everyone who went into it, but it was a financial disaster and lasted only two years.

London has seen and seen off larger, and more established businesses than those that rose to fame in the 1960s. Gone are the Lyons teashops and corner houses, the ABC tea rooms, the Black & White coffee shops, the butchers and fishmongers that were an essential part of every high street, the ironmongers' stores with their mysterious shelves and drawers of tools, the milliners, the shoemakers, hosiers and laundry chains. Only the funeral directors remain untouched though most have lost their independence.

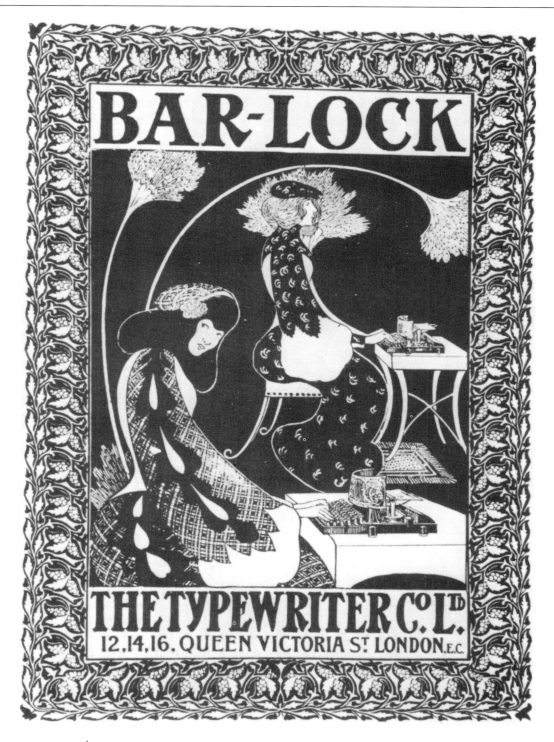

A BEAUTIFULLY (if unrealistically) designed advertisement for Barlock typewriters before the First World War.

CHAPTER XXIV

SOME WORKING LIVES

MORE IS KNOWN OF THE WORKING HOURS AND CONDITIONS OF THE POORER CLASSES of the nineteenth and twentieth centuries than of those slightly better off. This is in part due to Parliamentary inquiries when governments could bear to have their consciences aroused; but it is also due to surveys compiled by Henry Mayhew and Booth, the zeal of philanthropists and a modern output of theses and books that neatly knit together an academic bent and a retrospective social concern. Servants, shop assistants, manual workers and the destitute we know about, but rarely do we find revealed the clerk in a City office with enough income and ambition to buy a small house in Tottenham or Stockwell. The Grossmiths' hero, Mr Pooter, in *Diary of a Nobody*, is the famous exception, his office life and marital home in Holloway form the basis of a classic book; and Dickens conveys the strict and punctual lives these workers led. But on the whole the working environment of this class of Londoner is poorly dealt with.

OFFICE WORKERS

IT WAS IN THE VICTORIAN PERIOD THAT THE 'OFFICE' OF DESKS, ledgers and invoices began to assume so much importance and the workers themselves became clerks instead of scribes. A hundred years earlier men of business gathered in coffee-houses or inns and did their transactions with a minimum of paperwork, perhaps assisted by a literate scribe to record them. A man's place of business was often his own residence and the office, therefore, was merely a piece of furniture in which papers, pens and sealing wax were kept. All was transformed as the Industrial Revolution quickened and commerce and trade expanded and become more complex. A man with pretensions could not possibly contain a business and the staff required in his own house and, in any case, the existence of separate premises was itself an advertisement of substance.

Gradually, some uniformity of office practice was established. Double-entry bookkeeping became common, spelling was standardized as educational facilities and dictionaries became more available, but the clerk's life was generally one that lacked variety. In the 1840s an assistant clerk in the St Pancras Vestry rooms spent the entire year just writing up lists of ratepayers in ledgers, and nor was his task altered with the advent of typewriters. In most businesses the managing clerk reigned supreme beneath the owner. It was he that opened the post, delegated the work, made up the confidential ledgers, had charge of the safe in the proprietor's absence, and opened up the office in the morning while casting a rheumy eye over those who signed in just before the fixed time of arrival. In these gaslit offices, with coal fires kept in order by the office boy, the deference to status rarely lapsed.

The miserably stunted life of Dickens's Bob Cratchit, Scrooge's clerk, is well known, and in *Sketches by Boz*, describing a clerk, Dickens writes:

> *The dingy little back office into which he walks every morning, hanging his hat on the same peg, and placing his legs beneath the same desk: first, taking off that black coat which lasts the year through, and putting on one which did duty last year, and which he keeps in his desk to save the other. There he sits till five o'clock, working on, all days, as regularly as the dial over the mantel-piece, whose loud ticking is as monotonous as his whole existence: only raising his head when some one enters the counting house, or when, in the midst of some difficult calculation, he looks up at the ceiling as if there were inspiration in the dusty sky-light with a green knot in the centre of every pane of glass. About five, or half-past, he slowly dismounts from his accustomed stool, and again changing his coat, proceeds to his usual dining place, somewhere near Bucklersbury.*

We may see from this that the hours of work, though monotonous, were not exploitive: his clerk finished at around five, which is more than could be said for servants or shop assistants. The hours of clerical employees appear, in fact, to have been much the same as they are now and sometimes even better. In 1870 the clerical staff of the vestries of Lambeth and Hampstead worked 10–4, Islington 9–5, Chelsea 9.30–5.30, Southwark 10–6 and St Pancras 9–5 but with, in all cases, work on Saturday mornings as well.

A significant labour, before typewriters and carbon paper, was the copying of documents, a task that demanded legible handwriting and suppressed ambition. Or else a clerk, usually a junior one, had to learn the complexities of the Copying Press, a device which with the use of water, blotting paper and an oilskin sheet, could transfer a purple image of a document into the office Letter Book, that residuum of all information. Clerical workers received a salary of at least £80 per annum, just enough to get married on and rent a house, but not enough for extravagance, and barely enough to keep up appearances. Poor V.S. Pritchett, in his autobiography *A Cab at the Door*, recalls that when once applying for a job he was 'wearing a new suit, a stiff collar that choked me, a bowler hat which bit hard into my forehead and kept slipping over my ears.' And C.H. Rolph in his memorable autobiography, *London Particulars*, recalls how the constant opening and shutting of the vast ledgers in offices projected a thin cloud of dust over everyone's clothing so that, at two minutes to five 'there occurred a concerted and vigorous brushing of jackets and trousers, some men even brushing inside their permanent turn-ups', although Rolph came to suspect that this orchestrated noise was merely to alert the chief clerk that it was time to go home, just as football crowds whistle nervously to remind the referee of full time. Rolph's first office suit was bought (towards the end of the First World War) from a bespoke tailor who looked like 'H.G. Wells with an inch tape round his neck' and for the first few weeks he stood up to work in it (high desks then being normal) so as to avoid shining the seat of the trousers.

The lives of such a level of clerks if they were married were fiercely limited. The magazine *Everybody's* in 1911 described the financial circumstances of a family called Pennington who lived in a six-room house in Stamford Hill and whose income of £200 per annum would be 'luxury to the workman and beggary to the stockbroker'. Expenditure included school fees of £18 but did not include any allowance for a maidservant, which many clerks aspired to have.

Until the end of the nineteenth century the City was almost entirely a man's world – although typewriters had been invented they were still a rarity and women had not then begun to supplant men in day-to-day office tasks. Yet while men still dominated the Post Office letter sorting, or else the tedious business of the Railway Clearing House where credits and debits were balanced by hundreds of clerks between the various railway companies, women were soon found to be better suited in the telegraph offices. When typewriters were taken seriously women were thought to be more adept at using them and at the learning of shorthand: 'Short-hand writing is peculiarly suited to the light touch of a lady's hand, and the graceful suppleness of her fingers' asserted Pitman's in 1887. Moreover, their labour was cheaper – women were seldom paid more than £60-£80 per annum. In 1881 there were about 7,000 women clerks in England and Wales, and this had risen to 146,000 thirty years later; by 1920 there were about 170,000 women working in the Civil Service alone. By this time the typing pool had been invented, bringing into existence women whose job was to oversee these vast enterprises, regulating the work flow, dealing with the demands and complaints of the male clerks, ensuring that their charges were punctual and did not fraternize with office men.

Thus the First World War neatly marked, and speeded up, a transformation in office labour that would have happened anyway. From the 1920s typewriting was regarded as women's work with the result that it was thought odd, even demeaning, for a man to master a keyboard let alone shorthand, and from this the segregation of work in offices, with all that that has meant in terms of salaries and careers for the two sexes, has amplified.

DOMESTICS

At the same time there was also concern, even at government level, at the increasing difficulty of finding domestic servants. A special Women's Advisory Committee was established to report on this matter to Parliament and eventually concluded that there was a dearth of training facilities for servants and 'As a result the occupation is mainly carried on by unskilled workers who are unable on the one hand, to command for themselves satisfactory conditions of employment or, on the other, to fulfil their tasks efficiently.'

The 'servant problem' was in reality an 'employer problem'. The employers had made the situation of a domestic servant so unattractive that girls and young women of little education preferred the more glamorous, but still exploitative, life of shop assistants or factory workers. And those of better education opted for the freedom, the company and the shorter hours of office work. Though there must have been thousands of cases of humane treatment of servants, so that they felt as one (if an inferior one) of the family, there is, however, no lack of evidence that domestic service entailed long hours, primitive living conditions, paltry remuneration, a demeaning existence and a lack of free time. These drawbacks are so well and so frequently documented, that it is difficult not to draw the conclusion that middle-class employers subscribed to a general consensus as to how servants should be treated. A modern writer of some distinction has claimed that it was wrong to 'think of domestic servants as slaves. They were very far from that.' But later he relates that the 'general servant had one evening a week and every other Sunday as time off'.

The arduous physical conditions endured by servants were deterrent enough but there was also a distinct nip of social equality in the air. Why be a servant at all? Why be deferential? In 1901 it was still appropriate for the Ladies' Sanitary Association to advise servants, in a summary of behaviour expected of them, that they should not walk in the garden, that they were to wash all over every day, call the children Master or Miss, and make little noise about the house. But by 1919 the Women's Advisory Committee, in making a rather divided report, was suggesting that domestic servants might at some time

This advertisement for polish from the Illustrated London News *shows a maid happy in the work of making her face reflect in the floor. However, households were finding that women prepared to do this work were becoming increasingly scarce, and after the First World War the lack of servants had a profound influence on the design and size of houses as the wealthier population moved out into the suburbs.*

be unionized. This drew a stinging addenda to the report from the one committee member, the Marchioness of Londonderry, who had not attended any of its meetings, that she considered 'any possibility of the introduction into the conditions of domestic service of the type of relations now obtainable between employers and workers in industrial life as extremely undesirable and liable to react in a disastrous manner on the whole foundation of home life'. Other members thought that there should be more social clubs for servants. That same year the Highgate 1919 Club was formed at the Highgate Literary & Scientific Institution, for the 'recreation and amusement of domestic servants' with the wife of a wealthy coal merchant presiding. But the report made no recommendations about pay and hours and therefore ensured its own oblivion.

Most of the houses of central London and the inner suburbs had been built on the assumption that servants would be on hand to overcome their vertical layouts. In fact, the architecture of London is partly a result of that ready availability of domestics. In the outer suburbs, built in an age when a servant was unavailable even if affordable, the houses are horizontally planned. The growth in the number of servants in the nineteenth century reflected the larger families and the lower infant mortality rates that had become common. There was simply not enough employment, particularly for girls, and numerous charities, orphanages and workhouses had children who needed work and security. It was, of course, security at a price in a household, since the child once taken in had few rights and could be called upon to work at any hour of the day, and for as many hours as wanted. They worked in damp basements and slept in cold attics, sometimes sharing a bed with another servant. When they entered service they were at the lowest rung in a hierarchical system which gave comfort and order not only to the employers but to the servants as well.

In the grander establishments menservants were both ornamental and superior. A butler ruled the household in conjunction with the housekeeper whose charges were strictly those of the various maids, cooks and scullery maids. There were various undercurrents of status in this arrangement, for a lady's maid could claim by her personal and sometimes intimate association with the lady of the house an undefined superiority over the housekeeper; and a governess, neither servant nor member of the family, but usually of a class superior to the servants, was in an entirely invidious position; she was matched in this by the 'lady's help', almost invariably a middle-class woman in reduced circumstances obliged to act as companion, usually to a widow. In middle-class establishments the cook and the housekeeper would often be the same person, assisted by a parlour maid and a scullery maid; here too might be one manservant who acted as butler and carriage driver. A middling household was portrayed in the entertaining memoirs (1837) of William Tayler, who worked in a six-storey house in Great Cumberland Street, on whose site the Cumberland Hotel now stands. Here the family consisted of only two people, a wealthy widow and her unmarried daughter, but the staff for this large house and its frequent entertaining consisted of Tayler and three women.

The worst situation, and the fate of many of those sent out by workhouses and orphanages, was the maid-of-all-work who served in the households of modestly paid clerks who aimed to impress friends and neighbours. There were in these households all of the disadvantages of being in service and few of the occasional bonuses, since the income of the clerk and those of his visitors precluded any lavish disbursements.

The rapid decrease in the number of servants available had far-reaching consequences for London. Whatever their merits or demerits as employers, it was unrealistic to expect a late middle-aged couple to manage a five-storey house on their own before labour-saving devices were fully available. Not even a large expenditure of money on the typical London terrace house would have made that possible and certainly in their eyes it was not socially desirable anyway. Many of them were eager buyers of the service flats, which were easier to run and had the availability of a hall porter, cleaners and general help, built between the wars. The houses they left behind in places like Islington, Camden Town, Notting Hill, Bayswater and Kennington were let out in rooms. Gradually the housing fabric of inner London, the squares and terraces whose addresses were once so proudly embossed on notepaper, deteriorated, blackened with London's soot, wanting care and commitment, damaged by war. They were unconverted and unmodernized until gentrification rescued them.

A bus blown into a house in Harrington Square, Camden Town, in 1940.

CHAPTER XXV

TIME AFTER WAR

THE BLITZ

THE BOMBING BEGAN ON 25 AUGUST 1940, WHEN THE CHURCH OF ST GILES
Cripplegate was virtually destroyed, and it came again in earnest on 7
September. The defenceless London docks were attacked without respite by 400
German planes in broad daylight and again the same evening in darkness by
another 250 bombers. Over 400 civilians were killed and about 1,600 were wounded. The
East End, with its docks and factories, was a prime target and would continue to be so.
Yet deep shelter accommodation in the area was inadequate, so much so that a week later
East Enders marched to the Savoy Hotel to demand shelter there, which could not legally
be refused.

The solution for many Londoners, reluctantly conceded by London Transport, was the
use of Underground railway stations, but there were few of these in East London and they
were not everyone's choice in any case. Short of washing and lavatory facilities, they were
also crowded and noisy. They were not impenetrable either. In September seventeen
people died when a bomb got into Marble Arch station, and there were numerous deaths
at Sloane Square station in November; in January 1941 a bomb bounced down the
escalator stairs at Bank station and exploded on a platform, killing 117 people. During
this first bombing campaign, lasting throughout September and October, about 9,500
people were killed. The blitz of 1941 destroyed much of the area around St Paul's, the
House of Commons and again much of the East End.

By comparison, 1943 and 1944 were quiet. A last burst of German bombing at the
beginning of 1944 was ineffectual but on 13 June 1944 the first V1 flying bombs,
unmanned and inexactly programmed, caused enormous consternation on their first
appearance. Five days later the Guards Chapel at Wellington Barracks was hit and 119
people killed.

The anonymity and unpredictability of these bombs made them the more terrible.
They came with an ominous grinding noise and descended with an even louder silence.
By the time the Air Force had mastered a way of intercepting them the V2 rocket was
introduced, a missile that travelled too fast to engage. It is estimated that 518 V2s fell on
London during the blitz, resulting in the deaths of 2,724 people: the last ones fell on 25
March 1945.

THE PEACE

DEMOBILIZATION WAS A STRANGE AFFAIR: men, a mass of khaki, disgorging at docks and railway stations, saying goodbye to close friends, on their way to intimacy with strangers at home. They often arrived unannounced in the chaos of postal services from abroad and the absence of telephones in most houses. They came with kit bag on shoulder, walking with trepidation in familiar territory, fearing and wanting reunion. In hallways wide-eyed, almost unknown children waited their turn for his embrace and he, close to tears, would try to encompass them all. War, perversely, was more about meetings than partings. Men came back with addresses and plans for reunions, and found their wives and children with friendships established outside the perimeters of pre-war life, begun in public air-raid shelters, or in towns where they had been evacuated, or in factories where they worked.

POST-WAR HOUSING

THESE EMOTIONAL TIMES WERE SOON ECLIPSED BY REALITIES. London was a battered city, particularly in the east. It was also an old city, its housing stock decrepid and unsuited to its occupants, its factories full of equipment already out of date when war began. It was, after the rush of victory parties, a joyless place, obsessed with shortages and priorities and an eking out of old resources. There was no sudden injection of capital, no explosive regeneration that might have fired the spirit, only a relentlessly economical recovery, fraught with labour disputes and arguments as to the disposal of new bricks and mortar.

Impatient with the speed of things, squatters took over empty premises and there was particular resentment that thousands of buildings requisitioned by the government during the war stood empty: in Kensington alone about 8,000 hotels and houses were still in government hands in 1947. Pre-fabs – fabricated housing cheaply and quickly erected after the war – were regarded as a very temporary measure when they made their appearance, but they lasted in many areas certainly into the seventies. In these unusual circumstances London's local authorities were given great powers of comprehensive purchase so that they could rebuild effectively, but unfortunately this opportunity coincided with a shortage of building materials, an urgency of construction and the least attractive architectural period in our history.

GOING TO THE DOGS

IN THIS GREY ATMOSPHERE CINEMA AND SPORT DID WELL. Cinema provided fantasy and a semblance of luxury that radio, under its Presbyterian Director General, Lord Reith, declined to promote. No amount of Tommy Handley and BBC drama could match the make-believe of cinema, in which a lust for things American could be indulged. The cinema programmes were long – at least two films, one of which would be of lamentable quality – and on Saturday mornings there were Laurel & Hardy and cowboys for children.

Greyhound racing was a different love affair. Meetings took place all over London. They were floodlit occasions at which the smoke from thousands of Woodbines and

LONDON at the end of the Second World War had inherited a vast array of cinemas, some with exotic names, and some with the most fanciful architecture that many Londoners had seen. This cinema at Finsbury Park (which may still be discerned but only just) had strong oriental influences. some went for Egyptian themes and others adopted modern architectural styles.

Weights hung in a haze above the track, around which intelligent dogs were persistently fooled into chasing an object that they would have found inedible. At these tracks, before restaurants and corporate entertaining were needed to prop the sport up, there was a remarkably uncontrived atmosphere. Laura Thompson in her evocative book *Dogs* sums this up:

> *From the first, the dog men actually created their sport, it was not something that they knew as an image before they knew its reality; they made its reality. And because it was created a very short time ago, and it has been handed down through the dog men to the descendants who comprise so much of the dog world today, greyhound racing still retains traces of its true atmosphere.*

Speedway, a sport that mushroomed in the 1950s, had much the same atmosphere except that there was no gambling. The races, held in the same arenas in which the greyhounds ran, lasted slightly longer, mostly under floodlights but, unless there was a spill, were more predictable. Football stadiums too were crowded – it was not uncommon to have attendances at Arsenal or Chelsea of around 60,000, mostly standing, and fiercely partisan but without the squalid bravura of modern fans. London also hosted the 1948 Olympic Games, a brave gesture given the financial situation and the poor amenities available, but in those days of rare air travel, there were few visitors from overseas to accommodate, and the modest media circus was easy to contain. The Americans did well, as did Sweden and Holland, and the Russians and Eastern bloc countries were yet to shine; the host country, to no one's surprise, did badly.

THE FESTIVAL OF BRITAIN

IT IS INDICATIVE OF THE MELANCHOLY OF THAT POST-WAR PERIOD that the Festival of Britain in 1951 was dubbed 'A Tonic to the Nation'. The event, intended as a showcase one hundred years after the Great Exhibition in Hyde Park, was sniped at by MPs of all persuasions and by right-wing newspapers in particular. Nor was the artistic world without criticism. While men as disparate as Malcolm Sargent, A.P. Herbert, John Gielgud and Kenneth Clark were happy to sit on the Festival committee, Sir Thomas Beecham described it as a 'monumental piece of imbecility' and Evelyn Waugh and Noël Coward predictably despised it. No one in the Labour Government, with the exception of Herbert Morrison, was anxious to claim either its genesis or promotion in case it went disastrously wrong.

*T*HE *Dome of Discovery at the Festival of Britain in 1951. A concerted attempt was made to brighten up the south bank and to funnel 'culture' south of the river and away from the West End. Unfortunately, the architecture which followed the Festival has deterred many people from using the auditoria there.*

In the event it went splendidly right. Its main site was the derelict land to the north of County Hall and on this the Festival Hall was built; in Battersea Park a funfair and pleasure gardens were established, and elsewhere in London borough councils were invited to make their own contributions. The great and the good of modern art, architecture and design were involved: Hugh Casson, John Piper, Ben Nicholson, Keith Vaughan, Henry Moore, Barbara Hepworth and many more. They promoted, under difficult conditions, a new style of design that will forever be associated with that year. A Dome of Discovery housed exhibits of British inventiveness: a Skylon, a slim 296-foot pencil of a structure supported by cables, seemed to be suspended in space, and the Festival Hall itself, with its large and open spaces, so different from the minuscule foyers, lounges and bars of theatres and halls around London, was an immediate success. Over eight million people came to see them.

THE ANGRY YOUNG MEN

THE PRESS CREATED BOHEMIANS AND ANGRY YOUNG MEN from about 1954; they were, it seemed, a threat to social stability that frequented London coffee bars. They were not quite the same thing, although one person could be both, and eventually they were all to be classified as beatniks. The new Bohemians represented the rumblings of a fresh generation, many of them an educated working class, the product of art schools or new universities; in a few spirited years they reinvented the Bohemian lifestyle that existed in Fitzrovia before the Second World War and at the same time paved the way for the artistic anarchy of the 1960s. In truth, it was a rather dull Bohemianism, devoid of the larger-than-life personalities that made Fitzrovia legendary, and much too earnest to be fun. It was centred on Hampstead and Soho, but there were a lot of coffee bars in the West End, many occupied by vicarious tourists anxious to glimpse this new manifestation of revolt. Bohemians coincided with the staging of John Osborne's play, *Look Back in Anger*, at the Royal Court Theatre in 1956, and Colin Wilson's book, *The Outsider*, which, together with his personal life, made him famous. The Bohemians were not particularly rebellious, although in opting for a dress style of duffle-coats and casual trousers they could be taken as such: their very scruffiness, when most young men still wore suits or sports jackets and grey flannels, was a sufficient statement of revolt to convince most people. It was not a way of life that lasted long and it did not throw up the personalities and artistic work that could sustain its attraction, but Bohemians were probably at the heart of the Campaign for Nuclear Disarmament which gathered force within a few years.

The Moka in Frith Street, established by 1953, was probably the first of the new style coffee bars in London, using an espresso machine. They made their appearance at a time when it was unusual for Londoners to eat out and long before the vast increase of ethnic and fast-food restaurants in areas of London which in the 1950s had nothing more adventurous than a café. Proprietors eventually found, as rents went up in the 1960s, that coffee bars were not particularly profitable because not much food was consumed in them, but for seven or eight years Soho was renowned for them. The Moka was joined by Le Macabre in Meard Street, where coffins were used for tables, and in Old Compton Street were the Heaven and Hell and Act One Scene One; the Partisan in Carlisle Street was thought to be political and in the early 1960s the magazine *Private Eye* was published in the same tiny street; in nearby Greek Street the Establishment Club reintroduced satire to a nation whose sense of humour had been blunted by the bland standards permitted by the BBC. At the 2i's coffee bar, also in Old Compton Street, live music brought queues to its doors. Here there was a resident band and a frequent introduction of new talents.

One of the first coffee bars in London was established by George Hoskins, who later in his career was to be the Administrator of Centre 42. This second project was a venture in which the playwright Arnold Wesker hoped to bring art and theatre to a population which lacked its provision or else had resisted it. It began at the Trades Union Congress of 1960 when Wesker persuaded the delegates to pass an innocuous resolution, no. 42 on the agenda, 'to make proposals to future Congress to ensure a greater participation by the trade-union movement in all cultural activities'. It was hardly a resolution that could be turned down, especially one that was backed by so famous a person, but it was also loose enough in its wording to bind the TUC and its constituents to very little indeed. Wesker's vision was one of artists of different disciplines working together in circumstances in which the public might also be involved. To that end he obtained a lease on the old Roundhouse engine shed at Chalk Farm, a circular building which had been used as a warehouse almost since its erection in the mid-nineteenth-century and which was in bad repair. The building was transformed into a magical arena, but financial and artistic disagreements later led to Wesker resigning and by then the interest of the TUC had waned anyway. The importance of Centre 42 is not in what it did but in what it represented – an attempt not only to mix disciplines and to extend the arts to a working-class audience. The latter was not a new preoccupation: the LCC had hoped that the building of concert halls and other arts facilities on the South Bank would do much the same thing and there is no doubt that many in the audiences there saw orchestral performances for the first time. But on the whole they were not working class.

Otherwise, the most active of those promoting arts among the working classes were Labour councils in London, of which Camden (and prior to that St Pancras) Council was pre-eminent, but the drive for *new* audiences was not particularly successful. A further attempt was made by the Greater London Arts Association with the establishment in the 1970s of the Bubble Theatre, a portable dome which was erected, often in inclement weather, in London's parks, and in which a mix of popular and classic drama was attempted. It genuinely did and still does attract a working-class clientele, partly because its venue is not offputting. Another successful theatre in this sense was and is the Albany in Deptford, but the Greenwich Theatre, which set off with egalitarian hopes under the directorship of Ewan Hooper, has now a more conventional audience.

Fringe theatres had even less success in attracting a new audience. Even those in pubs, such as the Bush at Shepherd's Bush, or the King's Head in Islington, were unable to capitalize on their informal ambience. They were, however, part of a rich flowering of such venues. Joan Littlewood's Theatre Workshop at Stratford East was the earliest and the most famous, founded in 1953 in an unpromising part of London. In a safer theatrical area was the Hampstead Theatre Club, formed by James Roose-Evans in an old church hall in 1959 with professional but virtually unpaid actors. The Orange Tree at Richmond graduated from a pub to a purpose-built theatre and in the East End the Half Moon Theatre juggled a bill of populist and serious drama.

The surge of artistic innovation that overtook London in the 1960s was possible because the participants had little cultural baggage. The six years of the war and the arid years before and after them formed a creative fire break so that a new generation, as far as any generation may, started afresh. This commercially inspired transformation covering the fields of clothes, music, visual arts, entertainment and shopping fed voraciously on itself and spread quickly because of the availability of television.

The Property Boom

WHILE THE HEADLINES FOCUSED ON REBELLIOUS YOUTH, other young men, mostly former estate agents, were quietly changing London physically. Once the government abandoned its system of building licences in 1954 (a system by which it was hoped to divert scarce building materials to projects defined as essential), a spurt of development unparalleled since the Great Fire of 1666 took place. There were rich and numerous pickings to be had. Housing by now offered few incentives to private developers since rent controls restricted profit margins, but offices were a different matter. The old height limit of 80 feet (plus up to 20 feet of accommodation at the top set back from the visible walls) had been abandoned and new building techniques were already in place to build towers; Castrol House in Marylebone Road and New Zealand House in Haymarket demonstrated a way of maximizing a site by placing a tower on top of a podium block, a style which was to be copied all over London.

The business of property development required a strong nerve and good contacts. Most of the entrepreneurs were themselves estate agents – Max Rayne, a coat manufacturer, and Charles Clore, financier and owner of innumerable clothes and shoe shops, were notable exceptions in the big league of developers – who had inside knowledge of available sites. They also had contacts in the banks, building societies and insurance companies. A coterie of about ten architectural firms, which had expertise in planning regulations and the erection of economic blocks, designed much of the work, and a small number of wealthy construction companies, who often had an investment themselves, erected most of the blocks. Provided that the developer knew his business and was able to extract the highest plot ratio possible, he could hardly fail to make money since usually the funds for buying the site and the construction were put up by a financial institution or the builder. All the developer had to do after putting the deal together was to find a tenant – preferably a large company – who would in themselves provide sufficient reassurance for the lenders. There was no shortage of international and national companies wanting new office space and, in effect, the developer was borrowing money at a fixed cost against the construction of premises which multiplied in value as rents escalated in the late 1950s. It was possible, without any kind of investment other than talent and time, to make millions of pounds using other people's money, gambling on a rising market. The buildings themselves were of no architectural merit, nor were they intended to be, and London is still scarred by this outrageous burst of profit-taking.

Sometimes the local authority colluded with developers. The LCC, for example, was a vital and willing instrument in the two most profitable schemes in London – Centre Point and Euston Centre – where the Council's own plans for road schemes could not be pursued without the resources and ingenuity that a private developer could introduce. In the case of Centre Point the LCC planned a traffic roundabout at the junction of Tottenham Court Road and New Oxford Street, but could not afford to buy out the premises required. In a deal with Harry Hyams the Council got its roundabout (it was never used as such because in the meantime Charing Cross Road and Tottenham Court Road were made one-way, rendering a roundabout obsolete) but in return for his investment Hyams got one of the tallest and most valuable towers in London, so profitable that he was content to leave it empty for several years, awaiting a suitable tenant, while it increased in nominal value as office rents soared. The loss of rents was more than offset by increased valuation of the building and, at that time, no rates were paid on empty blocks.

The site of Euston Centre on Euston Road was occupied by run down shops and terraces of sub-standard houses behind. The LCC wanted an underpass at the junction of Euston Road and Tottenham Court Road which it found would breach planning consent outlines it had already given to Joe Levy, a developer who owned a number of strategic premises in the way of the new road. In a deal unknown to the general public, and working in tandem with the LCC, Levy bought up the numerous plots of land quietly and as cheaply as possible – many of the vendors unaware that anything was afoot. In return for the land the LCC needed Levy put together what was almost a small town of office accommodation which has always been immensely profitable.

Property developers became the new villains of the post-war era, held responsible for tearing down much-loved buildings, replacing them with impersonal blocks and making fortunes out of the public at the same time. All of these criticisms were true but at the same time they did find ways through the inertia of post-war London planning blight and confusion. The developers' activities may be compared with the inept way in which British Rail has used its valuable assets. Only in recent years has railway property in London been developed to any extent, and millions of pounds have been lost in the meantime from fallow land and premises. The consolation is that the lack of railway land development has left distinguished stations (with the exception of Euston) intact and no heritage of architecture of the 1960s and 1970s.

The demand for offices commercialized London with a force that no amount of legislation and local controls could have withstood and it enticed owners of large estates in London as diverse as City livery companies, the Church Commissioners, the Portman Estate and the Grosvenor Estate to look again at their landholdings. Owners of Victorian offices, particularly in the City, began to imagine their old-fashioned buildings as a fount of riches instead of a drain on their resources. Families with death duties to pay discovered that their solicitor just happened to know someone in the property business who might be interested in their run-down properties. Not even the desperate measure introduced by George Brown in 1964, which banned further office building in London, had any effect, since all that happened for the time being was that rents for existing accommodation went up, and in anticipation of a relaxation of the legislation the buying up of properties continued.

In the City, badly bombed during the war, the Corporation used its new powers of compulsory purchase to great effect, adding over 100 acres to its already substantial holdings. The City was able to construct the Barbican scheme in this bonanza, though it has to be said that the previously unadventurous Corporation endowed it with arts facilities and a museum of a quality well beyond the call of civic duty. With the exception of the South Bank arts complex the LCC and borough councils concentrated on housing for rent, a sector of the market for which only they had the resources and appetite. Unfortunately, the solution chosen was tower blocks and estates which had the effect of segregating their tenants from private accommodation – a policy that, in hindsight, was to cost London dear. Scarcely a building in all the flurry of local authority activity in the 1960s and 1970s could now be singled out for the attention of an architectural student, except as a warning. The Elephant & Castle area, badly damaged in the war, was comprehensively redeveloped with a scheme grotesque in its size. In Stepney, where about one quarter of the housing stock had been damaged by bombing, estates of numbing predictability were hastily constructed.

It could be argued that the era of the 1960s, however superficial much of it may have been, was the last occasion when London presented a modern identity to the world. Of course, it was a commercially-led presentation, owing little to the real forces of power within the capital; and it was a transient phase in London's history, just as other world cities have gone in and out of fashion on the strength of their social or artistic life. It is rare indeed for a city to acquire a revised reputation from the concentrated efforts of its civic fathers, though in Britain Glasgow, Manchester and Birmingham have tried hard and in many respects have succeeded. The GLC under the leadership of Ken Livingstone in the 1980s was seen to be promoting the entity of London for the first time since the heyday of Labour's municipal socialism, but he had few of the powers that leaders of councils outside the metropolis have as a matter of course. Since Mrs Thatcher abolished the GLC in 1986 London has had no such opportunity to speak with one voice.

London is now a city in governmental disarray, fragmented and complex, powerless to formulate policies of its own or negotiate on matters which impinge upon it. Decisions, even of profound importance, affecting the metropolis have been purloined by central government and to all intents and purposes no reasoned response may be assembled to amend or oppose them. Even the crucial Channel Tunnel rail link is of no more concern to London as a whole than the parochial interests of the borough councils through which it goes.

One school of thought is that there are advantages to this ad hoc system, and that to revive a London authority with an overall, long-term vision for the capital will lead to the mistakes and bureaucratic slowness of the days of municipal socialism. Life, not just London, now moves at too fast a pace, making long-term planning not an advantage but a dangerous thing. People with vision and with plans rarely like them amended and resist new circumstances if only out of pique. Planners, it is suggested, could not and would not have anticipated such diverse things as the gentrification of inner London, the cosmopolitan nature of its present population, the vast change in entertainment fashions, the growth of eating out, the level of homelessness within a relatively prosperous society, the apparently undaunted thirst for car ownership and the popularity of out-of-town shopping facilities. It is better, then, not to have strategic plans, but to respond quickly and positively to emerging trends.

This then is the broad dilemma for London – how should it be governed and, just as importantly, how may its people contribute towards that government? In what way can an overall London authority have an independence of thought and action when confronted with government, miscellaneous quangos and borough councils? It is not, as we have seen, a new dilemma and in the past only reluctant compromises have been introduced to deal with it. History suggests that nothing satisfactory will be attempted.

EPILOGUE

I T IS NOT DIFFICULT, FOR ALL THE REASONS EXPRESSED AT THE END OF CHAPTER 25, TO BE gloomy about London's future. Social problems, seemingly insoluble, abound. Homelessness, crime, traffic congestion, pollution, wretched poverty, poor educational facilities in many areas, unemployment – all induce a growing unease among those who want to think about them. Almost certainly these concerns are to be found in every other city in the country and in much of Europe.

Numerous commentators have suggested that London's decline matches national decline, and as Britain's fortunes since the Second World War have stumbled, so those of London have become sluggish. This implies that London is a hapless pawn in the economic disarray of Great Britain, consigned to a downward spiral from which there is no independent escape; as the fortunes of London thrived with those of the country for all those centuries so, inextricably, the city is bound up with the nation's reverses.

The situation was made worse, as we have seen, by the abolition of the Greater London Council, the last form of overall London government. That this was a spiteful act on the part of Margaret Thatcher, piqued by an authority that, despite the best-laid plans, remained in the control of the Labour Party, there is no doubt. Yet its abolition was a continuation of the hostility between Westminster and London which fitfully emerged over centuries and which, since 1855, has intensified. The abolition of the GLC inevitably enlarged the role of borough councils, but the government has since reduced these to no more than tightly controlled spending agents. The apppointment of a minister to concern himself with London has emphasized a new policy of managing the capital from Whitehall. Yet, perversely, large schemes which affect the whole of London are dealt with in various ways although always without the consent of Londoners as a whole. The redevelopment of the King's Cross railway lands, for example, is mainly the concern of the two local councils most affected who, quite reasonably, judge it by purely local criteria. The rebuilding of Docklands is left to an autonomous development corporation which may, if it wishes, override local or all-London considerations. The proposals to build a Cross Link railway, or else an extended underground system, are the business of members of Parliament. Vital hospitals are facing closure by the government quite against the wishes and views of those local authorities concerned. There is no logic to this situation let alone democracy. And, as we have already noted, the route of the Channel Tunnel rail link is fixed by the government.

Since the resurrection of some form of London authority is popularly considered to be indispensable to any revival of the capital's fortunes, it is worth examining what form it might take and what its functions might be. It is unlikely that social services, such as education and housing, would be taken out of the hands of the boroughs and returned to a metropolitan body. Certainly, some advantages of scale, consistency and quality were obtained in the inner London boroughs when the GLC was responsible for education, but these are of minor consideration when compared with the potential advantages of local supervision of schools, at least where the schools have preferred to remain under local authority control. It is even more unlikely that any new London authority would resume responsibility for such things as fire services and ambulances, or of open spaces now devolved to local authorities and, less logically, to the City of London.

Vague functions for a London authority are suggested, with the words 'strategic planning' seemingly an invincible argument. The new body, it is claimed, would produce an overall planning blueprint, especially relevant to transportation, for the foreseeable future. However, it was precisely in the fields of social services – such as housing, health, education and the emergency services – that the old London County Council and Greater London Council were sometimes outstanding, and in the more nebulous areas of planning they were often misguided and least successful. The exodus of industry, officially encouraged by the LCC and the GLC, has seen the disappearance of both jobs and skilled workers, leaving London a city of 'professional', commercial and unskilled employees, the latter largely dependent upon part-time jobs in service industries. The enforced provision of car-parking spaces with offices has helped to increase congestion. The rigid zoning of areas produced inflexibility in land use, and the building plans of the LCC and GLC, especially in south London, resulted in dreary ghettos of local authority housing. The inability of the GLC to raise their sights beyond municipal socialism helped to lose control of the development of Docklands. It was the GLC which took the initiative in proposing the wholesale demolition of the Covent Garden area. It was the LCC and GLC which proposed motorways through London that were hopelessly at odds with the environment.

Long-term planning is a hazardous game: even a cursory look at the famous Abercrombie plan for central London, drawn up in the concluding years of the Second World War, will reveal proposals which we now know would have been quite wrong had they ever been implemented. His plan, compiled at a time when urban motorways were considered to be a positive advantage, would have carved up considerable areas of inner London and even then would not have coped with the unforeseen increase in the ownership of cars.

Overall plans are at once the ambition and the weakness of authorities and, more particularly, of their officers. Their formulation and then their periods of consultation are so long that they are out of date even by the time they are agreed, let alone put into operation. They should be discouraged.

It is fairly clear, however, that the present arrangement for the governance of London cannot go on. There are too many specific problems that need to be addressed which are beyond the capabilities or resources of either local boroughs or any other government agency. The wretched conditions of the East End is one of them, the inadequacy of the public transport system another; the half-hearted attempts to deal with homelessness is a third. Yet there is something else that needs to be remedied that is more intangible – the lack of a London leadership. Where are the people who represent London, who have a duty and willingness to present their solutions and visions? Where are the personalities who might return to Londoners a surge of optimism about the city's future? They are not apparent because they have no forum and this leads to scepticism that the problems will be tackled, and a belief that London can do little more than stumble into a bleak future.

A way must be found to revive London democracy but without the cumbersome and bureaucratic structures of the past. It must be an authority that is flexible in its response and has the right powers to deal simultaneously with hostile Whitehall and covetous local boroughs. It will, most probably, need to emulate democratic systems elsewhere in which the leader or mayor is elected as a separate entity, with a small body of councillors elected on a regional basis. All of them would be paid and would be full time. It would not, because of London's democratic history, be an easy solution, but it is preferable to government by stealth.

Lastly, the pressure to project London as one of the economically paramount cities of the world should be resisted – the city and its people should be free to assess its modern nature, to capitalize on its undoubted advantages, to deal with its drawbacks, without the weight of its history upon it. There are other ways of being a great city than by being the financial centre of the world.

FURTHER READING

CHAPTER I – LIFE WITHIN THE WALLS

The best authority on Roman London is the late Ralph Merrifield, whose books *The Roman City of London* (1965) and *City of the Romans* (1983) are standard works. Subsequent discoveries are summarized by him in an essay in *The British Atlas of Historic Towns* vol. 3, *The City of London From Prehistoric Times to c.1520* (Mary Lobel ed. 1989). Also informative are *Roman London* by Peter Marsden (1980) and *Londinium: London in the Roman Empire* by John Morris (1982). The most comprehensive account of the Roman wall around London is by Walter George Bell *et al*, *London Wall Through Eighteen Centuries* (1937).

The minor rivers of London are the subject of Nicholas Barton's *The Lost Rivers of London* (rev. ed. 1992). The river Fleet has more literature than the other lost rivers, most notably *The Fleet: its river, prison and marriages* by John Ashton (1988) and The "Hole-bourne' by John George Waller in *London and Middlesex Archaeological Society Transactions* IV (1875). This author deals with the Tyburn and Westbourne in the same publication Vol. VI (1890). See also *Book of the Wandle: the story of a Surrey river* by John Morrison Hobson (1924).

There are numerous books on the Thames. These include *The Golden Age of the Thames* by Patricia Burstall (1981), *London's River: the story of a city* by Eric Samuel De Mare (rev. ed. 1972), *London River: the Thames story* by Gavin Weightman (1990), and *The Thames about 1750* by Hugh Phillips (1951), which describes in meticulous detail the buildings along the river in the middle of the eighteenth century.

The early port of London is described by Gustav Milne in *The Port of Roman London* (1985), and by Milne and Damian Goodburn in 'The Early Medieval Port of London 700-1200' in *Antiquity* LXIV (1990). See also James Bird *The Geography of the Port of London* (1957).

The best work on medieval London is *London 800-1216: the shaping of a city* by Christopher Brooke and Gillian Keir (1975). This may be supplemented by two books by Charles Pendrill, *Old Parish Life in London* (1937) and *London Life in the 14th Century* (1925). Three important studies are 'King Alfred and the Restoration of London' in *London Journal* XV (1990), *The Commune of London* by J.H. Round (1899) and *The Turbulent London of Richard II* (1951). For Westminster of this period there is really only *The Westminster Corridor* by David Sullivan (1994) which takes the story of Westminster Abbey and its lands in London up to the Conquest, and *Medieval Westminster 1200-1540* by Gervase Rosser (1989). For a fascinating modern map of the City of London in c.1270, and for parish and ward maps, see *The City of London from Prehistoric Times to c.1520* ed. by Mary Lobel (1989), a volume which also contains a condensed history of London 800-1270 by Brooke, and an essay by Caroline Barron on London in 'The Later Middle Ages: 1270-1520'.

Most livery companies have histories, too numerous to detail here. A general and much respected history of the principal companies is contained in *The Guilds and Companies of London* by George Unwin (4th ed. 1973). *The Merchant Class of Medieval London* by Sylvia Thrupp (Chicago 1948) is an invaluable study.

The standard work on London Bridge is *Old London Bridge* by Gordon Home (1931). Detailed studies include 'The Saxon London Bridge' by Graham Dawson in *The London Archaeologist* I (1968-72 pp 300-2), 'The Pre-Norman Bridge of London' by Marjorie Honeybourne in *Studies in London History* (1969), and 'Old London Bridge' by Michael Brown Pearson in *London and Middlesex Archaeological Society Transactions* n.s. IV (1918-22).

Most City churches and old parish churches in the rest of London have their own histories. General works on pre-Fire City churches are *London Churches Before the Great Fire* by William Wilberforce Jenkinson (1917), and 'London City Churches that Escaped the Great Fire' by Philip Norman in *London Topographical Record* V (1908). The most comprehensive work on Westminster Abbey is *A House of Kings: the history of Westminster Abbey* by Edward Carpenter ed. (1966). Publications on St Paul's Cathedral include *A History of St Paul's Cathedral and the Men Associated with It*, edited by Walter Matthews and William Atkins (1957). The most comprehensive survey of monastic lands in London is a London University M.A. thesis compiled by Marjorie Honeybourne in 1929. Numerous histories of the various monastic houses exist.

Marjorie Honeybourne is also the authority on leper hospitals in London and Middlesex, detailing their where-abouts in *London and Middlesex Archaeological Society Transactions* XXI (1963-7). Much detail about bubonic plague in London is contained in *A History of Bubonic Plague in the British Isles* by John Shrewsbury (1970).

Andrew Prescott deals with the events and personalities involved in the Peasants' Revolt of 1381 in an essay in *London Journal* VII (1981). For a comprehensive work on prisons (which includes details of London prisons) see Ralph Pugh's *Imprisonment in Medieval England* (1968). Marjory Bassett has written two studies of early London prisons: 'The Fleet Prison in the Middle Ages', in the *Toronto University Law Journal* V (1944), and 'Newgate Prison in the Middle Ages' in *Speculum* XVIII (1943).

CHAPTER II – THE OTHER LONDON

The most detailed account of early Westminster is to be found in Gervase Rosser's *Medieval Westminster 1200-1540* (1989). To a greater or lesser extent the medieval history of the parishes around London are dealt with in area histories. A good example is provided by David Pam in volume one of his three-volume history of Enfield, *A Parish Near London* (1990). The Savoy Palace is described in *The Savoy, manor: hospital: chapel* by Sir Robert Somerville (1960).

Some court rolls of outer London parishes have been printed. Most notable are those for Hornsey, translated by William McBeath Marcham (1929), and those of Wimbledon manor from Edward IV to 1864, published in 1866 for the Wimbledon Common Committee.

For drinking habits see *The English Alehouse: a social history 1200-1830* by Peter Alan Clark (1983). A fascinating description of early London markets is to be found in Hugh Alley's *Caveat: the Markets of London in 1598*, published by the London Topographical Society in 1988. Otherwise, *London's Markets, their Origin and History* by William J. Passingham (1935) is still the most comprehensive work. The entertaining by William Bruges of the Emperor Sigismund at Kentish Town is mentioned in *The Life of William Bruges* by Hugh Stanford London (Camden Society 1970).

CHAPTER III – MERCHANTS AND PROFESSIONALS

The houses of prominent merchants of the period are dealt with in *The Building of London from the Conquest to the Great Fire* by John Schofield (1984). Crosby Hall is detailed by Philip Norman in 'Crosby Place' in the *London Topographical Record* VI (1909). The best account of Richard Whittington's London career is contained in 'Richard Whittington: the man behind the myth' by Caroline Barron in *Studies in London History* (1969).

For the College of Physicians see 'Thomas Linacre and the Foundation of the Royal College of Physicians' in *Essays on the life of Thomas Lincacre* ed. by F.R. Maddison *et al.* The practice of medicine is described in 'The Personnel and Practice of Medicine in Tudor and Stuart England' by Raymond Stanley Roberts in *Medical History* VIII (1964), 'The regulation of midwives in the 16th and 17th centuries; in *Medical History* VIII (1964), and *The Pepperers, Spicers and Apothecaries of London during the 13th and 14th Centuries* by L.G. Matthews (1980).

An established history of the Inns of Court is that by W.J. Loftie, *The Inns of Court and Chancery* (rev. ed. 1905). Accounts of the various inns exist.

CHAPTER IV – A BLOODY REFORMATION

The most important work is Susan Brigden's *London and the Reformation* (1989). More specific studies include Ida Darlington's 'The Reformation in Southwark' in *Huguenot Society of London Proceedings* XIX no.3 (1955).

CHAPTER V – A GATHERING PACE

An essay on John Stow appears in *London Topographical Record* XXIII (1972), by Marjorie Honeybourne. He is also featured in *Historians of London* by Stanley Rubinstein (1968). The two most useful editions of Stow's *Survey* are that published by Everyman in 1956, and that edited by C.L. Kingsford, republished in 1971, both based on the 1603 edition.

Many studies of Elizabethan theatre in London have been published. See particularly *Playgoing in Shakespeare's London* by Andrew Gurr (1987), and *English Dramatic Companies* Vol. 1 by John Tucker Murray (1910). Masques are dealt with in *Stuart Masques and the Renaissance Stage* by John Nicoll (1937). Animal baiting is covered by 'Paris Garden and the Bear-baiting' by C.L. Kingsford in *Archaeologia* LXX (1920) and 'The Popularity of Baiting in England before 1600: a study of social and theatrical history' in *Education Theatre Journal* XXI (1969).

Witchcraft is detailed in 'Popular Beliefs about Witches: the evidence from East London, 1645-60' by Robert Higgins in *East London Record* no. 4 (1981). The danger to local midwives of being accused of witchcraft is highlighted by Jean Donnison in her history of the profession, *Midwives and Medical Men* (rev. ed. 1988).

Nothing illustrates the crimes and punishments of Middlesex so well as the published extracts of Quarter Sessions, which are on the shelves of any good London local history library. The most comprehensive account of Bridewell is that by E.G. O'Donoghue, *Bridewell Hospital, Palace, Prison, Schools from the Death of Elizabeth to Modern Times*, published in 2 vols (1923, 1929).

For the Royal Exchange, see *The Life and Times of Sir Thomas Gresham, Founder of the Royal Exchange* by John William Burgon (2 vols 1839).

No major history of the New River has been published, other than *The New River: a legal history*, by Bernard Rudden (1985).

The Covent Garden estate is detailed in the *Survey of London* vol. 36: *St Paul's Covent Garden* (1970).

Chapter VI – Making a Living

See *Memoirs of Bartholomew Fair* by Henry Morley (4th ed. 1892), also 'Food Consumption and Internal Trade' in *London 1500-1700: the making of the metropolis* ed. A.L. Beier and R.A.P. Finlay (1986), and 'The Development of the London Food Market' by Frederick Fisher in *Economic History Review* V no. 2 (1935).

For a firsthand account of shipbuilding in the seventeenth century, with particular relevance to Rotherhithe, see *The Autobiography of Phineas Pett* ed. by W. Perrin (1918).

Chapter VII – War Around the City

Aspects of the Civil War are discussed in: 'The Civil War Politics of London's Merchant Community' by Robert Brenner in *Past and Present* no. 58 (1973); 'London During the Civil War: its contribution to the political changes of the 17th century', by Sir Charles Firth in *History* XI (1926); 'The Struggle for London in the Second Civil War', by Ian Gentles in *Hist. Journal* XXVI (1983); 'The Civil War Defences of London' by David Sturdy in *London Archaeologist* II (1975).

Chapter VIII – Death, Destruction and Revival

For atmosphere, if not accuracy, Daniel Defoe's *Journal of the Plague Year, 1665* (ed. 1969) is recommended. The classic study of the Great Plague is *The Great Plague in London in 1665* by Walter George Bell (rev. ed. 1951). For an interesting study on the roll of Searchers, who verified plague victims, see 'The Searchers' by Thomas Rogers Forbes in *New York Academy Medicine Bulletin* 2nd ser. L. (1974). William Boghurst, the brave physician who tended the sick of St Giles-in-the-Fields, has his memoirs of the event in *Loimographia: an account of the Great Plague in year 1665* ed. by J.F. Payne (1894). Walter Bell is also author of *The Great Fire of London in 1666* (rev. ed 1923). An archaeologist's view of the events and evidence of the Great Fire is contained in *The Great Fire of London*, by Gustav Milne (1986). John Evelyn's proposals for the rebuilding of London after the Great Fire are contained in his *London Revived: consideration for its rebuilding in 1666*, ed. by E.S. de Beer (1938). A major essay on the speculative builder who was to thrive in the rebuilding of London, Nicholas Barbon, is by Norman Brett-James, 'A Speculative London Builder of the 17th Century: Dr Nicholas Barbon' in *London and Middlesex Archaeological Society Transactions* n.s. VI (1933). The principal book on the rebuilding of London is *The Rebuilding of London after the Great Fire* by Thomas Reddaway (1940).

For financial background of the period there is *The Story of the Bank of England from its Foundation in 1694 until the Present Day*, by William Dodgson Bowman (1937), and *The South Sea Bubble* by John Carswell (1960). There are individual histories of The Russian Company, Hudson Bay Company etc.

Restoration theatre in London is featured in *The Playhouse of Pepys* by Montague Summers (1935) and, by the same author, *The Restoration Theatre* (1934). Eighteenth century London theatre may be seen through the various biographies of its leading figures, such as David Garrick, John Rich etc, or else in the pages of the plentiful histories of the Theatre Royal, Drury Lane and Covent Garden theatre.

Chapter IX – Passing the Time

The standard work on London pleasure gardens is still *The London Pleasure Gardens of the 18th Century* by Warwick Wroth (1896), though more perceptive writing is to be found in *The English Spa 1560-1815: a social history* by Phyllis Hembry (1980), which includes the London watering places. Individual histories exist for such places as Vauxhall, Ranelagh and Cremorne.

Other than *London Coffee Houses: a reference book of coffee houses of the 17th, 18th and 19th centuries* by Bryant Lilywhite (1963), literature on the subject is mainly anecdotal and centres on the better-known houses. Men's clubs all have their individual histories in a section of London literature that far exceeds the importance of the subject. A long account of the 'musical coal-man', Thomas Britton, is to be found in *The History of Clerkenwell* by W.J. Pinks (2nd ed. 1881). Mozart's stay in London is dealt with in *Mozart* by Charlotte Haldane (1960). Opera in London is to be found in histories of Covent Garden Theatre and in *A History of English Opera* by Eric Walter White (1983).

Cricket in London, needless to say, has a large literature, with individual histories of many of the local cricket clubs. The Marylebone Cricket Club and Lord's is prominent of course, with *Double Century: the story of*

M.C.C. and Cricket by Tony Field being the most recent and useful publication. The Oval is dealt with in *The Official History of Surrey County Cricket Club* by David Lemmon (1988).

CHAPTER X – INSTITUTIONS IN THE MAKING

The standard work on the British Museum is *That Noble Cabinet: a history of the British Museum* by Edward Miller (1973), but the Museum published *Sir Hans Sloane and the British Museum* by Sir Gavin de Beer in 1953.

There are two major histories of the Royal Society of Arts: *The Royal Society of Arts, 1754-1954* by Derek Hudson and Kenneth Luckhurst (1975) and *A History of the Royal Society of Arts* by Sir H.T. Wood (1913). An account of the interesting Spitalfields Mathematical Society appears in *London Mathematical Society Bulletin XI* (1979) by J.W.S. Cassels.

For newspapers of the period see *The English Press in the 18th Century* by Jeremy Black (1987).

CHAPTER XI – BUYING AND SELLING

The activities and churches of the Huguenot communities in London are well documented in the publications of the Huguenot Society of London. *A Dictionary of English Furniture Makers 1660-1840* ed. by Geoffrey Beard and Christopher Gilbert (1986) is a good reference book and there are several essays on prominent London makers, including Chippendale, published by the Furniture History Society. London shopping in this period is described in *A History of Shopping* by Dorothy Davis (1966) and in *Shopping in Style* (1979) by Alison Adburgham.

CHAPTER XII – A TROUBLED MULTITUDE

A phase in the gin epidemic is described in 'Mother Gin and the London Riots of 1746', by George Rudé in *Guildhall Miscellany* I (1959). The standard history of the Foundling Hospital is *The History of the Foundling Hospital* by R.H. Nichols and Francis Wray (1935). See also 'Philanthropy and Empire: Jonas Hanway and the infant poor of London' by J.S. Stephen in *Eighteenth Century Studies* XII (1979).

An early work on policing London is that by Patrick Colquhoun, *Treatise on the Commerce and Police of the River Thames* (1800). Early policing is dealt with in *The History of the Bow Street Runners, 1729-1829* by Gilbert Armitage (1932). The formation of the Metropolitan Police is featured in *The Queen's Peace: the origins and development of the Metropolitan Police 1829-1979* by David Ascoli (1979). The Corporation of London published *City of London Police: 150 years of service 1839-1989* (1989) by D.A. Rumbelow. See also *The Life and Work of Sir John Fielding* by R. Leslie-Melville (1934), and *The Thief-Taker General: The rise and fall of Jonathan Wild* by Gerald Howson (1979). For a substantial account of the epidemic of hangings in London see *The London Hanged: crime and civil society in the eighteenth century* by Peter Linebaugh (1991).

For late 18th and 19th century prisons see *A Just Measure of Pain: the penitentiary in the Industrial Revolution, 1750-1850* by Michael Ignatieff (New York 1978); *The Criminal Prisons of London* by Henry Mayhew and John Binny (repr 1971); *The English Prison Hulks* by W. Branch Johnson (1957).

CHAPTER XIII – A CITY IN MOTION

The best summary of London's canals is *London Waterways* by Martyn Denney (1977). A detailed essay on the Regent's Canal by Alan Faulkner is included in *Change at King's Cross* ed. Michael Hunter and Robert Thorne (1990). Most railway authors concentrate on engines, rolling stock and signalling apparatus and are quite unreadable. Jack Simmons is an exception. His book *The Railway in Town and Country 1830-1914* (1986) and his essay 'The Power of the Railway' in *The Victorian City* ed. H.J. Dyos and Michael Wolff (1973), are good introductions to the more specific histories that exist for each of the main railways that came into London. See also an essay by Robert Thorne in *Change at King's Cross* (see above) on the effect of the railways on the coal trade in London. An invaluable summary of the various forms of transport in Victorian London is *Locomotion in Victorian London* by G.A. Sekon (1938). This includes useful summaries of the advent of steamboats, trams, cabs and buses. There is a vast array of other literature about buses and trams. Booklets are available for each of the London Underground lines – the earlier ones written by Charles Lee with the exactitude for which he was well-known, but lacking social comment. *Moving Millions* by Theo Barker (1990) is a pictorial record of London transport with a good commentary, but the standard work for much of the subject is *A History of London Transport* by Barker and Michael Robbins (2 vols 1963 and 1974).

CHAPTER XIV – CLEANING UP THE CAPITAL

The best introduction to the administrative conditions that pertained in London and the events which led up to the formation of the Metropolitan Board of Works in 1855, is contained in *The Government of Victorian London 1855-1889* by David Owen (1982), which includes an essay by Francis Sheppard, whose book *Local Government in St Marylebone 1688-1835* (1958) is essential to understanding what went before in the parishes. A splendidly ascerbic account of the neglect of London's affairs is contained in *The Government and Misgovernment of London* by William A. Robson (1939).

For a survey of the battles with water companies see 'London in the Nineteenth Century. 3, The fight for a water supply' by T.F. Reddaway in *Nineteenth Century* CXLVIII (1950), and 'The politics of London water' by A.K. Mukhopadhyay in *London Journal* (1975). In the 1978 volume of the same publication is 'Free water: the public drinking fountain movement in Victorian London' by Howard Malchow. For history of the sewerage system see *The Main Drainage of London* by G.W. Humphreys (1930).

For a comprehensive survey see *A Social History of Housing* by John Burnett (1986), and *Cruel Habitations: a history of working-class housing 1780-1918* by Enid Gauldie (1974). On the same theme is 'The Housing of the Working-Classes in London, 1815-1914' in *The History of Working-Class Housing*, ed. S.D. Chapman (1971). Accounts of some of the model-dwelling companies have been published. See also *Social Work in London, 1869 to 1912: a history of the Charity Organisation Society* by Helen Bosanquet (1914). Of prime importance in London social history is Henry Mayhew's *London Labour and the London Poor* (4 vols repr. 1971), and Charles Booth's *Life and Labour of the People of London* (17 vols 1902-3), together with his map of London showing income groups, republished by the London Topographical Society. See also *Evangelicals in Action: an appraisal of their social work in the Victorian era* by Kathleen Heasman (1962). For literature on workhouses see *The Workhouse System 1834-1929: the history of an English social institution* by M. Anne Crowther (1981). A little-known aspect of workhouse life is revealed in Ruth Richardson's *Death, Dissection and the Destitute* (1987).

An old-fashioned guide to London burial grounds is contained in *London Burial Grounds* by Mrs Basil Holmes (1896). More up to date is Harvey Hackman's *Wates's Book of London Churchyards* (1981). Julian Litten's *The English Way of Death* (1991) is an entertaining yet academic description of funerals since 1450. Guides to cemeteries in London include *London Cemeteries* by Hugh Meller (rev. ed. 1985).

Histories of some London dispensaries exist. See also 'Medical Dispensaries in 18th Century London' by William Hartston in *Royal Society of Medicine Proceedings* LVI (1963). A good base for the study of hospitals is *The Metropolitan Asylums Board and its Work 1867-1930* (pub. by the Board in 1930). Histories of most of the principal London hospitals exist. The only overview book that seems to exist is *The Development of the London Hospital System 1823-1982* by G. Rivett, though this, of course, excludes the formation of a number of prominent London hospitals. The provision of maternity hospitals is dealt with in detail by Jean Donnison in *Midwives and Medical Men* (rev. ed. 1988).

The principal London parks are described in Neville Braybrooke's *London Green: the story of Kensington Gardens etc.* (1959), and municipal parks are well detailed in John James Sexby's *The Municipal Parks, Gardens and Open Spaces of London: their history and associations* (1898). Of particular merit because of the light it throws on the movements to save London's commons and open spaces is *Hampstead Heath* by Alan Farmer (1984).

The history of fire-fighting is contained in *A History of the British Fire Service* by Geoffrey Blackstone (1957). The early insurance companies are described in *An Account of the Fire Insurance Companies Established During the 17th and 18th Centuries* by Francis Relton (1893), and *The British Fire Mark* by Brian J. Wright (1982).

CHAPTER XV – MOVING SCENES, BRIGHT LIGHTS AND OTHER PLEASURES
For panoramas and dioramas see *Panoramania* by Ralph Hyde (1988). The same author also wrote 'Mr Wyld's monster globe' in *History Today* 1970 pp 118-23. For the Great Exhibition see *The Great Exhibition 1851* by Yvonne Ffrench (1950). The catalogue of exhibits has been reprinted and is available through Dover Books. The most accessible account of the People's Palace is Deborah Weiner's 'The People's Palace: an image for East London in the 1880s' in *Metropolis London* ed. by D.M. Feldman and G. Stedman Jones (1989).

The literature on theatres and music halls is large. As a starting point refer to Diana Howard's *London Theatres and Music Halls* (1970) which lists the available books and publications on each building. London Zoo is detailed in *Centenary History of the Zoological Society of London* by Sir Percy Chalmers Mitchell (1929), and more entertainingly by Wilfrid Blunt in *The Ark in the Park: the zoo in the 19th century* (1976).

CHAPTER XVI – A SPORTING LIFE
Joanne Hawley has written a thesis (City University M.A. 1984) on 'The development of indoor ice skating rinks in London before World War II'. For tennis, there are various publications on the Wimbledon championships, but see also *The Queen's Club 1886-1986* by Roy McKelvie (1986). All the professional (and many amateur) London football clubs have their own histories.

CHAPTER XVII – A MISSION TO SAVE
For a description of evangelical influence in London see *Lighten Their Darkness: the evangelical mission to working-class London, 1828-1860* by D.M. Lewis (1986). See also *Clapham and the Clapham Sect* by Edmund Baldwin (1927). For a history of temperance see *The Water Drinkers: a history of temperance* by Norman Longmate (1968) and *The Crusade Against Drink in Victorian England* by Lilian Shiman (1988).

Chapter XVIII – A Bit of Learning

See Margaret Bryant's *The London Experience of Secondary Education* (1986) for an overview. There are numerous histories of London schools and school societies, and many articles analysing the establishment and effect of the London School Board. These are comprehensively summarized in Heather Creaton's invaluable *Bibliography of Printed Works on London History to 1939* (1994).

Though accounts of the establishment of library services have been published for several areas, there is no published overview of the history of the London library service.

Chapter XIX – Striving for Utopias

Much material on the building of the LCC council estates is contained in *History of the London County Council* by Sir Gwilym Gibbon and Reginald Bell (1939). The subject is discussed in *A Social History of Housing 1815-1970* by John Burnett (1978). See also *John Bean and the Progressive Movement* by Alfred George Gardiner (1925) and *Becontree and Dagenham* by Terence Young (1934). Suburbia is dealt with in *Dunroamin: the suburban semi and its enemies* by Paul Oliver et al (1981), and *Semi-Detached London* by Alan Jackson (1973).

Chapter XX – Arousal of a Multitude

For an in-depth account of a campaign (that failed) to save an area, see *The Battle for Tolmers Square* by Nick Wates (1976).

Chapter XXI – Political Divides

The standard, though uncritical, history of the London County Council is *History of the London County Council 1889-1939* by Sir Gwilym Gibbon and Reginald Bell (1939). More insights may be gathered in works on the Webbs, the Fabian Society and Herbert Morrison. See also *Politics and the People of London: the London County Council 1889-1965* ed. by Andrew Saint (1989), and *Socialists, Liberals and Labour: the struggle for London 1885-1914* by Paul Richard Thompson (1967). For the principal strikes see Ann Stafford *A Match to Fire the Thames* (1961), Terry McCarthy *The Great Dock Strike 1889* (1988) and Julian Symons *The General Strike: a historical portrait* (1957). Robert Benewick's *The Fascist Movement in Britain* (rev. ed. 1972) contains a chapter on the East End troubles.

Chapter XXII – Strangers to Our Shores

The best summary of immigration to London is in the catalogue for the exhibition (ed. Nick Merriman) at the Museum of London called *The Peopling of London* (1993). It includes a comprehensive bibliography relevant to the different communities.

Chapter XXII – A City of Consumers

For Regent Street see *A History of Regent Street* by Hermione Hobhouse (1975). There are a good many histories of shops, but they tend to be uncritical. Books exist on all the main London stores, such as Selfridge's, Harrods, John Lewis, Sainsbury's etc.

Chapter XXV – Time After War

For this period see *The Making of Modern London 1945-1985* by Steve Humphries and John Taylor (1986). Of particular interest is Oliver Marriott's *The Property Boom* (1967) and *From Splendour to Banality: the rebuilding of the City of London 1945-1983* ed. by Oliver Leigh Wood (1983). Development is also central to the theme of *Landlords to London; the story of a capital and its growth* by Simon Jenkins (1975). For an assessment of London's future see *London – 2001* by Peter Hall (1989).

Standard Works

No study of London can be made without reference to maps. The London Topographical Society has published maps, fully indexed, of London from Elizabethan days onwards. For general reference works see *The London Encyclopedia* by Ben Weinreb and Christopher Hibbert (1983), and William Kent's *An Encyclopedia of London* (rev. ed. 1970). See also *A History of London Life* by R.J. Mitchell and M.D.R. Leys (1958) and *London Life in the Eighteenth Century* by M. Dorothy George (1925). For the nineteenth century, not to be missed are Donald Olsen's the *Growth of Victorian London* (1976), *Victorian Cities* by Asa Briggs (1967), and *The Victorian City: Images and Realities* (2 vols 1973) by H.J. Dyos and Michael Wolff.

INDEX

Numbers in italics refer to illustrations

ACKNOWLEDGEMENTS

The Author is indebted to Roger Cline, who kindly read through most of the manuscript and offered helpful comments. All illustrations were supplied by Historical Publications Ltd except for those reproduced by kind permission of:

London Borough of Camden: 160, 202, 326; Roger Cline: 122; London Borough of Ealing: 264; Greater London Record Office: 258, 260, 261, 263, 330; Highgate Literary and Scientific Institution: 244; Hulton Deutsch Collection: 305; David Ingham: 303; Peter Jackson Collection: 35, 76, 135, 140, 207, 208, 211 and the front jacket; Marks and Spencer plc: 316; Metropolitan Police: 204; Museum of London: 290; Newham Recorder: 269; Royal College of Physicians: 40 (Linacre); Zoological Society of London: 229